arihant
SUCCESS AND NOTHING LESS

AF819592

Be a TOP SCORER
in CBSE Exams 2025

i Succeed

15 Sample Question Papers

with Quick Study Notes

Biology 12th

AUTHORS
Richa Raj
Himanshi Gambhir

Arihant Prakashan
(School Division Series)

Administrative & Production Offices

Regd. Office
'Ramchhaya' 4577/15, Agarwal Road, Darya Ganj, New Delhi -110002
Tele: 011- 47630600, 43518550

Head Office
Kalindi, TP Nagar, Meerut (UP) - 250002
Tel: 0121-7156203, 7156204

Sales & Support Offices
Agra, Ahmedabad, Bengaluru, Bareilly, Chennai, Delhi, Guwahati, Hyderabad, Jaipur, Jhansi, Kolkata, Lucknow, Nagpur & Pune.

PRICE ₹225.00

PO No : TXT-59-T060857-9-24

Published by Arihant Publications (India) Ltd.

For further information about the books published by Arihant, log on to www.arihantbooks.com or e-mail at info@arihantbooks.com

Follow us on

i Succeed

SAMPLE QUESTION PAPERS

THE **BEST CHOICE** OF TEACHERS & STUDENTS, Why?

01 Exact Exam Pattern

All Sample Papers have been designed on the actual exam format of CBSE

02 Complete Syllabus

Complete coverage of syllabus through different types of questions across all the sample papers

03 50% CBQs

As per latest CBSE circular, each sample paper has 50% Competency based Questions of all types.

04 Detailed Solutions

Step-by-step solutions to help you understand concepts and improve problem-solving skills.

05 Quick Study Notes

Focused revision of the whole syllabus through Quick Study Notes.

06 50+ MPQs

A supplement of 50 Most Probable Questions (MPQs) to give you last minute practice & preparation.

With Free
DOUBT SOLVING APP

Free Doubt Solving APP

To help you sort out your doubts at any time any place.

i Succeed

Biology 12

PREPARATION ASSESSMENT ZONE 1-26

PROFICIENCY BUILDING ZONE 27-163

i Succeed

Course Structure
2024-25

Time: 3 Hrs **Max. Marks : 70**

Units		Marks
VI	Reproduction	16
VII	Genetics and Evolution	20
VIII	Biology and Human Welfare	12
IX	Biotechnology and its Applications	12
X	Ecology and Environment	10
	TOTAL	**70**

UNIT VI Reproduction

Chapter 2 : Sexual Reproduction in Flowering Plants
Flower structure; development of male and female gametophytes; pollination - types, agencies and examples; out breeding devices; pollen-pistil interaction; double fertilization; post-fertilization events - development of endosperm and embryo, development of seed and formation of fruit; special modes-apomixis, parthenocarpy, polyembryony; Significance of seed dispersal and fruit formation.

Chapter 3 : Human Reproduction
Male and female reproductive systems; microscopic anatomy of testis and ovary; gametogenesis-spermatogenesis and oogenesis; menstrual cycle; fertilisation, embryo development upto blastocyst formation, implantation; pregnancy and placenta formation (elementary idea); parturition (elementary idea); lactation (elementary idea).

Chapter 4 : Reproductive Health
Need for reproductive health and prevention of Sexually Transmitted Diseases (STDs); birth control - need and methods, contraception and medical termination of pregnancy (MTP); amniocentesis; infertility and assisted reproductive technologies - IVF, ZIFT, GIFT (elementary idea for general awareness).

UNIT VII Genetics and Evolution

Chapter 5 : Principles of Inheritance and Variation
Heredity and variation: Mendelian inheritance; deviations from Mendelism – incomplete dominance, co-dominance, multiple alleles and inheritance of blood groups, pleiotropy; elementary idea of polygenic inheritance; chromosome theory of inheritance; chromosomes and genes; Sex determination - in humans, birds and honeybee; linkage and crossing over; sex linked inheritance - haemophilia, colour blindness; Mendelian disorders in humans - thalassemia; chromosomal disorders in humans; Down's syndrome, Turner's and Klinefelter's syndromes.

Chapter 6 : Molecular Basis of Inheritance
Search for genetic material and DNA as genetic material; Structure of DNA and RNA; DNA packaging; DNA replication; Central Dogma; transcription, genetic code, translation; gene expression and regulation - *lac* operon; Genome, Human and rice genome projects; DNA fingerprinting.

Chapter 7 : Evolution
Origin of life; biological evolution and evidences for biological evolution (paleontology, comparative anatomy, embryology and molecular evidences); Darwin's contribution, modern synthetic theory of evolution; mechanism of evolution - variation (mutation and recombination) and natural selection with examples, types of natural selection; Gene flow and genetic drift; Hardy - Weinberg's principle; adaptive radiation; human evolution.

UNIT VIII Biology and Human Welfare

Chapter 8 : Human Health and Diseases
Pathogens; parasites causing human diseases (malaria, dengue, chikungunya, filariasis, ascariasis, typhoid, pneumonia, common cold, amoebiasis, ringworm) and their control; Basic concepts of immunology - vaccines; cancer, HIV and AIDS; Adolescence - drug and alcohol abuse.

Chapter 10 : Microbes in Human Welfare
Microbes in food processing, industrial production, sewage treatment, energy generation and microbes as bio-control agents and bio-fertilizers. Antibiotics; production and judicious use.

UNIT IX Biotechnology and Its Applications

Chapter 11 : Biotechnology - Principles and Processes
Genetic Engineering (Recombinant DNA Technology).

Chapter 12 : Biotechnology and Its Application
Application of biotechnology in health and agriculture: Human insulin and vaccine production, stem cell technology, gene therapy; genetically modified organisms - *Bt* crops; transgenic animals; biosafety issues, biopiracy and patents.

UNIT X Ecology and Environment

Chapter 13 : Organisms and Populations
Population interactions - mutualism, competition, predation, parasitism; population attributes - growth, birth rate and death rate, age distribution. (Topics excluded: Organism and its Environment, Major Aboitic Factors, Responses to Abioitic Factors, Adaptations)

Chapter 14 : Ecosystem
Ecosystems: Patterns, components; productivity and decomposition; energy flow; pyramids of number, biomass, energy (Topics excluded: Ecological Succession and Nutrient Cycles)

Chapter 15 : Biodiversity and Its Conservation
Biodiversity-Concept, patterns, importance; loss of biodiversity; biodiversity conservation; hotspots, endangered organisms, extinction, Red Data Book, Sacred Groves, biosphere reserves, national parks, wildlife, sanctuaries and Ramsar sites.

Preparation Assessment Zone

Welcome to the Preparation Assessment Zone !

In this section, you'll find **Latest CBSE Sample Paper** and **Board Examination Paper 2024** to help you assess your readiness. Attempt these papers to familiarise yourself with the exam format and identify areas that need improvement.

Progress Tracker Tick the papers as you complete them.

- ☐ Latest CBSE Sample Paper
- ☐ Board Examination Paper 2024

Latest CBSE Sample Paper

Session 2024-25

Biology (Code 044)

Class 12

General Instructions

1. All questions are compulsory.
2. The question paper has five sections and 33 questions.
3. Section-A has 16 questions of 1 mark each; Section-B has 5 questions of 2 marks each; Section-C has 7 questions of 3 marks each; Section-D has 2 case-based questions of 4 marks each; and Section-E has 3 questions of 5 marks each.
4. There is no overall choice. However, internal choices have been provided in some questions. A student has to attempt only one of the alternatives in such questions.
5. Wherever necessary, neat and properly labelled diagrams should be draw.

- No. of Questions : 33
- No. of Sections : 5
- Time Alloted : 3 Hrs.
- Max. Marks : 70

Section A Multiple Choice Type Questions

1. Signals for parturition in human female originate from
   (a) fully developed foetus only
   (b) both placenta as well as fully developed foetus
   (c) placenta only
   (d) oxytocin released from maternal pituitary

2. To produce 1600 seeds, the number of meiotic divisions required will be
   (a) 2400 (b) 2000
   (c) 1600 (d) 1800

3. A sample of normal double-stranded DNA was found to have thymine content of 27%. What will be the expected proportion of guanine in this strand?
   (a) 23% (b) 32%
   (c) 36% (d) 73%

4. Observe the schematic diagram that depicts a small section of nucleic acid. The bases in two strands are paired through hydrogen bonds that are shown by the dark lines. Identify the correct sequence of nucleotide in the 5′-3′ direction.

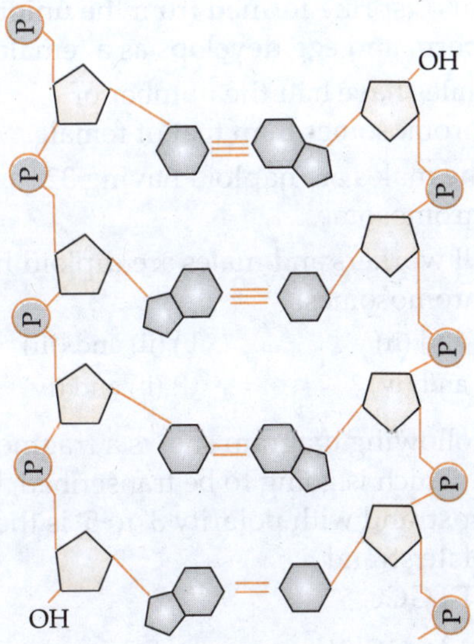

   (a) GCAT (b) CGTA
   (c) TAGC (d) ATCG

5. Suresh and Rajesh have defective haemoglobin due to genetic disorders. In Suresh, the problem is qualitative as he is having incorrectly functioning globin molecules while in Rajesh the problem is quantitative as he is having very few globin molecules. Identify the disorder they are suffering from.

	Suresh	Rajesh
(a)	Thalassemia - Autosomal dominant blood disorder	Sickle cell anaemia - Autosomal linked recessive trait
(b)	Sickle cell anaemia - autosomal linked dominant trait	Thalassemia - Autosomal Recessive blood disorder
(c)	Sickle Cell anaemia – autosomal linked recessive trait	Thalassemia – Autosomal Recessive blood disorder
(d)	Thalassemia - Autosomal dominant blood disorder	Sickle cell anaemia - Autosomal linked dominant trait

6. In *E.coli*, the *lac* operon gets switched on when lactose is

(a) present in the medium and it binds to the repressor

(b) not present in the medium and the repressor binds to the operator

(c) not present in the medium and RNA polymerase binds to the operator

(d) active lactose present in the medium binds to RNA polymerase

7. Which of the following features shows the mechanism of sex-determination in honey-bee?

(i) An offspring formed from the union of a sperm and egg develops as a female.

(ii) Males have half the number of chromosomes than that of female.

(iii) The males are haploid having 32 chromosomes.

(iv) All workers and males are diploid having 16 chromosomes.

(a) (i) and (ii) (b) (ii) and (iii)

(c) (i) and (iv) (d) (ii) and (iv)

8. The following diagram shows a fragment of DNA which is going to be transcribed, the upper strand with polarity 3′ to 5′ is the template strand

3′ ATTGCC 5′

5′ TAACGG 3′

After transcription the mRNA can be represented by

(a) 5′ AUUGCC 3′ (b) 5′ AUUGCC 3′

(c) 5′ UAACGG 3′ (d) 5′ GGCAAU 3′

9. Idli – dosa dough rises due to production of which of the following gas?

(a) CO (b) CO_2

(c) NO (d) NO_2

10. Adaptive radiation leads to which of the following?

(a) Increased competition among species

(b) Decreased speciation rates

(c) Limited morphological diversity among species

(d) Rapid divergence of traits among populations inhabiting a given geographical area

11. *Eco*RI cuts the DNA between bases G and A only when the sequence of GAATTC is present. The number of nucleotides present in the resultant sticky ends that will be formed in each of the two strands of DNA after this enzyme cuts the DNA will be:

	Vector DNA	Foreign DNA
(a)	1 & 5	5 &1
(b)	2 & 4	4 &2
(c)	2 & 5	5 & 2
(d)	3 & 4	4 & 3

12. During the secondary treatment of sewage, which of the following change in the effluent occur due to flocs?

(a) Reduction in BOD

(b) Increase in BOD

(c) Decrease in DO

(d) No change in DO or BOD

***Question Nos.** 13 to 16 consist of two statements – Assertion (A) and Reason (R). Answer these questions by selecting the appropriate option given below:*

(a) Both A and R are true and R is the correct explanation of A.

(b) Both A and R are true, but R is not the correct explanation of A.

(c) A is true, but R is false.

(d) A is false, but R is true.

13. **Assertion** (A) Cells of tapetum have more than one nucleus.

Reason (R) They undergo meiosis without cytokinesis.

14. **Assertion** (A) Deoxyribonucleoside triphosphates serve dual purposes.

Reason (R) They act as proofreaders and provide energy.

15. **Assertion** (A) A floating cover placed over the slurry in a biogas plant keeps on rising.

Reason (R) This cover keeps on rising due to the gas produced in the tank by the microbial activity.

16. **Assertion** (A) DNA fragments can be isolated by gel electrophoresis on the basis of their size.

Reason (R) The larger the fragment size, the faster it moves.

Section B Very Short Answer Type Questions

17. *Attempt either option A or B.*

A. (i) A blood test reported negative for hCG. What does negative hCG imply? Name the tissue which produces hCG?

(ii) If a blood test reported positive for hCG in a person, then which other hormones would also be secreted by the tissue secreting hCG?

Or

B. (i) The human male ejaculates about 200 to 300 million sperm during a coitus, however the ovum is fertilised by only one sperm. How does the ovum block the entry of additional sperms?

(ii) All copulations will not lead to fertilisation. Why?

18. *Attempt either option A or B.*

A. The schematic representation given below shows a DNA strand and two types of mutations in the DNA strand.

Original template

A	U	G	C	A	G	A	C	A	U	C	U	U	A	G
	Met			Gin			Thr			Ser			Stop	

Mutation I

A	U	G	A	A	G	A	C	A	U	C	U	U	A	G
	Met			Lys			Thr			Ser			Stop	

Mutation II

A	U	G	A	G	A	C	A	U	C	U	U	A	G	
	Met			Arg			His			Leu				

(i) Identify the type of mutation exhibited in I and II.

(ii) Which of the above mutation is more harmful? Give reason.

Or

B. Given below is a schematic representation of a *m*RNA strand

*m*RNA

5'————————————————————3'

AGGAGGUAUGAUCUCGUAAAAUAAA

(i) In the above sequence identify the translational unit in *m*RNA.

(ii) Where are UTRs found and what is their significance?

19. Given below is the relationship between the HIV levels in the blood and helper T cell count in a person detected with AIDS. Study the relationship and answer the questions that follow.

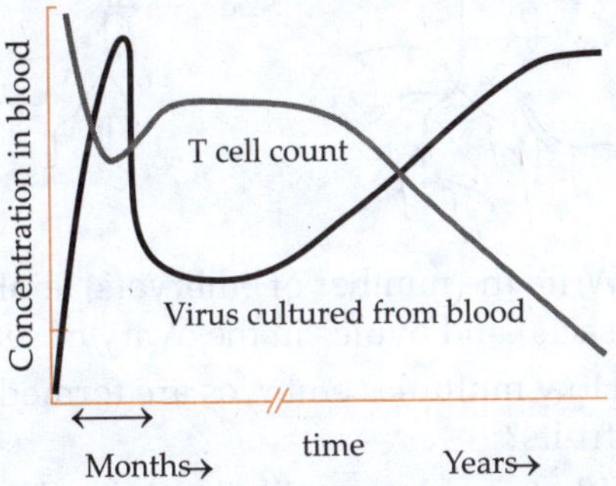

A. What kind of relationship is observed in the virus levels and the immune response after some days of the initial infection?

B. Does it completely clear the virus from the body permanently? Give reason for your answer.

20. A culture plate of *Lactobacillus* shows blue-coloured colonies and colourless colonies. Explain the principle involved in the formation of such variance in the colour of colonies.

21. *Attempt either option A or B.*

A. (i) It was estimated that if an evergreen forest has a GPP of 400 J/m^2/day and 150 J/m^2/day worth of carbon dioxide flows out of that forest, what is the NPP in that forest?

(ii) Explain why pyramids of energy must always be upright?

Or B. (i) Assume that, GPP Forest A = GPP Forest B = GPP Forest C, If Forest A has NPP = 1254 J/ m^2/day; Forest B, NPP = 2157 J/ m^2/day; and Forest C, NPP = 779 J/ m^2/day, which one of these forests has maximum energy loss by respiration? Give reason.

(ii) Draw an ecological pyramid of number of the following food chains
   (a) Grass-Animal-Fleas on the host animal
   (b) Tree-Insects-Woodpecker

Section C Short Answer Type Questions

22. The image below shows two germinated seeds *X* and *Y* which belong to the same species. Seed *X* is produced by apomixis whereas seed *Y* is a product of sexual reproduction.

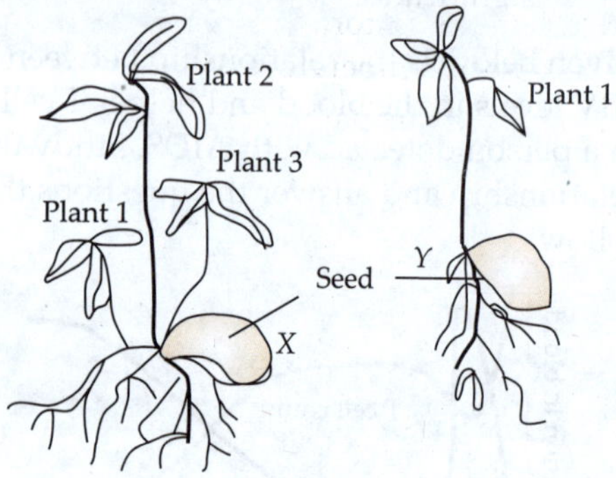

A. Write the number of embryo(s), embryo sac(s) and ovules in the ovary of seed *X*.

B. How multiples embryos are formed in citrus fruits?

C. What advantage will plants developed from seed *Y* have over seed *X*?

23. Name the place in human ovary where the first meiotic division is completed during oogenesis. What are the products of this division? Give the chromosome number of each type of cells involved in the process.

24. The schematic representation given below shows the concept of central dogma.

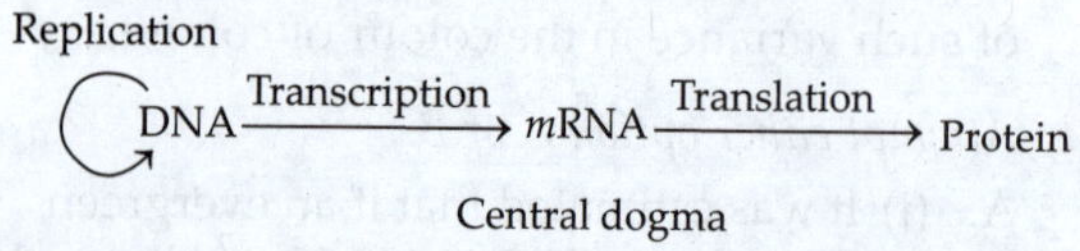

A. During the process of replication and transcription the pairing of nitrogenous bases is not similar. Explain.

B. How is the above process modified in a retrovirus? Name the process.

C. Justify why during the process of transcription only a segment of DNA is copied into RNA?

25. Describe the steps involved in Southern blot hybridisation using radiolabeled VNTR as a probe.

26. Bio-fertilisers are organisms that enrich the nutrient quality in the soil. Explain the role of three main sources of bio-fertilisers.

27. Explain how PCR technique can be used for amplification of a small amount of DNA template?

28. A. Diagram given below depicts different species of Warbler birds feeding on different regions on a Spruce tree. Explain the mechanism which helps them to co-exist.

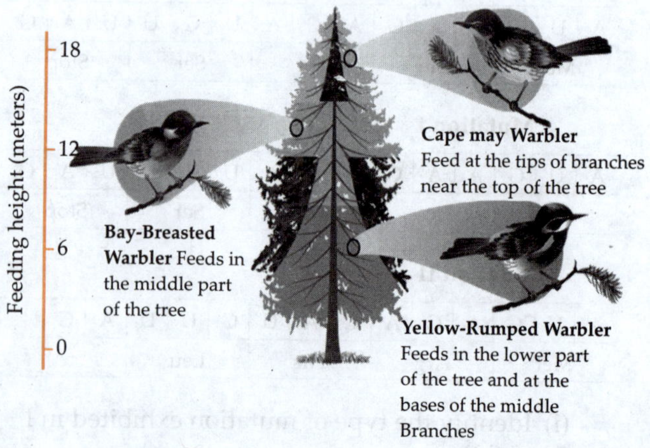

B. What does Gause's exclusion principle state? Does it apply in the case shown above? Explain.

Section D Case Based Questions

Q. Nos. 29 and 30 are case-based questions. Each question has 3 subparts with internal choice in one subpart.

29. Assuming that within a population of beetles where Hardy Weinberg conditions are met, the colour black (B) is dominant over the colour red (b). 40% of all beetles are red (bb).

Given this information, answer the questions below:

A. What is the frequency of red beetles?

B. Calculate is the percentage of beetles in the population that are heterozygous.

Attempt either subpart C or D.

C. What is the frequency of homozygous dominant individuals?

Or

D. Assuming that Hardy Weinberg conditions are met in the beetle population consisting of 1500 beetles. How many beetles would you expect to be black and red in colour respectively?

30. Given below is the pattern of temperature in a person suffering from a non-viral disease transmitted by mosquitoes. Study the graph and answer the questions that follow:

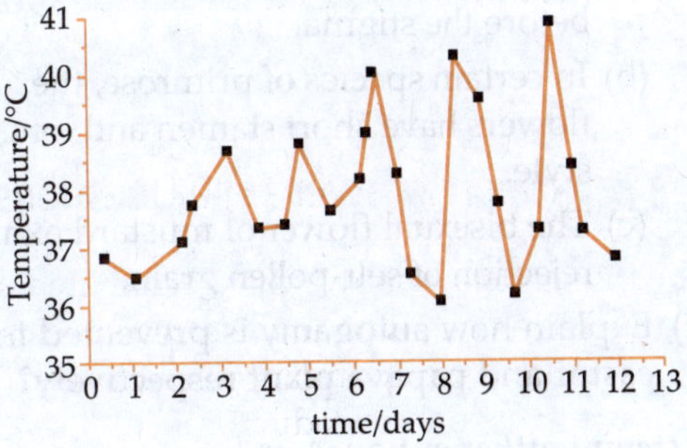

A. Explain the factor(s) responsible for this pattern of temperature.

B. How does this pathogen multiply in the human body?

Attempt either subpart C or D.

C. How is this infection transmitted to humans?

Or

D. Which stages of the life cycle of this pathogen are completed in the mosquito's gut?

Section E Long Answer Type Questions

31. *Attempt either option A or B.*

A. Cryptorchidism is a condition in which the testes fail to descend into the scrotum. It can also lead to compromised Sertoli cell function and has an impact on Leydig cell function.

(i) Identify at least 3 parameters of male fertility which get affected due to cryptorchidism.

(ii) Which process will be affected if mature spermatids are not released from Sertoli cells?

(iii) Name and explain one assisted reproductive technology (ART process) in which the sperm/semen is used to assist fertilisation.

(iv) Name and explain the assisted reproductive technology that should be used to complete the development of embryos I and II shown in the figure given below.

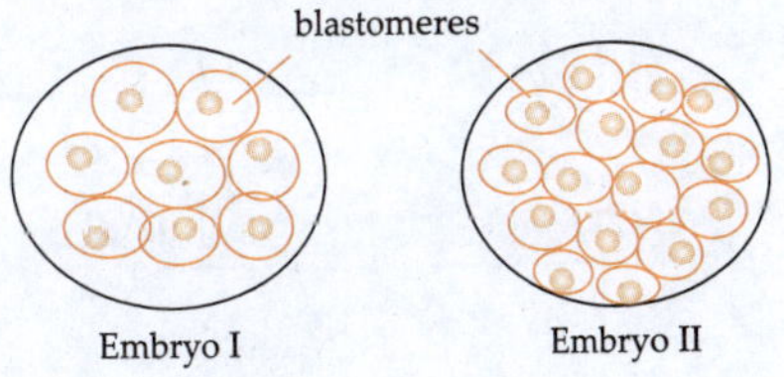

Or

B. (i) Explain the significance of each of the following features present in plants given below.

(a) In rose-bay plant the stamens ripen before the stigma.

(b) In certain species of primrose, the flowers have short stamen and long style.

(c) The bisexual flower of mustard exhibits rejection of self-pollen grain.

(ii) Explain how autogamy is prevented in castor and papaya plant respectively?

32. *Attempt either option A or B. .*

A. Explain how advent of biotechnology has helped in preventing infestation by nematodes and thereby increasing crop yield?

Or

B. In the future, genetic therapies may be used to prevent, treat, or cure certain inherited disorders in humans. Justify the statement with a suitable example.

33. *Attempt either option A or B.*

A. (i) Why is there a need to conserve biodiversity? (Any two reasons)

(ii) Name and explain any two causes that are responsible for the loss of biodiversity.

Or

B. (i) Name the two types of desirable approaches to conserve biodiversity? Explain with examples bringing out the difference between the two types.

(ii) State the features of a stable biological community.

Explanations in Topper's Style

1. (b) The signals for parturition originates from both placenta as well as fully developed foetus. [1]

2. (b) Formation of one seed requires fertilsation between one pollen grain and one egg. To produce 1600 seeds, 1600 pollen grains and 1600 eggs will be required.Each microspore mother cell results in the formation of 4 pollen grains after one cycle of meiotic division. So, 400 meiotic divisions will result in the production of 1600 pollen grains.

   One megaspore mother cell after one cycle of meiotic division results in the formation of 1 egg. So, 1600 meiotic divisions will take place to form 1600 eggs. Thus, total number of meiotic divisions required for the formation of 1600 seeds will be 400 + 1600 =2000. [1]

3. (a) According to Chargaff's rules, in DNA, A =T and G=C;

   Thus, A +T+G+C =100

   Given T = 27% so A=T =27%

   Thus A+T = 27 +27 =54%

   Thus, G+C =100 – 54 = 46%

   Since G = C so G = 46/2 =23% [1]

4. (b) The sequence of DNA from 5′-3′ direction will be CGTA as the triple hydrogen bond is present between cytosine and guanine and the double hydrogen bond is present between adenine and thymine. The purines (A and G) have two ringed structure, while pyrimidines (C and T) have one. [1]

5. (c) Sickle-cell anaemia is an autosomal linked recessive trait whereas thalassemia is an autosomal linked recessive blood disease. Thalassemia differs from sickle cell anaemia in that the former is a quantitative problem involving the synthesis of too few globin molecules, while the latter is a qualitative problem involving the synthesis of incorrectly functioning globin molecules. [1]

6. (a) In *E.coli*, the *lac* operon gets switched on when lactose is present in the medium and it binds to the repressor. [1]

7. (a) Statements (i) and (ii) are correctly represents the features that show the mechanism of sex determination in honey bee. The sex-determination in honey bee is based on the number of sets of chromosomes an individual receives. [1]

8. (c) After transcription the *m*RNA can be represented by 5′ UAACGG 3′ [1]

9. (b) The dough that is used for making foods such as dosa and idli is fermented by bacteria. The puffed-up appearance of dough is due to the production of CO_2 gas. [1]

10. (d) Adaptive radiation leads to rapid divergence of traits among populations inhabiting a given geographical area. [1]

11. (a) *Eco*RI is a restriction enzyme that specifically recognises and cuts DNA at the sequence GAATTC. The enzyme creates sticky ends by cutting between the G and A on each strand of the DNA, leaving overhangs. It will create a 1 nucleotide sticky end with overhang of G and a 5 nucleotide sticky end with overhangs of AATTC.

    Hence, the number of present in the resultant sticky ends that will be formed in each of the two strands of DNA after this enzyme cuts the DNA will be 1 & 5 in the vector DNA and 5 & 1 in the foreign DNA. [1]

12. (a) During the secondary treatment of sewage, the reduction in BOD (Biochemical Oxygen Demand) occurs in the effluent due to flocs.

    The flocs are masses of bacteria associated with fungal filaments that form mesh-like structures. As they grow in the effluent, these microbes consume a major portion of the organic matter, thereby reducing the BOD of the effluent. [1]

13. (c) A is true, but R is false. R can be corrected as The cells of tapetum undergo mitosis without cytokinesis. [1]

14. (c) A is true, but R is false. R can be corrected as Deoxyribonucleoside triphosphates act as substrate and provide energy for polymerisation reaction. [1]

15. (a) Both A and R are true and R is the correct explanation of A. [1]

16. (c) A is true, but R is false. R can be corrected as The smaller the fragment size, the farther it moves. [1]

17. A. (i) The hormone, human Chorionic Gonadotropin (hCG) is produced in women only during pregnancy. The negative hCG implies no pregnancy. It is produced by placenta. [1]

    (ii) If a blood test report is positive for hCG in a person then other hormones such as human placental lactogen (hPL), Estrogen, progestogens and relaxin would also be secreted by the tissue secreting hCG (placenta). [1]

Or

B. (i) During fertilisation, a sperm comes in the contact with zona pellucida layer of the ovum and induces changes in its membrane that blocks the entry of additional sperms. This mechanism ensures that only one sperm fertilises the ovum. [1]

(ii) Not all copulations lead to fertilisation, as the ovum and sperm must be transported simultaneously to the ampullary region for fertilisation to occur. [1]

18. A. (i) In I, the mutation is a point mutation, whereas in II, it is a frameshift mutation. [1]

(ii) Mutation II is more harmful as more codons are affected. Frameshift mutations can lead to large-scale changes in the length and chemical composition of a polypeptide, resulting in a non-functional protein that often disrupts the biochemical processes of a cell. Sometimes, incorrect amino acids can be inserted, or premature termination can also occur when a nonsense codon is encountered. Frameshifts generally have very severe phenotypic effects. [1]

Or

B. (i) A translational unit in mRNA is the sequence of RNA that is flanked by the start codon (AUG) and the stop codon (UAA) and codes for a polypeptide. In the given sequence, 5′ AUG AUC UCG UAA 3′ is a translational unit. [1]

(ii) The untranslated regions (UTRs) are present at both 5′-end (before start codon) and at 3′-end (after stop codon). They are required for an efficient translation process. [1]

19. A. As the acquired immune response gears up, there is a reciprocal relationship between virus levels in the blood and helper T lymphocytes levels. As the level of helper T levels rises, the virus levels decline. [1]

B. No, the immune response does not completely clear the virus from the body permanently. After several years, if the HIV patient remains untreated, the patient will lose the adaptive immune response, including the ability to produce antibodies. This occurs because HIV progressively infects and destroys helper T lymphocytes, leading to a progressive decrease in the number of these cells. [1]

20. The variance in the colour of colonies on a culture plate of *Lactobacillus* is based on the principle of insertional inactivation.

In this, a recombinant DNA is inserted within the coding sequence of an enzyme, β-galactosidase. This results into inactivation of the enzyme, a phenomenon known as insertional inactivation.

When the plasmid in the *Lactobacillus* bacteria does not have an insert, the β-galactosidase enzyme remains functional. This enzyme interacts with the chromogenic substrate in the medium and results in the formation of blue coloured colonies. In contrast, when an insert is present, it causes insertional inactivation of β-galactosidase, preventing the enzyme from interacting with the substrate. As a result, the colonies do not produce any colour and are identified as recombinant colonies. [2]

21. A. (i) Given, GPP = 400 J/m²/day

R = 150 J/m²/day

NPP can be calculated using given equation.

NPP = GPP – R

NPP = 400 J/m²/day – 150 J/m²/day

NPP = 250 J/m²/day [1]

(ii) Pyramid of energy is always upright. As energy flows from one trophic level to the next trophic level, some amount of energy is lost, in each trophic level, in the form of heat. Therefore, the pyramid of energy is always upright and can never be inverted.

Or B. (i) Given that Gross Primary Productivity (GPP) is equal for all forests, the equation for Net Primary Productivity (NPP) is:

NPP = GPP - Respiration of plants

Therefore, Respiration of Plants = GPP – NPP.

Given,

NPP Forest A = 1254 J/m²/day

NPP Forest B = 2157 J/m²/day

NPP Forest C = 779 J/m²/day

The smallest NPP corresponds to the largest respiration. Hence, forest C has the maximum energy loss by respiration because it has the lowest NPP, indicating the largest difference between GPP and NPP. [1]

(ii)

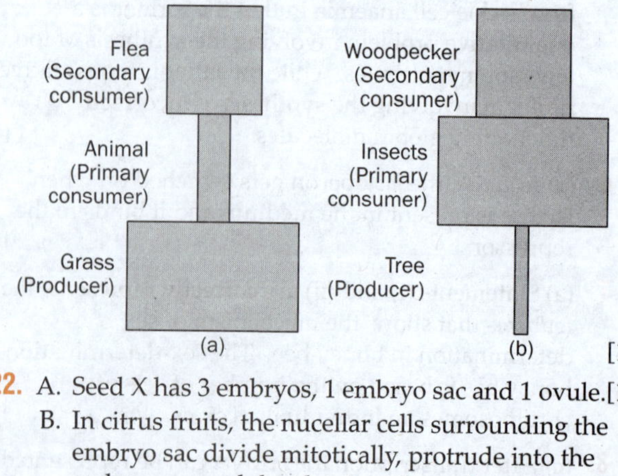

[1]

22. A. Seed X has 3 embryos, 1 embryo sac and 1 ovule.[1]

B. In citrus fruits, the nucellar cells surrounding the embryo sac divide mitotically, protrude into the embryo sac and develop into the embryos by asexual reproduction. [1]

C. The plants developed from seed Y will have following advantages over seed X:
- **Resource Utilisation** The plants growing from seed X share the nutrients from the endosperm, which can result in some plants being undernourished. On the other hand, a single plant from seed Y will utilise all the available endosperm, ensuring optimal growth.
- **Genetic Variation** The plants from seed X are clones, so they do not exhibit genetic variation. In contrast, plants from seed Y have genetic variation, which allows them to show greater adaptability. [1]

23. In human ovary, the first meiotic division is completed in the primary oocyte during oogenesis. [1]

The primary oocyte undergoes first meiotic division to form a large haploid secondary oocyte and a tiny first polar body. The primary oocyte comprises of 46 chromosomes, whereas secondary oocyte and first polar body have 23 chromosomes each. [2]

24. A. The pairing of nitrogenous bases differs between replication and transcription. During replication, adenine pairs with thymine in DNA, while during transcription, adenine pairs with uracil in RNA. [1]

B. In retroviruses, the nucleic acid is RNA and it is used to synthesise DNA. This process involves a reverse flow of information, from RNA to DNA, and is known as reverse transcription.

C. During the process of transcription only a segment of DNA is copied into RNA as it is a highly energy-rich process and as per the need, only the gene coding for a specific protein is transcribed. [1]

25. The steps involved in Southern blot hybridisation using radiolabeled VNTR as a probe are as follows:
- Isolation of DNA.
- Digestion of DNA by restriction endonucleases.
- Separation of DNA fragments by gel. electrophoresis.
- Transferring (blotting) of separated DNA fragments to synthetic membranes, such as nitrocellulose or nylon.
- Hybridisation using labelled VNTR probe.
- Detection of hybridised DNA fragments by autoradiography. [3]

26. The three main sources of biofertilisers are bacteria, fungi and cyanobacteria.
- **Bacteria** The nodules on the roots of leguminous plants are formed by the symbiotic association of *Rhizobium* (bacteria). These bacteria fix atmospheric nitrogen into organic forms. Other bacteria such as *Azospirillum* and *Azotobacter* can fix atmospheric nitrogen while free-living in the soil. [1]
- **Fungi** They are also known to form symbiotic associations with plants (mycorrhiza). Many members of the genus *Glomus* form mycorrhiza. The fungal symbiont in these associations absorbs phosphorus from soil and passes it to the plant. [1]
- **Cyanobacteria** They are autotrophic microbes widely distributed in aquatic and terrestrial environments, many of which can fix atmospheric nitrogen, e.g. *Anabaena, Nostoc, Oscillatoria*, etc. Blue-green algae also add organic matter to the soil and increase its fertility. [1]

27. PCR stands for Polymerase Chain Reaction. In this reaction, multiple copies of the gene (or DNA) of interest are synthesised *in vitro* using two sets of primers (small chemically synthesised oligonucleotides that are complementary to the regions of DNA) and the enzyme DNA polymerase. The enzyme extends the primers using the nucleotides provided in the reaction and the genomic DNA as template.

If the process of replication of DNA is repeated many times, the segment of DNA can be amplified to approximately billion times, i.e., 1 billion copies are made. Such repeated amplification is achieved by the use of a thermostable DNA polymerase (isolated from a bacterium, *Thermus aquaticus*), which remains active during the high temperature induced denaturation of double stranded DNA.

Each cycle has three steps: (i) Denaturation, (ii) Annealing and (iii) Extension

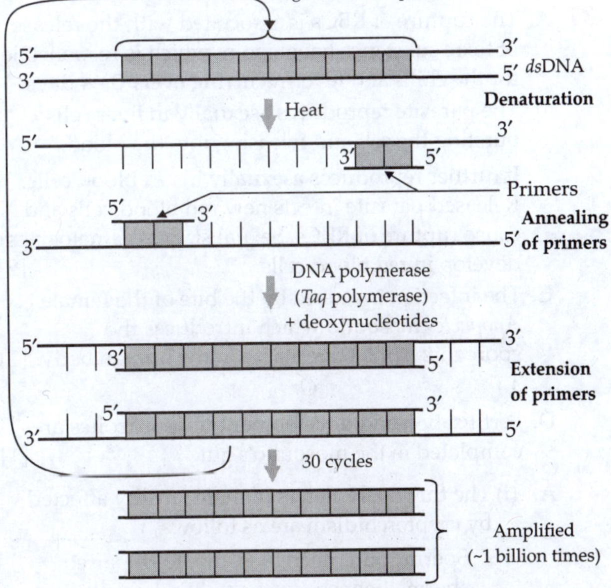

28. A. Different species of Warbler birds feeding on different regions of spruce tree are able to co-exist by mechanism of 'resource partitioning'. If two species compete for the same resource, they could avoid competition by choosing different foraging patterns. This is known as resource partitioning.

MacArthur showed that five closely related species of Warblers living on the same tree were able to avoid competition and co-exist due to behavioural differences in their foraging activities. [1.5]

B. Gause's 'Competitive Exclusion Principle' states that two closely related species competing for the same resources cannot co-exist indefinitely and the competitively inferior one will be eliminated eventually. This principle does not apply in the given case because the birds avoid direct competition by feeding in different parts of the same tree. [1.5]

29. A. Given is bb = q^2 = 0.4 (40%)

To determine q, the frequency of the recessive allele in the population, take the square root of q^2 which equals 0.632. So, q = 0.63 [1]

B. Accordign to Hardy Weinberg principle p + q = 1, then p must be 1 - 0.63 = 0.37.

The percentage of beetles in the population that are heterozygous would be 2pq.

2 (0.37) (0.63) = 0.47 [2]

C. Given is BB= p^2 = $(0.37)^2$= 0.14 [1]

Or

D. As, 1500 is the total population and E 40% of beetle population is red.

Hence, the number of beetles with red colour will be 1500x0.4= 600

If total population is 1500 and red is 600 then black would be 1500-600=900. [1]

30. A. The rupture of RBCs is associated with the release of toxic substance haemozoin, which is responsible for the chills and fever/recurring every 3 - 4 days.

B. The parasite reproduces asexually in liver cells, bursting the cell and releasing into the blood.

It further reproduces asexually in red blood cells. Released parasite infects new red blood cells and cause rupture of RBCs. Sexual stages (gametocytes) develop in red blood cells. [2]

C. The infection is caused by the bite of the female *Anopheles* mosquito which introduces the sporozoites (infective stage) in the human body. [1]

Or

D. Fertilisation and development of sporozoites are completed in the mosquito's gut. [1]

31. A. (i) The three parameters of male fertility affected by cryptorchidism are as follows

- Sperm count decreases, due to impaired spermatogenesis.
- Spermatids fail to receive the necessary nourishment for their development into spermatozoa, thereby affecting spermiogenesis.
- Leydig cells, which are responsible for synthesising and secreting androgen hormones like testosterone, will have reduced androgen secretion. [1.5]

(ii) The process of spermiation will be affected if mature spermatids are not released from Sertoli cells. [0.5]

(iii) Artificial insemination (AI) technique is an assisted reproductive technology in which the sperm/semen is used to assist fertilisation. In this technique, the semen collected either from the husband or a healthy donor is artificially introduced either into the vagina or into the uterus (IUI – Intra Uterine Insemination) of the female. [1]

(iv) The zygote or early embryos (with upto 8 blastomeres, i.e, embryo I) could be transferred into the Fallopian tube (ZIFT–Zygote Intra Fallopian Transfer) and embryos with more than 8 blastomeres (i.e, embryo II) , into the uterus (IUT – Intra Uterine Transfer), to complete its further development. [2]

Or

B. (i) (a) In the rose-bay plant, the maturation times of the stamen and pistil are not the same. As a result, pollen cannot germinate on the stigma, preventing autogamy in rose-bay. [1]

(b) Different position and incompatible placement of the reproductive structure prevent autogamy in primrose. [1]

(c) By rejecting the self-pollen grain, the mustard flower exhibits self- incompatibility. This is a genetic mechanism which prevent the pollen grain from forming pollen tube on the pistil of the same flower. [1]

(ii) In castor, although the male and female flowers are present on the same plant but are not in close proximity, thereby preventing self-fertilisation (autogamy). In papaya, the male and female flowers are on different plants, thereby preventing autogamy. [2]

32. A. Several nematodes parasite infects a wide variety of plants and animals including human beings. For instance, a nematode *Meloidegyne incognitia* infects the roots of tobacco plants and causes a great reduction in yield. A novel strategy was adopted to prevent this infestation which was based on the process of RNA interference (RNA*i*). RNA*i* takes place in all eukaryotic organisms as a method of cellular defense. This method involves silencing of a specific *m*RNA due to a complementary *ds*RNA molecule that binds to and prevents translation of the *m*RNA (silencing). The source of this complementary RNA could be from an infection by viruses having RNA genomes or mobile genetic elements (transposons) that replicate via an RNA intermediate.

Using *Agrobacterium* vectors, nematode-specific genes were introduced into the host plant. The introduction of DNA was such that it produced both sense and anti-sense RNA in the host cells. These two RNAs being complementary to each other formed a double stranded (*ds*RNA) that initiated RNA*i* and thus, silenced the specific *m*RNA of the nematode. The consequence was that the parasite could not survive in a transgenic host expressing specific interfering RNA. The transgenic plant therefore got itself protected from the parasite. [5]

Or

B. Gene therapy is a collection of methods that allows correction of a gene defect that has been diagnosed in a child/embryo. Here genes are inserted into a person's cells and tissues to treat a disease. Correction of a genetic defect involves delivery of a normal gene into the individual or embryo to take over the function of and compensate for the non-functional gene.

The first clinical gene therapy was given in 1990 to a 4-year old girl with adenosine deaminase (ADA) deficiency. The disorder is caused due to the deletion of the gene for adenosine deaminase. This enzyme is crucial for the immune system to function.

In some children ADA deficiency can be cured by bone marrow transplantation; in others it can be treated by enzyme replacement therapy, in which functional ADA is given to the patient by injection. But the problem with both of these approaches is that they are not completely curative. The gene therapy procedure involves the following steps

- The lymphocytes from the blood of the patient are grown in a culture outside the body.
- A functional ADA cDNA (using a retroviral vector) is then introduced into these lymphocytes, which are subsequently returned to the patient.
- However, as these cells are not immortal, the patient requires periodic infusion of such genetically engineered lymphocytes. However, if the gene isolate from marrow cells producing ADA is introduced into cells at early embryonic stages, it could be a permanent cure.

33. A. (i) The two reasons for conserving the biodiversity are as follows

1. **Narrowly utilitarian arguments** Human beings derive direct economic benefits from nature, like food, firewood, fibre, construction material, industrial products (resins, gums, dyes, tannins, etc.) and medicinally important products.
2. **Broadly utilitarian arguments** Biodiversity plays a major role in maintaining and sustaining supply of goods and services from various species as well as ecological systems. For instance,

- Amazon forest is estimated to contribute 20 per cent of the total oxygen in the atmosphere on earth.
- Pollinators like bee, bumble bees, birds and bats pollinate plants to form fruits and seeds.
- Aesthetic pleasures like bird watching, spring flowers in full bloom, walking through the thick forest, waking up to a bulbul's song, etc. are some other benefits of the ecosystem.

(ii) The two major causes of biodiversity loss are as follows

- **Habitat loss and fragmentation** Destruction of habitat is the primary cause of extinction of species. When large-sized habitats are broken or fragmented due to human settlements, building of roads, digging of canals, etc., the population of animals requiring large territories and some animals with migratory habitats declines.
- **Alien (exotic) species invasions** Some alien (exotic) species when introduced unintentionally or deliberately, become invasive and cause harmful impact, resulting in extinction of the indigenous species. For instance, the Nile perch, a large predator fish when introduced in Lake Victoria (East Africa) caused the extinction of an ecologically unique species of Cichlid fish in the lake.

Or B. (i) The two desirable approaches to conserve biodiversity includes *in situ* and *ex situ* conservation.

S. No.	*In situ* conservation	*Ex situ* conservation
(i)	It is conservation and protection of biodiversity in its natural habitat.	It is conservation of selected threatened plant and animal species in places outside their national habitat.
(ii)	Population is conserved in the surroundings where they have developed their distinctive features	Population is conserved under simulated conditions that closely resemble their natural habitat.
(ii)	e.g. national parks, biosphere reserves, wildlife sanctuaries, etc.	e.g. botanical gardens, zoological parks, wildlife safari, gene banks .

(ii) The features of a stable biological community are as follows

- It should not show too much variation in productivity from year to year.
- It must be either resistant or resilient to occasional disturbances (natural or man-made).
- It must also be resistant to invasions by alien species.

Write your Roll No.

Board Exam Paper 2024

Biology 12th (Code 044)

No. of Ques : 33 | No. of Sections : 5 | Time : 3 Hrs. | Max. Marks : 70

General Instructions

1. This question paper contains 33 questions. All questions are compulsory.
2. Question paper is divided into five sections-Sections A, B, C, D and E.
3. **Section-A**- question number 1 to 16 are Multiple choice type questions. Each question carries 1 mark each.
4. **Section-B**- question number 17 to 21 are very short answer type questions. Each question carries 2 marks each.
5. **Section-C**- question number 22 to 28 are short answer type questions. Each question carries 3 marks.
6. **Section-D**- question number 29 and 30 are case-based questions. Each question carries 4 marks. Each question has subparts with internal choice in one subpart.
7. **Section-E**- question number 31 to 33 are long answer type questions. Each question carries 5 marks.
8. There is no overall choice. However, an internal choice has been provided in Sections B, C and D of the question paper. A candidate has to write answer for only one of the alternatives in such questions.
9. Wherever necessary, neat and properly labelled diagrams should be drawn.

Section A Multiple Choice Type Questions

***Question nos.** 1 to 16 are multiple choice type questions, carrying 1 mark each.*

1. The type of bond represented by the dotted line '.........' in a schematic polynucleotide chain is

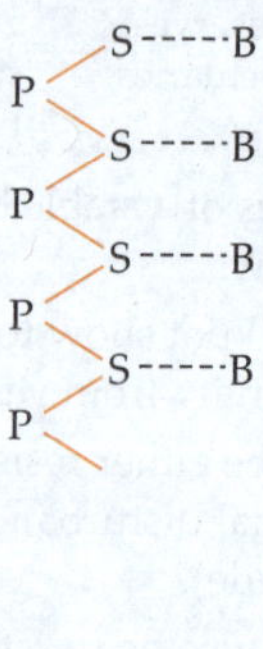

(a) hydrogen bond
(b) peptide bond
(c) N-glycosidic linkage
(d) phosphodiester bond

2. Select the option that has the correct sequence of events of human female reproductive cycle.

(i) Secretion of FSH
(ii) Ovulation
(iii) Growth of corpus luteum
(iv) Growth of follicle and oogenesis
(v) Sudden increase in LH

Options
(a) i-iii-v-iv-ii
(b) i-iv-v-ii-iii
(c) iv-i-v-iii-ii
(d) v-ii-iii-iv-i

3. *Lactobacillus* that sets milk into curd is categorised as
(a) cyanobacteria
(b) archaebacteria
(c) chemosynthetic bacteria
(d) heterotrophic bacteria

4. The specific *Bt* toxin genes which protect the cotton plants against the cotton bollworms are
(a) *cry* I Ac and *cry* II Ab (b) *cry* I Ab and *cry* I Bc
(c) *cry* II Ac and *cry* I Ac (d) *cry* II Ab and *cry* I Ab

5. Listed below are some amino acids and their corresponding *m*RNA codons.

Amino acid	*m*RNA codons
Phenylalanine	UUU
Lysine	AAG
Arginine	CGA
Alanine	GCA

Select the DNA sequence that would code for the following polypeptide sequence.

Polypeptide : Alanine - Arginine - Lysine - Phenylalanine
(a) CGT GCT TTC AAA
(b) CGT GCT TTC TTT
(c) CGU GCU UUC AAA
(d) CGU GCU UUC TTT

6. In which of the following plants are both male and female flowers born on the same plant and the mode of pollination can be geitonogamy or xenogamy?
(a) Papaya (b) Date palm
(c) Maize (d) Spinach

7. Which one of the following transgenic animals is being used to test the safety of the polio vaccine?
(a) Sheep (b) Goat
(c) Pig (d) Mice

8. In which of the following conditions/diseases is there a substantial increase in the activity of mast cells observed in the human body?
(a) Typhoid (b) Allergy
(c) Ascariasis (d) AIDS

9. The periodic abstinence by a couple for family planning should be from
(a) day 5 to 10 of menstrual cycle
(b) day 13 to 15 of menstrual cycle
(c) day 10 to 17 of menstrual cycle
(d) day 16 to 20 of menstrual cycle

10. Select the incorrect match from the following.

	Human karyotype	Characters
(a)	45+XX	Broad palm with characteristic palm crease
(b)	44+XXY	Overall feminine development
(c)	44+XO	Sterile females as ovaries are rudimentary
(d)	44+XY	Normal male

11. Using a DNA template, how many new DNA molecules would be generated after 10 cycles of amplification in PCR?
(a) 512 (b) 1024
(c) 2048 (d) 256

12. Read the four statements given below and select the option having two correct statements.
(i) A lion eating a deer and a sparrow feeding on grains are ecologically similar in being consumers.
(ii) Predator starfish *Pisaster* helps in maintaining species diversity of some invertebrates.
(iii) Predators ultimately lead to extinction of prey species.
(iv) Production of chemical nicotine and strychnine by plants are metabolic disorders.
(a) (i) and (iii) (b) (ii) and (iv)
(c) (i) and (ii) (d) (iii) and (iv)

Assertion-Reason Based Questions

For question nos. 13 to 16 two statements are given - one labelled as Assertion (A) and the other labelled as Reason (R). Select the correct answer to these questions from the codes (a), (b), (c) and (d) as given below

(a) Both Assertion (A) and Reason (R) are true and Reason (R) is the correct explanation of Assertion (A).

(b) Both Assertion (A) and Reason (R) are true, but Reason (R) is not the correct explanation of the Assertion (A).

(c) Assertion (A) is true, but Reason (R) is false.

(d) Assertion (A) is false, but Reason (R) is true.

13. **Assertion** (A) *Agrobacterium tumefaciens* is a pathogen of several monocot plants.

Reason (R) It is able to deliver a piece of DNA known as T-DNA to transform normal plant cells into a tumor.

14. **Assertion** (A) The laws of our country permit legal adoption and it is as yet, one of the best methods for childless couples looking for parenthood.

Reason (R) Emotional, religious and social factors are no deterrents to the legal adoption of orphaned and destitute children in India.

15. **Assertion** (A) Linked genes do not show dihybrid F_2 ratio 9 : 3 : 3 : 1.

Reason (R) Linked genes do not undergo independent assortment.

16. **Assertion** (A) Functional ADA cDNA genes must be inserted in the lymphocytes at the early embryonic stage in gene therapy for ADA deficiency.

Reason (R) Cells in the embryonic stage are immortal, differentiated and easy to manipulate.

Section B Very Short Answer Type Questions

17. Do you think apomixis can be compared to asexual reproduction? Justify your answer. State the benefits of apomixis to the farmers. (2)

18. (a) A farmer while working on his farm was bitten by a poisonous snake. He was rushed to a nearby health centre where the doctor gave him an injection to save his life.

(i) What did the doctor inject and why? (1½)

(ii) Name the kind of immunity provided by this injection. (½)

Or

(b) Why do organic farmers not recommend complete eradication of insect pests ? Explain giving reason. (2)

19. Observe the picture given below. Name the naturalist and write the explanation given by him that evolution of life forms had occurred on the basis of this example. (2)

20. Write the basic steps followed in the Assisted Reproductive Technologies (ART) programme to help childless couples. Why is it also known as test-tube baby programme? (2)

21. A specific plant species was introduced into Australia in 1920 and later it became invasive spreading over millions of hectares of rangeland.

(a) Name the plant that was introduced into Australia and mention the reason for its uncontrollable growth. (1)

(b) State how its spread was eventually brought under control? (1)

Section C Short Answer Type Questions

22. (a) (i) What are transgenic animals? (1)

(ii) Name the first transgenic cow and state its importance. (2)

Or

(b) (i) Explain the convention for naming *Eco*RI. (2)

(ii) With the help of an illustration only, show the action of *Eco*RI on a DNA polynucleotide. (1)

23. Identify *A*, *B*, *C*, *D*, *E* and *F* in the table given below (3)

Name of human diseases	Causative organisms	Symptoms
Pneumonia	*Streptococcus*	*A*
Typhoid	*B*	High fever, weakness headache, stomach pain
Common cold	Rhino virus	*C*
Ringworm	*D*	Dry scaly lesions on body parts, redness, itching
Ascariasis	*Ascaris*	*E*
F	*Entamoeba histolytica*	Constipation, cramps, stools with mucus and blood clots

24. Explain the mode of action of contraceptive pills taken by human females. Mention the schedule to be followed for effective outcome. (3)

25. (a) Name and write two characteristics of the type of DNA that forms the basis of DNA fingerprinting technique. (1+1)

(b) Mention any two applications of this technique. (½+½)

26. Given below is a picture that shows the magnified blood smear of a patient under a microscope.

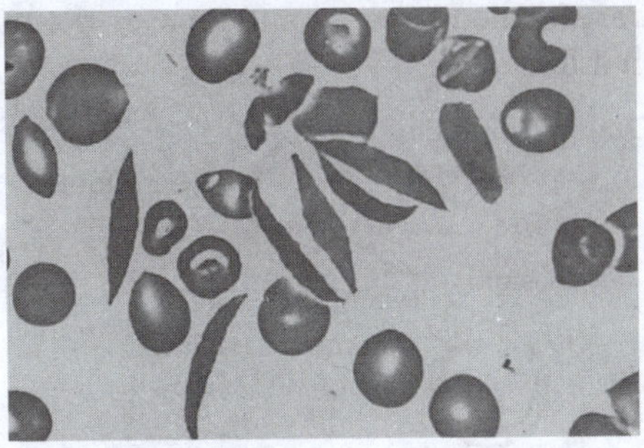

(a) Name the disease the blood smear is indicative of. Write the symptoms of the disease and its cause. (1)

(b) Explain the inheritance pattern of the disease with the help of a suitable cross. (2)

27. (a) Explain the significance of the experiment carried out by SL Miller. Name the scientists whose hypothesis prompted him to carry out this experiment. (2½)

(b) How does meteorite analysis favour this hypothesis? (½)

28. (a) State what is primary productivity and mention its units? (1½)

(b) Some ecologists observed that primary productivity of a place in Rajasthan was low as compared to a particular place in Kerala. Explain why? (1½)

Section D Case Based Questions

Question nos. 29 and 30 are case-based questions. Each question has 3 sub- questions with internal choice in one sub- question.

29. Study the diagram given below that shows the steps involved in the procedure of selecting transformed bacteria and answer the questions that follow

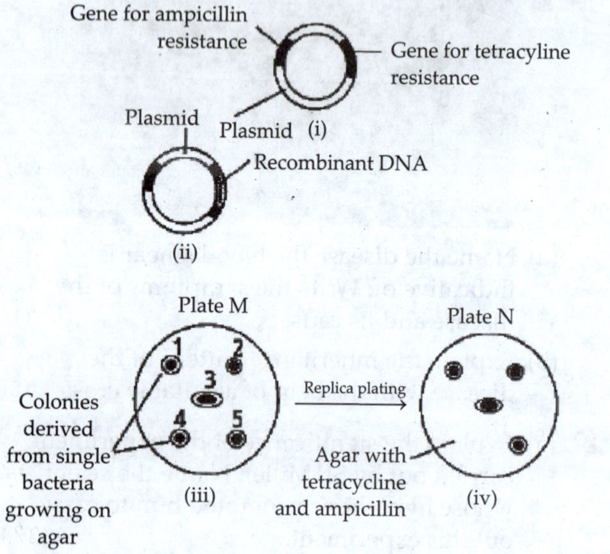

(a) Identify the colony that has got transformed. Justify your answer. (½+½)

(b) What are the sites in a plasmid called where ampicillin and tetracycline resistance genes are inserted? State their role in genetic engineering. (2)

(c) Name two enzymes playing an important role in genetic engineering. (1)

Or (c) State the role of β-galactosidase in insertional inactivation.

30. Read the following passage and answer the questions that follow

It incredible that India's land area is only 2.4 per cent of the world's total land area whereas its share of the global species diversity is an impressive 8.1 per cent. However, in these estimates of species, prokaryotes do not figure anywhere.

Biologists are always keen on collecting data with respect to species diversity observed in different regions of the world. The data collected based on the survey conducted for species richness of groups of mammals in three different regions of the world is shown in the bar graph given below

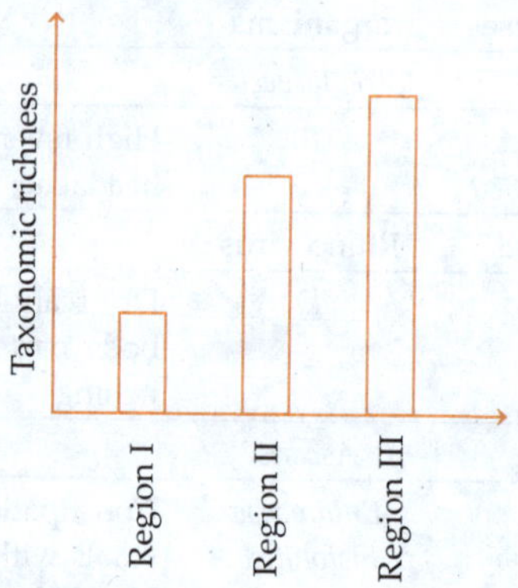

(a) Why is the species richness maximum in region III in the bar graph? (1)

Or

(a) Why is the species richness minimum in region I in the bar graph? (1)

(b) Plants and animals do not have uniform diversity in the world but show rather uneven distribution. Mention what this kind of diversity is referred to as? (1)

(c) Why is it that prokaryotes do not have an estimated number of their species diversity as seen in plants and animals? Explain. (2)

Section E Long Answer Type Questions

31. (a) (i) Name and explain the property present in normal cells but is lost in cancer cells. (1½)

(ii) All normal human cells have genes that may become cancerous under certain conditions. Name them and explain how? (1)

(iii) State the role of the following techniques in detection and diagnosis of cancer.

(1) Biopsy and histopathology (1)

(2) Magnetic resonance imaging (1½)

Or

(b) Large quantities of sewage are generated every day in cities as well as in towns and are treated in Sewage Treatment Plants (STPs) to make them less polluting. Given below is the flow diagram of stages of STP. Study the flow diagram and answer the questions that follow

Primary effluent passed into large aeration tanks
↓
Effluent passed into settling tanks to form 'sediment'

(i) (1) Why is primary effluent passed into large aeration tanks? (1)

(2) What is the 'sediment' formed, referred to as? Mention its significance. (1)

(3) Explain the final step in the settling tank before the treated effluent is released into water bodies. (1)

(ii) Name any two organisms commonly used as biofertilisers, belonging to different kingdoms. Write how each one acts as a biofertiliser? (2)

32. (a) Many patterns of inheritance deviate considerably from the pattern of inheritance as explained by Mendel. List any four such inheritance patterns and explain any three with the help of an example each. (2 + 3)

Or

(b) (i) Construct a transcription unit with a coding strand given below with proper labelling.

A T G C T G A T G C G A (2)

(ii) When does a coding strand become a template strand? (1)

(iii) Why does a double-helix DNA molecule transcribe into a single-stranded RNA molecule? (2)

33. (a) (i) Explain the development of male gametophyte in an angiosperm. (2½)

(ii) Draw a labelled diagram of a three-celled male gametophyte. (2½)

Or

(b) (i) Draw a diagrammatic sectional view of ovary of human female and label the following

(1) Blood vessels (2) Primary follicle

(3) Tertiary follicle (4) Ovum (2)

(ii) At which state of life are primary follicles formed in a human female? (½)

(iii) Explain the events (both hormonal and structural) that occur at the time of ovulation till the onset of the next menstrual cycle. (2½)

Explanations in Topper's Style

1. (c) A nitrogenous base (B) is linked to the OH of 1'C pentose sugar (S) through a N - glycosidic linkage.
2. (b) The correct sequence of events of human female reproductive cycle is as follows

   (i) Secretion of FSH $\rightarrow$ (iv) Growth of follicle and oogenesis $\rightarrow$ (v) Sudden increase in LH $\rightarrow$ (ii) Ovulation $\rightarrow$ (iii) Growth of corpus luteum.
3. (d) *Lactobacillus* is heterotrophic bacteria which convert milk into curd as they convert lactose into lactic acid.
4. (a) The specific *Bt* toxin genes which protect the cotton plants against cotton bollworms are *cry* IAc and *cry* II Ab, while *cry* IAb controls corn borer.
5. (a) Polypeptide sequence :

   Alanine - Arginine - Lysine - Phenylalanine

   *m*RNA : GCA - CGA - AAG - UUU

   DNA : CGT - GCT - TTC - AAA
6. (c) In maize plant, both male and female flowers are born on the same plant and the mode of pollination can be geitonogamy (pollination on same plant, different flowers) or xenogamy (pollination in different flower on different plant). Other plants mentioned in the options are all dioecious (bisexual) where no geitonogamy is possible.
7. (d) Transgenic mice are being used to test the safety of the polio vaccine.
8. (b) In allergy, release of the chemicals like histamine and serotonin from the mast cell (thus, its increased activity) is observed in the human body.
9. (c) The periodic abstinence is a natural method of birth control where couples avoid or abstain from coitus from day 10 to 17 of the menstrual cycle (i.e. fertile period) when ovulation could be expected.
10. (c) Option (c) is incorrect and can be corrected as

    Sterile females with rudimentary ovaries are seen in females with Turner's syndrome with karyotype of 45 + XO (absence of one of the X-chromosome).
11. (b) After 'n' number of PCR cycle, 2^n copies of DNA are produced. So, after 10 such cycle, number of DNA molecules generated would be 2^{10}, i.e. 1024 DNA molecules.
12. (c) Statements (i) and (ii) are correct, while statements (iii) and (iv) are incorrect and they can be corrected as
    - Predators generally maintain the equilibrium in the species diversity. It is only in the case when they over exploit the prey, the prey would become extinct and following it, the population of predator will also become extinct due to lack of food.
    - Production of chemicals nicotine and strychnine by plants are defence mechanisms against grazers and browsers.
13. (d) A is false, but R is true. A can be corrected as *Agrobacterium tumefaciens* is a pathogen of several dicot plants.
14. (a) Both A and R are true and R is the correct explanation of A.

    Our laws permit legal adoption and it is as yet, one of the best methods for couples looking for parenthood. Emotional, religious and social factors are no deterrents to the legal adoption of orphaned and destitute children in India unlike the Assisted Reproductive Technologies (ARTs) that face emotional, religious and social issues.
15. (a) Both A and R are true and R is the correct explanation of A.

    Linked genes do not show dihybrid F_2 ratio 9 : 3 : 3 : 1 as they do not follow independent assortment. Linked genes act and move as a unit rather than independently.
16. (c) A is true, but R is false. R can be corrected as

    Cells in the embryonic stage are immortal, undifferentiated and easy to manipulate. Embryonic cells are pluripotent, i.e. they can give rise to all somatic cell types.
17. Yes, apomixis can be compared to asexual reproduction. It is a form of asexual reproduction that mimics sexual reproduction as it involves seed formation, but do not involve fusion of gametes, e.g. grasses and Asteraceae.

    Apomixis is beneficial to the farmers as

    (i) It is genetically similar to the parents producing them. Thus, useful traits can be maintained over generations.

    (ii) It is a cost-effective method for producing seeds.

    (iii) Apomictic seeds can be used years after year to raise new crops.

18. (a) (i) The doctor injected anti-venom into the farmer's body as it contains preformed antibodies against the snake venom. These ready-made antibodies are directly given to protect the body against foreign agents.

(ii) When ready-made antibodies are provided by a patient to fight against foreign antigen, it is called passive immunity.

Or (b) Organic farmers do not recommend complete eradication of insect pests because without them, the beneficial predatory and parasitic insects which depend upon them as food or hosts would not be able to survive. The predators as well as parasites also act as biocontrol agents and help in the maintenance of ecological balance. Organic farmers believe that biodiversity furthers health. More the variety in a biodiversity, more is the sustainability it supports.

19. The given figure shows example of giraffes given by French naturalist **Lamarck** who explained his theory of evolution as

Evolution of life forms had occurred, but driven by use and disuse of organs. He gave the examples of giraffes who in attempt to forage leaves on tall trees had to adapt by elongation of their necks. As they passed on this acquired character of elongated neck to succeeding generations, giraffes, slowly, over the years, came to acquire long necks.

20. Assisted Reproductive Technologies (ARTs) programmes or *In Vitro* Fertilisation (IVF) is very helpful to such couples who cannot have a baby by natural means.

The steps of ART are as follows

(i) The sperm from male donor and ova from female donor is collected.

(ii) They are fertilised outside the body in similar condition as that of the body.

(iii) Embryo transfer takes place.
The early embryo sac upto 8 blastomeres is transferred into the Fallopian tube and more than 8 blastomeres embryos are transferred into uterus.

(iv) Further development of embryo takes place inside the womb of mother in usual manner. The baby formed by ARTs is called test tube baby because embryo is formed in the lab in a test tube, instead of the woman's Fallopian tube. The programme is thus called test tube baby programme.

21. (a) The prickly pear cactus was introduced into Australia in the early 1920's and caused havoc by spreading rapidly into millions of hectares of rangeland due to lack of any of its natural predators in the new land.

(b) The invasive prickly pear cactus was brought under control by introducing a cactus feeding predator (a moth) from its natural habitat.

22. (a) (i) **Transgenic Animals** These are animals that have had their DNA mainpulated to possess and express an extra (foreign) gene. Using *r*DNA technology many transgenic rats, rabbits pigs, sheeps, cows and fish have been produced.

(ii) The first transgenic cow (1997), Rosie produced human protein enriched mikl (2.4 g/L). This milk contained the human α-lactalbumin and was more nutritionally balanced for human babies than natural cow milk.

Or

(b) (i) The convention for naming *Eco*RI is as follows
First letter, $E \rightarrow$ *Escherichia* (genus)
Second two letters *co* $\rightarrow$ *coli* (species)
Fourth letter, R $\rightarrow$ name of the strain
Roman number I $\rightarrow$ order of isolation of enzymers (from that strain of bacteria)

(ii)

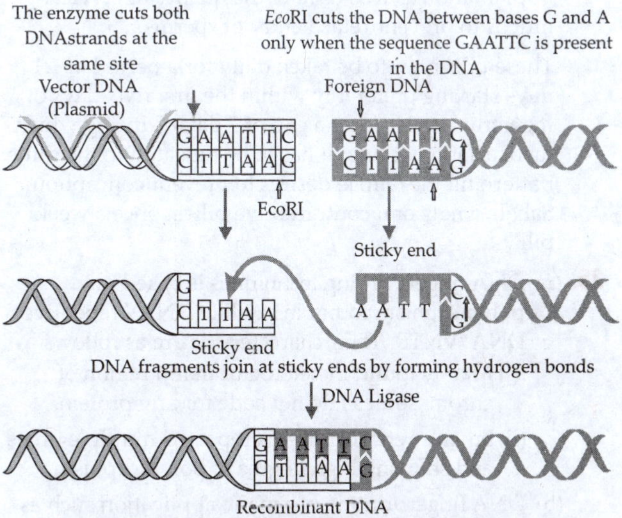

Steps in the formation of recombinant DNA by the action of restriction endonuclease enzyme *Eco*RI

23. Completed table is given as follows

Name of human diseases	Causative organisms	Symptoms
Pneumonia	*Streptococcus*	(*A*) Chills, fever, cough, headache, lips and fingers turning bluish.
Typhoid	*Salmonella typhi* (*B*)	High fever, weakeness, headache, stomach pain.
Common cold	*Rhinovirus*	(*C*) Nasal congestion and discharge, sore throat, hoarseness, cough, headache, tiredness, etc.
Ringworm	*Microsporum*, *Trichophyton* and *Epidermophyton* (*D*)	Dry scaly lesion on body parts, redness, itching.
Ascariasis	*Ascaris*	(*E*) Internal bleeding muscular pain, fever, anaemia and blockage of intestinal passage,
Amoebiasis (*F*)	*Entamoeba histolytica*	Constipation, cramps, stools with mucus and blood clots.

24. Contraceptive pills contain small dosage of either progestogens or progestogen - oestrogen combinations. These pills inhibit ovulation and implantation as well as alter the quality of cervical mucus to prevent/retard entry of sperms.

These pills have to be taken daily for a period of 21 days starting preferably within the first five days of menstrual cycle. After a gap of 7 days (during which menstruation occurs) it has to be repeated in the same pattern till the female desires to prevent conception. Saheli, a new oral contraceptive pill is 'once a week pill'.

25. (a) DNA fingerprinting techniques is based on polymorphism found in satellite DNA / repetitive DNA /VNTR. Their characteristic are as follows

(i) Mainly found in heterochromatin region of chromosomes ; do not code for any protein.

(ii) Small stretch of DNA is repeated multiple times and showing high degree of polymorphism.

(b) DNA fingerprinting has many application such as

(i) in forensic science (crime investigations, paternity tests, etc.)

(ii) in determining population and genetic diversities.

26. (a) The given blood smear shows sickle shaped RBCs and thus, is indicative of diseases called sickle-cell anaemia.

Symptoms Biconcave disc to elongated sickle like RBC, severe anaemia, shortness of breath, etc.

Cause substitution of glutamic acid (Glu) by valine (Val) at sixth position of beta globin chain of haemoglobin molecule.

(b) Sickle-cell anaemia is an autosomal recessive trait that can be transmitted from parents to the offspring, when both partners are carrier for the gene (heterozygous). This disease is controlled by a single pair of allele Hb^A and Hb^s, where Hb stands for haemoglobin , Hb^s represents the normal genotype of blood. Only homozygous individual for Hb^s ($Hb^S Hb^S$) show the diseased phenotype. The heterozygous individuals are carriers ($Hb^A Hb^S$).

(Carrier mother)(Carrier father)

$Hb^S Hb^A$ ↓ (Hb^S)(Hb^A) $Hb^S Hb^A$ ↓ (Hb^S)(Hb^A)

♀ \ ♂	Hb^S	Hb^A
Hb^S	$Hb^S Hb^S$ (Affected)	$Hb^S Hb^A$ (Carrier)
Hb^A	$Hb^S Hb^A$ (Carrier)	$Hb^A Hb^A$ (Normal)

Outcome : 1 Affected : 2 Carriers : 1 Normal

27. (a) SL Miller performed an experiment to demonstrate that UV radiations or electrical discharges or a combination of these can produce complex organic compounds from a mixture of CH_4 , NH_3 , H_2 and water vapour (H_2O) at 800°C. He observed the formation of amino acids, sugars, pigments, nitrogen bases and fats in the flask. This theory supported the theory of abiogenesis followed by chemical evolution. Scientists whose hypothesis prompted him to carry out this experiment were Oparin and Haldane who gave the theory that the first form of life came from pre-existing, non-living organic molecules (e.g. RNA, protein, etc.)

(b) Analysis of meteorite content also revealed similar compounds indicating that similar processes are occurring elsewhere in space.

28. (a) Primary productivity is the rate at which solar energy is converted into organic substances through the process of photosynthetic and chemosynthetic autotrophs. It is also referred as the production of organic compounds through the biological process of photosynthesis. Its unit is $gm^{-2}yr^{-1}$ or (k cal m^{-2}) yr^{-1}.

(b) Primary productivity depends on the plant species inhabiting a particular area, environmental factors, availability of nutrients and photosynthetic capacity of plants.

Primary productivity of a place in Rajasthan, i.e. an arid (dry) region has low primary productivity because of some unfavourable environmental conditions, like absence of water, high temperature and lack of vegetation. On the other hand, Kerala, i.e., a coastal area has more primary productivity because of favourable environmental conditions like availability of water, moderate temperature and moderate amount of vegetation.

29. (a) Colony 4 got transformed as it failed to grow on agar containing ampicillin and tetracycline. Since, it is transformed, its gene for tetracycline and ampicillin resistance became inactive, thus it lost its ability to grow in both of them (ampicillin and tetracycline).

(b) Selectable markers are sites where ampicillin and tetracycline resistance genes are inserted. They are very important in genetic engineering as they help in the selection of the transformants from those of the non- transformants.

(c) *Eco*RI, *Hind* III.

Or (c) β - galactosidase acts as a reporter enzyme. It is produced by *lac z*, a reporter gene. In insertional inactivation, when there is inactivation of *lac z* gene due to insert , no β - galactosidase is formed and thus no blue colour in formed. Thus, giving a white coloured colonies of transformants.

30. (a) Species richness is maximum in region III of the bar graph as it contains the maximum count of different species present in a region or ecological environment, i.e. taxonomical richness.

Or (a) Species richness is minimum in region I of the bar graph as it contains the least count of different species present in a region or ecological environment, i.e. taxonomical richness.

(b) This kind of diversity is referred to as species diversity.

(c) Prokaryotes do not have an estimated number of their species diversity as seen in plants and animals as

- It is difficult to study prokaryotic species diversity using conventional taxonomic methods.
- They are microscopic and thus, their estimation is difficult.
- Most prokaryotic organisms are impossible to culture *in vitro* and hence cannot be studied properly.

31. (a) (i) Normal cells in our body show a property called 'contact inhibition' that cancerous cells lack, contact inhibition is the property that prevents the uncontrolled proliferation of cells when they are in contact with other neighbouring cells. Cancerous cells have lost this property which leads to masses of cell called tumours.

(ii) Proto-oncogenes are genes that are present in normal human cells which, when activated under certain conditions, could lead to oncogenic transformation of the cells. Transformation of normal cells into cancerous cells may be induced by carcinogens (cancer causing agents) that may be physical, chemical or biological.

(iii) 1. In biopsy, a piece or the suspected tissue is cut into thin sections and then studied and examined under microscope (histopathological studies) by a pathologists.

2. MRI uses strong magnetic fields and non-ionising radiations to accurately detect pathological and physiological changes in the living tissue.

Or

(b) (i) 1. The primary effluent in passed into large aeration tank for aerobic digestion of effluent by flocs masses of bacteria associated with fungi in a mesh like structures to decrease its BOD by digesting the organic matter in it.

2. 'Sediment' formed is referred to as activated sludge. A part of this is pumped back into the aeration tank to serve as the inoculum.

3. The final step in the settling tank is anaerobic digestion by fungi and bacteria in anaerobic sludge digesters. After which, the treated effluent is generally released into natural water bodies.

(ii) *Rhizobium* fixes atmospheric nitrogen into plant usable organic forms by forming symbiotic association with legumes.

Azospirillum fixes atmospheric nitrogen while free living in the soil and enriching the nitrogen content of soil.

32. (a) Many patterns of inheritance deviated considerably from the pattern of inheritance as explained by Mendel. These deviation were due to different reasons and phenomena .

Four such inheritance patterns are

1. incomplete dominance
2. codominance
3. pleiotropy
4. linkage and recombination

The inheritance pattern explained by mend are as

(i) **Incomplete Dominance** It is a phenomenon in which the dominant allele is not able to mask the characters of recessive allele completely. This F_1-hybrid shows characters intermediate to the parental type. In this process, the phenotypic ratio of F_2-generation deviates from the Mendel's monohybrid ratio.

For example, inheritance of flower colour in the dog flower (snapdragon or *Antirrhinum* sp.) and four O' clock plant (*Mirabilis jalapa*).

(ii) **Codominance** It is a phenomenon in which two alleles are able to express themselves independently when present together. These alleles are called codominant alleles. The offsprings show resemblance to both the parents.

- A common example of codominance is ABO blood grouping in humans, which is controlled by the gene I (I^A, I^B and i).
- I^A and I^B (dominant alleles) produce RBC surface antigens A and B, respectively, whereas 'i' (recessive allele) does not produce any antigen.
- These three different alleles may produce six different genotypes of human ABO blood group that may show four phenotypes, i.e. A, B, AB and O.

(iii) **Linkage and Recombination** The physical association of two or more genes on a chromosome is called linkage. In other words, when two or more genes are closely located on a chromosome, then both the genes are passed on together in the next generation.
This type of inheritance of genes is known as linkage. It is an exception of Mendel's law of independent assortment.

Or

(b) (i)

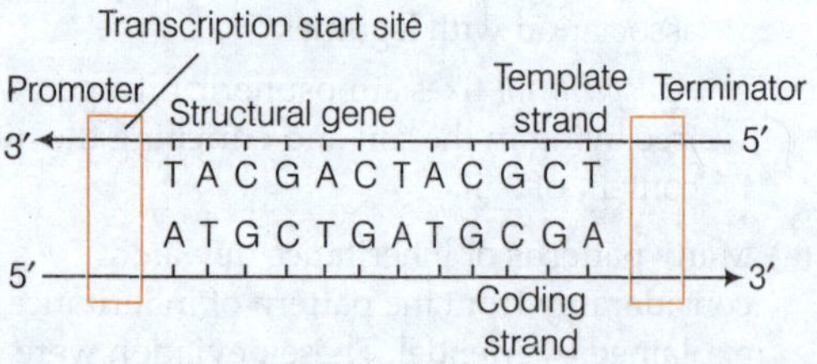

(ii) A coding strand becomes a template strand if the positions of promoter and terminator get exchanged. So, the position of promoter and terminator defines the template and coding strand.

(iii) A double-helix DNA molecule transcribe into a single-stranded RNA molecule because only one strand is transcribed to code for RNA. If both strands act as template, they would code for two RNA molecules. having different sequences and if these RNA molecules code for proteins, then the proteins will have different sequence of amino acid. Therefore, one segment of DNA would be coding for two different proteins.

If two RNA Molecules are produced simultaneously, they would be complementary to each other and hence would form a double strand RNA. Therefore, RNA would not be translated into protein .

33. (a) (i) Development of Male Gametophyte
Development of male gametophyte involves the study of following

Stamen

- It is the male reproductive unit of angiosperm. It consists of following two parts
- The long and slender stalk called the **filament**.
- The terminal generally bilobed structure called the **anther.**

Structure of Anther

It is a bilobed structure with each lobe having two **theca**, therefore it is called **dithecous**. In a cross-section, it appears four sided, i.e. tetragonal. It consists of four microsporangia, located at four corners (two in each lobe). **Microsporangia** after development become pollen sacs by producing pollen grains.

Microsporangium

Structure of microsporangium contains following features in a transverse section

- It appears nearly circular in outline.
- It is surrounded by four wall layers. The outer three layers are **epidermis, endothecium** and **middle layers**. These three wall layers are protective in function and they also help in dehiscence of anther to release the pollen. The fourth and innermost layer called the **tapetum**, which nourishes developing pollen grains. It contains cells with dense cytoplasm and more than one nuclei.
- The microsporangial wall layers enclose a mass of sporogenous tissue.
- Each cell of sporogenous tissue undergoes meiosis to form four cells, which remain associated in microspore tetrad.

Each cell of this tetrad after separation develops into pollen grains that represent male gametophyte.

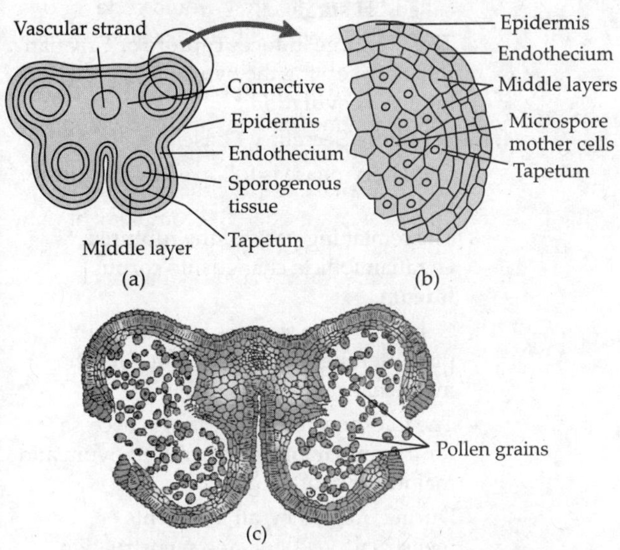

(a) TS of a young anther, (b) Enlarged view of one microsporangium, (c) TS of mature dehised anther

Microsporogenesis

The process of the formation of microspores from a **Pollen Mother Cell** (PMC) through meiosis is called microsporogenesis.

Microspores are arranged as tetrad. As the anthers mature and dehydrate, they dissociate from each other and develop into pollen grains. Pollen grains or the male gametophytes are later released during dehiscence of anther.

(ii) The labelled diagram of a mature microspore of an angiosperm with three celled male gametophyte.

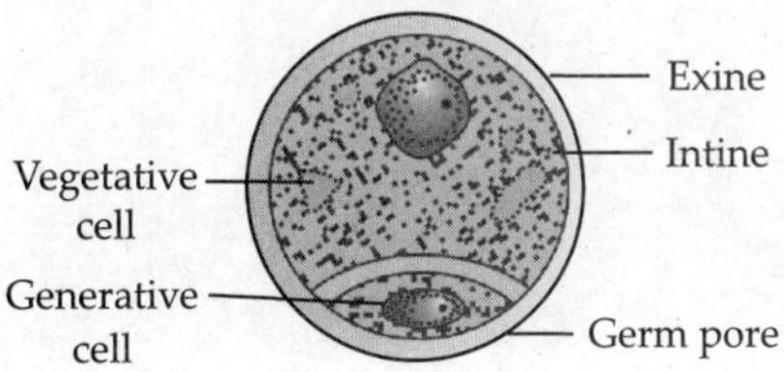

Or

(b) (i)

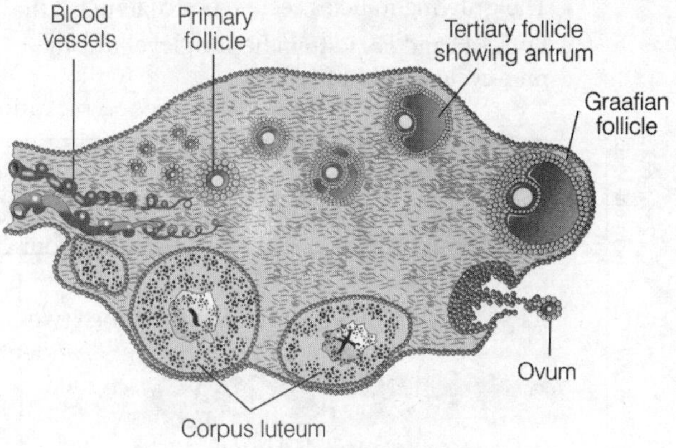

Diagrammatic sectional view of ovary showing different stages

(ii) Primary follicles are formed in a human female at the foetal stage only.

(iii) The four phases of menstrual cycle are as follows

1. **Menstrual Phase**
   - Cycle starts with this phase and the menstrual flow occurs for 3-5 days.
   - It occurs due to the breakdown of endometrial lining of the uterus and blood vessels which along with unfertilised ovum comes out through the vagina.
   - Menstruation occurs only if fertilisation does not take place.
   - Lack of menstruation generally indicates pregnancy. It may also be due to stress, poor health, diseases, etc.
2. **Follicular or Proliferative Phase**
   - Menstrual phase is followed by the follicular phase.
   - The primary follicle in the ovary grows to become a fully mature Graafian follicle and simultaneously the endometrium of uterus regenerates through proliferation.
   - Pituitary and ovarian hormones induce the changes in ovary and uterus.

- LH and FSH levels increase gradually during this phase and stimulate follicular development.
- The growing follicles secrete oestrogens.
- Both LH and FSH attain highest level during mid-cycle (about 14th day).

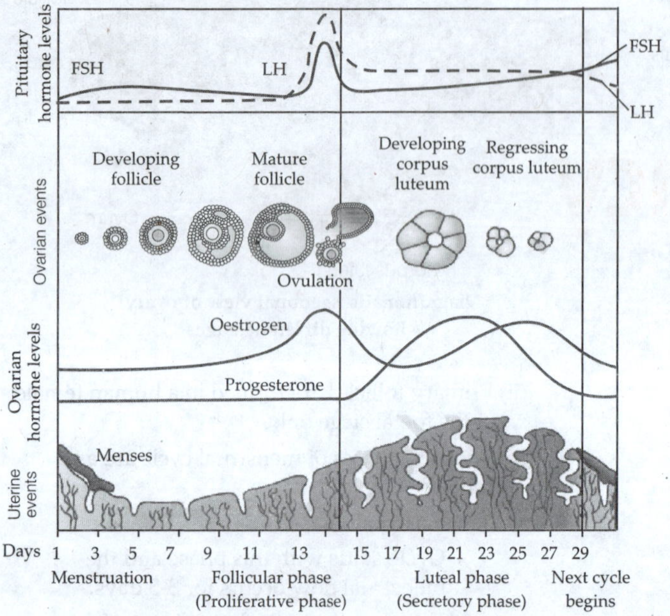

Diagrammatic representation of various events during a menstrual cycle

3. **Ovulatory Phase**
   - Rapid secretion of LH leading to its maximum level during the mid-cycle is called **LH surge**.
   - The LH surge induces rupture of Graafian follicle, releasing the ovum. This process is known as **ovulation**.
4. **Luteal Phase/Secretory Phase**
   - Ovulatory phase is followed by the luteal phase.
   - The remaining parts of the ruptured Graafian follicle change into **corpus luteum**.
   - Corpus luteum secretes large amount of progesterone, which is required for the maintenance of endometrium.
   - The thickened endometrium is necessary for the implantation of fertilised ovum and maintenance of pregnancy.
   - During pregnancy, all the events of menstrual cycle stop and menstruation does not occur.
   - If fertilisation does not occur, the corpus luteum degenerates to form **corpus albicans**, which does not secrete progesterone. This causes rupture of endometrium leading to menstruation, i.e. initiation of a new cycle.

Proficiency Building Zone

Welcome to the Proficiency Building Zone !

This section contains **15 Sample Question Papers** designed to enhance your problem-solving skills and proficiency. Use these papers to practice regularly and track your progress. Remember, consistent practice is key to mastering Biology.

Progress Tracker Tick the papers as you complete them.

- ☐ Sample Paper 1 _____ (Fill your score)
- ☐ Sample Paper 2 _____ (Fill your score)
- ☐ Sample Paper 3 _____ (Fill your score)
- ☐ Sample Paper 4 _____ (Fill your score)
- ☐ Sample Paper 5 _____ (Fill your score)
- ☐ Sample Paper 6 _____ (Fill your score)
- ☐ Sample Paper 7 _____ (Fill your score)
- ☐ Sample Paper 8 _____ (Fill your score)
- ☐ Sample Paper 9 _____ (Fill your score)
- ☐ Sample Paper 10 _____ (Fill your score)
- ☐ Sample Paper 11 _____ (Fill your score)
- ☐ Sample Paper 12 _____ (Fill your score)
- ☐ Sample Paper 13 _____ (Fill your score)
- ☐ Sample Paper 14 _____ (Fill your score)
- ☐ Sample Paper 15 _____ (Fill your score)

SQP Code : **PB-1/15**	Series *i*-**Succeed 1-25/15**	Roll No.

Sample Question Paper 01

Biology 12th (Code 044)

General Instructions

1. All questions are compulsory.
2. The question paper has five sections and 33 questions.
3. Section-A has 16 questions of 1 mark each; Section-B has 5 questions of 2 marks each; Section-C has 7 questions of 3 marks each; Section-D has 2 case-based questions of 4 marks each; and Section-E has 3 questions of 5 marks each.
4. There is no overall choice. However, internal choices have been provided in some questions. A student has to attempt only one of the alternatives in such questions.
5. Wherever necessary, neat and properly labelled diagrams should be draw.

Time : 3 Hrs.

Max. Marks : 70

Section A Multiple Choice Type Questions

1. Use of vaccines and immunisation programmes are done in maximum healthcare centres. Out of the options given below, select the correct infectious diseases that are controlled by this programme.
(a) Diphtheria and pneumonia
(b) Polio and tetanus
(c) Cancer and AIDS
(d) Both (a) and (b)

2. Which of the following RNA carries the amino acids from the amino acid pool to *m*RNA during protein synthesis?
(a) *m*RNA
(b) *hn*RNA
(c) *r*RNA
(d) *t*RNA

3. Given below are the different ART techniques with their correct procedure.

	ART	Procedure
A.	*In vivo* fertilisation	Fusion of the gametes in the female reproductive tract.
B.	ZIFT	Zygote with more than 8 blastomeres is transferred into the uterus.
C.	IUT	Zygote or early embryo with up to 8 blastomeres is transferred into the Fallopian tube.
D.	IVF	Collected gametes are made to form the zygote in laboratory.

Select how many techniques are correctly matched with their procedure?
(a) 3 (b) 4 (c) 2 (d) 1

SP-01

4. Red Data Book deals with
(a) organisms on the verge of extinction
(b) endemic plants
(c) organisms showing photoperiodism
(d) organism that are extinct

5. Read the four statements given below and select the option having two correct statements.
(i) Analogous structures are a result of divergent evolution.
(ii) Excess use of herbicides, pesticides has only resulted in selection of resistant varieties in a much lesser time scale.
(iii) The essence of Darwinian theory about evolution is natural selection.
(iv) According to Darwin, evolution occured due to a single step large mutation.
(a) (i) and (ii) (b) (ii) and (iii)
(c) (i) and (iv) (d) (iii) and (iv)

6. Rita was doing an experiment on linkage, which of the following cross is suitable for experiment on linkage?
(a) aaBB × aaBB (b) AABB × aabb
(c) AaBb × AaBb (d) AAbb × AaBB

7. Lichens show the symbiotic association between algae and fungi. The kind of interaction exhibited in this case is
(a) parasitism (b) mutualism
(c) predation (d) competition

8. Select the option that has the correct sequence of events of spermatogenesis in human male.
(i) Spermatozoa
(ii) Spermatogonia
(iii) Primary spermatocytes
(iv) Secondary spermatocytes
(v) Spermatids

Options
(a) (i) → (ii) → (iii) → (iv) → (v)
(b) (ii) → (i) → (iii) → (iv) → (v)
(c) (ii) → (iii) → (iv) → (v) → (i)
(d) (v) → (i) → (iii) → (iv) → (ii)

9. Which of the following factors has a negative effect on the population growth rate?
(a) Increased emigration
(b) Increased immigration
(c) Increased natality
(d) Decreased mortality

10. Statutory ban on amniocentesis in India was necessary because
(a) it is very expensive
(b) it can tell about chromosomal aberrations
(c) it is an invasive procedure and carries high risk of abortions
(d) it can be used for pre-natal sex-determination leading to female foeticides

11. Control of gene expression in prokaryotes takes place at the level of
(a) DNA replication (b) transcription
(c) translation (d) elongation

12. Which is the particular type of drug that is obtained from the plant whose one flowering branch is shown below?

(a) Hallucinogen (b) Depressant
(c) Stimulant (d) Pain killer

***Question** Nos. 13 to 16 consists of two statements- Assertion (A) and Reason (R). Answer these questions by selecting the appropriate option given below.*
(a) Both Assertion and Reason are true and Reason is the correct explanation of Assertion.
(b) Both Assertion and Reason are true, but Reason is not the correct explanation of Assertion.
(c) Assertion is true, but Reason is false.
(d) Assertion is false, but Reason is true.

13. Assertion (A) The edges of the infundibulum possess finger-like projections called fimbriae.

Reason (R) Fimbriae helps in collection of sperm during coitus.

14. **Assertion** (A) If the sequence of bases of one DNA strand is known then the sequence of other strand can be predicted.

Reason (R) Both the strands of DNA are complementary to each other.

15. **Assertion** (A) Bone marrow transplantation and enzyme replacement are always curative for ADA deficiency.

Reason (R) Bone marrow transplantation do not address the underlying genetic cause of ADA deficiency.

16. **Assertion** (A) A constant input of solar energy is the basic requirement for any ecosystem to function.

Reason (R) Solar energy powers the primary production of organic matter through photosynthesis and derives energy through food webs.

Section B Very Short Answer Type Questions

17. A plasmid DNA and a linear DNA (both of the same size) have one site for a restriction endonuclease. When cut and separated on agarose gel-electrophoresis, plasmid shows one DNA band, while linear DNA shows two fragments. Explain.

Or *Eco*RI is used to cut a segment of foreign DNA and that of the vector DNA to form recombinant DNA.
Show the following with the help of schematic diagrams.

(i) The site at which *Eco*RI act and cut both the segments.

(ii) Sticky ends formed on both the segments where the two DNA segments join to form a recombinant DNA.

18. Explain how surgery may be used as an effective method of birth control in a man and women?

Or

In a survey, to a district of Madhya Pradesh the medical authorities found that the population is increasing rapidly. They made the couples aware about the various contraceptive methods like the permanent and temporary methods in order to control the population.

(i) State any two temporary contraceptive methods.

(ii) Does sterilisation or surgical method of contraception do cause any side effects?

19. Name the plant source of the drug popularly called smack. How does it affect the body of the abuser?

20. Typical pyramids of biomass (g/m^2) of three different ecosystems are shown below as

1-Producers, 2-Herbivores, 3-Carnivores

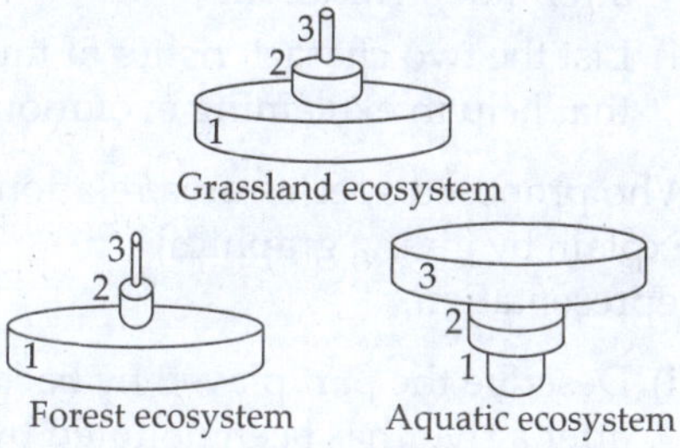

(i) In aquatic ecosystem, an inverted pyramid is observed. Suggest a possible reason for this.

(ii) What will be the pyramid of energy for all three ecosystems be like?

21. Given below is the ladder of human evolution.

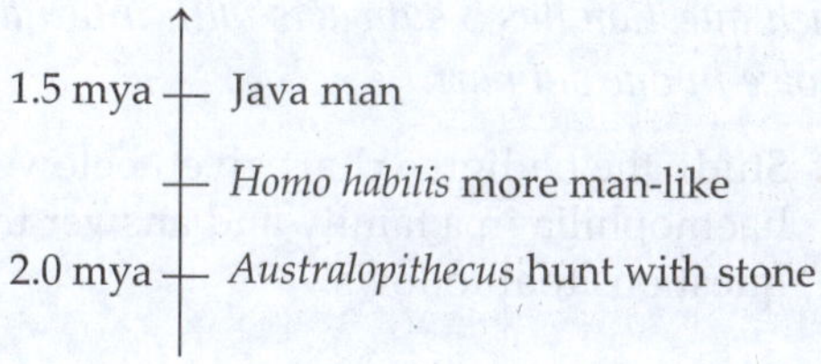

(i) What is the scientific name of Java man? Where did the *Australopithecus* evolve?

(ii) What are the characteristics of *Australopithecus*?

Or In a typical nucleus, some regions of chromatin are stained light and other dark. Explain why is it so and what is its significance?

Section C Short Answer Type Questions

22. Study the schematic representation of the genes involved in the *lac* operon given below, which is a group of genes with a single promoter.

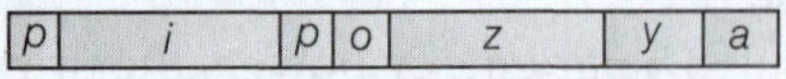

(i) Identify and name the regulatory gene in this operon. Also explain its role in switching off the operon.

(ii) This kind of regulation is called as negative regulation. Analyse the reason for this kind of regulation.

23. (i) Why does the population of dark-winged moth become more than that of white-winged moth become after industrilisation?

(ii) List the two characteristics of mutation that help in explaining evolution.

24. Who proposed species-area relationship? Explain by giving graphical representation.

25. (i) Describe the part played by bacteria after a river has been polluted by sewage.

(ii) Why is sewage water treated until the BOD is reduced? Give a reason.

26. Name two end products of double fertilisation in angiosperms. How are they formed? Write their fate during the development of seed.

27. Observe the figure and answer the questions that follows

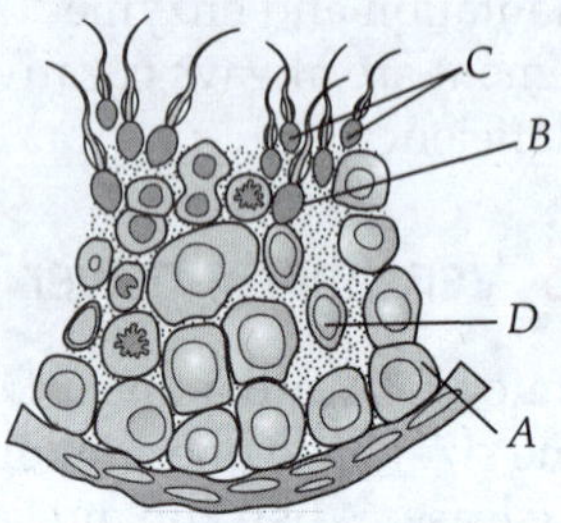

(i) Identify the parts *A*, *B*, *C* and *D* from the figure of seminiferous tubule given below.

(ii) Write the functions of *A* and *D*.

(iii) When do the oogenesis and the spermatogenesis initiate in human females and males, respectively?

28. Why must a cell be made 'competent' in biotechnology experiments? How does the cell can be made competent? Also state the role of 'biolistic gun' in biotechnology experiments.

Section D Case Based Questions

Q. Nos. 29 and 30 are case-based questions. Each question has 3 subparts with internal choice in one subpart.

29. Study the pedigree chart given below for haemophilia in a family and answer the questions that follows.

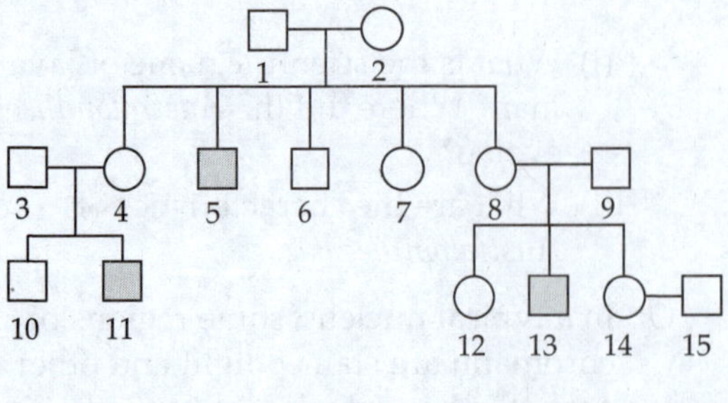

(i) On the basis of the inheritance pattern exhibited in this pedigree chart, what conclusion can you draw about the pattern of inheritance? [1]

(ii) What would be the possible genotype of members 4 and 5? [1]

(iii) A blood test shows that member 14 has haemophilic gene. What would be the probability that her child will be a haemophilic boy if she marry a normal male? [2]

Or

(iii) If the individual 5 marries a carrier female, what would be the probability of their child having haemophilia? [2]

30. The data below shows the new case and deaths from AIDS, worldwide.

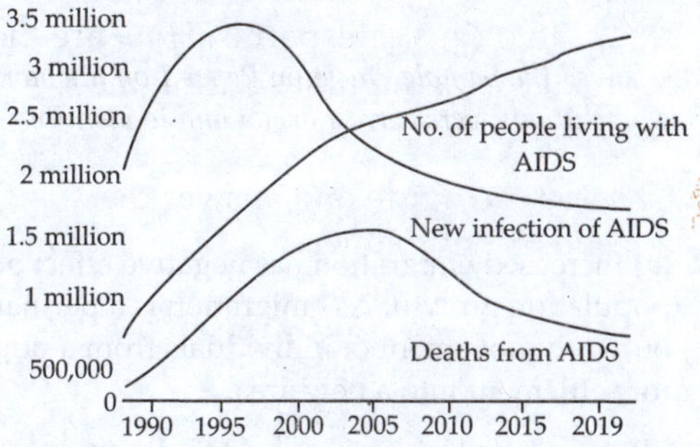

(i) With reference to the above graph which cases are decreasing? Explain. [1]

(ii) What is the cause of this disease? Mention the causative organism. [1]

(iii) Explain why the people living with AIDS are in increasing number? [2]

Or

(iii) What safety measure can be followed by the people for the prevention of HIV? [2]

Section E Long Answer Type Questions

31. Observe the diagram shown below for the process of humulin production and answer the questions that follows.

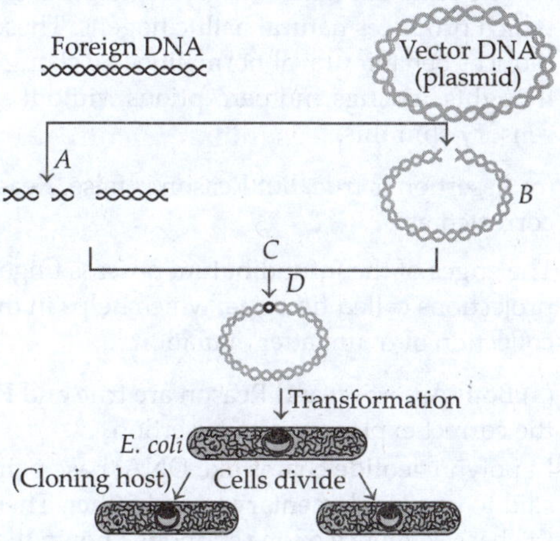

(i) What does label 'C' represent and what is its role? Also, identify the label which represents an enzyme that is utilised for cutting the molecule of DNA.

(ii) What purpose is humulin term used for? Through which bond chains *A* and *B* of humulin are bonded? Which DNA sequence will be introduced in label *B* to produce humulin?

Or (i) What are *cry* genes? In which organisms are they present?

(ii) How does 'RNA interference' takes place in eukaryotes? Mention its importance.

(iii) Why does *Bt* toxin does not kill the bacterium that produces it, but kills the insect that ingests it?

32. DNA fingerprinting focuses on regions of the DNA that are highly variable between individuals. These regions include, Short Tandem Repeats and (STR) and Variable Number Tandem Repeats (VNTRs).

(i) For the process of DNA fingerprinting, from where does the DNA obtained from?

(ii) VNTR are used in the process of DNA fingerprinting. Describe its role in DNA fingerprinting.

(iii) List any two application of DNA fingerprinting technique.

Or (i) Discuss in detail about the contribution of Morgan and Sturtevant in the area of genetics.

(ii) Why are grasshopper and *Drosophila* said to show male heterogamety? Explain.

(iii) Give two examples fo female heterogamety.

33. Explain the development of the primary endospermic nucleus into an endosperm and the development of the zygote into an embryo in a fertilised embryo sac of a dicot plant.

Or Describe the embryonic development in humans.

Explanations in Topper's Style

My Commitment *I affirm that I am reviewing these solutions only after I have solved the Sample Question Paper 1 on my own. My purpose of looking the solutions is solely to verify whether my answers/solutions were correct or not and to identify my mistakes in case my solutions were wrong or I could not solve that.*

1. (d) Diseases like polio, tetanus, diphtheria and pneumonia are controlled with the help of vaccines and immunisation programmes. [1]

2. (d) *t*RNA carries the amino acids from amino acid pool to *m*RNA during protein synthesis. Each *t*RNA is specific to amino acid, as *t*RNAs are added to the sequence, amino acids are linked together by peptide bonds. [1]

3. (c) The correct option is 'c' as *In vivo* fertilisation and IVF are correctly matched with their procedure while the rest are incorrectly matched and can be corrected as

When zygote or early embryo with upto 8 blastomeres is transferred into the Fallopian tube, it is termed as ZIFT (Zygote Intra Fallopian Transfer).

When the zygote with more than 8 blastomeres stage is transferred into the uterus is termed as IUT (Intra Uterine Transfer). [1]

4. (a) Red Data Book is a catalogue of taxa facing risk of extinction. It is maintained by IUCN. [1]

5. (b) Statements (ii) and (iii) are correct, while statements (i) and (iv) are incorrect and can be corrected as

Analogous structures are a result of convergent evolution - different structures evolving for the same function and hence having similarity.

According to Darwin, evolution was gradual, while de Vries believed that mutation is caused speciation and hence called it saltation (single step large mutation). [1]

6. (b) The most suitable cross for experiment on linkage given in options (b) i.e. AABB × aabb, because the parent organisms have clear and distinguishable genotypes for both genes, making it easier to follow the inheritance of each gene. [1]

7. (b) Lichens show mutualistic relationship by mutually benefitting two individuals of different species like fungi and algae. [1]

8. (c) The correct sequence of events of spermatogenesis in human male is as follows

(ii) → (iii) → (iv) → (v) → (i) Spermatozoa. [1]

9. (a) Increased emigration has negative effect on the population growth. As emigration is a permanent outward movement of individuals from a population for settlement into a new area. [1]

10. (d) Amniocentesis can be used to detect developing foetus in a mother's womb, people started getting the test done to kill the developing female foetus.

This resulted in the decline in gender ratio in some parts of the country. [1]

11. (b) Control of gene expression in prokaryotes takes place at the level of transcription. [1]

12. (a) The plant shown in the given picture is *Datura*, which produces natural hallucinogens. These drugs induces behavioural abnormalities by changing thoughts, feelings and perceptions without any actual sensory stimulus. [1]

13. (c) Assertion is true, but Reason is false. Reason can be corrected as

The edges of the infundibulum possess finger-like projections called fimbriae, which helps in the collection of ovum after ovulation. [1]

14. (a) Both Assertion and Reason are true and Reason is the correct explanation of Assertion.

In polynucleotide chains like DNA, base pairing are said to be complementary to each other. Therefore, if the base sequence of one strand is known then the sequence of other strand can be predicted. [1]

15. (d) Assertion is false, but Reason is true. Assertion can be corrected as

Bone marrow transplantation and enzyme replacement therapy are not always curative for ADA deficiency. [1]

16. (a) Both Assertion and Reason are true and Reason is the correct explanation of Assertion. [1]

17. A single DNA band is observed in plasmid DNA, while two DNA bands are observed in the linear DNA in an agarose gel because plasmid is a circular DNA molecule and when cut with the enzyme, it becomes linear, but does not get fragmented.

Whereas, a linear DNA molecule can gets cut into two fragments. [2]

Or

EcoRI recognises the palindromic sequence $\begin{matrix}\text{GAATTC}\\ \text{CTTAAG}\end{matrix}$ in a given fragment of DNA.

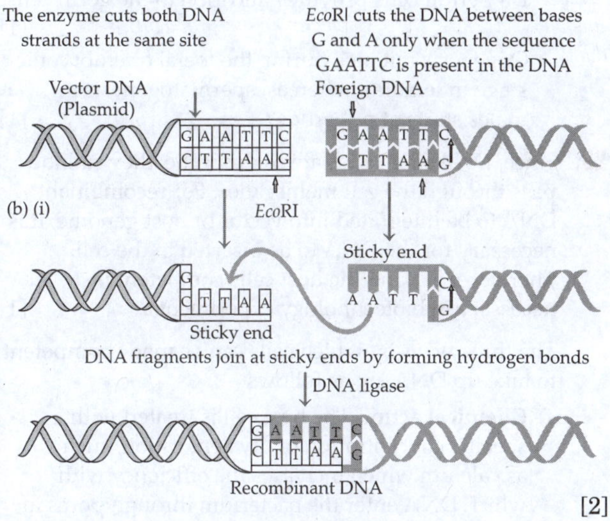

[2]

18. In a man, vas deferens or sperm ducts are cut, clipped or tied by a ligature, so no sperms are released in the semen. Hence, no fertilisation or fusion of gametes occur.
In a women, Fallopian tube or oviduct are tied or ligated. As a result ovum or egg does not reach the uterus, so fertilisation is not possible. [2]

Or (i) The two temporary contraceptive methods includes

- **Condoms** These are barrier contraceptives that prevent sperm from entering the uterus.
- **Birth control pills** Oral contraceptive pills contain hormones that prevent ovulation or fertilisation. [1]

(ii) **Sterilisation** or **surgical methods** are those methods that are involved in the terminal and permanent modification of reproductive ducts.
Yes, these methods that are known to cause some side effects including irregular menstruation, nausea, abdominal pain, etc. [1]

19. Smack is obtained from *Papaver somniferum* (poppy plant).
Smack affects the abuser body by the following way
(i) binding to specific opioid receptors present in our central nervous system and gastrointestinal tract.
(ii) acting as a depressant and slows down the body function. [2]

20. (i) In aquatic ecosystem, an inverted pyramid is observed, because the biomass of primary producer, (i.e. phytoplankton) is much lesser than the consumers, i.e. small fishes. [1]

(ii) The pyramid of energy for each of these ecosystem will be upright as energy flows from producers to consumers. [1]

21. (i) The scientific name of Java man is *Homo erectus*, *Australopithecus* evolved in East African grasslands. [1]

(ii) The characteristics of *Australopithecus* are as follows

- They were the first human-like beings.
- They have brain capacities between 650-800 cc.
- They hunted with stone, weapons but essentially ate fruit. [1]

Or

In a typical nucleus, light staining of chromatin indicates loosely packed euchromatin, facilitating gene expression, while dark staining reflects the densely packed' heterochromatin, often associated with inactive genes or structural roles in chromosome maintenance. Thus, spatial variation regulates the gene activity and maintains chromosome structure. [2]

22. (i) *i* gene is the regulatory gene in this operon.
Role of regulatory gene in switching off operon is as follows

- It codes for the repressor protein of the operon, which is synthesised constitutively.
- The repressor has the affinity for the operator gene. It binds to the operator and prevents RNA polymerase from transcribing the structural genes. [2]

(ii) When repressor binds to the operator, the operon is switched off and transcription is stopped so, it is called a negative regulation. [1]

23. (i) After industrialisation, the population of dark-winged moths become more than that of white - winged moths.
This is because the tree trunks covered by lichens become dark due to the air pollution during industrialisation. White-winged moths fail to camouflage and thus, decreased in number whereas dark-winged moths were able to escape predation. [2]

(ii) According to mutation theory of evolution

- Mutations are random, inheritable and appear in all conceivable directions.
- Same type of mutations can appear in the number of individuals of a species. [1]

24. Species - area relationship was given by Alexander von Humboldt.

According to this, within a region species richness increased with the increasing explored area, but only upto a limit. [1½]

On a logarithmic scale, the relationship is a straight line described by the equation

$\log S = \log C + Z \log A$

where, S = species, A = Area, Z = slope of the line, $c = y$ – intercept.

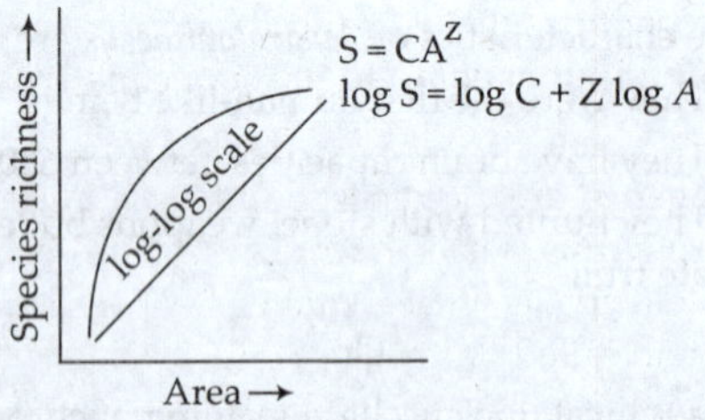

[1½]

25. (i) Pollution by sewage causes growth of the decomposer bacteria that causes decay or breakdown of organic matter from faeces and urea etc. These bacteria thrive in aerobic conditions utilising dissolved oxygen in water for respiration. Consequently, dissolved O_2 in water gets decreased.

As a result of lack of O_2, anaerobic conditions develop which are unfavourable for other organisms. This process ultimately contributes to eutrophication. [1½]

(ii) The higher the BOD of sewage water, more is its polluting potential. Therefore, the sewage water is treated, till its BOD is reduced which further indicates the reduction in the organic matter present in it. [1½]

26. The two end products of double fertilisation in angiosperms are diploid **zygote** and a triploid **Primary Endosperm Nucleus** (PEN). [1]

A diploid zygote is formed by the process of syngamy through the fusion of haploid gametes, (i.e. male gamete and egg). Simultaneously, another male gamete and two polar nuclei of central cell fuse to form triploid primary endosperm nucleus. This latter process is known as triple fusion. [1]

During the development of seed, the zygote undergoes mitotic divisions to form a mature embryo while, the primary endosperm cell gives rise to nutritive tissue called endosperm, which provides nourishment to growing embryo. [1]

Value Points For getting maximum marks, following value point should be added in the answer.

Students should mention the terms like syngamy and triple fusion.

27. (i) A - Spermatogonia, B - Spermatid, C - Spermatozoa, D - Sertoli cells [1]

(ii) A - Spermatogonia undergo mitosis and meiosis to produce spermatozoa (sperms).

D - Sertoli cells provides nutrition to the germ cells. [1]

(iii) Oogenesis initiates during the foetal or embryonic stage in females, whereas, spermatogenesis in males starts at puberty. [1]

28. Since, DNA molecules are hydrophilic, they cannot pass through the cell membranes. For recombinant DNA to be integrated into vector or host genome, it is necessary for the DNA to be inserted in the cell. Therefore, making the host cells competent is necessary in biotechnology experiments. [1]

The three ways by which cells can be made competent to take up DNA are as follows

(i) **Chemical action** The host cell is treated with a specific concentration of divalent cation, such as calcium which increases the efficiency with which DNA enter the bacterium through pores in its cell wall.

(ii) **Heat shock treatment** Incubating the cells with recombinant DNA on ice, followed by brief treatment of heat at 42°C and again putting them back on ice.

(iii) **Biolistic gun** or **gene gun** Method are used to bombard *r*DNA loaded on gold or tungsten particles with high velocity into host cells. In this way, the *r*DNA is delivered to the desired host cells. [2]

29. (i) The conclusion drawn from the given pedigree is that, haemophilia is a sex-linked recessive disorder. [1]

(ii) The genotype of members 4 and 5 will be XX^h (carrier) and X^hY (affected), respectively. [1]

(iii) Member 14 has haemophilia gene which means she is a carrier (XX^h) of the disease.

Cross

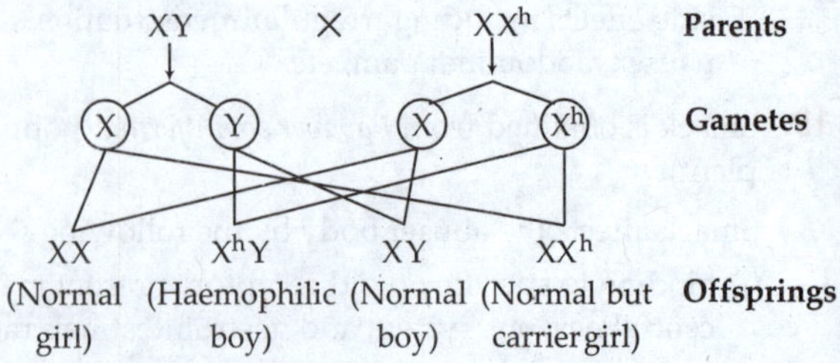

The probability that her child (boy/son) will be a haemophilic will be $1/4 = 0.25 = 25\%$ [2]

Or

(iii) If 5, i.e. affected male (X^hY) marries a carrier female (X^hX) than the probability of affected child will be 50%. This can be explained by the cross below

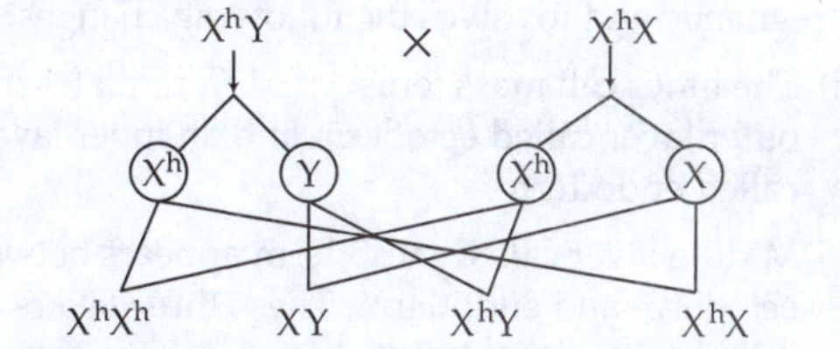

(Haemophilic girl) (Normal boy) (Haemophilic boy) (Carrier but normal girl)

Out of 4 children, 1 son and 1 daughter will be haemophilic and 1 daughter can be carrier while, 1 son will be completely normal. So, the probability is 50%. [2]

Common Mistake

Generally students gets confused between autosomal and sex-linked recessive disorders. In autosomal recessive disorder, unaffected parents can have affected offspring. In contrast, sex-linked recessive disorder is usually observed where sons are affected.

30. (i) With reference to the above graph the new cases of infection from AIDS and the death cases are seen to be decreasing due to usage of medicines and increased awareness about the disease. [1]

(ii) AIDS is caused by Human Immunodeficiency Virus (HIV). This virus attacks the helper T-cells of immune system and weakens it. [1]

(iii) Although there is no cure for AIDS, there are medicines that help people with AIDS to live longer and healthier lives by lowering the amount of virus in the body. So, the graph is seen to be increasing. [2]

Or

(iii) The prevention for AIDS includes the following
- Use of condoms during sexual contact.
- Avoid sex with unknown partners/multiple partners.
- Do not share syringes or needles. [2]

31. (i) Label *C* represents the DNA ligase which is an enzyme that is used to join together two different types of DNA molecules.

Label *A* depicts restriction endonuclease, which is utilised for cutting the molecule of DNA. [2]

(ii) The term humulin is used for human insulin made from recombinant DNA that is identical to the insulin present in humans and is used to treat diabetes.

Both chains *A* and *B* are produced separately and are combined by creating the disulphide bonds to form humulin.

DNA sequences corresponding to the two polypeptides that is *A* and *B* chains of insulin are synthesised *in vitro* and introduced into label *B*. [3]

Or

(i) '*cry* genes' are the genes found in *Bacillus thuringiensis*, a bacterium. These genes-encode for protein crystals that contain a toxic insecticidal protein called *Bt* toxin. [1]

(ii) The strategy to prevent nematode infestation in tobacco plant is **RNA interference**.

It involves silencing of a specific *m*RNA due to a complementary *ds*RNA which binds and prevent translation of *m*RNA. [2]

(iii) *Bt* toxin does not kill bacteria because in bacteria it exists in inactive state.

When *Bt* toxin is ingested by an insect, it gets converted into its active form due to the alkaline pH of the gut. The activated toxin binds to the surface of the epithelial cells of the midgut and creates pores. Water enters through these pores and causes swelling and lysis of cells in insect body. [2]

32. (i) In DNA fingerprinting, DNA is obtained from white blood corpuscles, hair root cells, etc. [1]

(ii) VNTR is Variable Number of Tandem Repeats. These are short nucleotides repeats found within the DNA. VNTRs are highly specific for individuals, i.e. no two individuals have the same VNTR.

VNTRs are used as probe in the identification because of their uniqueness, making them effective in distinguishing between different individuals. [2]

(iii) Two applications of DNA fingerprinting are as follows

(a) It can help identify the (genetic mother and genetic father) offspring.

(b) It is very useful in the detection of crime and legal pursuits. [2]

Or

(i) Morgan worked on a fruit fly. He stated and established that genes are located on the chromosomes. He also established the principle of linkage.

Sturtevant was a student of Morgan. His contributions were that he constructed the first genetic map of a chromosome while working on the *Drosophila* genome. He also established concept of the linkage group. [2]

(ii) In male heterogamety, males produces two different types of gametes. In humans and *Drosophila*, the males have *X* and *Y* chromosomes, whereas in grasshopper, the male have only one X-chromosome (XO type). Thus, the males of these organisms show male heterogamety as they produce two types of gametes either with or without X-chromosome. [2]

(iii) In some organisms, female produce two different types of gametes. This is termed as female heterogamety. For example, lizards and some reptiles. [1]

33. In a fertilised embryo sac of a dicot plant two major processes occur, i.e. the development of primary endospermic nucleus into the endosperm and the development of zygote into embryo.
The development of primary endospermic nucleus into endosperm takes places when the primary endospermic nucleus undergoes successive mitotic divisions without cytokinesis and forms a multinucleate structure. In dicots this multinucleate structure undergoes cellularisation forming a cellular endosperm. This endosperm provides nutrition to the developing embryo. [2]

Embryo Development in Dicot Seed

(a) Embryo formation starts after a certain amount of endosperm is formed.

(b) Zygote divides by mitosis to form a proembryo.

(c) Formation of globular and heart-shaped embryo occurs, which finally becomes mature embryo.

(d) In dicot plant, embryo consists of two cotyledons and an embryonal axis between them.

(e) The portion of embryonal axis above the level of attachment of cotyledons is epicotyl and terminates in the plumule.

(f) The portion of embryonal axis below the level of attachment of cotyledon is the hypocotyl, it becomes radicle (root tip). [3]

Or

Embryonic development in humans starts after pregnancy and involves the following changes

(i) The inner cell mass (embryo) differentiates into an outer layer called ectoderm and an inner layer called endoderm.

(ii) Middle layer called mesoderm appears between the ectoderm and endoderm. These three layers are called primary germ layers.

(iii) Primary germ layers give rise to all the tissues and organs of the adult. The inner cell mass contains certain cells called stem cells, which have the potency to give rise to all the tissues and organs.

(iv) In humans, after one month of pregnancy, the embryo's heart is formed. The sign of growing foetus can be ensured by listening to the heartbeat after 5-7 week of pregnancy.

(v) By the end of second month, limbs and digits develop.

(vi) By the end of third month (first trimester), most of the major organ systems are formed.

(vii) During the fifth month, the first movement of foetus and appearance of hair on the head are observed.

(viii) By the end of sixth month (second trimester), the body gets covered with fine hair, eyelids separate and eyelashes are formed.

(ix) By the end of eight months, the testes in male foetus descend into the scrotum.

(x) By the end of nine months, the foetus is fully developed and ready for the birth. [½×10=5]

SQP Code : **PB-2/15** Series ***i*-Succeed 2-25/15** Roll No.

Sample Question Paper 02

Biology 12th (Code 044)

General Instructions

1. All questions are compulsory.
2. The question paper has five sections and 33 questions.
3. Section-A has 16 questions of 1 mark each; Section-B has 5 questions of 2 marks each; Section-C has 7 questions of 3 marks each; Section-D has 2 case-based questions of 4 marks each; and Section-E has 3 questions of 5 marks each.
4. There is no overall choice. However, internal choices have been provided in some questions. A student has to attempt only one of the alternatives in such questions.
5. Wherever necessary, neat and properly labelled diagrams should be draw.

Time : 3 Hrs.

Max. Marks : 70

Section A Multiple Choice Type Questions

1. Among the following crosses, which cross will yield recessive progeny in F_1-generation?

(a) TT × tt

(b) Tt × tt

(c) tt × tt

(d) TT × TT

2. Select the option that has the correct sequence of occurrence of origin and evolution of man.

(i) *Homo erectus*

(ii) Neanderthal man

(iii) *Homo habilis*

(iv) *Homo sapiens*

Options

(a) (i) → (ii) → (iii) → (iv)

(b) (iii) → (i) → (ii) → (iv)

(c) (iii) → (ii) → (i) → (iv)

(d) (iv) → (iii) → (i) → (ii)

3. Select the incorrect match from the following.

	Methods	Agent required
(a)	Anemophily	Pollination takes place *via* the wind
(b)	Hydrophily	Pollination by bats
(c)	Ornithophily	Pollination performed by birds
(d)	Entomophily	Pollination by insects

4. The equation of Verhulst - Pearl logistic growth model is

$$\frac{dN}{dt} = rN\left[\frac{K-N}{K}\right]$$

In this equation, *K* indicates

(a) biotic potential

(b) carrying capacity

(c) population density

(d) intrinsic rate of natural increase

5. A patient is admitted for myocardial infarction. Which of the following bioactive molecule can improve his condition?
(a) Cyclosporin-A (b) Statins
(c) Protease and pectinase (d) Streptokinase

6. Stability of DNA is impacted by
(a) deoxyribose sugar
(b) presence of thymine in place of uracil
(c) Both (a) and (b)
(d) None of the above

7. Which of the following is false regarding the gene therapy?
(a) Gene therapy may be effective in the treatment of cancer
(b) It could be used to treat genetic diseases caused by single gene effect
(c) Gene therapy replaces faulty genes with functional genes
(d) It is widely used everywhere with great success

8. DNA - dependent RNA polymerase catalyses transcription on one strand of the DNA which is known as
(a) coding strand (b) alpha strand
(c) template strand (d) anti strand

9. Having become an expert on gel electrophoresis, you are asked to examine a gel for a colleague. Where would you find the smallest fragments of DNA?
(a) Near the positive electrode, farthest away from the wells
(b) Near the negative electrode, close to the wells
(c) Near the top, near the negative pole
(d) Near the middle they tend to slow-down after the first few minutes

10. Read the four statements given below and select the option having two correct statements.
(i) *Trichophyton* and *Epidermophyton* causes most common infections diseases in man.
(ii) *Entamoeba histolytica* is a protozoan parasite in the small intestine of human.
(iii) Sexual stage (gametocyte) of *Plasmodium* develop in RBC.
(iv) Interferons protect infected cells from further viral infection.
(a) (i) and (iii) (b) (ii) and (iv)
(c) (i) and (iii) (d) (iii) and (iv)

SP-02

11. Bacteria possessing restriction endonuclease enzyme remains
(a) affected by bacteriophages
(b) unaffected by bacteriophages
(c) resistant to drugs and heat
(d) None of the above

12. The diagram given below shows the inheritance of haemophilia in a family. What will be the genotype of the individual marked M?

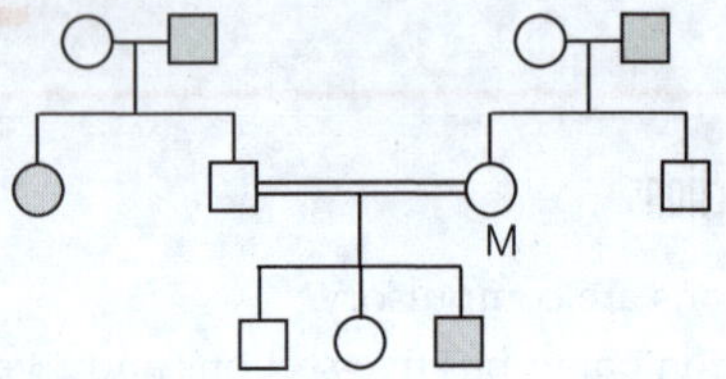

(a) M – XY (b) M – XX
(c) M – X^hX^h (d) M – X^hX

***Question** Nos. 13 to 16 consists of two statements, Assertion (A) and Reason (R). Answer these questions by selecting the appropriate option given below.*
(a) Both Assertion and Reason are true and Reason is the correct explanation of Assertion
(b) Both Assertion and Reason are true, but Reason is not the correct explanation of Assertion
(c) Assertion is true, but Reason is false
(d) Assertion is false, but Reason is true

13. **Assertion** (A) The most commonly used bioreactors are stirring type.
Reason (R) The stirrer facilitates mixing and oxygen availability throughout the bioreactor.

14. **Assertion** (A) Mutation, genetic recombination, natural selection and isolation form the most essential process for evolution.
Reason (R) All new traits arise from these processes.

15. **Assertion** (A) Traits like height and skin colour are the examples of polygenic inheritance.
Reason (R) In polygenic inheritance single gene influences multiple phenotypic traits.

16. **Assertion** (A) Menstrual phase is analogous to shedding tears over the lost ovum.

Reason (R) During the menstrual phase, the endometrial lining shed because of reduced hormonal support.

Section B Very Short Answer Type Questions

17. The daughter born to a couple where father is haemophilic and mother is normal, could be a carrier/normal. Show with the help of a Punnett cross. Give reason for your answer.

Or A normal couple gave birth to one haemophilic son and two normal daughters. Work out the cross to show the genotypes of the parents and their progeny.

18. Refer to the following diagram of the side view of the male reproductive system to answer the following questions.

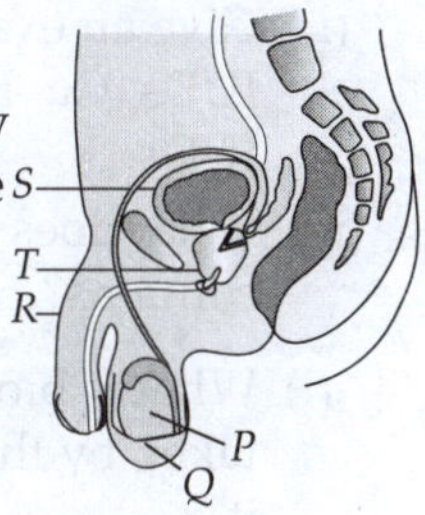

(i) Name the organs labelled as *P*, *Q* and *R*.

(ii) State the function of parts labelled as *S* and *T*.

Or Differentiate between spermatogenesis and spermiogenesis.

19. Why are cancer patients often given α–interferon as part of the treatment?

20. (i) Why is it essential to have a selectable marker in a cloning vector?

(ii) Mention the uses of cloning vector in biotechnology.

21. For a species-area relationship, *Z* (indicates species richness), is calculated as

- 0.7 for area *P*
- 0.16 for area *Q*

Which area has higher species richness and a steeper slope? What is the significance of species-area relationship?

Or

The following graph shows the species-area relationship. Answer the following questions as directed.

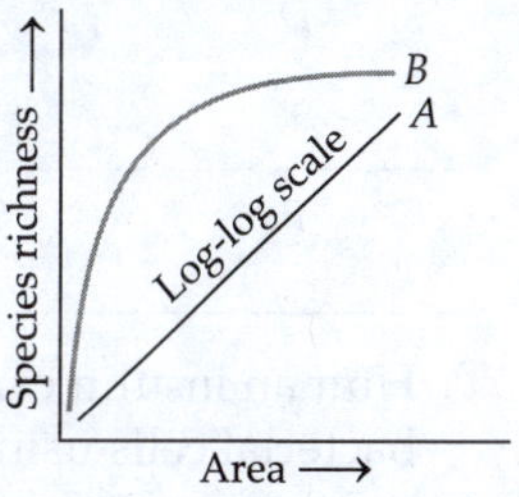

(i) Name the naturalist who studied the kind of relationship shown in the graph. Write the observations made by him.

(ii) Write the situations as discovered by the ecologists when the value of *Z* (slope of the line) lies between (a) 0.1 and 0.2 (b) 0.6 and 1.2. What does *Z* stand for?

SP-02

Section C Short Answer Type Questions

22. The ability of the body (host) to fight against the disease causing agents is called immunity. It is of two types, i.e. innate immunity and acquired immunity.

(i) Describe any two situations in which preformed antibodies are given to a person. What kind of immunisation is it?

Also, discuss its advantages.

(ii) Describe autoimmunity.

23. (i) State the use of biodiversity in modern agriculture.

(ii) Why Western ghats in India have been declared as biological hotspot?

24. Carefully observe the pyramid of number shown below.

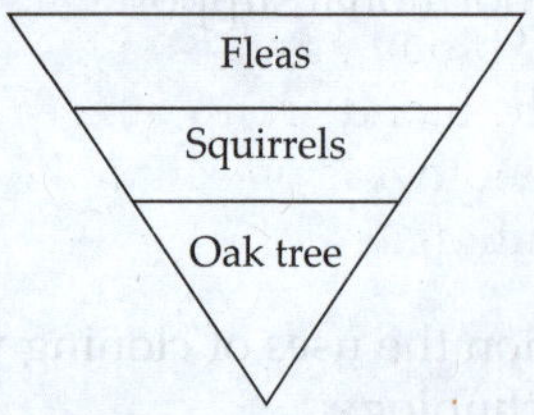

(i) Why is this pyramid inverted?

(ii) How much energy is being transferred at each level? Will the pyramid of energy if drawn for this food chain also be inverted? Give reason.

25. Identify *A*, *B*, *C*, *D*, E and *F* in the table given below.

Human ancestors	Cranial capacities	General features
A	650-800 cc	*B*
Homo sapiens	1300-1400 cc	C
D	*E*	Use hides to protect their body
F	900 cc	Probably ate meat.

26. Human insulin can be produced in bacterial cells using biotechnology. What are the steps involved in extracting and combining the polypeptides from bacterial cells to create human insulin? List any two applications of recombinant DNA technology, each in medical diagnosis and agriculture.

27. A newly married couple was afraid of using contraceptive and IUDs. So, they opted for natural methods of contraception.

During a random counselling session, the couple found that natural contraception is not reliable, instead they can use barrier contraceptives.

(i) Name two barrier methods of contraception that could be used by this couple.

(ii) Give an example each of hormonal IUDs, Cu–IUDs and non-medicated IUDs.

(iii) What does the contraceptive pill Saheli contains?

28. (i) What is biopiracy? State the intiative taken by the Indian Parliament against it.

(ii) Name any two techniques that serve the purpose of early diagnosis of some bacterial/viral human diseases.

Section D Case Based Questions

Q. Nos. 29 and 30 are case-based questions. Each question has 3 subparts with internal choice in one subpart.

29. A 35 years old man undergoes a surgical procedure that blocks gametes transport. However, he regretted his decission only after six months, felling he had not been adequately counseled.

(i) What procedure has been done to him? Explain. [2]

Or

(i) Compare the surgical method of contraception with barrier method [2]

(ii) Is this process effective against STD? [1]

(ii) Does reversal of this surgery is possible? [1]

30. The cross below shows the blood group phenotypes for mother and her two children. Observe the same carefully and answer the questions that follow.

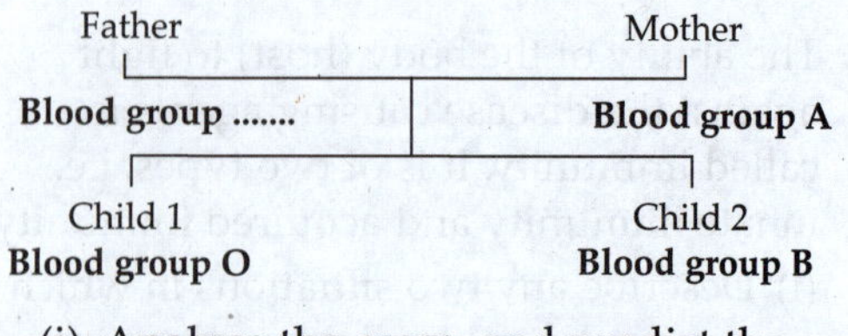

(i) Analyse the cross and predict the blood group genotype of the father. [1]

(ii) Explain the phenomenon of codominance in regard of the above given cross. [1]

(iii) State the basis behind the occurrence of different genotypes of blood types in human beings. [2]

Or (iii) Prepare a cross to show the genotypes of children born to the parents where father has blood group A and mother has B blood group and the genotype for the blood group of both, i.e. father and mother is present in heterozygous condition. [2]

Section E Long Answer Type Questions

31. Three different type of crosses were made between plants P_1 and P_2 for different characters. The F_1-generation obtained is tabulated below.
Mention the various laws of inheritance associated with cross 1 and cross 2.

Also find the phenotypic ratio of F_2-generation of each cross.

Crosses	Parent (P_1)	Parent (P_2)	F_1	F_2
1.	YYRR (Yellow, round)	yyrr (Green, wrinkled)	YyRr (Yellow, round)	–
2.	RR (Red)	rr (White)	Rr (Pink)	–

Or (i) Explain the methodology included in DNA fingerprinting.

(ii) Mention the cause of DNA polymorphism.

32. Antibiotic production by microorganisms is one of their interesting features, particularly from a medical and commercial point of view. More than 10,000 antibiotics and similar bioactive metabolites have been isolated from microbes, with approximately 500 new classes of low molecular weight compounds published every year.

(i) What is antibiotic and give one example?

(ii) How antibiotics are produced?

(iii) What is an issue with overuse of antibiotics?

Or

(i) Write the source and the effect on the human body of the following drugs
(a) Morphine
(b) Cocaine
(c) Marijuana

(ii) Name the drug used for helping patients to cope with mental illness like depression, but often misused.

(iii) How does moderate and high dosage of cocaine affect the human body?

33. Trace the events of the implantation of zygote in uterus.

Or

(i) Draw the diagram of a pistil where pollination has successfully occurred.

Label the parts involved in reaching the male gametes to its desired destination.

(ii) Write the functions of the following.
(a) Synergids
(b) Micropyle
(c) What is pollen-pistil interaction and how is it mediated?

Explanations *in Topper's Style*

My Commitment *I affirm that I am reviewing these solutions only after I have solved the Sample Question Paper 2 on my own. My purpose of looking the solutions is solely to verify whether my answers/solutions were correct or not and to identify my mistakes in case my solutions were wrong or I could not solve that.*

1. (c) A cross between homozygous recessive parents, i.e. tt × tt will yield $_1$ recessive progeny.

Parents → tt × tt

Gametes → t × t

$_1$ → tt (Recessive homozygous trait) [1]

2. (b) The correct order of sequence of occurrence of origin and evolution of man is as follows

(iii) *Homo habilis* → (i) *Homo erectus* → (ii) Neanderthal man → (iv) *Homo sapiens*. [1]

3. (b) Option (b) is incorrectly matched and can be corrected as

In hydrophily, water is the medium for pollination. [1]

4. (b) The '*K*' in the equation of Verhulst - Pearl logistic growth represents the carrying capacity of the environment. [1]

5. (d) Streptokinase is derived from the bacteria, *Streptococcus*. It is used to remove blood clots from the vessels of patients suffering from myocardial infarction. [1]

6. (c) DNA contains deoxyribose sugar and thymine instead of uracil. Along with these two factors the double helical structure also impacts the stability of a DNA molecules. [1]

7. (d) Option (d) is false regarding the gene therapy and can be corrected as

Gene therapy is not widely used everywhere with great success because, it is still in trial and in testing stages for many diseases. [1]

8. (c) The strand of DNA from which the *m*RNA is formed after transcription is known as the template strand or the anti-sense strand. The template strand is usually directed from 3′ to 5′ direction. [1]

9. (a) The smallest fragments of DNA are found near the positive electrodes as

DNA is negatively charged. These fragments travel towards the anode (farthest away from the loading wells). [1]

10. (a) Statements (i) and (iii) are correct. Rest statements (ii) and (iv) are incorrect and can be corrected as

Entamoeba histolytica is a protozoan parasite in the large intestine of human which causes amoebiasis (amoebic dysentery). In cytokine barriers, virus - infected cells secrete proteins called interferons which protects the non-infected cells from further viral infection. [1]

11. (b) The bacteria possessing restriction endonucleases remains unaffected by bacteriophages because these enzymes can cut foreign DNA, such as that from bacteriophages, thereby protecting the bacteria from infection. [1]

12. (d) The genotype of the individual marked 'M' has to be X^hX, i.e. she has to be the carrier, so as to produce an individual who is affected, in the last generation. [1]

13. (a) Both Assertion and Reason are true and Reason is the correct explanation of Assertion.

The most commonly used bioreactors are stirring type. A stirred - tank bioreactor is usually cylindrical or with a curved base to facilitate the mixing of the reactor contents. The stirrer facilitates mixing and oxygen availability throughout the bioreactor. [1]

14. (a) Both Assertion and Reason are true and Reason is the correct explanation of Assertion.

For evolution to occur, changes in gene frequency is essential. These changes are brought about by mutation, natural selection, isolation (reproductive as well as geographic) resulting in the formation of new species over a longer span of time. [1]

15. (c) Assertion is true, but Reason is false. Reason can be corrected as

Polygenic inheritance involves the contribution of multiple genes to a single phenotypic traits. [1]

16. (a) Both Assertion and Reason are true and Reason is the correct explanation of Assertion.

Menstrual phase is the phase of menstrual flow/ menses which continues for 3-5 days and involves discharge of blood (a total of 50-100 mL) along with the shedding of endometrial lining (uterus, Fallopian tube and vagina) due to reduced levels of both oestrogen and progesterone hormones.

The menstrual phase is also known as funeral of unfertilised egg or shedding tears over the lost ovum. [1]

17. The daughter born to a haemophilic father and normal mother would be a carrier. This is because haemophilia is a sex linked (X-linked) recessive disorder which follows the *criss-cross* inheritance.

X^hY (Haemophilic father) XX (Normal mother)

♀ ♂	X^h	Y
X	XX^h	XY
X	XX^h	XY

Carrier daughter; Normal sons [2]

Or

Haemophilia is a X- linked recessive disease. The gene responsible for haemophilia is located on X-chromosome.

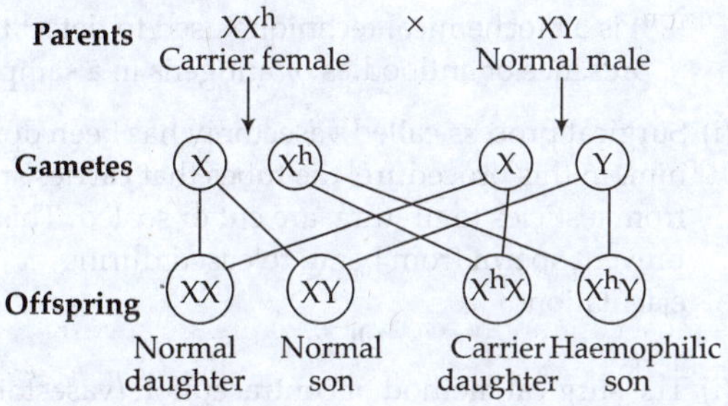

[2]

18. (i) The organs labelled *P*, *Q* and *R* are identified as testis, scrotum and penis, respectively. [1]

(ii) Part *S* is urinary bladder which is meant for the temporarily storage of urine.

While, part *T* is the prostate gland, which is an accessory gland of male reproductive system. It produces nutrients and enzymes required for sperm activation. [1]

Or

Differences between spermatogenesis and spermiogenesis are

Spermatogenesis	Spermiogenesis
It is a process of formation of sperms from immature germ cells.	It is a process of transformation of a circular spermatid to a motile spermatozoa.
Number of cells increases as each spermatogonium produces four spermatids.	No change in number of cells as only one spermatid develops into a spermatozoa.

[2]

19. The tumour cells are capable of avoiding recognition and destruction by immune system therefore, the cancer patients are given α–interferons, which are biological response modifiers. It helps in activating the immune system and destroy tumours. [2]

20. (i) Selectable marker in a cloning vector helps in identifying and selecting recombinants and eliminating the non - recombinants. [1]

(ii) The uses of cloning vector in biotechnology are as follows

(a) It helps in linking the foreign/alien DNA with the hosts DNA.

(b) It used to replicate and propagate specific DNA sequence. [1]

21. According to Alexander van Humboldt, species richness increases with the explored area.

Thus, area *P* with species richness (*Z*), 0.7 will have more species and steeper slope. [1]

Species-area relationship helps in understanding the structure of a habitat and study of factors which impact the survival of a species. [1]

Or (i) Alexander von Humboldt studied the relationship shown in the graph. He observed that species richness increased within an explored area, but only upto a limit. [1]

(ii) (a) Value of *Z* lies between 0.1-0.2, when area is small to normal.

(b) Value of *Z* lies between 0.6-1.2, when area is very large.

Z is slope of the line, which is regression coefficient. [1]

22. (i) The two situations in which preformed antibodies are given to a person are as follows

- In the case of snake bites, an antitoxin against venom is directly given.
- In case of injury, tetanus injection is given to avoid muscle spasms.

This kind of immunisation is known as passive immunisation.

In the passive immunisation, preformed antibodies are introduced in the body for the immediate immune response.

Advantages of passive immunisation are as follows

The preformed antibodies develop quick immune response in the recipient against the infective agents. [2]

(ii) Autoimmunity is the state in which the body loses its ability to distinguish between the self and non-self cells.

The body's immune system starts destroying its own cells which leads to fatal malfunctions called autoimmune diseases, e.g. rheumatoid arthritis, Grave's disease, haemolytic anaemia, etc. [1]

23. (i) The uses of biodiversity in modern agriculture are as follows

(a) Human obtain food, fibres, medicines and many industrial products from plants.

(b) Wild varieties of plants are used for breeding to obtain disease and pest resistant crops with many desirable traits. [2]

(ii) Western ghats have been declared as biological hotspot due to its rich biodiversity and ecological condition favouring many species of plants and animals. Many endemic species of amphibians, reptiles and fishes are found in these regions. [1]

24. (i) The pyramid of number is inverted because the oak tree is only one in number as compared to the squirrels and fleas. Pyramid of number does not account for the relative size of organisms present at each trophic level. [1]

(ii) Total 10% of the energy is transferred to each level from the lower trophic level.
No, pyramid of energy will not be inverted because the producers will always have more energy than other level, which continuously decreases as it passes from one trophic level to next. [2]

25. In the given table *A*, *B*, *C*, *D*, *E* and *F* are identified as

A → *Homo habilis*

B → First human - like being

C → Arose during ice age

D → Neanderthal

E → 1400 cc

F → *Homo erectus* [3]

26. Transgenic bacteria have been produced that translate the constituting polypeptide chains of human insulin. These polypeptides can be extracted from the bacterial cells and combined by creating disulphide bonds to produce human insulin.

In humans, insulin is produced as a prohormone with three polypeptides A, B and C.
After processing, the C-peptide is removed and the mature insulin is formed. When transgenic bacteria are used, instead of producing an extra stretch of C-peptide, only A and B polypeptides are produced and then linked to produce mature insulin directly. [2]

Two important applications of recombinant DNA technology are as follows

(i) **Medical diagnosis** It is used to detect HIV infection using ELISA.

(ii) **Agricultures** It is used in agriculture to produce genetically modified organisms such as Golden rice, *Bt* cotton, etc. These are either nutritionally enriched or resistant to pests, worms, etc. [1]

27. (i) Condoms and cervical caps are the two barrier methods of contraception that could be used by this couple. [1]

(ii) **Hormonal IUD** — Progestasert and LNG-20
Cu-IUDs – Multiload-375 and Cu-T,
Non-medicated IUDs – Lippes loop, [1]

(iii) Saheli is once a week contraceptive pill which contains a non-steroidal preparation, centchroman. [1]

28. (i) Biopiracy is the unauthorised use of biological resources by multinationals or other organisations, i.e., without proper permissions from the relevant authorities or people concerned with it.
Indian Parliament has recently passed the second amendment of Indian patents bill, which considers various issues related with biopiracy, e.g., terms of patent, emergency provisions, research and development initiative. [2]

(ii) Two techniques that serves the purpose of early diagnosis of some bacterial/viral human diseases are as follows

- **PCR** (Polymerase Chain Reaction) It is used to amplify and detect small amount of DNA or RNA.
- **ELISA** (Enzyme Linked Immunosorbent Assay) It is a biochemical technique used to detect the presence of antibodies or antigens in a sample.[1]

29. (i) Surgical process called vasectomy has been done to him. In this procedure, the tubes that carries sperm from testicles to urethra, are cut or sealed. This prevent sperm from being released during ejaculation. [2]

Or

(i) The surgical method of contraception (vasectomy or tubectomy) is highly effective and considered permanent, while the barrier method (e.g. condoms) varies in effectiveness and offers reversible contraception without affecting long term fertility. [2]

(ii) Vasectomy does not offer any protection against the Sexually Transmitted Diseases (STDs). The STDs are transmitted through the sexual contact involving bodily fluids and vasectomy does not affect this transmission. [1]

(iii) Surgical methods have poor reversibility and cannot be reversed. [1]

30. (i) In the cross given, the child 1 has blood group O, (i.e. is recessive in nature). Thus, father needs to have allele i, while, child 2 has blood group B, so father need to have I^B. Hence, the blood group of father would be B and the genotype will be I^Bi. [1]

(ii) Codominance is the phenomenon in which two alleles expresses themselves independently when present together in an organism. [1]

(iii) The gene I is responsible for ABO blood group in humans have three alleles, i.e. I^A, I^B, i.
In this, the alleles I^A and I^B are dominant over i and produces slightly different sugar in comparison to *i* which does not produces any sugar. Therefore, I^AI^B when present together in a single organism expresses their own genotypes due to codominance.

Hence, persons can have both A and B types of sugars. Hence, total different six genotypes are present in human beings. [2]

Or

(iii)

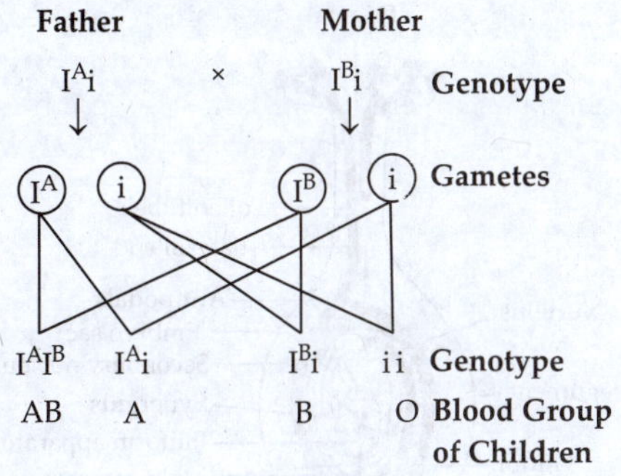

[2]

31. **Cross 1** is associated with the law of independent assortment.

According to this law, when two pairs of traits are combined in a hybrid, segregation of one pair of character is independent of other pair of characters. In a dihybrid cross, the phenotype of F_2-generation is round yellow, wrinkled yellow, round green and wrinkled green that appears in the ratio of 9 : 3 : 3 : 1. [2½]

Cross 2 is associated with the law of incomplete dominance.

Incomplete dominance is a form of gene interaction in which both alleles of a gene at a locus are partially expressed, often resulting in an intermediate or different phenotype. It is also known as partial dominance.

For example, in snapdragon, the allele for red colour is dominant over the allele for white colour. But the heterozygous flower with both the alleles are pink in colour.

The F_2-generation obtained by self-crossing the F_1-generation are as follows

Red : Pink : White

1 : 2 : 1 [2½]

Or

(i) The methodology included in DNA fingerprinting are as follows

(a) DNA is isolated and digested by the restriction endonucleases.

(b) DNA fragments are separated by gel electrophoresis.

(c) Separated DNA fragments are transferred to the synthetic membranes like nitrocellulose or nylon.

(d) Hybridisation using labelled VNTR probe.

(e) Hybridised DNA fragments are detected by autoradiography.

The sensitivity has been increased by the use of polymerase chain reaction. [3]

(ii) DNA polymorphism occurs due to mutation. The mutations keep on accumulating generation after generation and form one of the basis of variability / polymorphism. [2]

32. (i) Antibiotics are the substances produced by bacteria or fungi which can kill other microorganisms, especially bacteria. One of the well-known antibiotic is penicillin. [1]

(ii) Antibiotics are produced on a large scale by the process of fermentation. This is a chemical process which is induced by the microorganisms in a large tank. A tank contains a growth medium that provides nutrition for the microorganisms growth. Optimising temperature, pH levels, oxygen and nutrient in the fermentation tank is very crucial for antibiotic production.

After production, the antibiotics are extracted and purified through multiple physical processes. [2]

(iii) Taking antibiotics too often or for the wrong reason can cause the bacteria to change, so much that antibiotics do not work against them. This is called bacterial resistance or antibiotic resistance. Some bacteria are now resistant to even the most powerful antibiotics as available as antibiotic resistance is a growing problem. [2]

Or

(i) (a) **Morphine** is obtained from the latex of *Papaver somniferum*. It is a depressant, which slows down the body functions. [1]

(b) **Cocaine** is obtained from *Erythroxylum coca*. It is a stimulant and produces a sense of euphoria and increased energy. [1]

(c) **Marijuana** is obtained from the inflorescence of *Cannabis sativa*. It affects the cardiovascular system of the body. [1]

(ii) **Lysergic Acid Diethylamides** (LAD) or barbiturates are often misused. [1]

(iii) Moderate dose of cocaine has stimulating action on central nervous system. It produces a sense of euphoria and increased energy. High dosage of cocaine causes hallucinations. [1]

33. The implantation of zygote in uterus occurs in the following steps

(i) The mitotic division within the zygote called cleavage starts as the zygote moves towards the uterus through the isthmus of the oviduct.

(ii) It forms 2, 4, 8 and 16 daughter cells called blastomeres.

(iii) The embryo with 8-16 blastomeres is called morula.

(iv) Morula continues to divide and transforms into blastocyst as it moves further into the uterus.

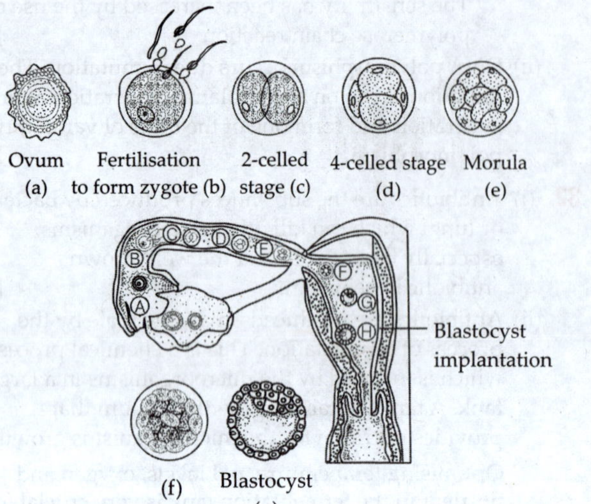

(v) Blastomeres in the blastocyst are arranged into an outer layer called trophoblast.

(vi) The inner group of cells attached to trophoblast constitute the inner cell mass.

(vii) Trophoblast layer then gets attached to the endometrium and the inner cell mass gets differentiated in the form of embryo.

(viii) After attachment, the uterine cells divide rapidly and cover the blastocyst. This leads to embedding of blastocyst in the endometrium of the uterus. This is called implantation. [5]

Or

(i) The parts involved in transferring the male gametes to its desired destination are stigma, style, micropyle, filiform apparatus and synergids.

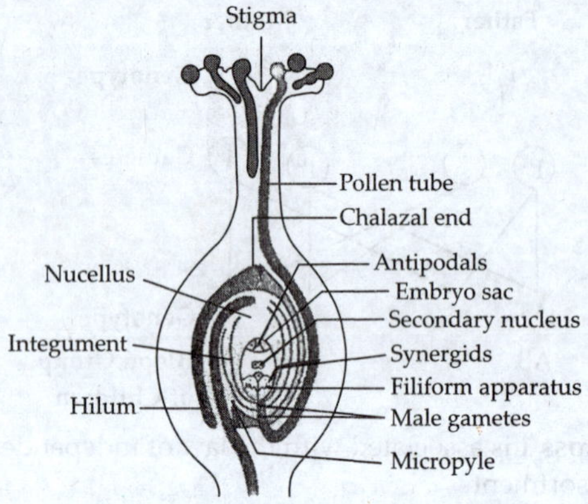

Longitudinal Section (LS) of a post-pollinated pistil

[3]

(ii) (a) **Synergids** These possess special cellular thickenings at their micropylar tip called filiform apparatus. That often guides the pollen tube to enter embryo sac.

(b) **Micropyle** It facilitates the entry of pollen tube and thus fertilisation.

(c) Pollen-pistil interaction is a chain or group of events that takes place from the falling of pollen over the stigma to the formation of pollen tube and its entry into the ovule. It is mediated by chemical components. [2]

SQP Code : **PB-3/15** Series ***i*-Succeed 3-25/15** Roll No.

Sample Question Paper 03

Biology 12th (Code 044)

General Instructions

1. All questions are compulsory.
2. The question paper has five sections and 33 questions.
3. Section-A has 16 questions of 1 mark each; Section-B has 5 questions of 2 marks each; Section-C has 7 questions of 3 marks each; Section-D has 2 case-based questions of 4 marks each; and Section-E has 3 questions of 5 marks each.
4. There is no overall choice. However, internal choices have been provided in some questions. A student has to attempt only one of the alternatives in such questions.
5. Wherever necessary, neat and properly labelled diagrams should be draw.

Time : 3 Hrs.

Max. Marks : 70

Section A Multiple Choice Type Questions

1. Which among the following diseases causes internal bleeding, muscular pain, anaemia and blockage of intestinal passage?

(a) Filariasis (b) Ascariasis
(c) Amoebiasis (d) Ringworm

2. Select the option that has the correct sequence with respect to structure of mammary gland.

(i) Mammary alveolus
(ii) Mammary duct
(iii) Mammary lobe
(iv) Areola
(v) Lactiferous duct

Options

(a) (ii) → (iv) → (v) → (iii) → (i)
(b) (iv) → (i) → (v) → (ii) → (iii)
(c) (iii) → (i) → (ii) → (v) → (iv)
(d) (iii) → (ii) → (i) → (iv) → (v)

3. Select the correct match from the following.

	Enzymes	Functions
(a)	Restriction endonuclease	Removes nucleotides from the ends of DNA
(b)	Restriction exonuclease	Cuts DNA at specific position
(c)	DNA ligase	Cuts DNA at non-specific position
(d)	*Taq* polymerase	Extends primers on genomic DNA template

4. $p^2 + 2pq + q^2 = 1$, this equation cannot operate in a population if

(a) frequent mutations occur among the gene pool
(b) there is no migration to a new habitat for a long time
(c) free interbreeding occurs among all individuals
(d) is isolated from other populations

5. *Bt* toxin gene isolated from a bacterium, is cloned and inserted in plants like cotton, soybean, tobacco to develop resistance to insects. The bacteria is
(a) *Bacillus subtilis*
(b) *Bacillus thermusaquaticus*
(c) *Bacillus thuringiensis*
(d) *Meloidogyne incognita*

6. A male having abnormal arrangement of chromosome is sterile. He also shows feminine development due to unnatural presence of a X-chromosome. Mention the chromosomal disorder from which he suffers.
(a) Turner's syndrome
(b) Down's syndrome
(c) Klinefelter's syndrome
(d) Haemophilia

7. Read the four statements given below and select the option having two correct statements.
(i) Smallpox can be completely eradicated by the use of vaccines and immunisation programmes.
(ii) The thymus is the main lymphoid organ where all blood cells including lymphocytes are produced.
(iii) AIDS is caused by retrovirus, which have an envelope enclosing the DNA genome.
(iv) Non-ionizing radiations like UV cause DNA damage leading to neoplastic transformation.

Options
(a) (i) and (ii) (b) (ii) and (iii)
(c) (i) and (iv) (d) (iii) and (iv)

8. Consider the formula given below.

$$N_t = N_o e^{rt}$$

what does '*e*' in this formula signifies?
(a) Population density after time *t*
(b) Population density at time zero
(c) The base at natural logarithms
(d) Intrinsic rate of natural increase

9. A specific recognition sequence identified by endonuclease as to make cut at specific positions within the DNA is
(a) poly (A) tail sequences
(b) degenerate primer sequence
(c) okazaki sequences
(d) palindromic nucleotide sequences

10. Which of the following codon is not a stop terminator codons?
(a) UAA (b) UUU
(c) UAG (d) UGA

11. BOD of waste water is estimated by measuring the amount of
(a) total inorganic matter
(b) oxygen evolution
(c) biodegradable organic matter
(d) oxygen consumption

12. The given figure is the diagrammatic representation of the vector pBR322. Which one of the given options correctly identifies its certain component(s)?

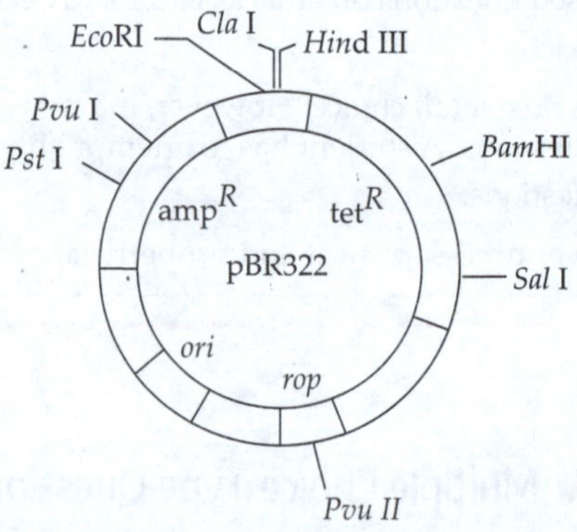

(a) *ori*–original restriction enzymes
(b) *rop*–reduced osmotic pressure
(c) *Hind* III, *Eco*RI–selectable markers
(d) amp^R, tet^R–antibiotic resistance genes

***Question** Nos. 13 to 16 consist of two statements, Assertion (A) and Reason (R) answer these questions by selecting the appropriate option given below.*
(a) Both Assertion and Reason are true and Reason is the correct explanation of Assertion
(b) Both Assertion and Reason are true, but Reason is not the correct explanation of Assertion
(c) Assertion is true, but Reason is false
(d) Assertion is false, but Reason is true

13. **Assertion** (A) Diaphragms, cervical caps and vaults are the barriers made up of rubber.

SP-03

Reason (R) Diaphragms, cervical caps and vaults are used to cover the male copulatory organ during coitus.

14. **Assertion** (A) Turner's syndrome is caused due to the presence of extra X-chromosome.

Reason (R) Individuals suffering from Turner's syndrome have rudimentary ovaries and lack secondary sexual characteristics.

15. **Assertion** (A) *t*RNA recognises its corresponding codon in *m*RNA.

Reason (R) For each codon, there is an individual RNA.

16. **Assertion** (A) Mycorrhiza is a mutualistic inter-relationship.

Reason (R) Mycorrhiza is an association between fungi and roots of higher plants.

Section B Very Short Answer Type Questions

17. Explain when is a genetic code is said to be

(i) degenerate?

(ii) universal?

Or Carefully examine structures A and B of pentose sugar given below. Which one of the two is more reactive? Give reasons.

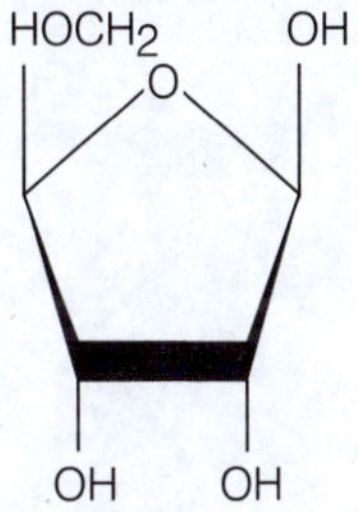

A

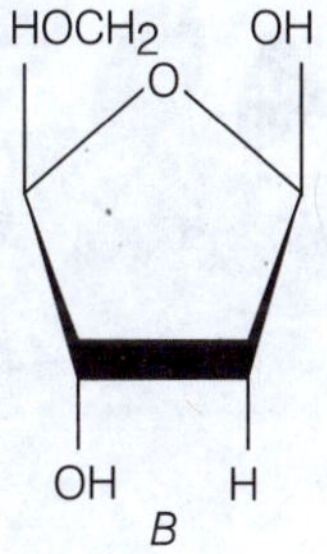

B

18. A woman took a pregnancy test, which showed a positive result.
Pregnancy tests typically give positive result after implantation.

(i) Name the site where implantation of blastocyst occur in the female reproductive system.

(ii) Name the structure that supports the developing embryo after implantation.

Or (i) Where do the signals for parturition originate in humans?

(ii) Why is it important to feed the newborn babies on colostrum?

19. (i) State what does standing crop of a trophic level represent?

(ii) What is a detritus food chain made up of? How does the organisms in detritus food chain meet their energy and nutritional requirements?

20. (i) Give the name of the source organism of the gene *cry* IAC and its target pest.

(ii) Mention the uses of cloning vector in biotechnology.

21.

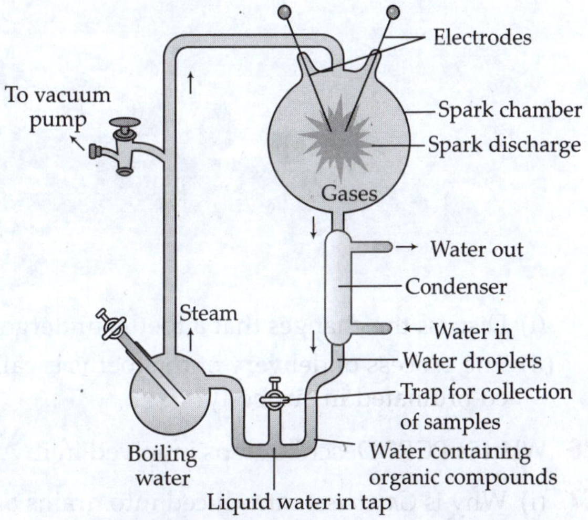

(i) In the experiment, shown above, name the gases used in order to simulate the primitive atmosphere.

(ii) State the significance of the experiment done by Miller and Urey.

Or The distance between genes *A* and *B* is 20 map units, genes *B* and *C* is 10 map units, while between genes *A* and *C* is 30 map units. Based on the above information, construct a linkage map and find out the possible order of the genes *A*, *B* and *C* in the map.

SP-03

Section C Short Answer Type Questions

22. (i) List the changes the primary oocyte undergoes in the tertiary follicular stage in human embryo.

(ii) Write the function of the seminal vesicle.

23. Identify *A, B, C, D, E* and *F* in the table given below

Phenomenon	Examples	Characteristics
A	*B*	fruit develop without fertilisation
C	*Citrus* and Mango	*D*
Apomixis	*E*	*F*

24. Evolution is any cumulative change in the characteristics of organisms over many generations. Based on this, answer the questions related to evolution.

(i) How does homology leads to divergent evolution?

(ii) Give an example of analogy in plants.

25. The graph below shows the stages of pregnancy and the changes observed in the developing foetus.

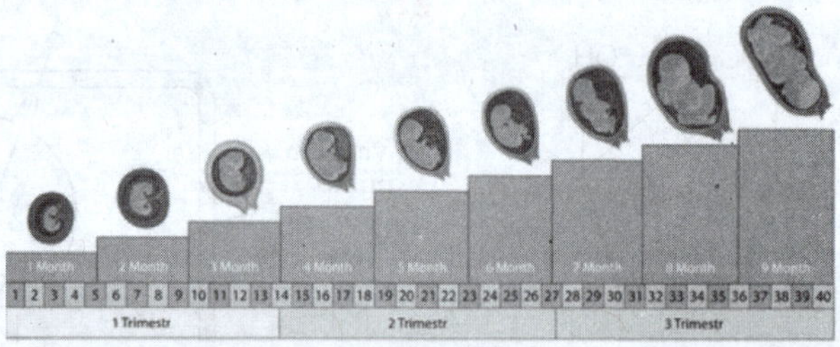

STAGES OF PREGNANCY

(i) Discuss the changes that a foetus undergoes by the end of 12th week.

(ii) The process of delivery of the foetus is called parturition. How is this process co-ordinated in our body?

26. What is PCR? Describe steps involved in it. Also mention any two of its applications.

27. (i) Why is *Gambusia* introduced into drains and ponds?

(ii) Mention one application for each of the following.

(a) Passive immunisation

(b) Antihistamine

(c) Colostrum

(d) Cytokinin-barrier

28. (i) When does a geneticist need to carry a test cross?

(ii) Why is pedigree analysis done in the study of human genetics? State the conclusion that can be drawn from it.

Section D Case Based Questions

Q. Nos. 29 and 30 are case-based questions. Each question has 3 subparts with internal choice in one subpart.

29. The diagram given below is that of a typical biogas plant

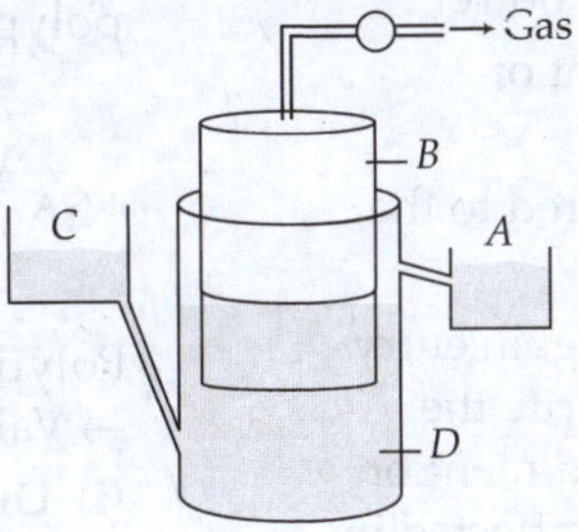

(i) Identify *A*, *B* and *C*. [1]

Or (i) What is the main function of biogas plant? [1]

(ii) (a) Describe how biogas is generated from activated sludge?

(b) List the components of biogas. [2]

(iii) Expand KVIC. [1]

30. Observe the graph below and answer the questions that follows..

The graph represents the variations in the number of cases of amniocentesis observed over the years.

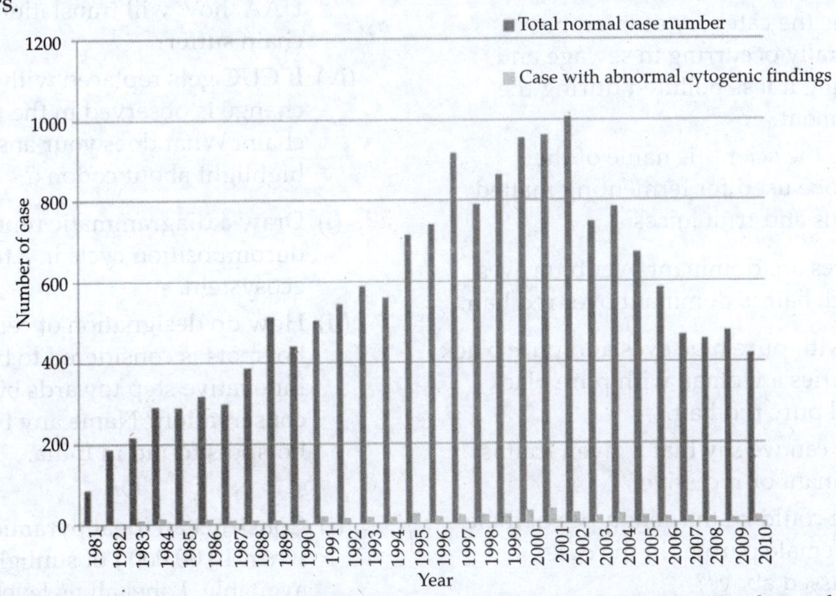

(i) After 2002, cases of amniocentesis were observed to be declining. Explain why? [1]

(ii) After amniocentesis evaluation, the doctor advised a pregnant women to terminate the pregnancy. Explain what could be the reason behind this decision? [1]

(iii) 'Unfortunately this technique is being misused'. Elaborate the context of this statement. [2]

Or

(iii) Amniocentesis is a pre-natal diagnostic procedure to assess chromosomal abnormalities and foetal infections. How is this made possible? [2]

Section E Long Answer Type Questions

31. (i) How does smoking tobacco in human lead to oxygen deficiency in their body?

(ii) How does moderate and high dosage of cocaine affect the human body?

(iii) (a) Name the causative agent of typhoid in humans.

(b) Name the test administered to the confirm the disease.

(c) How does the pathogen gain entry into the human body? Write the diagnostic symptoms and mention the body organ that gets affected in severe cases?

Or

(i) The three microbes are listed below. Name the product produced by each one of them and mention their use.

(a) *Aspergillus niger*

(b) *Trichoderma polysporum*

(c) *Monascus purpureus*

(ii) Name the category of microbes naturally occurring in sewage and making it less polluted during the treatment.

(iii) Write the scientific name of the microbe used for fermenting malted cereals and fruit juices.

32. Black eyes are dominant over blue eyes and black hair is dominant over red hair.

A man with pure blue eyes and pure black hair marries a woman with pure black eyes and pure red hair.

(i) How can we say that a given trait is dominant or recessive?

(ii) What could be the genotypes of male and female partner in the case discussed above?

(iii) What will be the probabilities of phenotypes of the children of this couple?

Or

Read the sequence of the nucleotides in the given segment of *m*RNA and the respective amino acid sequence in the polypeptide chain.

									X
*m*RNA	AUG	UAC	CCU	AAU	GGC	GUU	UCU	CUC	UGA
	1	2	3	4	5	6	7	8	

Polypeptide P $\rightarrow$ Tyr $\rightarrow$ Pro $\rightarrow$ Asp $\rightarrow$ Gly $\rightarrow$ Val $\rightarrow$ Ser $\rightarrow$ Leu

(i) Draw the nucleotide sequence of the DNA strand from which this *m*RNA was transcribed.

(ii) A mutation occurred at 6th codon in the *m*RNA where 'G' was replaced by 'A'. What is this type of mutation called and how will it affect the polypeptide chain?

(iii) What does P coded by AUG represents? If AUG is replaced by UAA, how will translation of *m*RNA chain suffer?

(iv) If CUC gets replaced with CUG, no change is observed in the polypeptide chain. What does your answer highlight about codons?

33. (i) Draw a diagrammatic representation of decomposition cycle in a terrestratal ecosystem.

(ii) How do designation of certain areas as hotspots is considered to be the innovative step towards biodiversity conservation? Name any two famous hotspots found in India.

Or

(i) Construct an ideal pyramid of energy when 10,00,000 J of sunlight is available. Label all its levels.

(ii) Why are the pyramids referred to as upright or inverted? Explain.

Explanations in Topper's Style

My Commitment *I affirm that I am reviewing these solutions only after I have solved the Sample Question Paper 3 on my own. My purpose of looking the solutions is solely to verify whether my answers/solutions were correct or not and to identify my mistakes in case my solutions were wrong or I could not solve that.*

1. (b) *Ascaris*, the common roundworm causes ascariasis. Symptoms of this disease includes the internal bleeding, muscular pain, fever, anaemia and of intestinal blockage. [1]

2. (c) The correct sequence of order of mammary gland starting from the top is as follows
(iii) Mammary lobe → (i) Mammary alveolus → (ii) Mammary duct → (v) Lactiferous duct → (iv) Areola. [1]

3. (d) Option (d) is correctly matched. Rest all are incorrect and can be corrected as
Restriction endonuclease cuts the DNA at a specific position.
Restriction exonucleases removes the nucleotides from the end of DNA.
DNA ligase joins the DNA fragments. [1]

4. (a) Hardy-Weinberg equation $(p^2 + 2pq + q^2 = 1)$ applies to a population where the allelic frequencies are stable from one generation to the next. The Hardy-Weinberg principle cannot be applied to a population where frequent mutations arise, as these will keep changing, leading to new phenotypes. [1]

5. (c) *Bacillus thuringiensis* is a soil bacterium which produces *Bt* toxin protein as crystals in an inactive form. These proteins are often extracted from bacteria, cloned and are inserted in different crop plants to develop resistance against insect pests. [1]

6. (c) A male having abnormal arrangement of chromosome, (i.e. 47; XXY) is sterile and shows the feminine development due to the presence of extra X-chromosome. The male here is suffering from the chromosomal disorder called Klinefelter's syndrome. [1]

7. (c) Statements (i) and (iv) are correct, while statements (ii) and (iii) are incorrect and can be corrected as
The bone morrow is the main lymphoid organ where all blood cells including lymphocyte are produced.
AIDS is caused by the Human Immunodeficiency Virus (HIV), a member of a group of virus called retrovirus, which have an envelope enclosing the RNA genome. [1]

8. (c) '*e*' in the formula $N_t = N_o e^{rt}$ signifies the base at natural logarithms. [1]

9. (d) Restriction endonuclease recognises a specific sequence of DNA that is called palindromic nucleotide sequence. [1]

10. (b) UAA, UAG, UGA are stop codons or (terminator codon). UUU would code for phenylalanine (Phe). Thus, UUU is not a stop terminator codon. [1]

11. (d) BOD of waste water is estimated by measuring the amount of consumption of oxygen. [1]

12. (d) Option (d) contains the correctly identified components as amp^R (ampicillin resistance gene) and tet^R (tetracycline resistance gene) are antibiotic resistance genes. Rest all options are incorrect and can be corrected as
ori is the origin of replication, *rop* codes for proteins involved in replication of the plasmid.
Hind III as well as *Eco*RI are restriction sites. [1]

13. (c) Assertion is true, but Reason is false. Reason can be corrected as
Diaphragms, cervical caps and vaults are the contraceptive barriers which are made up of rubber. They are inserted into the female reproductive tract to cover the cervix during coitus. These barriers helps to prevent conception by blocking the entry of sperms through the cervix. [1]

14. (d) Assertion is false, but Reason is true. Assertion can be correct as
Turner's syndrome is caused due to the absence of X-chromosome. Individuals having single X-chromosome, [i.e. 2A + XO (45)] have female sexual differentiation, but ovaries are rudimentary. Other associated phenotypes of this condition are short stature, webbed neck, broad chest, lack of secondary sexual characteristics and sterility. [1]

15. (c) Assertion is true, but Reason is false. Reason can be corrected as
As there are 61 codons specifying amino acids, the cell should contain 61 different *t*RNA molecules, each with a different anticodon.

The number of *t*RNA molecule discovered is much less than 61. This implies that the anticodons of some *t*RNAs read more than one codon on *m*RNA. [1]

16. (b) Both Assertion and Reason are true, but Reason is not the correct explanation of Assertion.

Mutualism is a type of positive interaction, in which the organisms, forming an association are benefitted. For example, mycorrhiza is an association of fungi and roots of higher plants. In this association, fungi helps in water and mineral absorption by the plant. In exchange of this, fungi obtain prepared food material. [1]

17. (i) Genetic code is said to be degenerate when some amino acids are coded by more than one codon, e.g, UUU and UUC, both code for phenylalanine[1]

(ii) Genetic code is said to be universal when a particular codon codes for the same amino acid in all organisms, for example, from bacteria to human UUU codes for phenylalanine. [1]

Or

Structure *A* represents ribose sugar and structure *B* represents deoxyribose sugar.

Structure *A*, i.e. ribose sugar present in every nucleotide of RNA is more reactive making RNA highly reactive, labile and easily degradable compared to DNA.

18. (i) The site where implantation of blastocyst occurs in the female reproductive system is the uterine wall. [1]

(ii) Placenta supports the developing embryo after implantation. The placenta also facilitate the supply of oxygen and nutrients to the embryo. [1]

Or

(i) The signals for parturition originate from the fully developed foetus and the placenta, which induces mild uterine contraction called foetal-ejection reflex. [1]

(ii) Colostrum contains necessary antibodies (IgA) that provide protection against disease to infants. [1]

19. (i) Standing crop of a trophic level represents the total mass of living material or energy content of all the organisms of a trophic level at a particular time and location.

(ii) Detritus food chain is made up of decomposers i.e. some bacteria and fungi. Organisms in detritus food chain meet their energy and nutrient requirements by degrading the dead organic matter or detritus. [1]

20. (i) The source organism of the gene *cry* IAC is *Bacillus thuringiensis* and its target is cotton bollworms. [1]

(ii) Cloning vector in biotechnology helps in linking the foreign/alien DNA with the host's DNA and helps in the selection of recombinants from the non-recombinants. [1]

21. (i) In this experiment, the main objective was to create the atmospheric conditions that are prevalent on the primitive earth. Hence, gases used in this experiment were a mixture of NH_3, H_2O, CH_4 and H_2. [1]

(ii) The Miller and Urey's experiment was conducted to provide validation to Oparin–Haldane's theory of chemical theory of life.

It provided the first evidence that organic molecules needed for life could be formed from inorganic components and confirms that abiotic synthesis may have occurred in primitive atmospheric conditions. [1]

Value Points For obtaining maximum marks, students should write the purpose of those gases choosen instead of giving direct answer

Or If we assume that gene *B* is present in the middle of *A* and *C*, then the correct order of genes *A*, *B* and *C* is

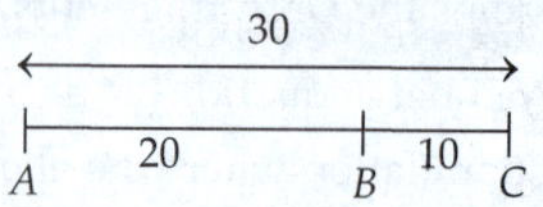

This arrangement satisfies all the stated conditions, i.e.

$A - B = 20$ map units , $B - C = 10$ map units

$A - C = 30$ map units [2]

22. (i) The primary oocyte within the tertiary follicle grows in size. The fully grown primary oocyte completes its first meiotic division to produce two daughter nuclei in which larger haploid cell is called secondary oocyte and the tiny one is called first polar body. The secondary oocyte retains bulk of nutrient rich cytoplasm of primary oocyte. [2]

(ii) Seminal vesicle produces an alkaline secretion containing prostaglandins, proteins and fructose. The high fructose content provides energy to the spermatozoa. These secretions form 60-70% of the fluid found in the semen. [1]

23. In the given table *A*, *B*, *C*, *D*, *E* and *F* are identified as

$A \rightarrow$ Parthenocarpy

$B \rightarrow$ Banana

$C \rightarrow$ Polyembryony

$D \rightarrow$ nucellar cells develop into embryo

$E \rightarrow$ Grasses

$F \rightarrow$ Production of seeds without fertilisation [3]

24. (i) In divergent evolution, the same basic organ in animals or plants of same ancestory become specialised to perform different functions, (i.e. exhibits homology) in order to adapt different environmental conditions, prevailing in their habitats.
For example, the forelimbs of vertebrates like whale's front flipper, bat's wings, cat's paw, etc. [2]

(ii) Examples of analogy in plants is the sweet potato and potato. Here, the sweet potato is a modified root, while the potato is a modified stem tuber. Despite their different origins, both serve the function of storing food. [1]

25. (i) By the end of 12 weeks, foetus undergoes following changes
- Foetus is fully formed with all the organs, muscles and bones.
- Sex organs are well-developed. [1]

(ii) Parturition is induced by a complex neuro-endocrine mechanism. The signals for parturition originates from the fully developed foetus and placenta that induces the uterine contractions called **foetal-ejection reflex**.
The stimulatory reflex between uterine contractions and oxytocin secretions create stronger contraction and this leads to the expulsion of the baby. [2]

26. PCR (Polymerase Chain Reaction) is a technique which is used to amplify specific DNA sequences.

Steps involved in PCR

The procedure of PCR involves 3 steps described below

(i) **Denaturation** The double-stranded DNA is separated by subjecting it to the high temperature (95°C) for 2 minutes. This breaks the H-bonds between nucleotides.

(ii) **Annealing** It involves hybridisation of primer to *ss*DNA. The temperature is maintained at 50°C, which allows annealing of primers with their complementary sequences on separated DNA strands.

(iii) **Extension** *Taq* DNA polymerase enzyme extends the primers. Thus, this completes one PCR cycle. Completing the replication of the rest of the DNA. [2]

Applications of PCR

(i) PCR helps in an early detection of infectious agents present in low numbers to rule out any possible infections.

(ii) PCR is used to copy DNA from fossils discovered which help in evolutionary studies. [1]

27. (i) *Gambusia* is a fish that feed upon mosquito larvae. Thus, it is introduced in drains and ponds to destroy disease vector. [1]

(ii) *Applications of given components are as follows*

(a) Passive immunisation provides a faster immune response.

(b) Antihistamine is used to reduce the symptoms of allergy, such as sneezing, watery eyes, rashes, running nose, etc.

(c) Colostrum consists of antibodies (e.g. IgA) that provide immunity to an infant against infections.

(d) Cytokinin barrier produces interferons and protects non-infected cells from further viral infections. [2]

28. (i) A geneticist needs to carry a test cross when he/she wants to determine the genotype of an organism, with a dominant phenotype trait, whether it is homozygous or heterozygous. [1]

(ii) The study of inheritance of genetic traits in several generations of a human family in the form of a family diagram is called pedigree analysis.
Inheritance pattern of traits in human beings cannot be studied by crosses. Thus, pedigree analysis is done. Based on the pedigree studies, inheritance of a specific trait, abnormality or disease can be easily traced. [2]

29. (i) In the given diagram *A*, *B* and *C* are identified as
A – Sludge tank
B – Gas holder
C – Slurry (dung + water) [1]

Or (i) The main function of biogas plant is to produce biogas through the anaerobic digestion of organic waste materials, which can be used as a renewable energy source for cooking, heating and electricity. [1]

(ii) (a) Biogas is produced from the activated sludge through anaerobic digestion, where bacteria breakdown organic matter in the absence of oxygen. This process generates methane (CH_4) and CO_2, forming biogas. It's primarily used as renewable source for heat, electricity.

(b) Biogas is a mixture of gases (methane 60%, CO_2 40%, traces of hydrogen and several other gases) produced by the microbial activity and may be used as fuel. [2]

(iii) KVIC stands for Khadi and Village Industries Commission [1]

30. (i) After 2002, cases of amniocentesis were observed to be declining due to the strict steps taken by the government against it. Moreover, in many countries the amniotic fluid test was also banned by the government. [1]

(ii) The doctor advised medical termination of pregnancy (MTP) as the foetus may be unviable or the pregnancy is harmful for mother or foetus (or both). [1]

(iii) The techniques of amniocentesis is being misused to know about the sex of an unborn baby. If the baby turns out to be female, in many cases the pregancy is medically or illegally terminated. It has indirectly caused an increase in female foeticides. [2]

Or

(iii) In amniocentesis, a small amount of amniotic fluid containing foetal cells is extracted from the amnion surrounding the developing foetus. These cells are then cultured and karyotype analysis is carried out. This reveals any genetic abnormality if present in the foetus, such as Down's syndrome, cystic fibrosis, etc. [2]

31. (i) Smoking increases carbon monoxide content in blood and reduces the concentration of haem-bound oxygen. This causes oxygen deficiency in the body. [1]

(ii) Moderate dosage of cocaine have a stimulating action on control nervous system. It produces a sense of euphoria and increased energy. However, high dosage of cocaine causes hallucinations. [1]

(iii) (a) Typhoid is caused by a bacteria *Salmonella typhi*. [1]

(b) Typhoid is confirmed by the widal test. [1]

(c) Pathogens enter the human body through contaminated food and water.

Diagnostic symptoms includes high fever, weakness, stomach pain, etc. The body organ affected in severe cases is small intestine. [1]

Or

(i) (a) The product obtained by *Aspergillus niger* is citric acid. [1]

(b) The product obtained by *Trichoderma polysporum* is cyclosporin-A. [1]

(c) The product obtained by *Monascus purpureus* is statins. [1]

(ii) The category of microbes naturally occurring in sewage and making it less polluted are bacteria and fungi, wherein masses of bacteria get associated with filaments of fungi to form mesh - like structure called flocks. [1]

(iii) *Saccharomyces cerevisiae* also called Brewer's yeast is the microbe used for fermenting malted cereals and fruit juices. [1]

32. (i) The given trait is dominant as any trait which expresses itself in the homozygous condition is dominant, e.g. BB (pure black), bb (pure blue). [1]

(ii) The genotype of parents will be

Man		**Woman**
bbRR	×	BBrr
(Pure blue eyes, Pure black hairs)		(Pure black eyes, Pure red hairs)

[1]

(iii) The probable phenotypes of their children can be

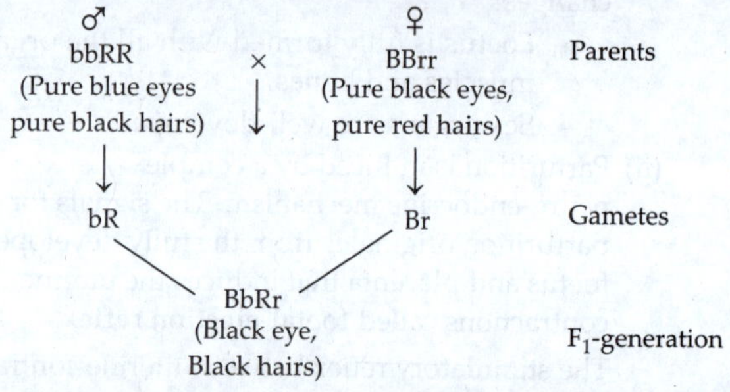

The probability of their children will be 100% black eyes and black hairs. [3]

Or

(i) TAC-ATG-GGA-TTA-CCG-CAA-AGA- GAG-ACT is the DNA sequence from which *m*RNA was transcribed. [1]

(ii) At 6th place, GUU codon is present, a mutation replacing G with A is called a point mutation.

The new codon will become AUU. The original codon GUU codes for valine while the mutated codon AUU codes for isoleucine.

By altering just one amino acid, the entire peptide may change, thereby changing the entire protein. It may alter some other characteristics or function of the protein formed. [2]

(iii) P is methionine coded by AUG. It starts the translation of *m*RNA sequence. AUG is start codon while UAA is the stop condon. If UAA appears at the beginning, the translation of *m*RNA chain will not initiate. [1]

(iv) CUC and CUG both codons code for leucine amino acid. Thus, there will no change in polypeptide synthesis if CUC gets replaced with CUG.

This indicates that genetic codons are degenerative, i.e. more than one codon can code for a given amino acid. [1]

33. (i)

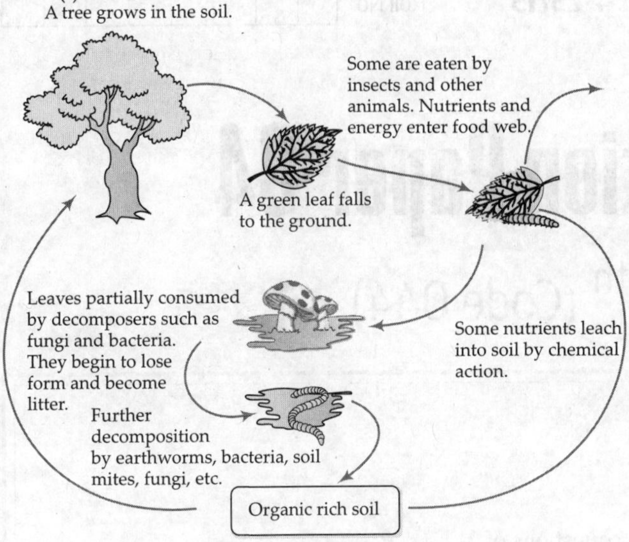

Diagrammatic representation of decomposition cycle in a terrestrial ecosystem

[3]

(ii) Hotspots are the regions that exhibits high degree of endemism and great species richness, therefore, designating these areas as 'biodiversity hotspots' allow their maximum protection and reduce the ongoing extinction by about 30%. [1]

The famous hotspot regions in India are Western Ghats and Himalayas. [1]

Or

(i)

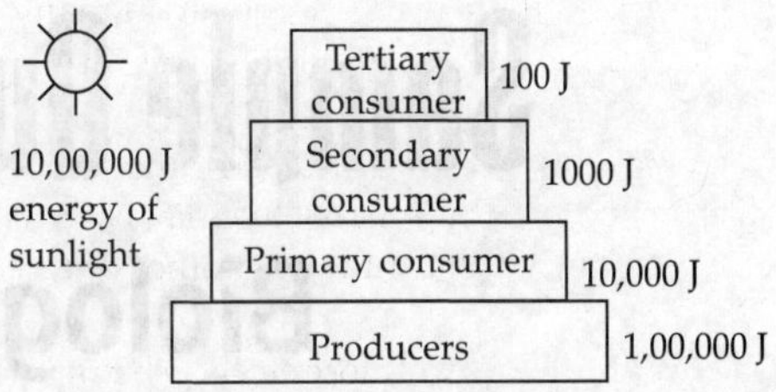

Ideal pyramid of energy

[3]

(ii) When producers are more in number and biomass than the herbivores and the herbivores on the contrary are more in number and biomass than the carnivores, such pyramids is referred to as upright. For example Energy at a lower trophic level is always more than at a higher trophic level. Therefore, pyramid of energy is referred to as always upright.

When the numbers and biomass of producers are less, and consumers increase, becomes largestest at the top consumer level, the pyramid of numbers and biomass is referred to as inverted. [2]

SQP Code : **PB-4/15** Series ***i*-Succeed 4-25/15** Roll No.

Sample Question Paper 04

Biology 12th (Code 044)

General Instructions

1. All questions are compulsory.
2. The question paper has five sections and 33 questions.
3. Section-A has 16 questions of 1 mark each; Section-B has 5 questions of 2 marks each; Section-C has 7 questions of 3 marks each; Section-D has 2 case-based questions of 4 marks each; and Section-E has 3 questions of 5 marks each.
4. There is no overall choice. However, internal choices have been provided in some questions. A student has to attempt only one of the alternatives in such questions.
5. Wherever necessary, neat and properly labelled diagrams should be draw.

Time : 3 Hrs.
Max. Marks : 70

Section A Multiple Choice Type Questions

1. A test tube baby programme was suggested to an infertile couple by the doctor. Out of the options given below, select the correct technique that is used in this programme.

(a) Zygote Intra Fallopian Transfer (ZIFT)
(b) Intra Uterine Insemination (IUI)
(c) Gamete Intra Fallopian Transfer (GIFT)
(d) All of the above

2. Which of the following options represents a test cross correctly?

(a) Pp × pp (b) Pp × PP
(c) Pp × Pp (d) PP × pp

3. Select the correct match from the following.

	Terms		Definition
(a)	Parturition	1.	The uterine contractions developed by foetus and placenta.
(b)	Ovulation	2.	Release of egg from the corpus luteum.
(c)	Implantation	3.	Attachment of embryo to the myometrium.
(d)	Gestation	4.	Period of time between conception and birth.

4. Select the option that has the correct sequence of LS of an embryo of grass (from top to bottom).

(i) Epiblast
(ii) Radicle
(iii) Scutellum
(iv) Coleoptile
(v) Coleorhiza

Option

(a) (i) → (ii) → (iv) → (iii) → (v)
(b) (iii) → (iv) → (i) → (ii) → (v)
(c) (iv) → (iii) → (ii) → (i) → (v)
(b) (iii) → (iv) → (ii) → (i) → (v)

5. Yeast respires using sugar. Identify the conditions required and the products formed from the options given below.

(a) It respires under anaerobic condition and produces lactic acid
(b) It respires under aerobic condition and produces alcohol
(c) It respires under anaerobic condition and produces alcohol
(d) It respires under aerobic condition and produces lactic acid

6. If N = Population density at time t, then population density at time $t+1$ can be written as $N_{t+1} = N_t + [(A+B)-(C+D)]$.

Which of the following option is correct for A, B, C and D in the above equation.

(a) A can be mortality and B can be natality
(b) B can be immigration and C can be natality
(c) C can be mortality and D can be immigration
(d) A can be natality and D can be emigration

7. Read the four statements given below and select the option having two correct statements.

(i) Biodiversity is the term popularised by the sociobiologist Edward Wilson.
(ii) India has more than 1,000 genetically different strains of rice.
(iii) The number of fungi species in the world is more than the combined total of the species of fishes, amphibians, reptiles and mammals.
(iv) India has 8.1 per cent of the world's land area.

(a) (i) and (ii) (b) (ii) and (iv)
(c) (i) and (iii) (d) (iii) and (iv)

8. The figure shows action of restriction enzyme.

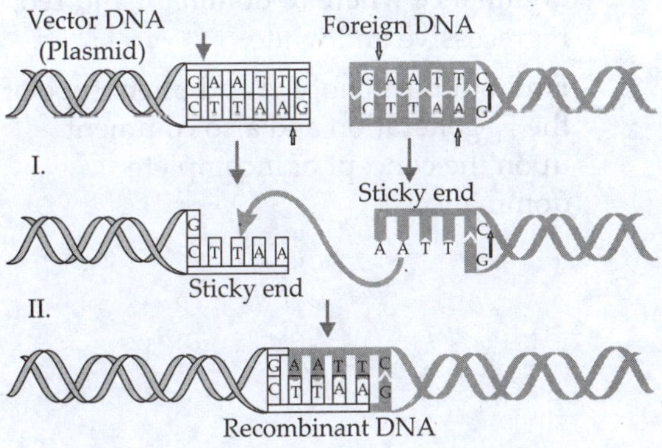

Different enzymes (I and II) are involved in this action. Choose the correct enzymes that are involved in this process.

	Enzyme I	Enzyme II
(a)	*Eco*RI	DNA ligase
(b)	*Hind* II	DNA ligase
(c)	*Eco*RI	*Hind* III
(d)	Endonuclease	Exonuclease

9. Saliva in the mouth and tears from the eyes belong to which type of innate immunity barriers?

(a) Cytosine barriers
(b) Cellular barriers
(c) Physiological barriers
(d) Physical barriers

10. Which of the following microbes gives nutritional supplement, i.e. protein as a product?

(a) *Acetobacter* (b) *Chlorella*
(c) *Pseudomonas* (d) *Corynebacterium*

11. The cells of which of the following layers of the anther wall are multinucleated?

(a) Epidermis
(b) Endothecium
(c) Middle layer
(d) Tapetum

12. An inverted pyramid of biomass can be found in which of the following ecosystem?

(a) Tundra (b) Marine
(c) Forest (d) Grassland

Question Nos. 13 to 16 consists of two statements, Assertion (A) and Reason (R). Answer the questions by selecting the appropriate option given below.

(a) Both Assertion and Reason are true and Reason is the correct explanation of Assertion
(b) Both Assertion and Reason are true, but Reason is not the correct explanation of Assertion
(c) Assertion is true, but Reason is false
(d) Assertion is false, but Reason is true

13. **Assertion** (A) Endosperm is formed by the fusion of one male gamete and two polar nuclei.

SP-04

Reason (R) In pea, the endosperm remains as part of seed as it is not completely consumed up during embryo formation.

14. **Assertion** (A) In humans, the gamete contributed by the male determines whether the child will be male or female.
Reason (R) Sex in humans is a polygenic trait depending upon a cumulative effect of some genes on X-chromosome and some on Y-chromosome.

15. **Assertion** (A) Biotechnology produces transgenic microorganisms that function as microfactories for proteins.
Reason (R) Transgenic microorganisms can be developed to produce proteins of human use like insulin.

16. **Assertion** (A) Herbivores are also called as first order consumers.
Reason (R) Herbivores obtain their food directly from plants.

Section B Very Short Answer Type Questions

17. How are sticky ends formed on a DNA strand? Why are they so called?

Or (a) Which conditions apart from the temperature, pH and substrate are provided by the bioreactor?

(b) Name the components of a bioreactor.

18. Write the characteristic features of anther, pollen and stigma of wind pollinated flowers.

Or Write the difference between the tender coconut water and the thick, white kernel of a mature coconut and their ploidy.

19. Due to improper functioning gland *'X'* was removed from the body of a 15-year-old person. Identify *'X'*, can you predict the effects that will be observed in the immune functions of this individual?

20. Organisms occupy a place in the natural surroundings or in a community according to their feeding relationships with other organisms.

Based on the source of the nutrition or food, organisms occupy a specific place in a food chain.

(i) Can we say that 'man can be primary as well as secondary consumer'? Justify this statement.

(ii) Which trophic level do zooplanktons and phytoplankton occupy?

21. Explain the role of initiator *t*RNA in initiation of protein synthesis.

Or

All pattern of inheritance could not be explained exclusively on the basis of Mendel's original principles alone. Certain complexities were observed by later workers which deviated them from Mendel's laws or Mendelism.
Draw a cross showing incomplete dominance where R=dominant and red, r = recessive and white.

Find out the genotype and phenotype of the F_1-generation and also comment upon the concept of incomplete dominance.

SP-04

Section C Short Answer Type Questions

22. The figure given below shows the LS of an anatropous ovule.

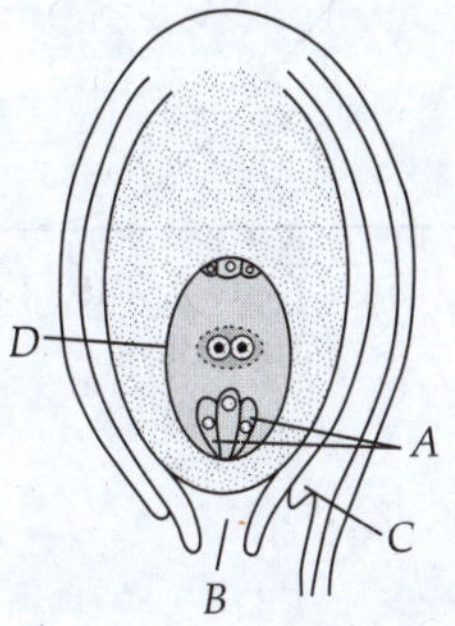

(i) Label the parts *A*, *B* and *C*.

(ii) Write the function/role played by the label '*A*' in the process fertilisation.

23. (i) Name the stage of cell division where segregation of an independent pair of chromosome occurs.

(ii) Why do normal RBC become elongated and sickle shaped in structure in a person suffering from sickle-cell anaemia?

24. While studying an article on human evolution, Sita got to know about the common ancestors of human and apes.

(i) Write two differences between *Homo erectus* and *Homo habilis*.

(ii) Rearrange the following from early to late geological period, Carboniferous, Silurian and Jurassic.

25. (i) Why does *hn*RNA undergo splicing? Where does splicing occur in the cell?

(ii) What will happen if DNA replication is not followed by cell division in a eukaryotic cell?

26. *A* and *B* are two different cloning vectors in two different bacterial colonies cultured in chromogenic substrate. Bacterial colonies with cloning vector *A* were colourless, whereas those with B were blue coloured. Explain by giving reasons for the difference in colour that appeared.

27. Identify *A*, *B*, *C*, *D*, *E* and *F* in the table given below.

Name of human diseases	Causative organisms	Symptoms
Typhoid	*A*	*B*
C	*P. falciparum*	Fever recurring every three to four days
Ascariasis	*D*	*E*
F	Epidermophyton	Scaly lesions on various body

28. (i) Write the importance of cryopreservation in conservation of biodiversity.

(ii) List the features that make a stable biological community.

Section D Case Based Questions

Q. Nos. 29 and 30 are case-based questions. Each question has 3 subparts with internal choice in one subpart.

29. Study the given pedigree chart showing the pattern of blood group inheritance in a family.

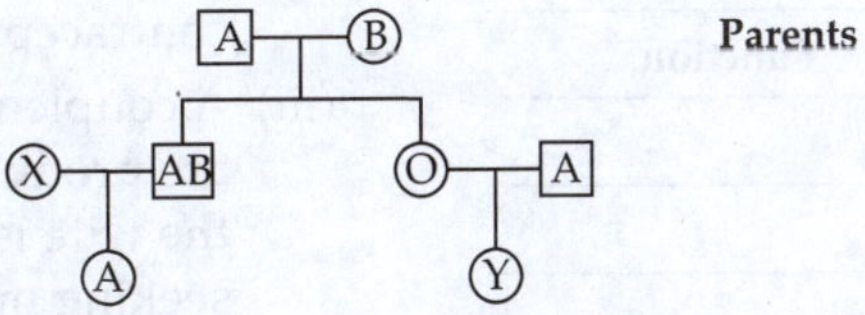

(i) On the basis of the inheritance pattern exhibited in this pedigree chart, what conclusion can you draw about the genotype of the parents (A and B)? [1]

(ii) If the individual in the second generation shows dominant allele I^A and I^B.

(a) What genotype is shown by the individual X.

(b) Also tell the possible blood group shown by it. [1]

(iii) If the parents in the second generation shows both dominant and recessive allele, what possible blood groups can be shown by the individual 'Y' in third generation? [2]

Or

(iii) If the individual in the second generation has blood group B instead of A, what possible blood groups can be seen of the individual 'Y' in third generation? [2]

30. The two graphs given below show the comparison of two people who took part in a study to find out the effectiveness of two types of immunisation. Person *A* received an injection of antibodies against tetanus and person *B* received a tetanus vaccination. A blood test was analysed after few weeks for the presence of antibodies to tetanus.

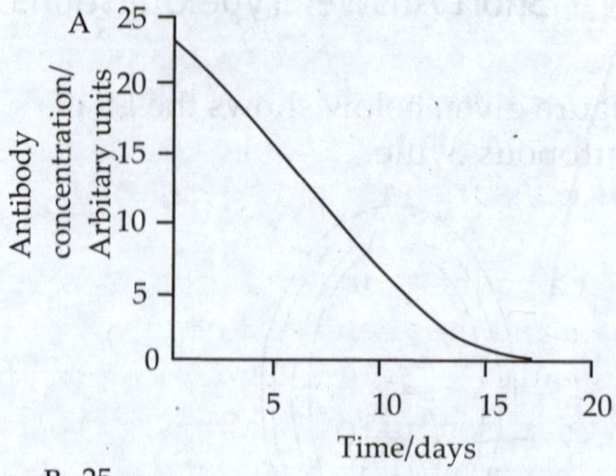

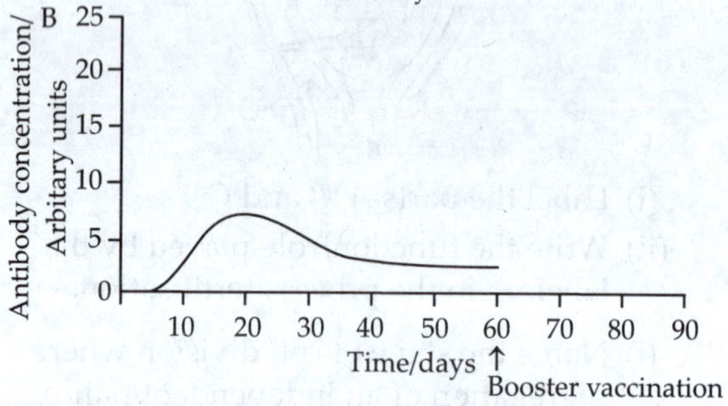

(i) With reference to the above graph explain, why the antibody concentration in person *A* decreased during the study period? [1]

(ii) What are the types of immunity that are shown in the person *A* and *B*, respectively? [1]

(iii) How will you explain that the antibody concentration in person *A* did not increase? [2]

Or (iii) Explain why the experiments had to measure the concentration of antibodies to tetanus rather than the concentration of all antibodies in the blood *A* and *B*. [2]

SP-04

Section E Long Answer Type Questions

31. Given below are organs of female reproductive system. Identify and write their location and function.

Organs	Location	Function
Ovaries		
Uterus		
Mammary glands		
Fimbriae		
Fallopian tube		

Or (i) Mention one positive and one negative application of amniocentesis.

(ii) Why is saheli a well-accepted contraceptive pill?

(iii) A couple where both husband and wife are producing functional gametes, but the wife is still unable to conceive, is seeking medical aid.

Describe any one method that you can suggest to this couple to become happy parents.

32. Scientists have long been altering the genes of food crops to boost food production and to make crops more pest or cold resistant. Proponents of GMO says that these crops are environmental friendly and safe to eat. However, critics claim that GM crops require increased amount of pesticides and herbicides and thus damages the environment.

(i) Giving an example of *Bt* cotton, prove the critics point invalid.

(ii) (a) Name the Indian organisation which make decisions regarding the validity of GM research.

(b) Mention any two advantage of genetically modified (GM) plants.

(iii) Name two Indian crops which were biopirated by some multinational companies.

Or

In genetic engineering there are various enzymes involved which simplify this complex process. These enzymes are used for cutting of DNA at specific location during *r*DNA technology.

(i) Do eukaryotic cells have restriction endonucleases? Justify your answer.

(ii) Name the first restriction endonuclease discoverd.

(iii) (a) Mention the difference in the mode of action of exonuclease and endonuclease.

(b) How does restriction endonuclease *Eco*RI function?

33. (i) 'Process of transcription and translation are coupled in prokaryotes, but not in eukaryotes'. Explain.

(ii) Draw a diagram depicting the Hershey-Chase experiment.

Or

(i) Write the term used for the resemblance of varieties of placental mammals to corresponding marsupials in Australia.

(ii) Why are wings of butterfly and birds said to be analogous organs ?

(iii) Draw a diagrammatic representation of Miller's experiment.

Explanations in Topper's Style

My Commitment *I affirm that I am reviewing these solutions only after I have solved the Sample Question Paper 4 on my own. My purpose of looking the solutions is solely to verify whether my answers/solutions were correct or not and to identify my mistakes in case my solutions were wrong or I could not solve that.*

1. (a) In test tube baby programme, the zygote is allowed to divide upto 8-celled blastomeres in the laboratory, then it is transferred into the Fallopian tube. This technique is called ZIFT (Zygote Intra Fallopian Transfer). [1]

2. (a) A test cross is a type of cross done between the heterozygous F_1-generation and recessive parent, i.e.

$$\underset{(F_1\text{-generation})}{Pp} \times \underset{(\text{Recessive parent})}{pp}$$ [1]

3. (d) The correct match given in option (d).
Rest are incorrect and can be corrected as

The process of delivery of foetus (childbirth) is called parturition.

The release of egg from the Graaffian follicle is known as ovulation.

Implantation is the attachment of embryo to the endometrium. [1]

4. (b) The correct sequence of LS of an embryo of grass (from top to bottom) are as follows

(iii) Scutellum → (iv) Coleoptile → (i) Epiblast → (ii) Radicle → (v) Coleorhiza. [1]

5. (c) Yeast respires under anaerobic conditions and converts glucose to alcohol and CO_2. [1]

6. (d) *A* and *B* are natality and immigration that increases the population density. Whereas, *C* and *D* are mortality and emigration that decreases population density. [1]

7. (c) Statements (i) and (iii) are correct, while statements (ii) and (iv) are incorrect and can be corrected as

India has more than 50,000 genetically different strains of rice and 1000 varieties of mango.

India has only 2.4 per cent of the world's land area, its share of the global species diversity is an impressive 8.1 per cent. [1]

8. (a) *Eco*RI is a restriction enzyme (endonuclease) that cuts the DNA segment at specific location during *r*DNA technology. Whereas, DNA ligase (molecular scissor) is an enzyme that joins two separated strands of plasmid and foreign DNA. [1]

9. (c) The saliva in the mouth and the tears from the eyes belongs to the physiological barriers. They both prevents microbial growth. [1]

10. (b) *Chlorella* gives nutritional supplement, i.e. protein as a product. [1]

11. (d) Tapetum is the innermost layer of the anther wall. The cells of this layer have dense cytoplasm and generally have more than one nucleus. This arises when the nuclear division during mitosis is not followed by cell wall formation. [1]

12. (b) An inverted pyramid of biomass can be found in marine ecosystem. [1]

13. (c) Assertion is true, but Reason is false. Reason can be corrected as

In dicot seed, there is no residual endosperm as it is completely consumed during the embryo formation. Hence, its considered as non-endospermic seed. [1]

14. (c) Assertion is true, but Reason is false. The reason can be corrected as

In humans, sex is determined by sex chromosomes. Sex chromosomes in human females are XX and in human males are XY which means that human male produces X and Y-chromosomes containing gametes, while human females produces only X-containing gametes. Therefore, males determine the sex of offspring. Sex in humans is a monogenic trait due to the lack of interaction between the genes on X and Y-chromosomes, which is required for a trait to be polygenic. [1]

15. (b) Both Assertion and Reason are true, but Reason is not the correct explanation of Assertion.

Transgenic microorganisms can be developed by inserting genes encoding for desired protein products using recombinant DNA technology. These transgenic organisms function as living microfactories that produces proteins like human insulin, human growth hormone, etc. [1]

16. (a) Both Assertion and Reason are true and Reason is the correct explanation of Assertion. [1]

17. Restriction enzymes cut the strands of the DNA a little away from the centre of the palindromic sites, but between the same two bases on the opposite strands. This leaves the single-stranded position at the ends. These overhanging stretches are called **sticky ends**. These are named so because they forms hydrogen bonds with their complementary cut counterparts. [1 + 1]

Or (a) Apart from temperature, pH and substrate, a bioreactor provides oxygen, salts and vitamins. [1]

(b) Components of a bioreactor are as follows
- an agitator system
- an oxygen delivery system
- foam control system
- temperature control system
- pH control system
- sampling parts to withdraw the culture. [1]

18. In wind pollinated flowers,

(a) Anthers are well-exposed for the easy dispersal of pollen grains.

(b) Pollen grains are light and non-sticky, so that they can be transported by wind currents.

(c) Stigma is large and feathery to trap pollens. [2]

Or The tender coconut water represents the free nuclear endosperm while, the white kernel is the cellular endosperm. The water and kernel of the endosperm are both triploid. [2]

19. Here, *X* refers to thymus gland, which is the primary lymphoid organ. In thymus gland, the immature lymphocytes such as B-lymphocytes differentiate into an antigen-sensitive lymphocytes. Hence, when the thymus gland is removed from the body of a person, his immune system will become weak. As a result, of which the individual's body becomes prone to the infectious diseases easily. [2]

20. (i) Yes, man can be a primary as well as secondary consumer because man can consume both plants as well as meat of other animals. So, man is herbivore as well as carnivore. [1]

(ii) Phytoplanktons occupy the first trophic level, while the zooplanktons occupy the second trophic level. [1]

21. The initiator tRNA binds to the amino acid methionine at its amino acid acceptor site. It has anticodon loop, which has anticodon for methionine, (i.e., UAC). It recognises the start codon (AUG) and binds to it according to the complementarity of bases. [2]

Or In snapdragon (*Antirrhinum majus*), on crossing the pure breeding red flowered and white flowered plants produces the hybrid of F_1-generation possesing pink flowers.

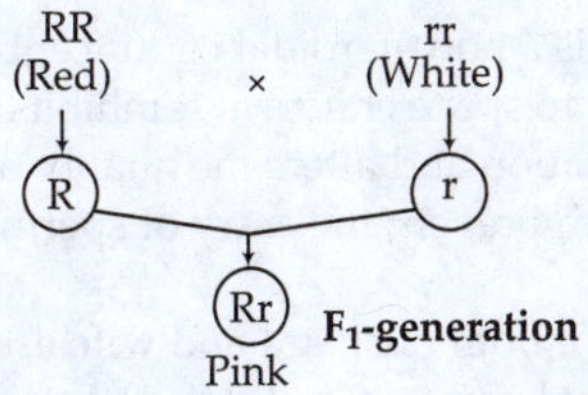

The genotype of F_1-generation is Rr and the phenotype is pink.

Incomplete dominance is a form of gene interaction in which both alleles of a gene at a locus are partially expressed, often resulting in an intermediate of different phenotype. [2]

22. (i) The parts *A*, *B* and *C* are identified as *A* – Synergids, *B* – Micropyle, *C* – Hilum [1]

(ii) The part labelled as *A* represents synergids. They possess special cellular thickenings at their micropylar tip called filiform apparatus. This apparatus guides the pollen tube to enter into the embryo sac. Once the tip of pollen tube enters one of the synergids, it begins to degenerate. [2]

23. (i) During meiotic anaphase-I of cell division, the separation of independent pair of chromosomes occurs. [1]

(ii) In sickle-cell anaemia, substitution of valine occurs in place of glutamic acid at the sixth position of haemoglobin chain. The mutant haemoglobin molecule undergoes polymerisation under low oxygen tension, causing the change in the shape of the RBCs from biconcave disc to the elongated sickle-like structure. [2]

24. (i) Differences between *Homo erectus* and *Homo habilis* are as follows

Homo erectus	*Homo habilis*
Origin period is 1.5 mya.	Origin period is about 2 mya.
Brain capacity is 900 cc, meat eater, fossils are found in Java.	First human like being, brain capacity is 650-800 cc, herbivorous and fossils are found in East Africa.

[1 + 1]

(ii) The correct sequence from early to late geological period is
Silurian → Carboniferous → Jurassic. [1]

25. (i) *hn*RNA undergoes splicing to remove non-coding sequence, (i.e., introns) and joins exons. Splicing occurs in the nucleus of the cell. [1]

(ii) If cell division is not followed after DNA replication then the replicated chromosomes (DNA) would not be distributed to daughter nuclei. A continued replication of DNA without subsequent cell division results in the accumulation of DNA inside the cell. This would increase the volume of the cell nucleus, thereby causing cell expansion further, it will lead to polyploidy. [2]

26. On the basis of colour production in the presence of chromogenic substrate, the recombinants and non-recombinants can be differentiated. In this method, a recombinant DNA is inserted within the

coding sequence of an enzyme β-galactosidase, which results in the inactivation of enzyme.
In plate with cloning vector *A*, the bacterial colonies with inserted plasmids, shows no colouration. While in plate with cloning vector B, insertion of plasmid does not occur, therefore it shows blue colour. [3]

27. In the given table, *A, B, C, D, E* and *F* are identified as

A → *Salmonella typhi*
B → High fever, weakness, constipation and stomach pain.
C → Malaria
D → *Ascaris*
E → Internal bleeding
F → Filariasis [3]

28. (i) The importantce of cryopreservation in the conservation of biodiversity is that gametes of threatened species can be preserved in viable and fertile conditions for long periods. [1]

(ii) Features of stable biological community are as follows

(a) It should not show much variation in terms of productivity from year - to - year.
(b) It should be resistant or resilient to occasional disturbances both natural and man - made.
(c) It must be resistant to invasions of alien species. [2]

29. (i) The genotype of the parents can be

$I^Ai \rightarrow$ A and $I^Bi \rightarrow$ B [1]

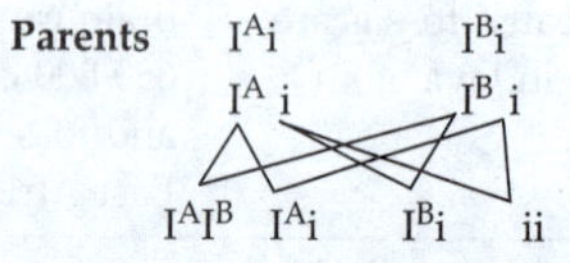

(ii) Now

(a) I^AI^B is married to X and produces child A. i.e. X can be I^Ai or I^AI^A or I^oI^o.
(b) The possible blood group will be A or O. [1]

(iii) The individual '*Y*' in the third generation will have two possible groups as group A or O. [2]

Or

(iii) When the individual in the second generation has blood group B, then the individual '*Y*' in the third generation will have possible groups as B or O. [2]

30. (i) After introducing antibodies into the body, their concentration decreases over time due to natural degradation, metabolism and clearance by the immune system. [1]

(ii) The types of immunity shown in person *A* is artificial passive immunity and person *B* is artificial active immunity. [1]

(iii) The person *A* shows no antigen entering the body, resulting in no immune response.
The B-lymphocytes are not activated and not differentiated into the plasma cells and memory cells in his body. Thus, no antibody is formed. [2]

Or

(iii) Antibodies are always specific for the specific antigens/proteins of a pathogen. There is a variable region in the structure of antibody which, makes a specific antigen binding site for a specific antigen. [2]

31. (i) **Ovaries**

Location These are primary sex organ been located on the upper pelvic cavity on both lateral sides of uterus.
Function Production of ova (gametes) and female sex hormones oestrogen and progesterone. [1]

(ii) **Uterus**

Location It is maintained in position within the pelvic cavity by muscles and ligaments.
Function It is the site of implantation and plays active role in parturition. [1]

(iii) **Mammary Glands**

Location Composed of lobes within the breasts.
Function Produces and secrete milk for nourishment of an infant. [1]

(iv) **Fimbriae**

Location Finger-like projections, located at the end of Fallopian tubes.
Function During ovulation, the fimbriae sweep over the surface of the ovary to capture the released egg (ovum). [1]

(v) **Fallopian tube**

Location Open-ended tubes that extend from the ovaries to the uterus.
Function Site of fertilisation, conveys ova toward uterus. [1]

Or

(i) Applications of amniocentesis are as follows

(a) **Positive application** It can be used to diagnose any chromosomal abnormality or genetic disorder in foetus.
(b) **Negative application** It can be used to determine the sex of foetus and lead to female foeticide. [1+1]

(ii) 'Saheli' is a non-steroidal contraceptive pill used by females to space children. It inhibits ovulation and implantation and alters the quality of cervical mucus to prevent the entry of sperms into cervix. [1]

(iii) In case, if both husband and wife are producing functional gametes, but wife is not able to conceive, the IVF technique can be employed to bless them with child.

In *in vitro* fertilisation gametes from both husband and wife are collected, i.e. sperm and ova and are fused to form zygote under laboratory conditions. [2]

32. (i) *Bt* cotton produces toxin proteins that kill certain insects like lepidopterans, coleopterans and dipterans. Thus, this crop does not require the application of herbicides and pesticides. [1]

(ii) (a) GEAC is an Indian organisation that makes decisions regarding the validity of GM research. [1]

(b) The two advantages of genetically modified (GM) plants are as follows

- Genetic modification has made crops more tolerant to a biotic stresses (cold, draught, salt, heat).
- It has reduced releliance of plants on chemical pesticides. [2]

(iii) Basmati rice, turmeric and neem. [1]

Or

(i) No, eukaryotic cells do not have restriction endonucleases. All the restriction endonucleases have been isolated from various strains of bacteria. Prokaryotes (bacteria) have this enzyme as a defence mechanism to destroy the foreign DNA or to restrict the growth of bacteriophages. [2]

(ii) First restriction endonuclease *Hind* II was discovered by Smith, Wilcox and Kelley in 1968. [1]

(iii) (a) **Exonucleases** cleave base pairs of DNA at their terminal ends while, **endonucleases** cleave DNA at any point within the DNA segment at specific position except terminal ends.

(b) **Restriction endonuclease** are the enzymes produced mainly by certain bacteria.

These recognises a specific sequence called restriction site. The *Eco*RI cuts the DNA strand a little away from the palindromic sequence, but between the same two bases on the two strands

*Eco*RI ↓

5′–G – A – A – T – T – C – 3′

3′–C – T – T – A – A – G – 5′

↑ *Eco*RI [1+1]

33. (i) In prokaryotes, the processes of transcription and translation are coupled, which means that the translation begins while *m*RNA is still being synthesised. This coupling occurs because prokaryotic cell lacks a defined nucleus. In contrast, eukaryotes have a defined nucleus, that separates the processes of transcription and translation. And therefore, transcription occurs in the nucleus of a cell whereas translation occurs in the cytoplasm of a cell. [2]

(ii)

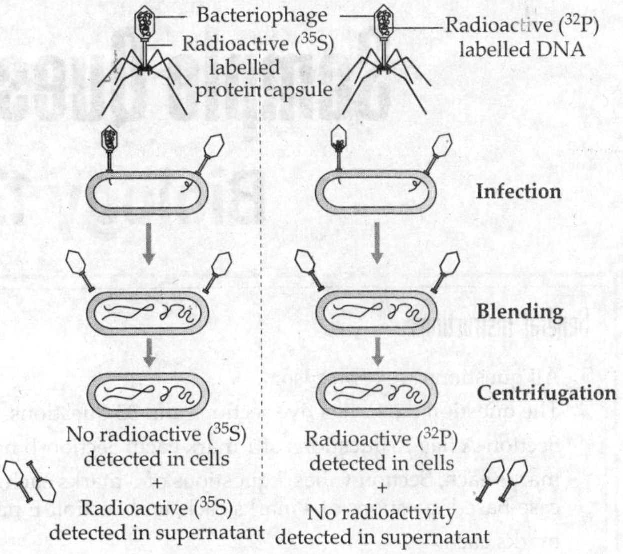

The Hershey-Chase experiment [3]

Or

(i) Adaptive radiation occurring through parallel evolution results in the resemblance of placental mammals to the corresponding marsupials in Australia. [1]

(ii) Wings of butterfly and birds are said to be analogous organs because they perform similar functions, but are dissimilar in their basic structure and development. [1]

(iii)

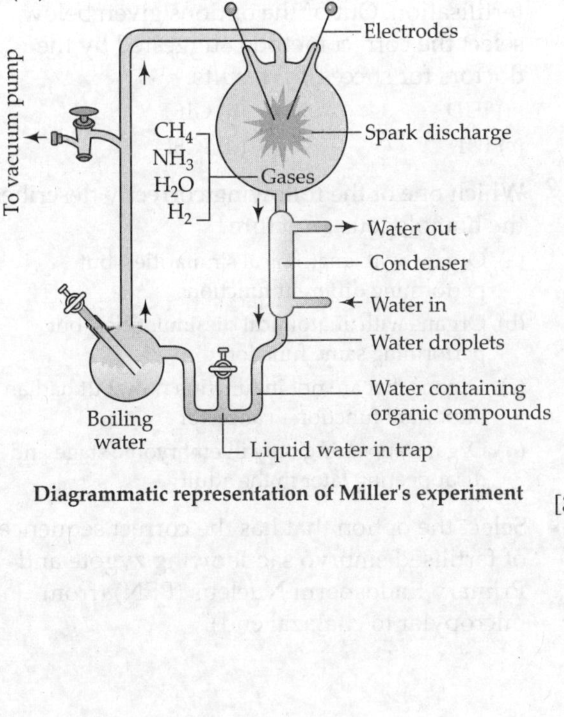

Diagrammatic representation of Miller's experiment [3]

SQP Code : **PB-5/15** Series ***i*-Succeed 5-25/15** Roll No.

Sample Question Paper 05

Biology 12th (Code 044)

General Instructions

1. All questions are compulsory.
2. The question paper has five sections and 33 questions.
3. Section-A has 16 questions of 1 mark each; Section-B has 5 questions of 2 marks each; Section-C has 7 questions of 3 marks each; Section-D has 2 case-based questions of 4 marks each; and Section-E has 3 questions of 5 marks each.
4. There is no overall choice. However, internal choices have been provided in some questions. A student has to attempt only one of the alternatives in such questions.
5. Wherever necessary, neat and properly labelled diagrams should be draw.

Time : 3 Hrs.

Max. Marks : 70

Section A Multiple Choice Type Questions

1. A female was incapable of producing ovum, but could provide suitable environment for fertilisation. Out of the options given below, select the correct method suggested by the doctors for successful results.

(a) IUD (b) GIFT
(c) IUI (d) ICSI

2. Which one of the following correctly describes the homologous structure?

(a) Organs with anatomical similarities, but performing different functions
(b) Organs with anatomical dissimilarities, but performing same function
(c) Organs that are not in function now, but had an important function in ancestor
(d) Organs appearing only in embryonic stage and disappearing later in the adult

3. Select the option that has the correct sequence of fertilised embryo sac showing zygote and Primary Endosperm Nucleus (PEN) (from micropylar to chalazal end).

(i) Zygote
(ii) Degenerating synergids
(iii) Degenerating antipodal cells
(iv) Primary endosperm cell
(v) Primary endosperm nucleus

Options

(a) (i) → (iii) → (iv) → (ii) → (v)
(b) (iii) → (i) → (ii) → (iv) → (v)
(c) (ii) → (i) → (iv) → (v) → (iii)
(d) (ii) → (i) → (v) → (iv) → (iii)

4. Read the four statements given below and select the option having two correct statements.

(i) Lactational amenorrhea is effective only upto a maximum period of 12 months following parturition.
(ii) Lippes loop is a non-medicated IUDs.
(iii) MTPs are considered relatively safe during second trimester, i.e upto 12 weeks of pregnancy.

(iv) Periodic abstinence is one such method in which the couples avoid from coitus from day 10 to 17 of the menstrual cycle.

(a) (i) and (ii) (b) (ii) and (iii)
(c) (ii) and (iv) (d) (iii) and (iv)

5. In order to activate the immune system and destroy tumour, which of the following substance is given to cancer patients?

(a) Histamine (b) Interleukin
(c) α-interferon (d) Morphine

6. Smita was doing an experiment where she was observing the growth of yeast. Which of the following equation correctly represents the exponential population growth curve?

(Where, N = Population density at time t, r = Intrinsic rate of natural increase.

(a) $dN/dt = rN$ (b) $dN/dt = rN\left(\frac{K-N}{K}\right)$

(c) $N_t = N_0 e^{rt}$ (d) Both (a) and (c)

7. Select the incorrect match from the following.

(a) *Saccharomyces cerevisiae* - Commercial production of ethanol
(b) *Acetobacter aceti* - Production of blood cholesterol lowering agents
(c) *Trichoderma polysporum* - Production of immuno suppressive agents
(d) Propionibacterium shermani - Ripening of swiss cheese

8. Which statement regarding the restriction endonucleases is not correct?

(a) They recognise a specific base sequence in the DNA
(b) They are produced by bacterial cells as a primitive immune system
(c) They digest DNA by removing nucleotides from a free 3 'end'
(d) They often generate sticky ends

9. In grasslands, cows belong to a particular trophic level. Identify the organism present that are equivalent to this trophic level in an aquatic ecosystem.

(a) Phytoplanktons (b) Large fishes
(c) Sea gulls (d) Zooplanktons

10. Smoking is not socially acceptable as it has greater risk to human health. Identify the type of cancer caused by smoking and the main component for this case.

	Cancer	Components
(a)	Lung	Carbon dioxide
(b)	Throat	Carbon monoxide
(c)	Lung	Tar
(d)	Throat	Nicotine

11. Vertical distribution of different species occupying different levels in a biotic community is known as

(a) divergence (b) stratification
(c) zonation (d) pyramid

12. Given below is an imaginary pyramid of numbers. What could be one of the possibilities about certain organisms at some of the different levels?

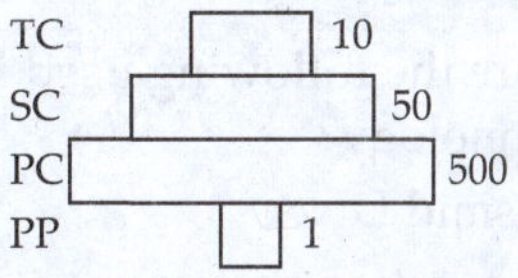

(a) Level PC is insects and level SC is small insectivorous birds
(b) Level PP is phytoplanktons in sea and whale on top level TC
(c) Level one PP is pipal trees and the level SC is sheep
(d) Level PC is rats and level SC is cats

Question Nos. 13 to 16 consist of two statements, Assertion (A) and Reason (R). Answer these questions by selecting the appropriate option given below.

(a) Both Assertion and Reason are true and Reason is the correct explanation of Assertion
(b) Both Assertion and Reason are true, but Reason is not the correct explanation of Assertion
(c) Assertion is true, but Reason is false
(d) Assertion is false, but Reason is true

13. **Assertion** (A) In females, parturition is the act of giving birth to a baby.
Reason (R) Signals for parturition originates only from a fully developed foetus.

14. **Assertion** (A) In pigeons, females are heterogametic and males are homogametic.
Reason (R) In pigeons, females have ZW sex chromosomes and males have ZZ sex chromosomes.

15. Assertion (A) A bacterial cell with no restriction enzyme can easily be infected and lysed by bacteriophages.

Reason (R) Restriction enzymes catalyse the synthesis of protection coat around bacterial cells that prevent bacteriophage attack.

16. Assertion (A) Tropical latitudes have greater biological diversity than temperate latitudes.

Reason (R) Tropical regions remain relatively undisturbed for millions of years.

Section B Very Short Answer Type Questions

17. In a habitat with unlimited resources, which type of population growth can be observed? Support your answer with a graphical representation.

Or Why are herbivores considered similar to predators in the ecological context? Explain.

18. How are the following used in biotechnology?

(i) Plasmid DNA

(ii) Recognition sequence

Or

What are bioreactors? Mention its significance.

19. (i) Write the scientific name of the microbe used for fermenting malted cereals and fruit juices.

(ii) Name the source of cyclosporin - A. How does this bioactive molecule function in our body?

20. Observe the structural representation of an apple and answer the questions that follows

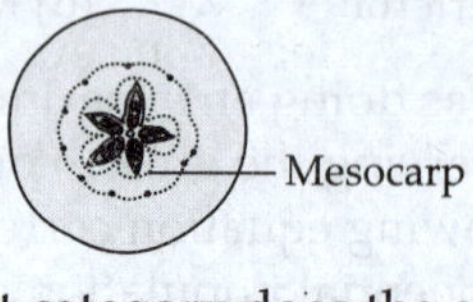

(i) What category does the above fruit (apple) come under and why?

(ii) What are the other examples that come under this category?

21. (i) Name the specific components and the linkage between them that forms deoxyadenosine.

(ii) Mention the role of the codon AUG and UGA during protein synthesis.

Or While teaching about transcription Miss Mona taught her class how it is similar in both prokaryotes and eukaryotes with only some minor differences?

(i) What are the transcriptional products of RNA polymerase-III?

(ii) What is the difference between capping and tailing?

SP-05

Section C Short Answer Type Questions

22. Study the schematic representation of gene involved in the *lac* operon given below which denotes group of gene with a single promoter.

p	*i*	*p*	*o*	*z*	*y*	*a*

(i) Identify the region where the repressor protein will attach normally.

(ii) Under certain condition repressor is unable to bind at their site. Explain.

(iii) If repressor fails to bind to the said site what products will be formed by *z*, *y* and *a*?

23. (i) Differentiate between benign and malignant tumours.

(ii) Why is colostrum a boon to the newborn baby?

24. Identify *A*, *B*, *C*, *D*, *E* and *F* in table given below

Agents of pollination	Characteristics	Examples
Water	Long and ribbon like pollen	*A*
B	flower emerge above the level of water	*C*
Air	*D*	*E*
F	Flowers are large, colourful, fragrant and rich in nectar	Rose

25. Typhoid is a life threatening infection caused by certain bacteria. The global burden of it is increased due to urbanisation and climate change.

(i) Name the causative agent of typhoid in humans. Also name the test administered to confirm the disease.

(ii) How does the pathogen gain entry into the human body? Write the diagnostic symptoms and mention the body organ that gets affected in severe case?

26. State the functions of *t*RNA, *r*RNA and *m*RNA in prokaryotes.

27. *In situ* conservation can help endangered/ threatened species. Justify the statement.

Or

The loss of biological diversity is a global crisis with hardly any region on the earth not facing ecological catastrophes. Out of the 1.7 million species which are known to inhabit the earth, one-third to one-fourth is likely to get extinct with in the coming decades. Man's intervention has speeded up the extinction rate from one species every 1000 years to one species every 10 years.

(i) What do you understand by the term biodiversity?

(ii) State some of the possible reasons of depletion of biodiversity.

(iii) How has an increase in population led to an increased dependence on agriculture?

28. Name the two different categories of microbes naturally occurring in sewage water. Explain their role in cleaning sewage water into usable water.

Section D Case Based Questions

Q. Nos. 29 and 30 are case-based questions. Each question has 3 subparts with internal choice in one subpart.

29. Study the given pedigree chart which shows the occurrence of colour blindness in one family.

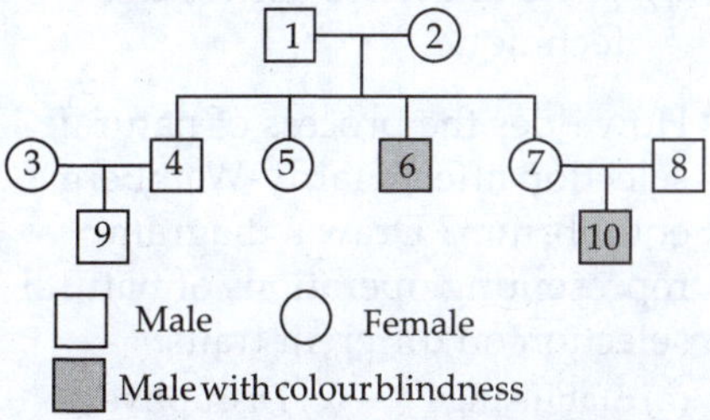

(i) On the basis of the inheritance pattern exhibited in this pedigree chart, what conclusion can be drawn about the allele of colour blindness? [1]

(ii) With reference to the above given pedigree, state the genotypes of the individuals shown in 2 and 4. [1]

(iii) It is often said that females are less likely to be affected by the disease than male. Explain why is it so in regard of the above drawn pedigree? [2]

Or (iii) If the individual in the first generation have a carrier female, then state the genotype of 6 and 7. [2]

30. The average length of the menstrual cycle is 28-29 days, but this can vary between woman and from one cycle to the next. The menstrual cycle is controlled by many different glands and the hormones that these glands produce. The menstrual cycle is a bio feedback system, which means-each structure and gland is affected by the activity of the others menstruation is the delimination of the thickened lining of the uterus from the body through vagina, menstrual fluid contains blood, cells from the lining of the uterus and mucus. The average length of a period is between three days and one week. The four phases of the menstrual cycle include menstruation, the follicular phase, ovulation and the luteal phase.

(i) Which is the shortest phase in menstrual cycle? [1]

(ii) What is the main function of corpus luteum? [2]

Or (ii) Which hormone level reached peak during luteal phase of menstrual cycle? [2]

(iii) Which area of the female reproductive system experiences the greatest change during menstrual cycle? [1]

Section E Long Answer Type Questions

31. A pregnant woman went to the hospital for an ultrasound. Where the doctor told her about the different changes occurring in the foetus developing inside her.

(i) Name the embryonic stage that gets implanted in the uterine wal.

(ii) Name the hormones that are produced by placenta.

(iii) Explain the process of implantation.

Or (i) Name an IUD that you would recommend to promote the cervix hostility to sperms.

(ii) What is amniocentesis? How is it misused?

(iii) List any two 'indicators' that indicate a reproductively healthy society.

32. The techniques of genetic engineering which include reaction of recombinant DNA using gene cloning and gene transfer, allows us to isolate and introduce only one or a set of desirable genes without introducing undesirable genes into the target organism. An alien DNA is linked with the origin of replication. So that, this alien piece of DNA can replicate and multiply itself in the host organisms. This can be called as cloning or making multiple identical copies of any template DNA. The cutting of DNA at specific locations become possible with the discovery of the so called–'molecular scissors restriction enzymes.

(i) How does exonuclease activity differ from endonuclease?

(ii) What will happen once a restriction enzyme find its recognition sequence?

(iii) Explain the action of the restriction endonuclease *Eco*RI.

Or Study the diagram given below that shows the DNA fragment seprated on gel, of suspects A, B and the DNA found on crime scene

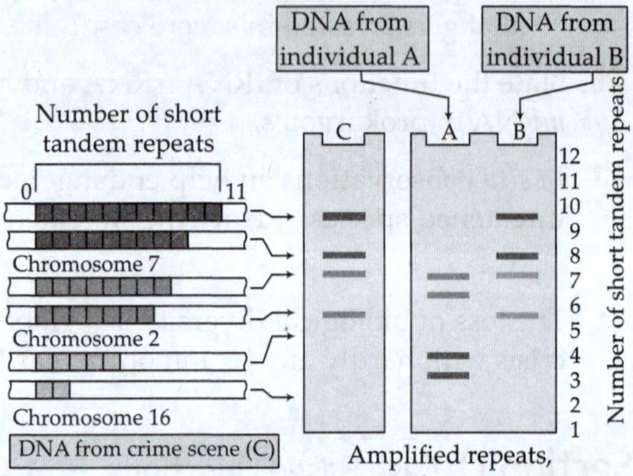

Amplified repeats, separated by size on a gel, give a DNA fingerprint

(i) Which of the suspects is likely to have committed the crime? Justify your answer.

(ii) Explain the technique included in the above figure.

(iii) Write one more uses of this technique.

33. How does the process of natural selection affect Hardy-Weinberg equilibrium? Draw a diagram representing operations of natural selection on different traits.

(a) Stabilising (c) Disruptive

(c) Directional

Or

(i) Differentiate between incomplete dominance and codominance.

(ii) A teacher wants his/her students to find the genotype of pea plants bearing purple coloured flowers in their school garden. Name and explain the cross that will make it possible.

Explanations in Topper's Style

My Commitment *I affirm that I am reviewing these solutions only after I have solved the Sample Question Paper 5 on my own. My purpose of looking the solutions is solely to verify whether my answers/solutions were correct or not and to identify my mistakes in case my solutions were wrong or I could not solve that.*

1. (b) Gamete Intra Fallopian Transfer (GIFT) is used in females who cannot produce ova, but can provide suitable environment for fertilisation. [1]

2. (a) Homologous organs are the organs that have the same fundamental structure or anatomical similarities, but are different in functions. Hence, such organs follows the same basic plans of organisation during their development. [1]

3. (c) The correct sequence of fertilised embryo sac showing zygote and primary endosperm nucleus are (ii) Degenerating synergids → (i) Zygote → (iv) Primary endosperm cell → (v) Primary endosperm nucleus → (iii) Degenerating antipodal cells. [1]

4. (c) Statements (ii) and (iv) are correct, while statements (i) and (iii) are incorrect and can be corrected as

- Lactational amenorrhea is effective only upto a maximum period of 6 months following parturition.
- MTPs are considered relatively safe during first trimester, i.e. upto 12 weeks of pregnancy. [1]

5. (c) Cancer patients are given substances called biological response modifiers such as α-interferon, which activates their immune system and helps in destroying the tumour. [1]

6. (d) Under unlimited resources, it would reach exponential growth which can be depicted by the following equation

$$dN/dt = rN$$

If we derive the integral form of the exponential growth equation, it can be written as

$$N_t = N_0 e^{rt}.$$ [1]

7. (b) Option (b) is an incorrect match. It can be corrected as *Monascus purpureus* is commercialised as blood - cholesterol lowering agents. It acts by competitively inhibiting the enzyme responsible for the synthesis of cholesterol. [1]

8. (c) Statement given in option (c) is not correct regarding the restriction endonuclease because restriction endonuclease is an enzyme that cleaves DNA at specific location called as restriction sites within the molecule. [1]

9. (d) In an aquatic ecosystem, the important herbivores are zooplanktons, larvae, tadpole, etc., equivalent to cows in grasslands. Thus, both cows and zooplanktons occupies the second trophic level in the terrestrial and aquatic ecosystems, respectively. [1]

10. (c) Smoking may often cause lung cancer. The carcinogen chemicals responsible for this is present in tar. [1]

11. (b) Stratification is the vertical distribution of different species occupying different levels in a biotic community. [1]

12. (a) The given figure shows the pyramid of number in single tree ecosystem. Here, a single large-sized tree provides food to a large number of herbivores which support few carnivores and the later are eaten (by small number of top carnivores.) So, here PP is used for Producer, i.e. single tree, PC is Primary Consumers, (i.e. large number of insects), SC is Secondary Consumers, i.e. small insectivorous birds and TC is Top Consumers, which may be eagle or falcon, etc. [1]

13. (c) Assertion is true, but Reason is false. Reason can be corrected as

The act of giving birth to a baby is called parturition. It is induced by a complex neuro-endocrine mechanism. The signals for childbirth originates from a fully developed foetus and the placenta that stimulates the release of oxytocin, leading to the vigorous uterine contractions also called foetal-ejection reflex. [1]

14. (a) Both Assertion and Reason are true and Reason is the correct explanation of Assertion.

In pigeons, ZW-ZZ type of sex-determination mechanism is found. In this type, the male has two homomorphic sex chromosomes (i.e. ZZ) and is homogametic in nature, while the female have two heteromorphic sex chromosomes (ZW) and is heterogametic. [1]

15. (c) Assertion is true, but Reason is false. Reason can be corrected as

Restriction enzymes produced in a bacterial cell, have the ability to recognise and cleave the foreign DNA introduced (such as from bacteriophage) into the host cell. Thus, bacterial cell cannot be infected and lysed by the bacteriophage. Hence, a bacterial cell lacking the restriction enzymes is easily susceptible to infection of phages when compared to the one with the restriction enzymes. [1]

16. (a) Both Assertion and Reason are true and Reason is the correct explanation of Assertion.

Tropical latitudes, have greater biological diversity than temperate latitudes because unlike temperate regions which were subjected to frequent glaciations in the past, tropical regions remained undisturbed for millions of years, where species continued to flourish. [1]

17. In a habitat where the resources needed for the survival are unlimited, the population growth occurs at an exponential rate.

This type of growth has two phases, i.e. **lag phase** (i.e. when organisms are adapting to environment) and **exponential phase** (i.e. rapid phase of reproduction).

Finally, when the supply of resources exhausts, it causes the growth to slow down.

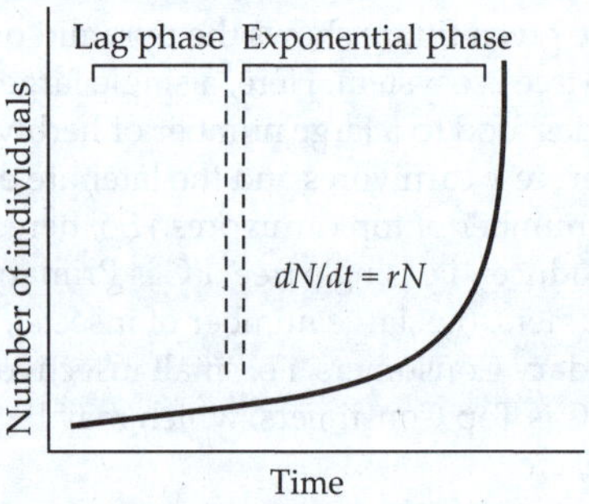

Population growth curve when resources are not limiting the

Hence, the growth can be expressed as

$$\frac{dN}{dt} = rN$$

Where, N = Population size

t = Time,

r = Intrinsic rate of natural increase. [2]

Or The herbivores feed on plants. They are considered as predators because they transfer energy across the trophic levels. Besides this, they also keep the population of their prey under control. For example, when the prickly pear cactus was introduced in Australia in early 1920, they spread rapidly causing havoc. Their population was controlled by introducing cactus-feeding predator (a moth). [2]

18. (i) Plasmid DNA → It is used for the construction of recombinant DNA, by ligating the alien piece of DNA with it. It is used as a cloning vector and helps in the selection of recombinants from non-recombinants. [1]

(ii) Recognition sequences - These are the specific base sequences of DNA, where restriction enzyme cuts the DNA.

They are utilised to extract the desired gene or fragments from DNA molecule. [1]

Or Bioreactors are large vessels in which raw materials are biologically converted into specific products such as enzymes using microbial, plant, animal or human cells. A bioreactor provides the optimal conditions for achieving the desired product by providing optimum growth conditions like temperature, pH, substrate, salts, vitamins and oxygen. [1+1]

19. (i) *Saccharomyces cerevisiae* also called brewers yeast is the microbe used for fermenting malted cereals and fruit juices. [1]

(ii) Cyclosporin - A is produced by the fungus *Trichoderma polysporum.* It is used as an immunosuppressive agent in organ - transplant patients as it suppresses the activation of T-cells in body. [1]

20. (i) In apple, the thalamus also contributes to fruit formation. So apples belongs to the category of fruits called false fruits. [1]

(ii) The fruits such as cashew, strawberry, etc., also belong to the same category as of apple. [1]

21. (i) The specific components of deoxyadenosine are adenine and deoxyribose. These are linked by N - glycosidic linkage. [1]

(ii) AUG acts as initiation codon and codes for amino acid methionine.

UGA acts as stop/termination codon that signals termination of polypeptide synthesis. [1]

Or (i) RNA polymerase-III is responsible for the transcription of *t*RNA, 5 S *r*RNA and *sn*RNAs (small nuclear RNAs). [1]

(ii) In capping process, an unusual nucleotide (methyl guanosine triphosphate) is added to 5′ end of *hn*RNA.

In tailing process, 200-300 adenylate residues are added at 3′ end of *hn*RNA. [1]

22. (i) The region where the repressor protein will bind normally is the 'operator region' or *O*. [1]

(ii) Repressor is unable to bind to the operator in the presence of an inducer which is lactose. [1]

(iii) If the repressor fails to bind to the operator region, then following products will form at the following sites

z - β - galactosidase, *y*- Permease

a - Transacetylase [1]

23. (i) Differences between benign and malignant tumours are as follows

Benign tumour	Malignant tumour
Tumour remains confined to the affected organ only.	The tumour spreads to other organs of the body.
The rate of tumour growth is usually slow.	Rate of tumour growth is usually rapid.
It is non-cancerous	It is cancerous.

[2]

(ii) The milk produced during the initial few days of lactation is called colostrum, which contains IgA antibodies. These are essential to develop resistance in newborn babies as they provide passive immunity and brings up a healthy baby. [1]

24. In the given table *A, B, C, D, E* and *F* are identified as

A → *Zostera*
B → Insect or wind
C → Water lily
D → Pollen grains are light and non-sticky; stigma is often large and feathery
E → Grasses or corn - cob
F → Insects [½×6=3]

25. (i) The causative agent of typhoid in humans is *Salmonella typhi*. Widal test is administered to confirm the disease. [1]

(ii) Pathogens gain entry into the human body through the contaminated food and water.

The diagnostic symptoms are high fever, weakness, stomach pain. The body organ affected in severe case is small intestine. [2]

26. (i) *t*RNA helps in the transferring of amino acids to ribosome for the synthesis of a polypeptide chain. [1]

(ii) *r*RNA plays both structural and catalytic role during translation. [1]

(iii) *m*RNA acts as an intermediary between DNA and protein. [1]

27. *In situ* conservation involves the protection of species in their natural habitats. It helps in the conservation of threatened/endangered species *via* following means

(i) Biodiversity hotspots are the regions with high levels of species richness and high degree of endemism. Hotspots cover less than 2% of the earth's land area. [1]

(ii) Protected areas are ecologically unique and biodiversity rich regions. These are legally protected as biosphere reserve, national parks and sanctuaries. [1]

(iii) Sacred groves are the forest areas that are set aside, all the trees and wildlife within it are venerated and given total protection. [1]

Or

(i) Biodiversity may be defined as the variety and variability of living organisms on the earth. In other words, it is defined as the variety of forms of life, gene pools and habitats found in an area. [1]

(ii) Some of the possible reasons why there is depletion of biodiversity are destruction of habitat, includes over-exploitation of resources, introduction of alien or exotic species and co-extinctions. [1]

(iii) With an increase in population, there is an increased demand for food, energy and income.

Thus, to fulfil the increasing demands of the growing population, there has been an increased indulgence in agricultural activities. [1]

28. Bacteria and fungi belongs to the category of naturally occurring microbes present in sewage. The bacteria along with the fungal mycelia forms flocs that are utilised during the secondary treatment of sewage. The primary effluent after separation of the grit and debris is taken for the secondary treatment.

Here, the effluent is passed into an aeration tank, where it is constantly agitated and air is pumped into it. This leads to vigorous growth of bacteria and floc formation. The bacteria in these flocs consumes organic matter, thus decreasing the BOD of the sewage.

Once the BOD is reduced the effluent is passed into a settling tank where the bacterial flocs are allowed to sediment. Then some part of this is pumped back into the aeration tank as inoculum while the remaining is transferred into the anaerobic sludge digester.

Here, the anaerobic bacteria digest the bacteria and fungi. Then, the effluent of secondary treatment is released into natural water bodies. [3]

29. (i) From the pedigree chart, it can be concluded that colour blindness is a sex-linked recessive disorder as the disease results from the recessive parent allele. [1]

(ii) The individual 2 will show the genotype as XX^C and individual 4 will show genotype XY. [1]

(iii) Gene controlling colour blindness are found on the X-chromosome. Female needs two alleles for colour blindness, (i.e. homozygous) for the trait, while male needs only one colourblind allele for the trait. So, females in the heterozygous form are protected from colour blindness but remain carrier. [2]

Common Mistake

Students are often mistaken and get confused in the fact that both parents in case of colour blindness can prove to be carriers. Now they should be clear that males cannot be carrier for colour blindness. They are either affected or unaffected, since trait for colour blindness is present on X-chromosome.

Or

(iii) The individual 6 will show genotype X^CY and individual 7 will show genotype XX^C. [2]

30. (i) The shortest phase in menstrual cycle is the ovulatory phase which last for 1 to 2 days. [1]

(ii) The corpus luteum makes uterus a healthy place for a foetus to grow. It releases a hormone called progesterone that prepares uterus for pregnancy. Corpus luteum is produced by ruptured Graafian follicle after ovulation. [2]

Or

(ii) During luteal phase of menstrual cycle, corpus luteum secretes large amount of progesterone. The latter reaches its peak at about 22nd day after the beginning of the cycle. In this phase uterus lining gets thickened further and becomes secretory. [2]

(iii) Endometrium wall of uterus periodically changes in different stages of menstrual cycle. [1]

31. (i) The embryonic stage that gets implanted in uterine wall is blastocyst. [1]

(ii) Placenta also acts as an endocrine tissue and produces several hormones like human chorionic gonadotropin (hCG), human placental lactogen (hPL), oestrogens, progestrons, etc. [1]

(iii) After fertilisation, the mitotic division starts as the zygote moves through the isthmus of the oviduct towards the uterus called cleavage.

Thus, forming 2, 4, 8, 16 daughter cells called blastomeres.

(a) The embryo with 8-16 blastomeres is called morula.

(b) The morula continues to divide and transforms into blastocyst as it moves further into the uterus.

(c) The blastomeres in the blastocyst gets arranged into an outer layer called trophoblast and the inner group of cells attached to the trophoblast called inner cell mass.

(d) The trophoblast layer then gets attached to the endometrium layer of the uterus and the inner cell mass differentiates into the embryo. After attachement, the uterine cells divide rapidly and covers the blastocyst.

As a result, the blastocyst becomes embedded in the endometrium of the uterus. This is called implantation and it leads to pregnancy. [3]

Common Mistake

Generally the students take into understanding that morula is 32-celled blastomere, while blastula is 8-16 celled blastomere.

However, this is not true. The former is 8-16 celled blastomere, while the later is 32-celled blastomere.

Or

(i) The hormone releasing IUDs, e.g. Progestasert and LNG - 20 are recommended to promote the cervix hostility to sperms. [1]

(ii) Amniocentesis is a prenatal diagnostic test. It is named so, because it is based on the chromosomal pattern of the cells in the amniotic fluid that surrounds the developing foetus in the womb.

It is misused to detect the sex of a pre-born child that leads to female foeticide. Hence, there is a statutory ban on amniocentesis. [2]

(iii) Two indicators that indicates a reproductively healthy society are as follows

(a) Increased number of medically assisted deliveries and better post-natal care leading to the decreased maternal and infant mortality rates.

(b) Awareness of problems due to uncontrolled population growth, social evils like sex abuse and sex related crimes, etc., should be created to enable people to think and take necessary step to prevent them. [2]

32. (i) Exonuclease removes nucleotide from the ends of DNA, whereas endonuclease make cuts at specific positions within DNA. [1]

(ii) Once restriction enzyme finds its recognition sequence, it binds to DNA and cuts each of the two strands of double helix at specific positions in their sugar-phosphate backbone. [1]

(iii) Restriction endonuclease *Eco*RI cuts DNA strands a little away from the centre of the palindromic sequence, but between the same two bases on the opposite strands, i.e. G and A, on both the strands. The site of action of enzyme in palindrome sequence is called recognition site.

(a) Due to this, single-stranded positions called sticky ends, overhangs at the end of each strand.

(b) Because of the stickiness, they form hydrogen bonds with their complementary cut counterparts. [3]

Or

(i) Suspect B is likely to have commited the crime. As the DNA of suspect B matches to the DNA found at the crime scene. [2]

(ii) The above figure depicts DNA fingerprinting. It involves the identifying differences in some specific regions in DNA sequence called as repetitive DNA, because in these sequence, a small stretch of DNA is repeated many times. [2]

(iii) DNA fingerprinting is used in

- Paternity and maternity testing to establish biological relationship in cases of disputed parentage. [1]

33. (i) Natural selection affects Hardy-Weinberg equilibrium in the following ways

(a) It is a process in which heritable variations help in the survival of an organism, enabling it to reproduce and give rise to a large number of offsprings.

(b) There may be change in the frequency of genes and alleles in the future generations.

(c) It leads to the formation of new species. [2]

(ii)

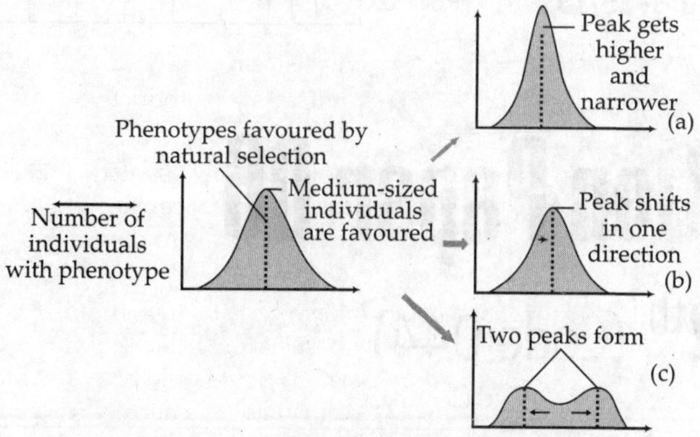

Diagrammatic representation of the operation of natural selection on different traits (a) Stabilising (b) Directional and (c) Disruptive

[3]

Or

(i) Differences between codominance and incomplete dominance are as follows

Codominance	Incomplete dominance
It is the appearance of both parental phenotypes together in the offspring when a cross is done between individuals with two different phenotypes.	It is the appearance of an intermediate phenotype, which is a combination of both parental alleles. When a cross is done between individuals with two different phenotypes.
Both parental alleles produce their effect independently, e.g. ABO blood group.	Effect of the two parental alleles is intermediate on the offspring. e.g. inheritance of flower colour in the dog flower.

[2]

(ii) Test cross is a method devised by Mendel to determine the genotype of a plant with dominant phenotype. In a test cross, the unknown dominant genotype is crosses with recessive parent. [1½]

(a) If the progeny consists of purple and white flowers in ratio of 1 : 1, the purple flower is a hybrid with PW genotype. It can be seen from the given cross.

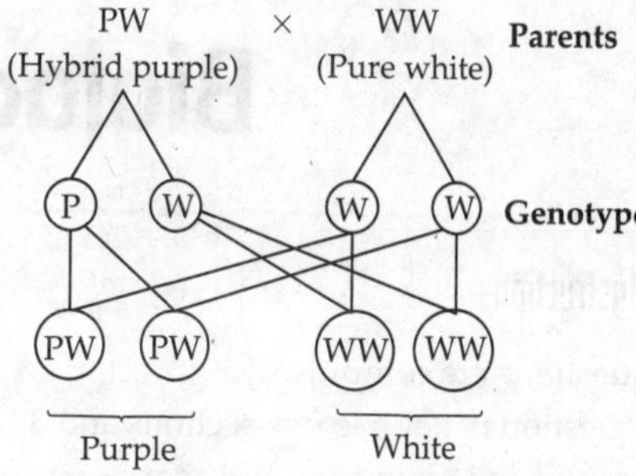

(ii) If the progeny obtained have all purple flowers, both parents are homozygous, i.e. genotype of purple flower is PP. It can be seen from the cross the follows.

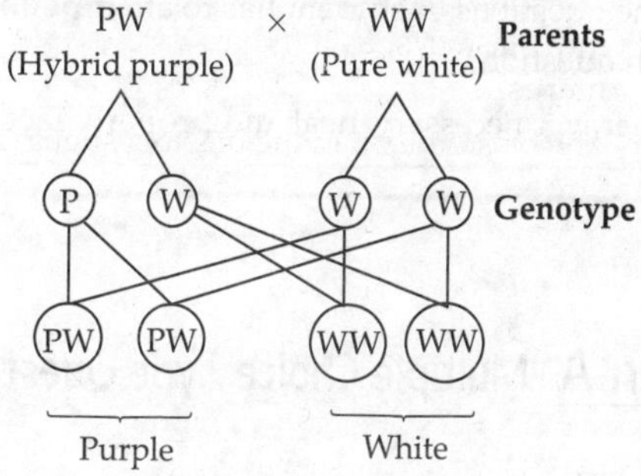

[1½]

SQP Code : **PB-6/15** Series ***i*-Succeed 6-25/15** Roll No.

Sample Question Paper 06

Biology 12th (Code 044)

General Instructions

1. All questions are compulsory.
2. The question paper has five sections and 33 questions.
3. Section-A has 16 questions of 1 mark each; Section-B has 5 questions of 2 marks each; Section-C has 7 questions of 3 marks each; Section-D has 2 case-based questions of 4 marks each; and Section-E has 3 questions of 5 marks each.
4. There is no overall choice. However, internal choices have been provided in some questions. A student has to attempt only one of the alternatives in such questions.
5. Wherever necessary, neat and properly labelled diagrams should be draw.

Time : 3 Hrs.

Max. Marks : 70

Section A Multiple Choice Type Questions

1. ZZ/ZW type of sex-determination is seen in
(a) platypus
(b) snails
(c) cockroach
(d) peacock

2. Which of the following aspects is not a component of functional unit of ecosystem?
(a) Productivity
(b) Energy flow
(c) Decomposition
(d) Ecological pyramids

3. Select the option that has the correct sequence of events of the evolution forms through geological periods.
(i) Devonian
(ii) Permian
(iii) Jurassic
(iv) Carboniferous
(v) Cretaceous

Options
(a) (i) → (ii) → (iv) → (iii) → (v)
(b) (ii) → (iv) → (i) → (iii) → (v)
(c) (i) → (iv) → (ii) → (iii) → (v)
(d) (i) → (iv) → (iii) → (ii) → (v)

4. The sticky ends of a fragmented DNA molecule are made up of
(a) calcium salts (b) methyl groups
(c) unpaired bases (d) endonuclease enzyme

5. Select the incorrect match from the following.
   (a) **Opioids** – Binds to receptor present in central nervous system.
   (b) **Cannabinoids** – Effect on cardiovascular system of the body.
   (c) **Cocaine** – Binds to receptor present in gastrointestinal tract.
   (d) **Morphine** – Effective sedative and pain killer.

6. Which of the following is not a characteristic of pBR322 vector?
   (a) It is the first artificial cloning vector constructed in 1977
   (b) It is the most widely used, versatile and easily manipulated vector
   (c) It does not have restriction site for Sal I
   (d) It has two antibiotic resistance gene, tet^R and amp^R

7. In sewage treatment, bacterial flocs are allowed to sediment in a settling tank. This sediment is called as
   (a) primary sludge
   (b) secondary sludge
   (c) activated sludge
   (d) inactivated sludge

8. Read the four statements given below and select the option having two correct statements.
   (i) The Eastern Ghats have a greater amphibian species diversity than the Western Ghats.
   (ii) *Rauwolfia vomitoria* is a medicinal plant which produces a active chemical reserpine.
   (iii) The largely tropical Amazonian rainforest in North America has more than 1,25,000 invertebrates.
   (iv) There is more solar energy available in the tropics, contribute indirectly to greater diversity.
   (a) (i) and (iii)
   (b) (ii) and (iv)
   (c) (i) and (ii)
   (d) (iii) and (iv)

9. Which of the following is one of the *ex situ* conservation methods for endangered species?
   (a) National parks
   (b) Cryopreservation
   (c) Wildlife sanctuaries
   (d) Biosphere reserves

10. The spermatids are transformed into spermatozoa by the process called
   (a) spermiation
   (b) spermatocytogenesis
   (c) spermiogenesis
   (d) spermatolysis

11. Identify the correct pair representing the causative agent of typhoid fever and the confirmatory test for typhoid.
   (a) *Streptococcus pneumoniae*/Widal test
   (b) *Salmonella typhi*/Anthrone test
   (c) *Salmonella typhi*/Widal test
   (d) *Plasmodium vivax*/UTI test

12. In the given diagram of pistil in which part fertilisation takes place?

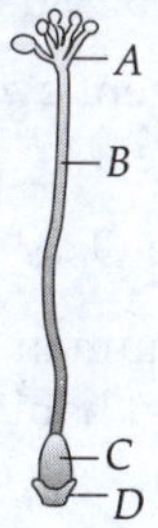

   (a) D (b) C (c) B (d) A

Question Nos. 13 to 16 consist of two statements - Assertion (A) and Reason (R), answer these questions by selecting the appropriate option given below.
   (a) Both Assertion and Reason are true and Reason is the correct explanation of Assertion
   (b) Both Assertion and Reason are true, but Reason is not the correct explanation of Assertion
   (c) Assertion is true, but Reason is false
   (d) Assertion is false, but Reason is true

13. Assertion (A) The female external genitalia includes mons pubis, labia majora and labia minora.

Reason (R) The glandular tissue of each breast contains single mammary lobe.

14. Assertion (A) Restriction enzyme is a type of endonuclease.

Reason (R) Restriction enzyme cuts the two strands of DNA at specific positions within the DNA.

15. Assertion (A) A single species does not show high diversity at the genetic level over its distributional range.

Reason (R) India has more than 50,000 genetically different strains of rice and 1,000 varieties of mango.

16. Assertion (A) Predation is an interspecific interaction with a feeding strategy.

Reason (R) Predators and their prey maintain fairly stable population through time and rarely one population become abundant or scarce.

Section B Very Short Answer Type Questions

17. 'The advent of birth control pills resulted in increased risks of sexually transmitted diseases'. Assess the fact given above and present your opinion on it.

Or

Mention the problems that are taken care by Reproduction and Child Healthcare Programme.

18. Explain convergent evolution by giving a suitable example.

Or

Name the first human-like hominid. Mention his food habit and brain capacity.

19. Name the cells, HIV (Human Immunodeficiency Virus) gains entry into after infecting the human body. Explain the events that occur in these cells.

20. In a court case seeking to determine the actual father of a baby, five samples were collected for DNA fingerprinting tests.

The samples were collected from the mother, the baby and three potential fathers namely Man-1, Man 2 and Man 3.

These samples are subjected to rigourous analysis to compare their genetic profiles and identify any similarities or differences for resolving the paternity dispute. The results of the tests are depicted in the diagram below.

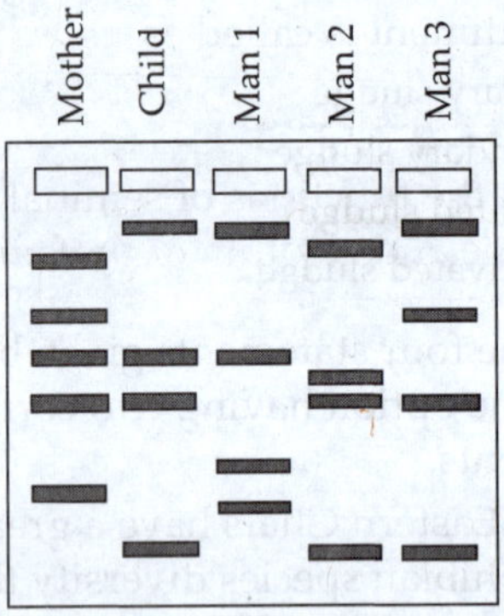

(i) Based on the result of DNA fingerprinting who is the father of child? Justify.

(ii) Is there any limitation on DNA fingerprinting? Support your answer with a suitable explanation.

21. (i) Write two places where methanogens can be found.

(ii) Mention two advantages of adding blue-green algae to paddy fields.

Or

Name the source of cyclosporin - A. How does this bioactive molecule function in our body?

SP-06

Section C Short Answer Type Questions

22. The figure given below shows a biogas plant.

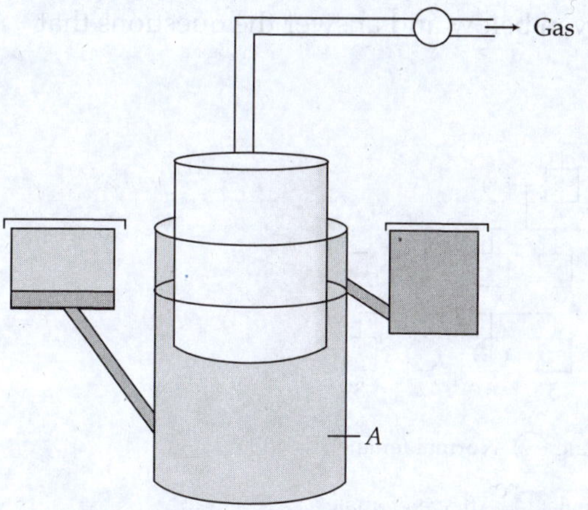

(i) Identify the part labelled as *A* in the above diagram and describe biogas.

(ii) Which group of microbes are observed in a biogas plant?

23. Explain the functions of seminal vesicle, acrosome and scrotum of the human male reproductive system.

24. (i) A young boy when brought a pet dog home started to complain of watery eyes and running nose. The symptoms disappeared when the boy was kept away from the pet.

(a) Name the type of antibody and the chemical responsible for such a response in the boy.

(b) Mention the name of any one drug that could be given to the boy for immediate relief from such a response.

(ii) State the function of mast cells in allergy response.

25. Since the origin of life on earth, there were five episodes of mass extinction of species.

(i) How is the 'Sixth extinction', presently in progress, different from the previous episodes?

(ii) Who is mainly responsible for 'Sixth Extinction'?

(iii) List any two points that can help to overcome this disaster.

26. Expand VNTR and describe its role in DNA fingerprinting. List any two applications of DNA fingerprinting technique.

27. Rita was 9 months pregnant, and wanted to know that how the foetus gets delivered after pregnancy period. So, she asked her gynaecologist to explain the process so that she could be mentally prepared for her delivery. Her gynaecologist explained the process in a very precise manner.

(i) What is the average duration of human pregnancy known as?

(ii) What is the term given to the process of delivery of foetus?

(iii) Which phenomenon is responsible for the term mentioned in (ii)?

28. Identify *A, B, C, D, E* and *F* in the table given below.

Evolutionary Phenomenon	Properties	Examples
A	Similar traits, different ancestors	*B*
C	Single ancestor, diverse species	*D*
E	*F*	Thorns of *Bouguinvillea* and tendrils of *Cucurbita*

SP-06

Section D Case Based Questions

Q. Nos. 29 and 30 are case-based questions. Each question has 3 subparts with internal choice in one subpart.

29. Study the pedigree chart for colour blindness given below and answer the questions that follows.

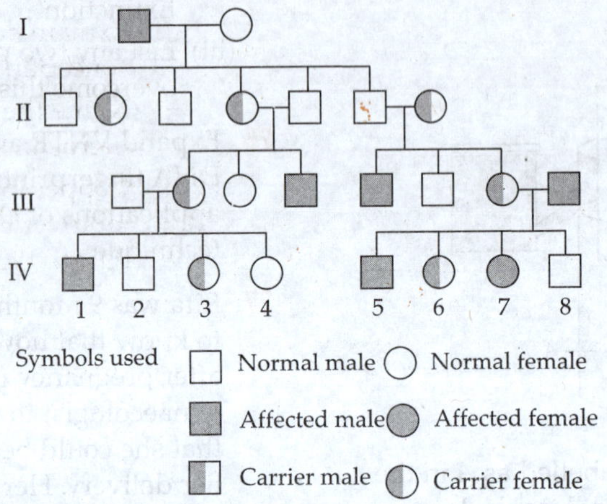

(i) On the basis of the inheritance pattern exhibited in this pedigree chart, what kind of trait is shown? [2]

(ii) Which sex, out of both can be the carrier of colour blindness? [1]

(iii) If individual 7 of IV generation had children, what percentage of her sons would you expect to be colourblind? [2]

Or

(iii) Why do all daughters in generation-II carry the colourblind gene? [2]

30. The data below show the number of patients that tested positive for dengue in the year 2005.

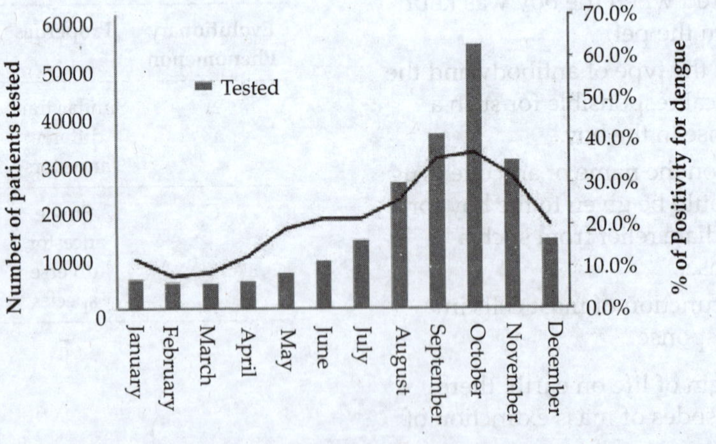

(i) With reference to the above graph, in which month did the outbreak of dengue fever occur? [1]

(ii) What type of mosquito is responsible for dengue? [1]

(iii) Explain why the outbreak of dengue fever usually occur in the time period that is depicted in the above graph? [2]

Or (iii) How can we control the spread of dengue? [2]

Section E Long Answer Type Questions

31. A schematic representation of Polymerase Chain Reaction (PCR) upto the extension stage is given below. Give answers of the following questions.

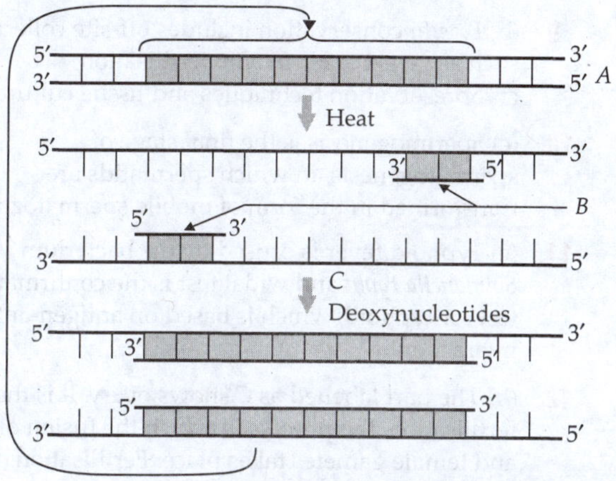

(i) Name the process *A* and identify *B*. Also identify C and mention its importance in PCR.

(ii) Describe the role of heat, primers and the bacterium *Thermus aquaticus* in the process of PCR.

Or

(i) Name the source from which insulin was extracted earlier. Why is this insulin no more in use by diabetic people?

(ii) Explain the process of synthesis of insulin by Eli Lilly company. Name the techniques used by the company.

32. Intra-uterine devices are the most widely accepted methods of contraception. These are used by females and are inserted by doctor or nurses in the uterus through vagina. However, these devices are not recommended for those who eventually intend to conceive.

(i) Explain how does Cu-T prevent conception?

(ii) Name the IUDs which makes uterus unsuitable for implantation.

(iii) Copper ions releasing IUDs are more efficient than hormonal IUD'S. Why?

Or

Angiospermic flowers may be monoecious, cleistogamous or show self-incompatibility. Describe the characteristic features of each one of them and state which one of these flowers promotes inbreeding and outbreeding, respectively.

33. Sketch a schematic diagram of *lac* operon in switched on position. How is the operon switched off? Explain.

Or

(i) State and explain the "Law of independent assortment'.

(ii) Using Punnett square show the F_2 result of a dihybrid cross where the pure breed parents have contrasting traits with reference to seed shape and seed colour in *Pisum sativum*. Give the phenotypic ratio.

Explanations in Topper's Style

My Commitment *I affirm that I am reviewing these solutions only after I have solved the Sample Question Paper 6 on my own. My purpose of looking the solutions is solely to verify whether my answers/solutions were correct or not and to identify my mistakes in case my solutions were wrong or I could not solve that.*

1. (d) Peacock shows ZZ/ZW sex determination type. In ZZ/ZW case, the female has heteromorphic (ZW) sex chromosomes and the male has homomorphic (ZZ) sex chromosomes. [1]

2. (d) The functional unit of ecosystem consists of productivity, decomposition, energy flow and nutrient cycling.

Thus, ecological pyramids are not a component of functional unit of ecosystem. [1]

3. (c) The correct order of events of the evolution forms through geological period is

(i) Devonian → (iv) Carboniferous → (ii) Permian → (iii) → Jurassic → (v) Cretaceous. [1]

4. (c) The single-stranded free ends that project from each fragment of DNA duplex are unpaired bases and are known as 'sticky-ends'. The sticky ends can join with similar complementary ends of DNA fragment from some other sources. [1]

5. (c) Option (c) is incorrectly matched and can be corrected as

Cocaine has a potent stimulating action on central nervous system. It interferes with the transport of the neuro-transmitter dopamine. [1]

6. (c) The pBR322 is the first artificial cloning vector. It is developed from *E.coli*. It contains restriction site (*Hind* III, *Eco*RI, *Bam*HI, *Sal* I, *Pvu* II, *Pst* I, *Cla* I), *ori* and two antibiotic resistance genes (amp^R and tet^R). [1]

7. (c) Activated sludge is formed during secondary sewage treatment through aeration. It possess flocs of decomposer microbes. [1]

8. (b) Statements (ii) and (iv) are correct, while statements (i) and (iii) are incorrect and these can be corrected as

- The Western Ghats have a greater amphibian species diversity than the Eastern Ghats.
- The largely tropical Amazonian rainforest in South American has the greatest biodiversity on earth- it is home to more than 40,000 species of plants, 3,000 fishes 1,300 of birds, 427 of mammals, 427 of amphibians, 378 of reptiles and of more than 1,25,000 invertebrates. [1]

9. (b) *Ex situ* conservation includes off-site collections, such as gene banks, *in vitro* fertilisation, cryopreservation techniques and tissue culture. [1]

10. (c) Spermiogenesis is the final stage of spermatogenesis, in which spermatids are transformed in the form of mobile spermatozoa. [1]

11. (c) Typhoid fever is caused by the bacterium *Salmonella typhi* and widal test is the confirmatory test for typhoid, which is based on antigen-antibody interaction. [1]

12. (b) The part labelled as C shows ovary. It is the site of fertilisation, the process in which the fusion of male and female gametes takes place. Fertilisation occurs in the ovary of a pistil. [1]

13. (c) Assertion is true, but Reason is false. Reason can be corrected as

The glandular tissue of each breast is divided into 15-20 mammary lobes containing clusters of cells called alveoli. [1]

14. (a) Both Assertion and Reason are true and Reason is the correct explanation of Assertion.

Restriction enzyme is a type of endonuclease that cuts the two strands of DNA at specific positions within the DNA. [1]

15. (d) Assertion is false, but Reason is true. Assertion can be corrected as
A single species might show high diversity at the genetic level over its distributional range. [1]

16. (a) Both Assertion and Reason are true and Reason is the correct explanation of Assertion.
Predation is an interspecific interaction with a feeding strategy. The number of predator usually depends upon the population of prey, but later is also controlled by predators.

Thus, predator and prey maintain a fairly stable population through time and rarely one population becomes scarce or abundant. [1]

17. The advent of birth control pills encouraged people to have unprotected sexual intercourse. Other means of contraception particularly condoms, are not used.

Thus, STDs are being more readily transmitted during sexual activities due to lack of any physical or mechanical barrier. [2]

Or Reproduction and Child Healthcare (RCH) programmes cover wide range of reproduction related areas. They include

(i) creating awareness among people about various reproduction related aspects. [1]

(ii) support for building up a reproductively healthy society by providing increased medical facilities, better postnatal care, better detection and cure of diseases like STDs, etc. [1]

18. When two different species with different ancestors tend to develop similar traits during the course of evolution is termed as convergent evolution. [1]

Example Some of the marsupials of Australia resemble placental mammals that live in similar habitats to other continents. [1]

Or *Homo habilis* were the first human-like hominid. They probably did not consume meat and their brain capacity was about 650-850 cc.

19. After infecting the human body, the HIV gains entry into macrophages.

Events occurring in these cells are as follows

(i) RNA genome of the virus replicates to form viral DNA by enzyme reverse transcriptase.

(ii) Viral DNA gets incorporated into the macrophage DNA and directs the infected cells to produce new viruses.

(iii) Macrophages continue to produce virus particles and thus called HIV factory. [2]

20. (i) Based on the above results it can be inferred that man 3 is father. As among the three man only man 3 has two bands that matches with the child. [1]

(ii) While DNA fingerprinting is highly accurate technique, it does not provide a 100% guarantee. As the accuracy results dependends on many factor such as quality of sample, and the selection of appropriate genetic markers for analysis. [1]

21. (i) The two places where methanogens can be found are

- Rice fields
- Ruminants alimentary canal [1]

(ii) In the paddy fields, cyanobacteria such as BGA fix atmospheric nitrogen to enrich the nitrogen content of soil. Therefore, the entire need of nitrogen to rice crop can be supplied by BGA, leading to increase in yield. [1]

Or **Cyclosporin** - A is produced by the fungus *Trichoderma polysporum*.

It is used as an immunosuppressive agent in organ - transplant patients as it suppresses the activation of T-cells in body. [2]

22. (i) *A* represents digester in the biogas plant, which is used to anaerobically decompose the biodegradable materials, and to produce biogas. Biogas is methane rich gas fuel produced primarily through the anaerobic breakdown of waste biomass by methanogenic bacteria. [1½]

(ii) The group of microbes observed in a biogas plants are called methanogens. These bacteria grows anaerobically on cellulosic material and produces large amounts of methane along with carbon dioxide and hydrogen gas. [1½]

23. The functions of seminal vesicle, acrosome and scrotum are as follows

(i) **Seminal vesicle** During spermatogenesis, it secretes an alkaline fluid rich in fructose and prostaglandins. High level of fructose are known to provide energy to the sperms. [1]

(ii) **Acrosome** It is a cap-like structure in the head region of the sperm. The acrosome contains hydrolytic enzyme, which help sperm to penetrate the cytoplasm of the ovum and thus facilitating fertilisation. [1]

(iii) **Scrotum** It is a bag-like structure made up of skin that holds and helps to protect testicles. [1]

24. (i) (a) In case of allergy, IgE antibodies are involved. histamine and serotonin are responsible for such responses.

(b) Anti-histamine could be given for immediate relief. [2]

(ii) The function of mast cells in allergy response is that it releases histamine, which causes inflammatory reactions in the body. [1]

25. (i) The current species extinction rate is estimated to be 100-1000 time faster than in the pre-human era. [1]

(ii) All activities performed by human beings for the survival and maintenance of their lifestyle are responsible for 'Sixth extinction', [1]

(iii) Points that can help to overcome this disaster are as follows

(a) Preventing habitat loss and fragmentation.

(b) Checking over-exploiting. [1]

26. The expanded form of VNTR is Variable Number of Tandem Repeats. These are short nucleotide repeats in DNA. These are highly specific for individuals.

Role of VNTR in Fingerprinting VNTRs are used as probe in the identification of DNA from different individuals because no two individuals can have the same VNTRs (except in case of monozygotic twins). [2]

Applications of DNA Fingerprinting

(a) DNA fingerprinting is a technique that involves identifying differences in same specific regions in DNA sequence called as repetitive DNA.

(b) DNA fingerprinting can identify the biological mother, father and offspring.

(c) DNA fingerprinting is very useful in the detection of crime and legal pursuits. (Any two) [1]

Value Points
In order to get maximum marks students should include following value points in the answer.
What actually is VNTR?
What is DNA fingerprinting?

27. (i) The average duration of human pregnancy is known as gestation period. It is approximately 270 days (i.e., 9 months) in humans. [1]

(ii) The term denoted to the process of delivery of foetus is called parturition. [1]

(iii) Parturition is induced by a complex neuro-endocrine mechanism. The signals for parturition originates from a fully developed foetus and the placenta which induces mild uterine contractions known as foetal-ejection reflex. [1]

28. In the given table *A, B, C, D, E* and *F* are identified as

$A \rightarrow$ Convergent evolution

$B \rightarrow$ Eye of octopus and mammals

$C \rightarrow$ Adaptive rdiation

$D \rightarrow$ Australian marsupials

$E \rightarrow$ Divergent evolution

$F \rightarrow$ Same ancestors, but different traits. [3]

29. (i) The trait that is shown in this pedigree chart is sex-linked and recessive. [1]

(ii) Females are usually the carriers of colour blindness, but they are usually not affected by it. [1]

(iii) As the 7 individual is an affected female. The expected percentage of her sons affected with colour blindness would be 100%. This can be explained as

X^CX^C (Female) $\downarrow$ XY (Male)

	X^C	X^C
X	X^CX	X^CX
Y	X^CY	X^CY

The possible gentoype of the offsprings will be X^CX, X^CX (carrier female) X^CY, X^CY (affected male). [2]

Or

(iii) All daughters in generation II carry the colourblind gene as they receive colourblind allele from the father. This can be explained as

X^CY (Father) $\downarrow$ XX (Mother)

	X^C	Y
X	X^CX	XY
X	X^CX	XY

The possible genotype of the offsprings will be X^CX, X^CX (carrier female) and XY, XY (normal male). [2]

Value Points
For getting maximum marks, following value point can be included in the answer.
Students should make the Punnett square.

30. (i) The outbreak of dengue fever occurred in the month of August to November, i.e. during rainy season. [1]

(ii) Dengue viruses are spread to people through the bites of infected *Aedes* species mosquitoes. [1]

(iii) The dengue fever outbreaks usually occur in the summer or during the rainy season because during this time period population of the vector mosquitoes are high. As, the combination of warm temperature and stagnant water provides ideal breeding condition for mosquitoes. [2]

Or

(iii) The spread of dengue can be controlled by the use of insect repellants, wearing long-sleeved shirts and long pants and by controlling mosquitoes inside and outside our houses. [2]

31. (i) *A* is a denaturation process and *B* are primers. *C* is *Taq* DNA polymerase, which is a thermostable enzyme, that remains active during the high temperature and amplify DNA sequences through polymerase chain reaction (PCR). [2]

(ii) **Role of Heat** In PCR (*in vitro*), the DNA strands are separated by heating at 95°C for 2 minutes. The heating causes the breakage of H-bonds between bases of two strands leading to its unwinding.

Role of Primers Primers are the short lengths of DNA of about 20 bp long that are required to start polymerisation of DNA in a PCR. The primers hybridise to their complementary sequence on the DNA strands at 40°-50°C temperature and help in DNA polymerisation.

Role of *Thermus aquaticus* An enzyme called *Taq* polymerase is isolated from *Thermus aquaticus*. Since, this bacteria thrives in temperature as high as 95°C, this enzyme can also tolerate high temperature without undergoing denaturation. Therefore, this enzyme is used in PCR instead of normal DNA polymerase. [3]

Or

(i) Insulin was extracted earlier from the pancreas of slaughtered pigs and cattle animals.

Insulin obtained from these source is no more in use by diabetic people because insulin from animal sources caused some patients to develop allergy or some other reactions to the foreign protein. [2]

(ii) Steps involved in insulin production by Eli Lilly company are as follows

(a) DNA sequences corresponding to the two polypeptide, A and B-chains of insulin were synthesised *in vitro*.

(b) They were introduced into plasmid DNA of *E. coli*.

(c) This bacterium was cloned under suitable conditions.

(d) The transgene was expressed in the form of polypeptides A and B, secreted into the medium.

(e) They were extracted and combined by creating disulphide bridge to form human insulin.

The recombinant DNA technique was used by the company. [3]

32. (i) Cu-T is placed in the uterus and proves to be an effective method of contraception in human females. It prevents implantation of the zygote on the uterine wall. It is a long lasting method of contraception. [2]

(ii) Hormone releasing IUDs are progestasert and LNG-20 which make uterus unsuitable for implantation. [1]

(iii) Cu ion releasing IUDs are more efficient methods of contraception because

(a) They suppress the sperm motility and capacity of fertilising ovum.

(b) It is the safest long term, least expensive, reversible contraceptives available.

The hormone releasing IUDs on the other hand, makes uterus unsuitable for implantation and the cervix hostile for sperms. [2]

Or (i) **Monoecious flowers** are unisexual, i.e. they have either the male reproductive or female reproductive part in separate flowers or both produced on same plant. The flowers (male and female)are separate. It prevents self-pollination and promotes cross-pollination.

(ii) **Cleistogamous flowers** are those flowers that does not open at all even at maturity. In such flowers anthers and stigmas lie close to each other. These flowers are invariably autogamous and promote inbreeding depression as there is no chance for cross-pollination at all.

(iii) **Self-incompatible** In angiospermic flowers, there is a genetic mechanism, where the flowers prevent the self pollens from fertilising the ovules or inhibit their germination on stigma. This device or mechanism promotes outbreeding. [5]

33. *Lac* operon consists of

(i) an operator, which controls all structural genes as a unit.

(ii) a regulatory gene (*i* gene).

(iii) three structural genes (*z*, *y*, *a*), which code for enzymes.

(iv) a promoter, where RNA polymerase binds for transcription.

The schematic diagram of *lac* operon in switched on position is given below

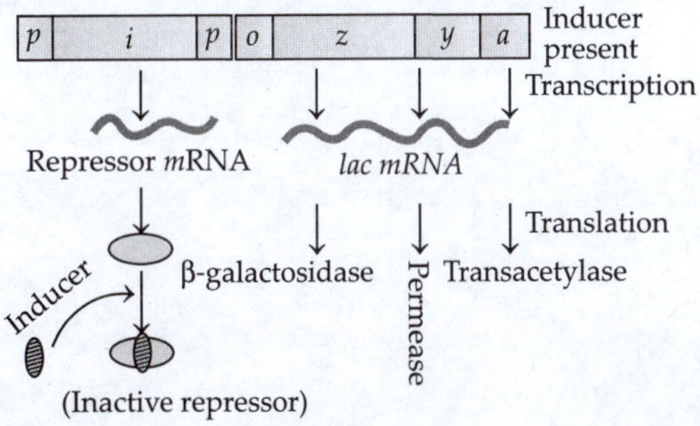

Lac* operon of *E. coli [3]

An operon is switched off through the action of a repressor protein. In *lac* operon *i* gene regulates and produces repressor *m*RNA. The repressor protein binds to the operator region of operon and as a result prevents RNA polymerase to bind to the operon. [2]

Or

(i) **Law of Independent Assortment** (Third law) is based on the inheritance of two genes, i.e., dihybrid cross which states that when two pairs of contrasting traits are combined in a hybrid, segregation of one pair of characters is independent of the other pair of characters. [2]

(ii)

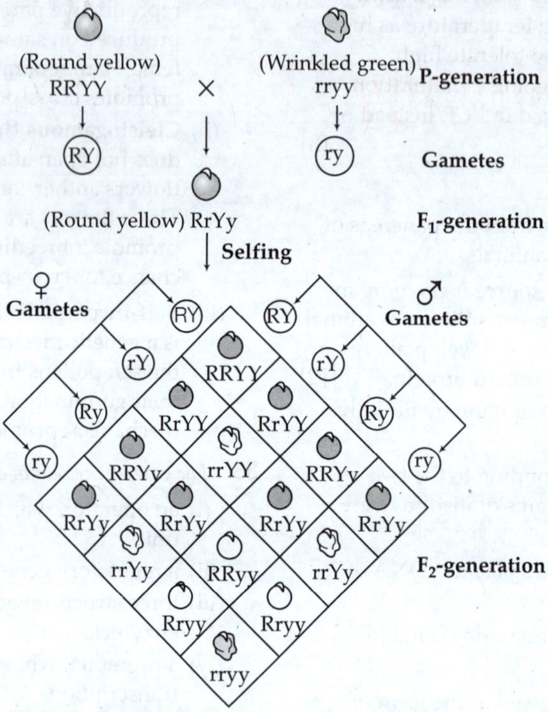

Phenotypic ratio Round yellow : Round green

9 : 3

Wrinkled yellow : Wrinkled green

3 : 1 [3]

SQP Code : **PB-7/15** Series ***i*-Succeed 7-25/15** Roll No.

Sample Question Paper 07

Biology 12th (Code 044)

General Instructions

1. All questions are compulsory.
2. The question paper has five sections and 33 questions.
3. Section-A has 16 questions of 1 mark each; Section-B has 5 questions of 2 marks each; Section-C has 7 questions of 3 marks each; Section-D has 2 case-based questions of 4 marks each; and Section-E has 3 questions of 5 marks each.
4. There is no overall choice. However, internal choices have been provided in some questions. A student has to attempt only one of the alternatives in such questions.
5. Wherever necessary, neat and properly labelled diagrams should be draw.

Time : 3 Hrs.

Max. Marks : 70

Section A Multiple Choice Type Questions

1. During the production of yogurt and cheese, the mixture undergoes a pH change. This change in pH is brought about by

(a) conversion of milk proteins to solid forms

(b) conversion of lactose to lactic acid

(c) release of CO_2

(d) ethanol production

2. Select the option that has the correct sequence of events of stages in the life cycle of *Plasmodium*.

(i) Parasite reach the liver through blood.

(ii) Sexual stage develop in red blood cell.

(iii) Parasites reproduce asexually in RBC, bursting the RBC cells and causing cycle of fever.

(iv) The parasite reproduces asexually in liver cells.

(v) When the mosquito bites human, sporozoites are injected with bite.

Options

(a) (i) → (v) → (ii) → (iv) → (iii)

(b) (v) → (i) → (ii) → (iv)→ (iii)

(c) (v) → (i) → (iv) → (iii) → (ii)

(d) (i) → (v) → (iii) → (iv) → (ii)

3. Population interactions

Organisms *A*	Organisms *B*	Names of interaction
+	+	Mutualism
–	–	*A*
+	–	Predation
+	–	*B*
+	0	Commensalism
–	0	*C*

'+' sign for beneficial interaction

'–' sign for harmful (detrimental) interaction

'0' sign for neutral interaction

Find out what could be *A*, *B* and *C*?

(a) *A*–Amensalism, *B*–Parasitism, *C*–Competition
(b) *A*–Competition, *B*–Parasitism, *C*–Amensalism
(c) *A*–Competition, *B*–Amensalism, *C*–Parasitism
(d) *A*–Amensalism, *B*–Competition, *C*–Competition

4. A pair of an animal and a plant which have been labelled as endangered (from India) in the Red Data Book are

(a) Banyan and Black buck
(b) Tamarind and Rhesus monkey
(c) *Bentinckia nicobarica* and Red panda
(d) *Azadirachta indica* and Deer

5. Read the four statements given below and select the option having two correct statements.

(i) Phenylketonuria is caused by mutation in the gene that codes for the enzyme phenylalanine hydroxylase.
(ii) Honeybee has a special characteristic features such as the males produce sperms by meiosis.
(iii) Colour blindness is a sex-linked recessive disorder.
(iv) Thalassemia is a qualitative problem of synthesising an incorrectly functioning globin.

(a) (i) and (ii) (b) (ii) and (iv)
(c) (i) and (iii) (d) (iii) and (iv)

6. Select the incorrect match from the following

(a) Fragmentation-Breakdown of detritus into smaller particles
(b) Humification- Result in accumulation of a dark coloured amorphous substance
(c) Mineralisation- Release of inorganic nutrients into soil
(d) Catabolism - Fungal enzymes degrade detritus into organic substances

7. Ecosystem need a constant supply of energy

(a) to counteract increasing disorderliness
(b) to counteract decreasing disorderliness
(c) to synthesise molecules
(d) Both (a) and (c)

8. The table below depicts the level of oxygen, numbers of aquatic plants and fishes and the level of organic matter in the rivers *P*, *Q*, *R* and *S* flowing across four towns. The water from which river is most polluted and requires urgent treatment?

	Rivers	Level of O_2	Aquatic plants	Fishes	Level of organic matter
(a)	*P*	High	4-5	< 10	Low
(b)	*Q*	High	30-45	< 100	High
(c)	*R*	Low	4-5	> 10	High
(d)	*S*	Low	30-45	> 100	Low

9. According to the Hugo de Vries variations occurs due to mutations. He worked on evening primrose and postulated that mutation is caused due to sudden variation and some time it led in the formation of new species. Formation of new species is termed as

(a) saltation (b) speciation
(c) founder effect (d) natality

10. A couple trying to have a child, recently found out, that the male partner has no sperm in his reproductive tract. Identify the ART which could help this couple to achieve conception.

	Method of ART	Specifics
(a)	Testicular sperm extraction	Collection of sperm from testis
(b)	Intra-cytoplasmic sperm injection	Directly injecting sperm into cytoplasm of ovule
(c)	Artificial donor insemination	Donated sperm is inseminated in woman's uterus
(d)	*In vitro* fertilisation	Fertilising sperm and ovule outside the body

SP-07

11. *Plasmodium falciparum* is an

(a) ectoparasite
(b) endoparasite
(c) obligate parasite
(d) facultative parasite

12. The figure below depicts the hormonal control of male reproductive system.

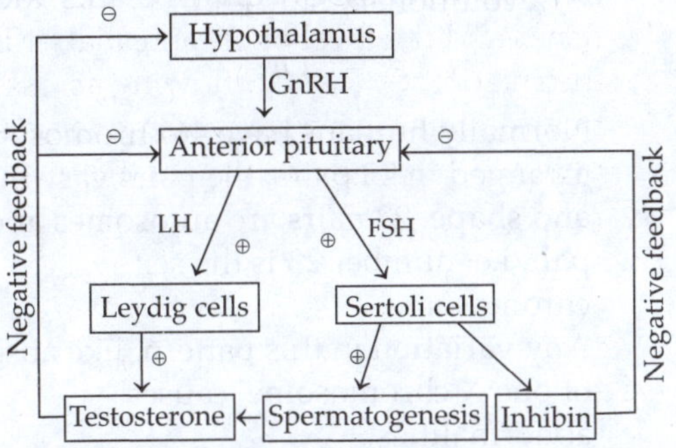

Due to a specific mutation in anterior pituitary, the secretion of GnRH gets reduced. Which of the following is the correct observation for this condition?

	Observations	Effects
(a)	Low levels of LH and FSH	Testosterone deficiency
(b)	Increased levels of LH and FSH	Enlarged testis
(c)	Low levels of LH and FSH	No oogenesis affecting the gamete production
(d)	Increased levels of gonadotropins	Sterile male

Question Nos. 13 to 16 consist of two statements, Assertion (A) and Reason (R). Answer these questions selecting the appropriate option given below.

(a) Both Assertion and Reason are true and Reason is the correct explanation of Assertion
(b) Both Assertion and Reason are true, but Reason is not the correct explanation of Assertion
(c) Assertion is true, but Reason is false
(d) Assertion is false, but Reason is true

13. Assertion (A) Mango is a false fruit.

Reason (R) Thalamus participates in false fruits formation.

14. Assertion (A) Polycistronic *m*RNA is capable of forming a number of different polypeptide chains.

Reason (R) Polycistronic *m*RNA has terminator codons.

15. Assertion (A) Plant with genetic modifications are more tolerant to abiotic stresses like drought and heat.

Reason (R) The plasmid vectors used for plant cell transformations are based on Ti-plasmids.

16. Assertion (A) Keystone species are not relevant to biodiversity conservation.

Reason (R) Keystone species have a significant impact on community structure and characteristics.

Section B Very Short Answer Type Questions

17. Cloning sites are required in a vector to facilitate the action of restriction enzymes during genetic engineering process. What will happen if many recognition sites are present within the vector?

Or β-galactosides enzyme is considered a better selectable marker. Justify the statement.

18. In the figure below, different methods of contraceptions are shown. Study them and answer the questions that follows.

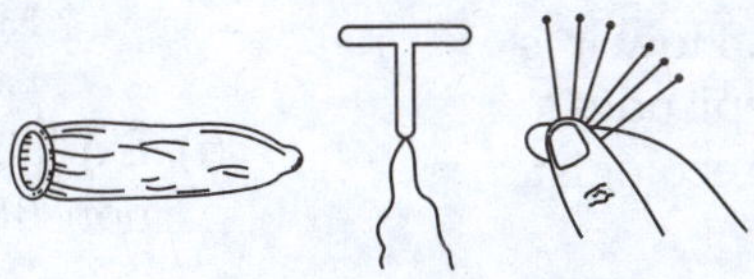

A B C

(i) Name these methods of contraceptive measures.
(ii) Mention which one of these is better suited for prevention against an STD.

Or

Describe the lactational amenorrhea method of birth control.

19. Describe stratification by citing three examples.

20. The cancer is the uncontrolled growth of cells which results in tumour. These can be either benign (stay in fix spot) or malignant (can move to other parts of the body) and can cause cancer.

Answer the following questions.
(i) Cancer is one of the most dreaded disease. Explain contact inhibition with respect to the disease.
(ii) Cancer patients often given α-interferon as a part of the treatment. Give reason.

21. The modifications in the wings of different organisms are also a part of evolution
(i) What conclusion can you derive with respect to these organisms?
(ii) How does the study of comparative morphology and anatomy help in evolutionary studies.

Or

Normally humans have 46 chromosomes arranged in 23 pairs, the pairs vary in size and shape. 22 pairs are autosomes and one pair, i.e. number 23 is the sex chromosome.
Any variation in this pattern, like absence of one *X* chromosome, causes abnormalities.
Identify the disease mentioned above and explain the causes of such chromosomal disorder. Also mention the diagnostic features of this disorder.

Section C Short Answer Type Questions

22. (i) Why tubectomy and vasectomy methods are known as the contraception?
(ii) Why these methods are generally not recommended to young couples?

23. Certain attributes of innate immunity are given in the table below. Identify *A*, *B*, *C*, *D*, E and *F* in the table given below.

Types of barrier	Example of the barrier	Functions
A	*B*	Prevent microbial growth
C	Polymorpho nuclear leucocytes	*D*
Cytokine	*E*	*F*

24. (i) Describe sixth extinction. How it is different from previous episodes? What is major concern of ecologist about sixth extinction?
(ii) "Amazonian rainforest in South America has the greatest biodiversity on earth". Justify the statement.

25. The graph given below shows the usage of pesticides on *Bt* crops and non-*Bt* crops, in four types of farm lands. Cotton bollworm were introduced as pest in all four farm lands.

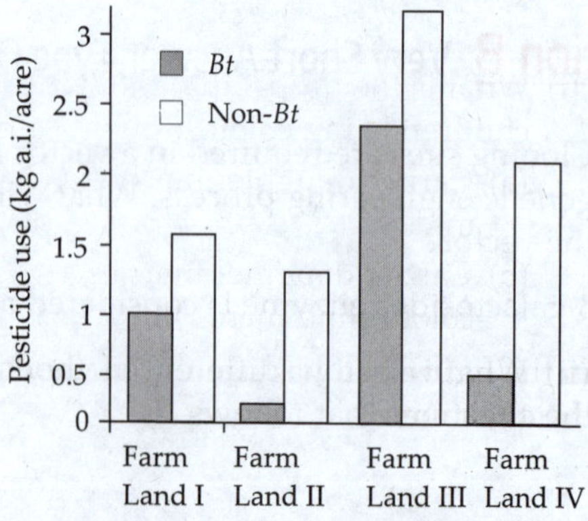

(i) Explain what effect would a *Bt* and non-*Bt* crop have on the pest?

(ii) Which of the below four farm lands have successfully applied the concepts of biotechnology to show better management practices and use of agrochemicals?

26. Highlight the structure of nucleosome and its importance in DNA packaging in eukaryotes.

27. Neha, a NGO worker is given the responsibility to educate the sex workers about sexually transmitted diseases. While the sex workers were initially hesitant and reluctant to attend Neha's session. Neha was patient and convinced them by explaining the importance of understanding STD so that they can protect themselves and lead healthy reproductive lives. The workers agreed and were happy to attend the session.

(i) Specify any two ways of prevention from such diseases.

(ii) What are STDs?

(iii) What are the symptoms of STDs?

28. (i) Explain the one advantage of using *Agrobacterium* in genetic engineering.

(ii) What are two core techniques that enabled the birth of modern biotechnology?

Or

(ii) The gene for colour blindness is present on X-chromosome. How does this affect its inheritance? [1]

(iii) Name another genetic disorder showing similar trait. [1]

Section D Case Based Questions

Q. Nos. 29 and 30 are case-based questions. Each question has 3 subparts with internal choice in one subpart.

29. Study the inheritance chart for colour blindness in a couple, where no history of this disease is present in the female partner.

Parents XX (Normal woman) X^cY (Colourblind man)

♀ \ ♂	X^c	Y
X	XX^c	XY
X	XX^c	XY

All carrier daughters — All normal sons

(i) What is the probability of their grand children being colourblind in case?

(a) Carrier daughter marries a normal man.

(b) Carrier daughter marries a colourblind man. [2]

(ii) What would happen to children of all their sons? [1]

30. Given below is the result of the survey done by MCD to analysis the breeding of mosquitoes. Observe the graph carefully and answer the questions that follows.

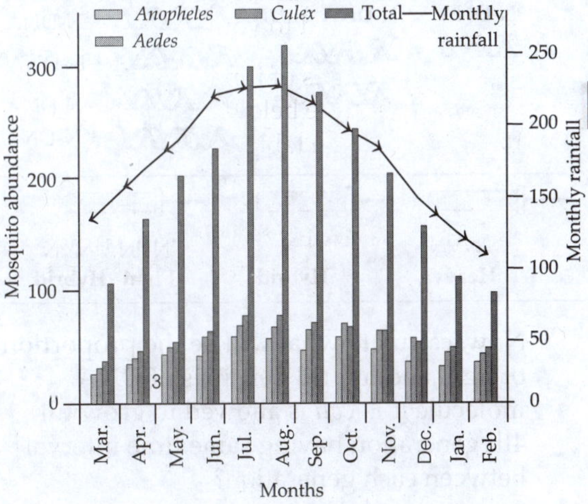

(i) According to the graph, in which month the mosquito breeding is at its peak? Also, give reason for it. [1]

(ii) If an individual gets bitten by a malarial parasite, what symptoms will he possess? [1]

(iii) Where does the fertilisation and development of malarial parasite take place in mosquito's body? Also mention what does the sexual stages of parasite are referred to as? [2]

Or (iii) What is the cause of cycle of fever during malaria? [2]

Section E Long Answer Type Questions

31. Mathew Meselson and Franklin Stahl perfomed an experiment, which proved that DNA replicates semi-conservatively for that, they grow *E. coli* in a medium containing $^{15}NH_4Cl$ which result in the incorporation of ^{15}N isotope into newly synthesised DNA.

They then transfered the cells into a medium with nomal $^{14}NH_4Cl$ and took samples at various definite time intervels as the cells multiplied and extracted the DNA that remained as double-stranded helices.

The DNA extracted from the culture at various time intervals are tabulated below

Separation of DNA by centrifugation

Parent DNA	Generation-I (20 min)	Generation-II (40 min)

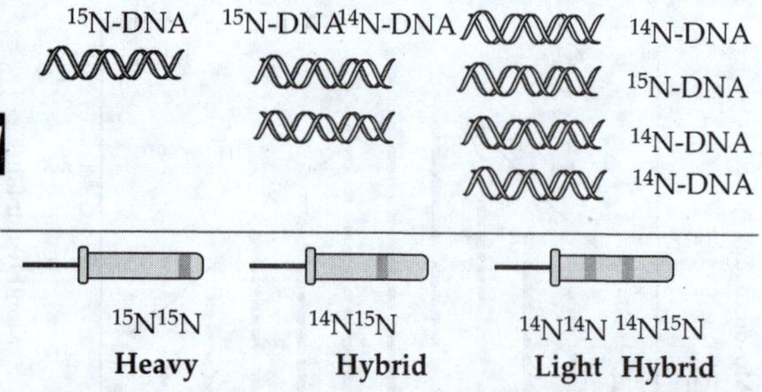

Now, calculate what will be the proportion of light and hybrid densities of DNA molecule if *E. coli* is allowed to grow till 4th generation having same time interval between each generation?

Or

(i) Name the kind of disease/ disorder and one symptom that are likely to occur in humans if

(a) Mutation in the gene that codes for an enzyme phenylalanine hydroxylase occurs.

(b) Trisomy of chromosome 21

(c) Presence of additional copy of X-chromosome

(ii) Mention the type of allele that expresses itself only in homozygous state in an organism.

(iii) Pea flowers produce assured seed sets. Give a reason.

32. Biotechnologists created *Bt* cotton by inserting DNA from a *Bt* bacterium into the cotton plant's DNA.

Following this insertion of modified *Bt* DNA into cotton plants, many companies moved the *Cry* protein into high performance cotton varieties for commercial benefits. *Bt* cotton offers a vastly improved methods of delivering *Cry* proteins to target insects compared to traditional methods thereby increasing the overall yield.

(i) List two advantages of using *Bt* cotton.

(ii) Write the mechanism of action for *Bt* toxin after its been consumed by a bollworm larvae.

(iii) Does *Bt* cotton affects beneficial insects?

Or The graph below depicts some of the GM crops being cultivated in the US.

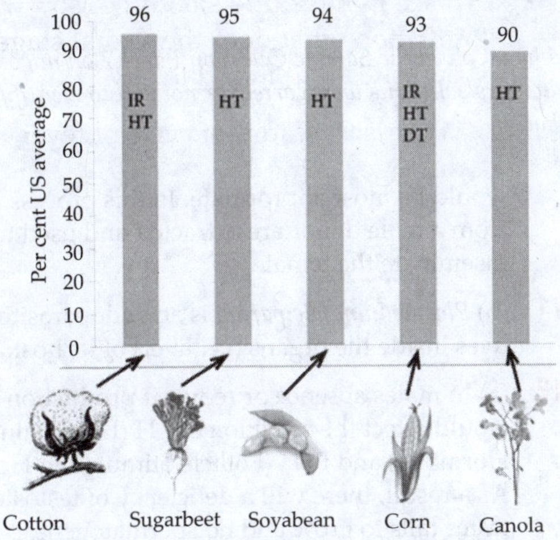

(i) Are you aware of the traits for which genetic modification is carried out in these crop plants?

(ii) The first stage in making a GM plant requires transfer of DNA into a plant cell. How is this achieved?

(iii) In India, the regulation of all activities related to GMOs and products are regulated as per the rules of the manufactures / use / import / storage of hazardous microorganisms, genetically engineered organisms or cells.

These rules are implemented by Ministry of environment, forests and climate change, Dept. of Biotechnology, Govt. of India with respect to GMOs. What is the agenda behind establishing such agencies?

33. (i) Explain the events in a normal woman during her menstrual cycle on the following days.

(a) Ovarian events from 13-15 days.

(b) Ovarian hormone level from 16-29 days.

(ii) Draw a diagrammatic sectional view of female reproductive system.

Or

(i) Although, seeds in general are the products of fertilisation, but a few flowering plants have evolved special mechanisms to produce seeds. Discuss any two mechanisms in brief.

(ii) Draw a diagrammatic representation of the mature embryo sac.

SP-07

Explanations in Topper's Style

My Commitment *I affirm that I am reviewing these solutions only after I have solved the Sample Question Paper 7 on my own. My purpose of looking the solutions is solely to verify whether my answers/solutions were correct or not and to identify my mistakes in case my solutions were wrong or I could not solve that.*

1. (b) The change in pH in the production of yogurt and cheese occurs due to the action of bacteria called *Lactobacillus*. These bacteria convert lactose present in milk to lactic acid, which, being acid lowers the pH of reaction mixture. [1]

2. (c) The correct order of events of stages in the life cycle of *Plasmodium* is as follows

(v)→(i)→(iv)→(iii)→(ii) [1]

3. (b) *A*, *B*, and C are identified as
A–Competition, *B*–Parasitism, *C*–Amensalism [1]

4. (c) A taxon is endangered when it is facing a very high risk of extinction in the wild, in near future.

In India, *Bentinckia nicobarica*, a species of flowering plant endemic to great Nicobar and Red panda has entered the endangered list. [1]

5. (c) Statements (i) and (iii) are correct, while statements (ii) and (iv) are incorrect and can be corrected as

Honeybee has a haplo-diploid sex - determination system and has a special characteristic features such as males produce sperms by mitosis.

Thalassemia is quantitative problem of synthesising too few globin molecule. [1]

6. (d) Match-pair given in option (d) is incorrect and can be corrected as

Catabolism include degradation of detritus into inorganic nutrients by bacterial and fungal enzymes. [1]

7. (d) Ecosystem need a constant supply of energy to counteract increasing disorderliness and to synthesise molecules. [1]

8. (c) Out of the all four rivers given (*P* to *S*), the river '*R*' is considered to be the most polluted one and need urgent treatment because here, the level of organic matter is high in which alga or other organism may grow on it. Thus, reduction in the level of O_2 in water. Due to which the aquatic plants and fishes are also affected which result in reduction in their population. [1]

9. (b) Speciation is the evolutionary process by which population evolve to become distinct species. It occurs when groups within a species become reproductively isolated from each other and genetic differences accumulates over time, leading to the emergence of new species. [1]

10. (c) For this couple where male partner has no sperm in his reproductive tract, artificial donor insemination would be most appropriate. In this process, sperms from a male donor are extracted and used to inseminate the female. [1]

11. (b) *Plasmodium falciparum* is an endoparasite, since it lives inside the organs (i.e. liver) of its host. [1]

12. (a) In males absence or reduced production of GnRH would affect the secretion of LH (Luteinizing Hormone) and FSH (Follicle Stimulating Hormone). As a result, there will a deficiency of testosterone, the testes fails to grow and no spermatogenesis will occur. Thus, affecting the production of sperms. [1]

13. (d) Assertion is false, but Reason is true. Assertion can be corrected as

Mango is a true fruit, as it is developed only from the ovary and there is no involvement of any accessory part. [1]

14. (b) Both Assertion and Reason are true, but Reason is not the correct explanation of Assertion. It can be explained as

Polycistronic *m*RNA is commonly found in prokaryotes. It contains two or more coding regions which can specify a number of different polypeptides chains. [1]

15. (b) Both Assertion and Reason are true, but Reason is not the correct explanation of Assertion.

In RDT, various GM plants have been undergone modification in their genomes to provide resistances from abiotic stresses. This is typically achieved by introducing genes that encode proteins involved in stress tolerance, improving plants's ability to withstand harsh environmental conditions. [1]

16. (d) Assertion is false, but Reason is true. Assertion can be corrected as

Keystone species are the important and relevant component of ecosystem balance and biodiversity conservation. These are species which have a significant and disproportionately large influence on community structure and characteristics. [1]

17. Cloning sites are required to link foreign DNA with the vector DNA. These sites are also called recognition sites as these are recognised by the restriction enzymes.

An ideal vector should have single or very few cloning sites. If more than one recognition sites are present within the vector, it will generate several fragments which will lead to more complications in gene cloning. [2]

Or Coding sequence of β-galactosidase is a better marker, as the recombinants and non-recombinants are differentiated on the basis of their ability to produce colour in the presence of a chromogenic substrate, while the selection of recombinants due to inactivation of antibiotic resistant gene is a tedous and time taking process as it include growing them simultaneously on two antibiotics containing media. [2]

18. (i) *A* – Condom, *B* – Copper-T
C – Implants [1]

(ii) Condoms are better for prevention against STDs. They are 98% effective against STD transmission. [1]

Or Lactation amenorrhea refers to the absence of menstruation during the period of intense lactation following parturition. It is a birth control method because

(i) ovulation and other events of menstrual cycle are stopped at this time. [1]

(ii) As long as the mother breastfeeds her child, chances of conception are nil because of the suppressed gonadotropin activity.

However, this method is generally reliable up to only six months after delivery. [1]

19. Vertical distribution of different species occupying different level is called stratification. [1]

For e.g. Trees occupy the top vertical strata of a forest, shrubs are the second and grasses occupy the bottom layers. [1]

20. (i) Contact inhibition is the property possessed by the normal cells. Due to this the growth of cells stops, when come in contact with other cells. But in case of cancer cells, this property is either inactive or lost.

As a result of it, cancer cells divide continuously to give rise to a mass of cells called tumours. [1]

(ii) Cancer patients are often given α-interferon (biological response modifies) as a part of their treatment because it activates patients's immune system and helps in destroying the tumour. [1]

21. (i) The wings of these organisms perform the same function, i.e. flight, although they have different origins and different structures. These organs are thus, identified as analogous. [1]

(ii) Comparitive morphology and anatomy help trace evolutionary relationships by identifying common structures among different species, indicating shared ancestry. [1]

Or

The chromosomal disease mentioned above is Turner's syndrome. It is caused by the non-disjunction of chromosomes. It is the phenomenon of failure of segregation of the members of homologous pairs of the chromosomes. The affected individual has underdeveloped feminine character. Females are sterile and ovaries are rudimentary. [2]

22. (i) Both vasectomy and tubectomy are the surgical methods of contraceptives. These are called so because these methods prevents the meeting of sperm with ovum.
In vasectomy a small portion from vas deferens is removed or tied up through a small incision on the scrotum. Similarly in female a small part of the Fallopian tube is removed or tied up with the incision in abdomen/vagina.

Due to the blockage in the accessory ducts, the gametes do not reach their destination, i.e. urethra in male and Fallopian tube in female. So, the surgical intervention block the gamete transport and thereby prevent conception. [2]

(ii) These methods are highly effective as they block transport and fusion of gametes, but are irreversible in nature. Hence, are not suggested to young couples. [1]

23. In the given table, A, B, C, D, E and *F* are identified as

A → Physiological

B → Lysozyme in saliva

C → Cellular

D → Phagocytose and destroy microbes

E → Interferons

F → Prevention of viral infections [3]

24. (i) The past five episode of mass extinction has been taken place. And in present sixth extinctions is in the process. The current species extinction rate are estimated to be 100 to 1,000 times faster than in the pre-human times. Ecologist warn that if the present trends continue, nearly half of all the species on earth might be wiped out within the next 100 years. [1½]

(ii) Amazonian rainforest in South America has the greatest biodiversity on earth; it harbors about 40,000 species of plants, 1,25,000 species of insects, 3000 species of fishes, 427 of amphibians, 378 of reptiles, 1300 of birds and 427 of mammals. [1½]

25. (i) In *Bt* cotton, a *cry* gene has been introduced from bacterium *Bacillus thuringiensis* (*Bt*) which causes synthesis of a toxic protein.

This protein becomes active in the alkaline gut of bollworm feeding on cotton and punches holes in the lining of the gut causing death of insect. However, a non-*Bt* crop will have no effect on the cotton bollworm, thus yield of cotton will decrease and non-*Bt* cotton crop will succumb to pest attack. [2]

(ii) Farm I and II have successfully applied the concepts of biotechnology because the use of pesticides is highly reduced for *Bt* crop. [1]

26. Nucleosome is a complex of negatively charged DNA wrapped around the positively charged histone octamer (unit of 8 molecules of histone). It is made up of four types of proteins, i.e. H_2A, H_2B, H_3 and H_4 occurring in pairs. H_1 acts as linker histone that connects one histone octamer to the another. A typical nucleosome consists of 200 base pairs of DNA helix.

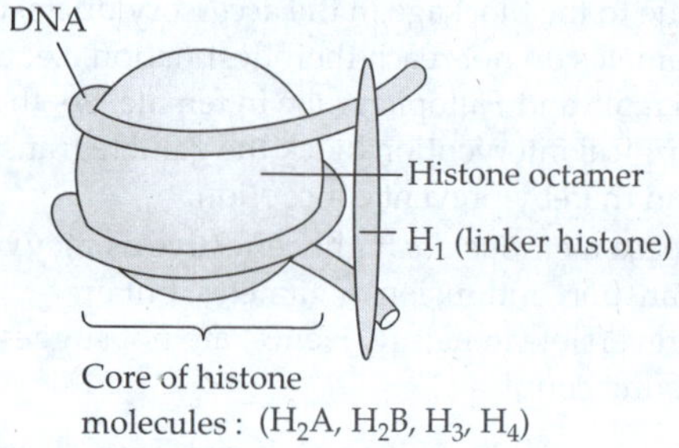

The length of DNA is 2.2 mm in a human diploid cell. This large-sized DNA is accommodated in the smaller area through packaging or compaction.

This is achieved by folding and attachment of DNA with basic proteins (e.g. histones in eukaryotes). [3]

27. (i) Condoms and cervical caps are the two barrier methods of contraception that could be used for the prevention of STDs. [1]

(ii) STDs or sexually transmitted diseases, are the infections that are primarily spread through sexual contact. They can be caused by bacteria, viruses or parasites. Common examples includes chlamydia, gonorrnea, syphilis, etc. [1]

(iii) Early symptoms of STDs are minor and include itching, fluid discharge, slight pain swelling, etc, in the genital region. [1]

28. (i) One advantage of using *Agrobacterium* in genetic engineering is its natural ability to transfer DNA to plant cells. This bacterium can introduce new genes into plant genome efficiently, making it a valuable tool for genetically modified plants with desired traits such as improved resistance to pests, disease or environmental conditions. [1½]

(ii) The two core techniques that enable the birth of modern biotechnology are as follows

(a) Genetic engineering → This technique alters the chemistry of genetic material, i.e. DNA and RNA.

(b) Bioprocess engineering → This technique is used in the maintenance of sterile conditions for the optimal growth of desired microbes. [1½]

29. (i) The probability of their grand children being colourblind is when

(a) **Carrier daughter marries a normal man.**

XX^c × XY
(Carrier woman)(Normal man)

♀ \ ♂	X	Y
X	XX	XY
X^c	XX^c	X^cY

Thus, 50% of their grandsons will be colourblind and 50% of their grand daughters will be carrier.

(b) **Carrier daughter marries a colourblind man**

XX^c × X^cY
(Carrier woman) (Colourblind man)

♀ \ ♂	X^c	Y
X	XX^c	XY
X^c	X^cX^c	X^cY

Thus, 50% of their grandson will be colourblind, 50% of their grand daughters will be colourblind, while rest 50% grand daughters will be carrier.

In both cases, 50% of grandsons will be colourblind. Thus, the probability (overall progenies) is 0.25%. [2]

(ii) The children of all their sons will be normal provided their wife is not a carrier or colourblind person. [1]

Or

(ii) The gene for colour blindness is present on X-chromosome. Thus, it is an X-linked trait. The inheritance of sex-linked traits occurs from father to daughter or mother to son. This is known as *criss-cross* inheritance. [1]

(iii) Haemophilia is another sex-linked recessive disease that shows transmission of disease from an unaffected carrier female to some of the male progeny. [1]

30. (i) During the month of August, (or a rainy season) the mosquito breeding is at its peak. This is because, the logged water and damp places provide suitable breeding environment for mosquitoes. [1]

(ii) Symptoms of malaria includes fever and flu-like illness, including shaking chills, headache, muscle aches and tiredness. [1]

(iii) The fertilisation and development of parasite takes place in the stomach of mosquito's body. The sexual stages of parasite are referred to as gametocytes. [2]

Or

(iii) At regular intervals, the parasite reproduces and causes bursting of RBCs. This rupturing of RBCs is associated with the release of a toxic substance called haemozoin, which is responsible for the chills and high fever recurring every three to four days. [2]

31. If *E. coli* is allowed to replicate till 4th generation, (i.e. 80 min) then it will divide four times, producing four generation.

In first generation, i.e. after 20 min, all strands will be hybrid density DNA molecules. [1]

In second generation, i.e. after 40 min 50% of the strands will be hybrid density molecule and remaining 50% will be light density molecule. [1]

In third generation, i.e. after 60 min 25% of the strands will be hybrid density molecule and remaining 75% will be light density molecules. [1]

In fourth generation, i.e. after 80 min 12.5% of the molecule will be hybrid density and 87.5% will be light density DNA molecule. [1]

Therefore, it can be concluded that after 80 min or at the end of the 4th generation 12.5% hybrid DNA and 87.5% light density DNA molecule will be produced.

Thus, the proportion of light density to hybrid will be 7 : 1. [1]

Or

(i) The following types of diseases are likely to occur in human

(a) Phenylketonuria

(b) Down's syndrome

(c) Klinefelter's syndrome

Symptoms of above disease are as follows

(a) Phenylketonuria - Accumulation of phenylalanine causes mental retardation.

(b) Down's syndrome - Affected individuals are short statured with small round head.

(c) Klinefelter's syndrome-The individual are sterile. [3]

(ii) Recessive allele expresses itself only in the homozygous condition because in the presence of a dominant allele its effect is masked. [1]

(iii) Pea flower produces assured seed set because they have cleistogamous flower, which undergo natural self-pollination. [1]

32. (i) The two advantages of using *Bt* cotton are as follows

(a) *Bt* cotton produces proteins (cry toxins) that specifically target and kill certain insect pest like bollworms. This reduces the damage caused by pest and improve crop yeild.

(b) *Bt* cotton lowers the use of chemical pesticides. Therefore, lowering the overall chemical inputs into environemnt, decreasing pollution and potential harm to non-target organisms. [2]

(ii) Mechanism of action for *Bt* toxin after its consumption by an insect is

Insect eats toxin. The enzymes get activated due to alkaline pH of gut

↓

Toxin binds to midgut epithelial cell surfaces

↓

Gut cells are perforated

↓

Death of the insect [2]

(iii) *Bt* cotton has minimal or no effect on other beneficial insects like bees, beetles, spiders, wasps, etc. However, it may indirectly lower the general abundance of some beneficial insects which prey upon caterpillars, since it causes a decline in caterpillars' numbers. [1]

Or (i) Most existing genetically modified crops have been created to

(a) develop resistance against pests, insects which can damage the crops, e.g. *Bt* gene from *Bacillus thuringinesis* has been inserted in crop plants to develop resistance against insects.

(b) develop herbicide tolerance which enable effective chemical control of weeds.

(c) develop disease resistance towards common pathogens like bacteria, virus, fungi, etc. [2]

(ii) It is achieved by virus / bacteria mediated DNA transfer. The bacteria most commonly used is *Agrobacterium tumefaciens*. The gene of interest is transferred to the bacterium, which is then made to infect the plant. This bacterium then delivers the DNA (Ti-plasmid mediated) to the host plant which then grows and express the trait for which it was modified. [2]

(iii) The government agencies reviews the information related with GM crops. For example, its nature, stability of transgene, effects on non-target organisms, potential for allergic reactions, etc. [1]

33. (i) The events in a normal woman during her menstrual cycle on the following days are as follows

(a) In the ovarian event from 13-15 days, a immature ovum (egg cell) is released from the

Graafian follicle. Both LH and FSH attains maximum peak.

FSH helps Graafian follicle to attain maturity and LH helps in its rupture. Ovum gets covered by a number of layer and a yellow fat layer forms corpus luteum. It releases progesterone.

(b) During menstrual cycle, the period level from 16-21 days is called luteal phase (secretory phase). The corpus luteum secretes large amount of progesterone which is essential for the maintenance of endometrium. [2]

(ii)

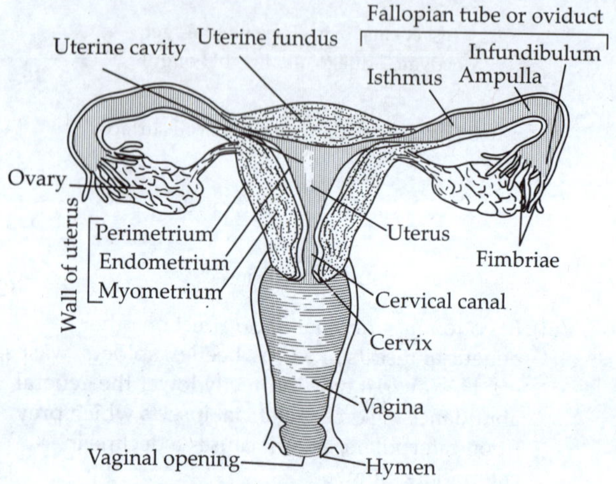

Diagrammatic sectional view of the female reproductive system

[3]

Or

(i) The special methods for seed production are discussed below

(a) **Apomixis** It is a form of asexual reproduction that mimics sexual reproduction and produces seeds without fertilisation. Thus, there is no gametic fusion or zygote formation. For example, Asteraceae and grasses. [1]

(b) **Polyembryony** It is the occurrence of more than one embryo in a seed. In gymnosperms, polyembryony can occur due to cleavage of growing embryo. It occurs in some species of *Citrus* (orange and lemon), onion, groundnut and mango varieties. [1]

(ii)

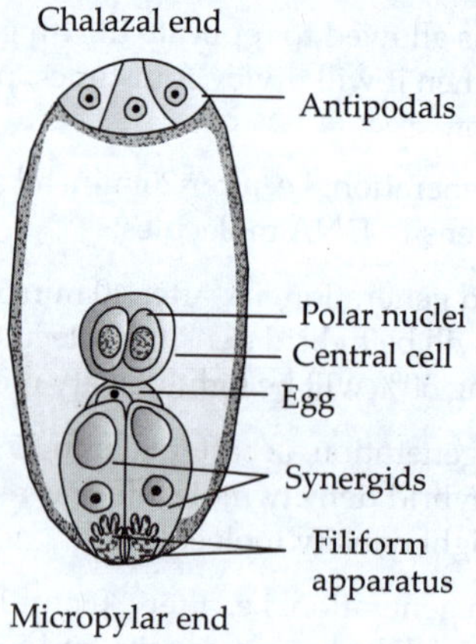

Diagrammatic representation of the mature embryo sac [3]

SQP Code : **PB-8/15**

Series ***i*-Succeed 8-25/15**

Roll No.

Sample Question Paper 08

Biology 12th (Code 044)

General Instructions

1. All questions are compulsory.
2. The question paper has five sections and 33 questions.
3. Section-A has 16 questions of 1 mark each; Section-B has 5 questions of 2 marks each; Section-C has 7 questions of 3 marks each; Section-D has 2 case-based questions of 4 marks each; and Section-E has 3 questions of 5 marks each.
4. There is no overall choice. However, internal choices have been provided in some questions. A student has to attempt only one of the alternatives in such questions.
5. Wherever necessary, neat and properly labelled diagrams should be draw.

Time : 3 Hrs.

Max. Marks : 70

Section A Multiple Choice Type Questions

1. Lactational amenorrhea as a means of contraception refers to

(a) absence of menstruation since ovulation does not occur during breastfeeding period

(b) reduced efficiency of pregnancy hormones

(c) unsuitable uterus

(d) suppressed sperm motility

2. When alleles of two contrasting characters are present together and one of the character expresses itself during the cross while the other remains hidden gives the

(a) law of purity of gametes

(b) law of segregation

(c) law of dominance

(d) law of independent assortment

3. Select the incorrect match-pair from the following

(a) Sickle-cell anaemia- base substitution at the sixth codon of beta globin gene

(b) Turner's syndrome- 45 + XO

(c) Klinefelter's syndrome – 44 +XXY

(d) Thalassemia- reduced rate of synthesis of globin chain of haemoglobin

4. The presence of both a leading and a lagging strand is observed during DNA replication. This is because

(a) RNA primers are not sufficient enough to facilitate replication of both strands

(b) only one DNA template is available for reading at a time

(c) DNA polymerase can catalyse synthesis of one strand at a time

(d) DNA polymerase reads only in $5' \rightarrow 3'$ direction

5. Transgenic animals are generally created for a variety of medical reasons except

(a) for testing vaccine safety

(b) for manufacturing of physiologically important proteins

(c) stimulation of pathogenicity

(d) for toxicity tests

6. Read the four statements given below and select the option having two correct statements.

(i) India has more than 50,000 genetically different strains of rice.

(ii) Species richness decrease with increasing explored area.

(iii) *Clarias gariepinus* is used for marine culture.

(iv) In Meghalaya, the sacred groves are the last refuges for a large number of rare and threatened plants.

(a) (i) and (iv) (b) (ii) and (iv)
(c) (i) and (iii) (d) (iii) and (iv)

7. Which of the following is an example of *ex situ* conservation strategy?

(a) Biosphere reserves (b) Sacred groves
(c) Hotspots (d) Zoological park

8. Select the option that has the correct sequence of events process of recombinant DNA technology.

(i) Isolation of the genetic material.

(ii) Amplification of gene of interest using PCR.

(iii) Cutting of DNA at specific location.

(iv) Obtaining the foreign gene product.

(v) Insertion of recombinant DNA into the host cell.

Options

(a) (i) → (ii) → (iv) → (iii) → (v)
(b) (ii) → (i) → (iv) → (v) → (iii)
(c) (i) → (iii) → (ii) → (v) → (iv)
(d) (i) → (iii) → (v) → (ii) → (iv)

SP-08

9. Given below are some statements derived from Darwin's theory of evolution. Select the one, which is incorrect.

(a) Darwin's variations were small and directional

(b) Fitness is the end result of the capability of an individual to get selected by nature

(c) New species evolves from ancestral forms by the struggle for limited resources

(d) Abrupt and drastic changes cause speciation

10. Which of the following is modified by genetic engineering is used as a 'clot buster' for removing clots from the blood vessels of patients who have undergone myocardial infarction leading to heart attack?

(a) *Streptococcus*
(b) Cyclosporin-A
(c) *Trichoderma polysporum*
(d) *Saccharomyces cerevisiae*

11. To protect tobacco against *Meloidogyne incognitia* using RNAi, nematode specific genes were introduced into the plant using

(a) transposons
(b) *Agrobacterium*
(c) virus with RNA genome
(d) retrotransposons

12. Study the given figure carefully.

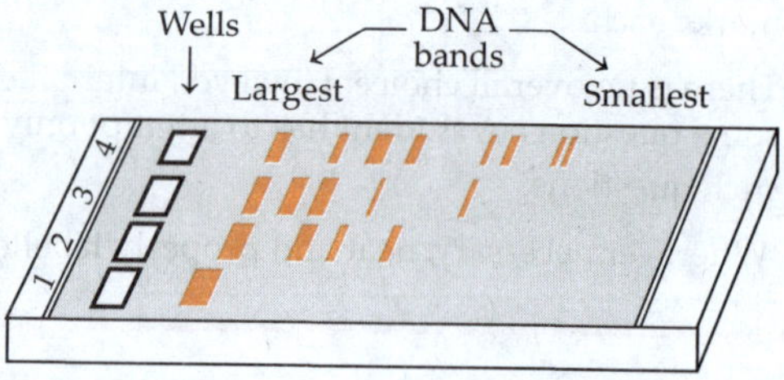

A fragment of DNA molecule on cutting with restriction enzyme yielded 4 fragments of sizes 3 kb, 2.5 kb, 8 kb and 6.7 kb. Having become an expert on gel electrophoresis, you are asked to examine a gel. Identify where would you find these segments of DNA.

	DNA fragments	Location
(a)	3 kb	Near the positive electrode, farthest from wells
(b)	6.7 kb	Near the negative electrode, closest to wells
(c)	8 kb	Near the positive electrode, farthest from wells
(d)	2.5 kb	In middle, slows down after few minutes

***Question** Nos. 13 to 16 consist of two statements, Assertion (A) and Reason (R). Answer these questions by selecting the appropriate option given below.*

(a) Both Assertion and Reason are true and Reason is the correct explanation of Assertion
(b) Both Assertion and Reason are true, but Reason is not the correct explanation of Assertion
(c) Assertion is true, but Reason is false
(d) Assertion is false, but Reason is true

13. **Assertion** (A) Our immune system always recognise the 'self cells' and destroys the foreign proteins.
Reason (R) When the system fails to recognise the 'self' from 'non-self', it starts destroying the body's own proteins. This is known as autoimmunity.

14. **Assertion** (A) The distance between two polynucleotide chains in DNA remains almost constant.
Reason (R) A purine is paired with pyrimidine with hydrogen bonds.

15. **Assertion** (A) Constant gene frequencies over several generations indicate an absence of evolutionary progress.
Reason (R) Evolution occurs when genetic equilibrium is absent.

16. **Assertion** (A) Meiosis is the cell division which occurs in the sexually reproducing organisms.
Reason (R) Meiotic cell division results into two cells having exactly same genetic makeup.

Section B Very Short Answer Type Questions

17. A cross is made between a tall plant with yellow seeds (genotype-TtYy) and a tall plant with green seeds (genotype - Ttyy). What will be the proportions of phenotypes of their offspring in F_1?

Or State what are Mendelian disorders. Both thalassemia and colour blindness categorised as Mendelian disorders. Justify.

18. In the figure below, the process of recombinant DNA technology is depicted.

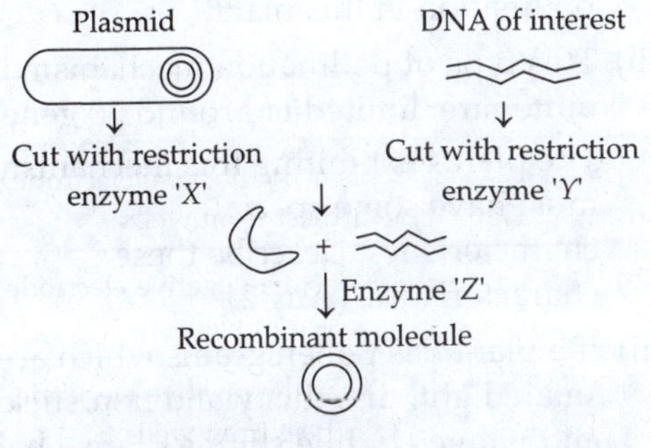

(i) What is the role of enzyme Z in the above experiment?
(ii) Will the outcome of this experiment be successful? Give your opinion along with your answer.

Or State how was *Agrobacterium tumefaciens* made as a useful cloning vector to transfer DNA to plant cells.

19. The formation of reproductive cells in human males takes place in the gonad while it is controlled by some other parts of the body. Justify the statement.

20. Name the bacterium responsible for the large holes seen in swiss cheese. What are these holes due to?

21. The density of a population in any given habitat during a specific period fluctuates. These changes are associated with the phenomenon *A* and *B* as shown below.

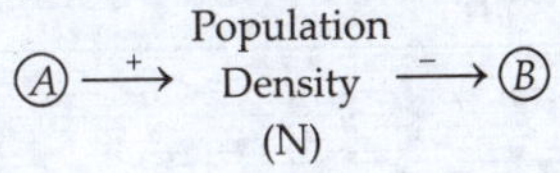

(i) What are *A* and *B*?
(ii) How do *A* and *B* affect the population density?

Or

Discuss one example based on your day to day observations, showing how does the loss of one species may lead to the extinction of another?

Section C Short Answer Type Questions

22. Identify *A, B, C, D, E* and *F* in the table given below.

Name of drugs	Obtained from	Causes
Opioids	*A*	*B*
C	*Cannabis sativa*	*D*
E	*F*	Sense of euphoria and hallucination

23. Explain the levels of biodiversity at genetic, specific and ecological levels with the help of one example each.

24. (i) What are the different diagnosis techniques to detect cancer in a patient?

(ii) Differentiate between the two different types of tumours. Which one is lethal and why?

25. Observe the given below diagram and answer the questions that follows.

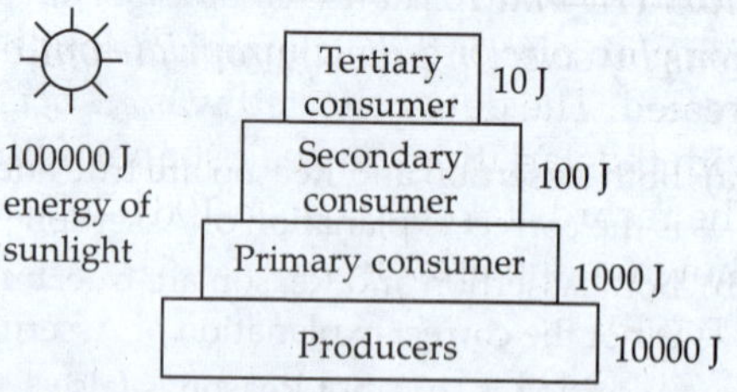

(i) Identify the type of pyramid given above. It is always upright.

(ii) Can a given species occupy more than one trophic level in the same ecosystem at the same time? Enlist one limitations of ecological pyramids.

26. Explain enzyme replacement therapy to treat adenosine deaminase deficiency. Mention two disadvantages of this procedure.

27. (i) What do oral pills contain and how do they act as effective contraceptives?

(ii) Mention simple principles by which one could be free of STDs.

28. Flowering plants have developed many devices to discourage self-pollination and to encourage cross-pollination. Explain two such devices.

Section D Case Based Questions

Q. Nos. 29 and 30 are case-based questions. Each question has 3 subparts with internal choice in one subpart.

29. Study the figure of a floating hydrophyte plant that grows in water bodies.

(i) On the basis of your knowledge about pollination, identify the mechanism of pollination in this plant. [1]

(ii) This type of pollination mechanism is quite rare, limited to around 30 genera. The plants exhibiting this mechanism must have some special characteristics. Describe these characteristics. (Any 2) [1]

(iii) If a plant has pollen grains which are small, light, dry, dusty and non-sticky and winged, while stigma - large, hairy and feathery, will they use a similar mechanism for exchanging gametes? [2]

Or (iii) If a plant has to get pollinated by insect, what characteristics should it exhibit? [2]

30. In order to build a longitudinal data set a record of adult finches *Geospiza fortis* living on one of the Galapagos islands was created. The data collected was associated with the variations in beak shape of birds. The records taken between 1981-2020 are shown in the graph.

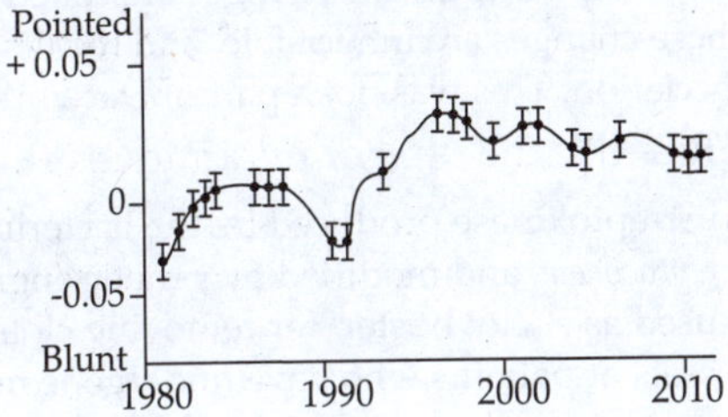

(i) What lead to the diversity in beak shape among the finches? [1]

(ii) The graph as a whole does not represent any evolutionary changes in the beaks since time interval is too small, where evolutionary progress can take thousands of years to occur. Is the above observation correct? Discuss your opinion on this. [1]

(iii) Galapagos finches offer an excellent example of adaptive radiation. Comment. [2]

Or (iii) 'Homology results in divergence'. Elaborate. [2]

Section E Long Answer Type Questions

31. (i) How flocs are formed during sewage treatment? Mention its application.

(ii) Why is the secondary treatment of water in sewage treatment plants called biological treatment?

(iii) Why are biofertilisers or biopesticides preferred to chemical fertilisers or pesticides?

Or

(i) How do normal cell become cancerous?

(ii) Cancer can be treated successfully only if detected at an early stage. How do the following help in detecting cancer?

(a) Biopsy (b) MRI

(iii) Name any two methods that can possibly cure cancer.

32. (i) Give two reasons why both the strands of DNA are not copied during the transcription process?

(ii) List two essential roles of ribosomes during translation.

(iii) Why is DNA molecules a more stable genetic material than RNA? Explain.

Or

Study the given pedigree chart showing the inheritance pattern of blood group in a family and answer the following questions.

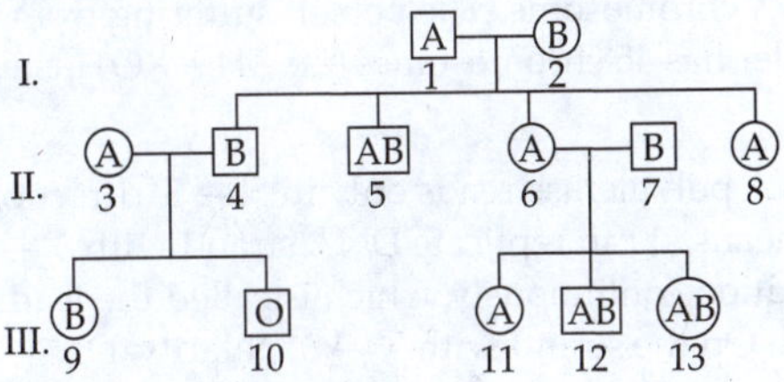

(i) Give the possible genotypes and phenotypes of the individual 1, 2, 3 and 4.

(ii) Which antigen(s) will be present on the plasma membranes of RBCs of individual 5 and 10?

(iii) Among the individuals in generations -II and III, who can be used as

(a) donor for any recipient?

(b) recipient for any donor. Give reason for your answer.

33. Trace the changes occurring in the oogonia during the transition of a primary follicle to Graafian follicle.

Or (i) Differentiate between autogamy, geitonogamy and xenogamy.

(ii) Draw a diagrammatic view of typical anatropous ovule and label the following

(a) Chalazal pole (b) Embryo sac

(c) Nucellus (d) Funicle

(e) Hilum

Explanations in Topper's Style

My Commitment *I affirm that I am reviewing these solutions only after I have solved the Sample Question Paper 8 on my own. My purpose of looking the solutions is solely to verify whether my answers/solutions were correct or not and to identify my mistakes in case my solutions were wrong or I could not solve that.*

1. (a) Lactational amenorrhea is described as a natural method of contraception. This is based on the fact that the menstrual cycle does not occur during the period of intense lactation following parturition. [1]

2. (c) Law of dominance states that when parents with pure, contrasting characters are crossed together , only one form of the trait appears in the next generation. The trait which appear in the next generation is known as dominant trait and which does not express itself is known as recessive trait. [1]

3. (b) The match-pair given in option (d) is incorrect and can be corrected as

   Turner's syndrome is caused due to the absence of one of the X chromosome. The person suffering from this disorder has 45 chromosomes (i.e., 44 + XO) instead of 46. [1]

4. (d)DNA polymerase reads only in $5' \rightarrow 3'$ direction that means, it can replicate DNA strand with $3' \rightarrow 5'$ orientation continuously, which is called the leading strand. On the strand with $5' \rightarrow 3'$ polarity, DNA replicates in the fragmented manner known as Okazaki fragments.
   This is called the lagging strand. Thus, both the leading and lagging strands are present together during DNA replication. [1]

5. (c) Transgenic animals are generally created for a variety of medical reasons such as the study of diseases, the production of pharmaceutical proteins and organs transplantation research. However, they are not generally created for stimulation of pathogenicity. Hence, option (c) is incorrect. [1]

6. (a) Statements (i) and (iv) are correct, while statements (ii) and (iii) are incorrect and can be corrected as
   - Species richness increases with increasing explored area, but only up to a limit.
   - *Clarias gariepinus* is used for aquaculture.

7. (d) *Ex situ* conservation involves protecting an organism outside its habitats by perpetuating sample population in resource centres. For example, a zoological park where wild animals are protected and also exhibited for public viewing. [1]

8. (c) The correct sequence of events of process of recombinant DNA technology is as follows

   (i) → (iii) → (ii) → (v) → (iv)

9. (d) Statement given in option (d) is incorrect and can be corrected as

   The abrupt and drastic changes are called as mutation. These changes are inheritable and results in speciation. This was not a part of Darwin's theory of evolution. [1]

10. (a) Streptokinase produced by the bacterium *Streptococcus* and modified by genetic engineering and is used as a 'clot buster' for removing clots from blood vessels of patients who have undergone myocardial infarction leading to heart attack. [1]

11. (b) By using *Agrobacterium* vector, nematode - specific genes can be introduced into the host plant which produces both sense and antisense RNA in the host cells. [1]

12. (a) Gel electrophoresis separates the fragments of DNA on the basis of size, shape, molecular weight, etc. Since, DNA has negative charge on it, the fragments of DNA under electric field will moves towards the anode. The smaller fragments move faster due to lesser friction, while larger fragments move slowly. Thus, the location of 3 kb is correct, as it will present nearest to the anode, i.e. near to positive electrode and farthest from well. [1]

13. (b) Both Assertion and Reason are true, but Reason is not the correct explanation of Assertion.

    Our immune system has the ability to distinguish between the self and non-self cells. Because every cell in the body has the presence of antigens. These antigens are particular and differs from one organism to another.

    Due to this, when the immune cells detect any other antigen a part from self antigen, they quickly initiate immune responses in the body. [1]

14. (a) Both Assertion and Reason are true and Reason is the correct explanation of Assertion.
    The distance between two polynucleotide chains is almost constant because the purines always pairs with pyrimidine with hydrogen bonds, i.e. Adenine always form two hydrogen bonds with Thymine ($A = T$) similarly guanine always form three hydrogen bonds with cytosine ($G \equiv C$). [1]

15. (a) Both Assertion and Reason are true and Reason is the correct explanation of Assertion. It can be explained as

    The constant gene frequencies ($p^2 + 2pq + q^2 = 1$) over several generations indicate that evolution is not taking place in the population.
    For evolutionary progress, changes in gene

frequencies is essential, this constant equilibrium is changed by random mating, mutation, gene flow, genetic drift and genetic recombination.

These processes introduce variations in a population which serves as raw material for evolution. [1]

16. (c) Assertion is true, but Reason is false. Reason can be corrected as

In meiosis, the resultant cells do not have exactly same genetic makeup due to the process of crossing over. [1]

17. Parents TtYy × Ttyy

(Tall, yellow seeds) (Tall, green seeds)

Gametes - TY, Ty, tY, ty Ty, ty

Progenies

♀/♂	Ty	ty
TY	TTYy (Tall and Yellow)	TtYy (Tall and Yellow)
Ty	TTyy (Tall and Green)	Ttyy (Tall and Green)
tY	TtYy (Tall and Yellow)	ttYy (Dwarf and Yellow)
ty	Ttyy (Tall and Green)	ttyy (Dwarf and Green)

Thus, the phenotypic ratio comes out to be

Tall and yellow : Tall and green : Dwarf and yellow : Dwarf and green 3 : 3 : 1 : 1. [2]

Or

The disorders that occur due to alternation in a single gene are called Mendelian disorders.

Both thalassemia and colour blindness are classified as Mendelian disorders.

- Colour blindness is a sex-linked recessive disorder occurs due to defect in either red or green cone cells of the eye. This results in failure to discriminate between these colours. [1]
- Thalassemia is an autosomal-linked recessive disorder resulting from mutation or deletion in either the α or β-chains of haemoglobin. [1]

18. (i) Enzyme Z joins the foreign DNA to the plasmid. [1]

(ii) To achieve recombinant both vector DNA and DNA/gene of interest should be cut with the same restriction enzymes which is not done in this experiment. Hence, this experiment will not yield successful results. [1]

Or

Agrobacterium infects plant tissues by transferring its plasmid T-DNA to the plant genome. This property of *Agrobacterium* was exploited to transfer desired gene to a particular plant. The desired gene is inserted in the plasmid T-DNA and the engineer *Agrobacterium* is allowed to infect that particular plant. Hence, it acts as a natural cloning vector. [2]

19. Gonadotropin Releasing Hormone (GnRH) is released significantly from hypothalamus during puberty. GnRH stimulates anterior pituitary to secrete LH and FSH. The LH acts on Leydig cells to stimulate the synthesis of androgen which then stimulates the process of spermatogenesis. FSH acts on Sertoli cells and stimulates secretion of some factors which helps in the process of spermiogenesis. [2]

20. Swiss cheese is produced by the bacterium *Propioni bacterium shermanii*. The large holes in Swiss cheese are due to the large amount of CO_2 production. [2]

21. (i) *A* is natality or immigration.

B is mortality or emigration.

(ii) **Natality** is the rate of production of new individuals per unit of population per unit time.

Immigration is defined as the permanent inward movement of individuals into a habitat.

Both these processes (A) add to the size of population.

Mortality is the number of patterns of deaths per unit time.

Emigration is the permanent outward movement of individuals from their habitat to elsewhere. Both these processes (B) decreases the size of a population. [2]

Or Co-extinction is the extinction of two mutually related or inter-related species, for instance extinction of fish species leads to the extinction of all those parasites exclusively found on it. Another example is plant pollinator where extinction of one leads to the extinction of other. [2]

22. Complete table is given as follows

Name of drugs	Obtained from	Causes
Opioids	Acetylation of morphine (*A*)	Slows down body function (*B*)
Cannabinoids (*C*)	*Cannabis sativa*	Effects on cardiovascular system (D)
Cocaine (*E*)	*Erythroxylum coca* (*F*)	Sense of euphoria and hallucination

[½×6=3]

23. Genetic diversity A single species shows diversity at the genetic level over its distributional range. For example, the genetic variation showed by the plant *Rauwolfia vomitoria* growing in the different Himalayan ranges might be in terms of the potency and concentration of reserpine. [1]

Species diversity It is the diversity at the species level or the measure of the variety of species and their relative abundance with the region. For example, the Western Ghats have a greater amphibian species diversity than the Eastern Ghats. [1]

Ecological diversity At the ecosystem level, India shows diversity with its deserts, rainforests, mangroves, coral reefs and alpine meadows. [1]

24. (i) To detect cancer in a patients various diagnostic techniques are used such as CT scan, MRI, biopsy, blood and bone marrow. [1]

(ii) The two different types of tumours are as follows

(a) **Benign tumour** It remains confined to the place of origin or affected organ. The rate of growth of tumour is low.

(b) **Malignant tumour** It invades surrounding tissue and spreads throughout the body. The rate of growth of the tumour is rapid.

Malignancy is lethal as it spreads all over the body through the process of **metastasis**. [2]

(iii) ***Saccharomyces cerevisiae*** Product is ethanol and it is used in making bread and beverages. [1]

25. (i) The pyramid given above is pyramid of energy. It is always upright. Because pyramid of energy states the relationship between the producers and consumers in an ecosystem in terms of flow of energy. Thus, it is always upright. [1]

(ii) Yes, a species can occupy more than one trophic level in the same ecosystem at the same time. For example, a sparrow is a primary consumer when it eats seeds, fruits, peas, etc. It is secondary consumer when it eats insects and worms.

One limitation of ecological pyramids is as follow It does not take into account the same species belonging to two or more trophic levels. [2]

26. Adenosine deaminase deficiency is a genetic disorder. The disorder is caused due to the deletion of the gene for adenosine deaminase, the enzyme crucial for the immune system to function. Adenosine deaminase deficiency in patients can be treated by enzyme replacement therapy. In this treatment, patients are regularly injected with the functional ADA enzyme. [2]

Two disadvantages of this procedure are as follows

(i) It does not completely eradicate the disease.

(ii) The requirement of repeated doses of the enzyme makes it expensive. [1]

27. (i) Oral contraceptives or pills are either progestogens or progestogen - oestrogen combination.

They function as effective contraceptive by inhibiting ovulation, inhibiting implantation, and by altering the quality of cervical mucus to prevent or stop the entry of sperm. [1½]

(ii) Simple principle by which one could be free of STDs are as follows

- avoid sex with unknown partner or multiple partner.
- Always use a barrier method of contraceptive.
- Consult a doctor in case of any symptom for early detection and treatment. [1½]

28. The mechanisms/processess that plants use to avoid self-pollination are known as outbreeding devices. The two outbreeding devices that flowering plants have developed to discourage self-pollination are as follows

(i) **Unisexuality** Flowers are unisexual, so that self-pollination is not possible. These plants may be monoecious (bearing both male and female flowers, e.g. maize) or dioecious (bearing male and female flowers on different plants, e.g. mulberry, papaya). [1½]

(ii) **Dichogamy** Anthers and stigmas mature at different times in a bisexual flower for preventing self-pollination.

(a) **Protandry** In some species anthers mature earlier than stigma of the same flower. The pollen thus become available to stigmas of the older flowers.

(b) **Protogyny** In some species stigmas mature earlier, so that they get pollinated before the anthers of the same flowers develop pollen grains. [1½]

Value Points In order to get maximum marks students should include following value points in the answer.

What are outbreeding devices?

29. (i) The plant is *Vallisneria*, where the flowers are borne underwater. For pollination, water is required as the agency or a medium. This mechanism is known as hydrophilly. [1]

(ii) Specific features associated with water pollinated plants are as follows

(a) stigma are long and sticky.

(b) pollen grains are long, ribbon like and coated by a mucilaginous covering. [1]

(iii) A plant with small, light, dry, non-sticky pollens and large, hairy, feathery stigma are adapted to get pollinated by wind. [2]

Or (iii) If a plant has to get pollinated by insect, it should exhibit the following characteristics

(a) Insect pollinated flowers should be large, colourful and fragrant.

(b) Flowers should have nectar glands, which secrete nectar to attract pollinators for feeding. [2]

30. (i) The diversity in the shape of the beak most probably due to changes in environment which lead to adaptive radiation. [1]

(ii) The graph indicates evolutionary change. It has been verified that evolution can occur with surprising speed based on the selection pressures. The selection in case of finches was strong and new populations evolved within a matter of generations. [1]

(iii) Galapagos finches offer an excellent example of adaptive radiation where an organism adapts to new ecological contexts. It is assumed that a stock of ancestral finches reached the islands from the mainland.

In the absence of much competition, they evolved to fill many of the empty ecological niches. During this process, their beaks changed in size and morphology as an adaptation towards different diets. [2]

Or

(iii) In divergent evolution, a same basic organ becomes adapted by specialisation to perform different functions in order to adapt to different environmental conditions in their habitat. Such organs are called as homologous organs . [2]

Common Mistake

Students often get confused between homology and analogy. They should remember structure with similar anatomy, morphology, embryology and genetics but dissimilar functions are known as homologous structures.

Structures that are superficially similar but anatomical dissimilar, performing the same function are known as analogous structures.

31. (i) Flocs are the mesh-like structure containing aerobic bacteria and fungal mycelium.

During sewage treatment , flocs are formed in aerobic tanks when organic matter is abundant. Flocs digest organic matter and reduce the BOD of sewage water. [2]

(ii) The secondary treatment of water in sewage treatment plants called biological treatment because in this treatment organic wastes of sewage water are decomposed by certain microbes present in water. [1]

(iii) Biofertilisers or biopesticides preferred to chemical fertilisers or pesticides because of the following

(a) They do not cause any pollution.

(b) They do not spoil the quality of the soil.

(c) Biopesticides are target specific.

(d) They are less expensive and biodegradable. [2]

Or

(i) Transformation of normal cells into neoplastic cells may be induced by the physical, chemical or biological agents. These agents are called **carcinogens**. Furthermore, several genes called **cellular oncogenes** (*c-onc*) or protooncogenes have been identified in normal cells which, when activated under certain conditions, could lead to oncogenic transformation of cells. [1]

(ii) Cancer can be detected by the following methods

(a) **Biopsy** In this, a suspected tissue is studied by cutting it into thin sections is stained and examined under microscope.

(b) **MRI** (Magnetic Resonance Imaging) It uses strong magnetic fields and non-ionising radiations to accurately detect pathological and physiological changes in the living tissue. (2)

(iii) Methods that can possibly cure cancer are as follows

(a) **Surgery** Tumours are removed by surgery to check further spread of cancer cells.

(b) **Radiation therapy** Tumour cells are irradiated by lethal doses of radiation, while taking care to protect the surrounding normal cells.

(c) **Chemotherapy** Several chemotherapeutic drugs are used to kill cancer cells. But, their side effects like hair loss, anaemia, etc., are also reported.

Most cancers are treated by the combination of the above three.

(d) **Immunotherapy** Biological modifiers like α-interferons are used to activate the immune system and help in destroying the tumour. [2]

32. (i) Both the strands of DNA are not copied during transcription process because of the following

(a) If the strands code for RNA, two different RNA molecules and two different proteins will be formed.

(b) The two RNA molecules if produced simultaneously would be complementary to each other, hence would form a double - stranded RNA. This would prevent RNA from being translated into protein. [2]

(ii) The two essential roles of ribosomes during translation are as follows

(a) It provides an attachment site for *m*RNA.

(b) It provide the site of polypeptide synthesis. [1]

(iii) The DNA molecule is more stable genetic material than RNA because of the following

(a) The hydrogen bond between purine and pyrimidine provides stability to the DNA.

(b) The DNA lacks a 2′OH group which makes it less reactive than RNA.

(c) The thymine in DNA is less reactive than uracil in RNA.

(d) RNA mutates easily. [2]

Or

(i) Possible genotypes and phenotypes of the individual 1, 3 and 4 are as follows

	Genotypes		Phenotypes
Individual 1	I^A i	⟶	Type A
Individual 2	I^B i	⟶	Type B
Individual 3	I^Ai	⟶	Type A
Individual 4	I^Bi	⟶	Type B

[2]

(ii) Individual 5 – Phenotype – AB

Antigen – A and B, Genotype – I^AI^B

Individual 10 – Phenotype – O

Antigen – None, Genotype – ii [1]

(iii) Among the individuals in generations II and III of this family tree.

(a) Donor for any recepient blood group is 10. This is because individuals produce neither A or B antigens.

(b) Recipient for any donor blood group are 5, 12 and 13. This is because AB individuals can produce both A and B antigens. [2]

33. The transition of an oogonium to a Graafian follicle involves several stages of development within the ovary. In fetal ovary, oogonia undergo mitosis to increase their numbers. Each primary oocyte then gets surrounded by a layer of granulosa cells called the primary follicle.

The primary follicles further get surrounded by more layers of granulosa cells and called secondary follicles. These secondary follicle soon transforms into a tertiary follicle which is characterised by a fluid-filled cavity called **antrum**.

The primary oocyte within the tertiary follicle undergoes meiotic division to become secondary oocyte and a first polar body (haploid). The tertiary follicle further changes into the mature follicle or Graafian follicle that ruptures

to release the secondary oocyte (ovum) from the ovary by the process called ovulation. [2½]

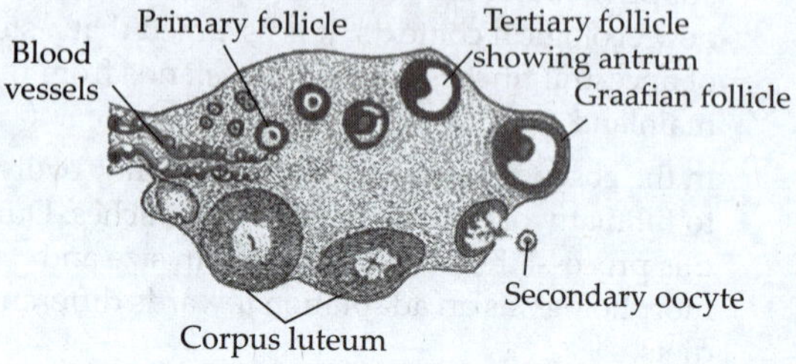

Diagrammatic sectional view of ovary showing different stages [2½]

Or

(i) (a) **Autogamy** It is the transfer of pollen grain from anther to the stigma of the same flower.

(b) **Geitonogamy** It is the transfer of pollen grains from anther of one flower to the stigma of another flower on the same plant.

Geitonogamy is functionally cross- pollination involving pollinating agent, but genetically it is equivalent to autogamy since, the pollen grains come from the same plant.

(c) **Xenogamy** It is the transfer of pollen grains from anther to the stigma of different plants of same species. It brings genetically different types of pollen grains to the stigma. [3]

(ii)

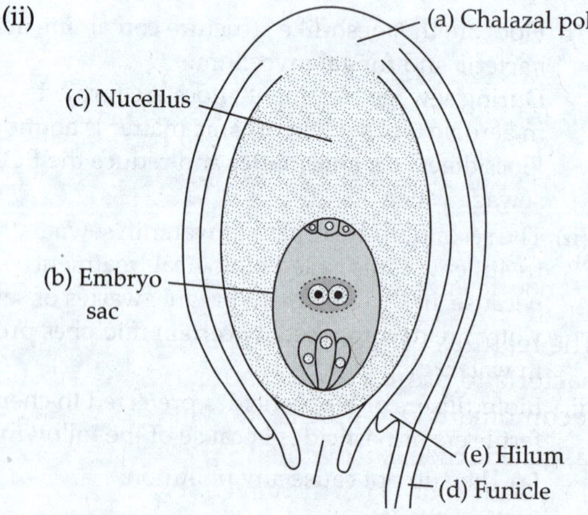

Diagrammatic view of typical anatropous ovule [2]

SQP Code : **PB-9/15** Series *i*-Succeed 9-25/15 Roll No. | | | | | | | | |

Sample Question Paper 09

Biology 12th (Code 044)

General Instructions

1. All questions are compulsory.
2. The question paper has five sections and 33 questions.
3. Section-A has 16 questions of 1 mark each; Section-B has 5 questions of 2 marks each; Section-C has 7 questions of 3 marks each; Section-D has 2 case-based questions of 4 marks each; and Section-E has 3 questions of 5 marks each.
4. There is no overall choice. However, internal choices have been provided in some questions. A student has to attempt only one of the alternatives in such questions.
5. Wherever necessary, neat and properly labelled diagrams should be draw.

Time : 3 Hrs.

Max. Marks : 70

Section A Multiple Choice Type Questions

1. Identify the role of polar bodies during oogenesis.
   (a) Polar bodies ensure that the ovum contains the most of cytoplasm
   (b) They get rid of defective sets of chromosomes, leaving the good set within the ovum
   (c) They are merely the byproduct of meiosis and serve no function
   (d) They prevent the development of secondary oocyte until fertilisation

2. The features of genetic code that allows bacteria to produce human insulin by recombinant DNA technology is
   (a) genetic code is redundant
   (b) genetic code is nearly universal
   (c) genetic code is specific
   (d) genetic code is not ambiguous

3. Given below are the phenomenon which deviates from Mendel's law of inheritance and their descriptions.

Phenomenon	Descriptions
A. Incomplete dominance	1. In heterozygous organisms both alleles expresses themselves completely.
B. Polygenic inheritance	2. Multiple genes govern a single character.
C. Codominance	3. F_1-hybrid does not resemble either of its parents.
D. Pleiotropy	4. A single gene influences many traits.

Select how many phenomenon are correctly matched with their descriptions?
(a) 1 (b) 3 (c) 2 (d) 4

4. Evolutionary divergence is marked by the development of
   (a) common set of structures in closely related groups
   (b) dissimilar set of functions in unrelated groups
   (c) common set of structures in unrelated groups
   (d) dissimilar set of functions in closely related groups

5. A biocontrol agent to be a part of an integrated pest management should be
(a) species-specific and symbiotic
(b) free-living and broad spectrum
(c) narrow spectrum and symbiotic
(d) species-specific and inactive on non-target organisms

6. Where will you look for the sporozoites of the malarial parasite?
(a) RBCs of humans suffering from malaria
(b) Spleen of infected person
(c) Salivary glands of freshly moulted female *Anopheles* mosquito
(d) Saliva of infected female *Anopheles* mosquito

7. The tropical Amazonian rainforest in South America has the greatest biodiversity on the earth. This is because of
(a) stable climate in tropics
(b) huge distance from the equator
(c) variation of climate in tropics
(d) higher altitudes

8. Select the option that has the correct sequence of events in genetically modifying an organism
(i) introduction of the identified DNA into the host
(ii) maintenance of introduced DNA into the host
(iii) identification of DNA with desirable genes
(iv) transfer of the DNA to its progeny.

Options
(a) (ii) → (i) → (iv) → (iii)
(b) (iii) → (i) → (ii) → (iv)
(c) (i) → (ii) → (iii) → (iv)
(d) (iii) → (ii) → (i) → (iv)

9. Genetic engineering techniques include
(a) altering genetic material
(b) sequencing genetic material
(c) studying genetic material
(d) None of the above

10. Select the incorrect match from the following options.
(a) Aleurone layer – Nutrition
(b) Ovule – seed
(c) Endosperm – Triple fertilisation
(d) Parthenocarpic fruit – without fertilisations

11. Read the four statements given below and select the option having two incorrect statements.
(i) The law of dominance is used to explain the expression of both the parental characters in a monohybrid cross in the F_1-generation.
(ii) Grasshopper is an example of XO type of sex determination in which the males have only one X - chromosome.
(iii) Thalassemia is transmitted when both the patners are unaffected carrier for the gene.
(iv) Turner's syndrome is caused due to the presence of additional copy of X chormosome.

(a) (i) and (ii) (b) (ii) and (iv)
(c) (i) and (iv) (d) (ii) and (iii)

12 Which of the following bacterium produce large holes in 'Swiss cheese' ?
(a) *Saccharomyces cerevisiae*
(b) *Propionibacterium shermanii*
(c) *Monascus purpureus*
(d) *Aspergillus niger*

***Question** Nos. 13 to 16 consist of two statements, Assertion (A) and Reason (R). Answer these questions by selecting the appropriate option given below.*
(a) Both Assertion and Reason are true and Reason is the correct explanation of Assertion
(b) Both Assertion and Reason are true, but Reason is not the correct explanation of Assertion
(c) Assertion is true, but Reason is false
(d) Assertion is false, but Reason is true

13. **Assertion** (A) Embryos of fish, salamander, tortoise, chick and a man of same age resemble each other closely.
Reason (R) This verifies that ontogeny recapitulates phylogeny.

14. **Assertion** (A) Sex education in schools is necessary.

Reason (R) Sex education will provide correct information and prevent any myths or misconceptions with respect to reproductive health.

15. **Assertion** (A) The pyramid of number of pond ecosystem is upright.

Reason (R) Phytoplanktons are maximum and secondary consumers are lesser in number.

16. **Assertion** (A) DNA has two chains having antiparallel polarity.

Reason (R) In a single strand of DNA, one end has a free phosphate group attached to the 5′ carbon of the deoxyribose sugar, while the other end has free hydroxyl group attached to the 3′ carbon of deoxyribose sugar.

Section B Very Short Answer Type Questions

17. A true-breeding tall pea plant is crossed with a true-breeding dwarf variety of pea plant. With the help of Punnett square show the above cross and mention the results obtained with respect to genotype and phenotype in F_2-generation.

Or Write the genotypes of the parents of a child suffering from thalassemia. State the cause of this disease.

18. In the figure below, parts *A*, *B* and *C* are very essential for this structure and influences the process of fertilisation. Study the figure and answer the questions that follows.

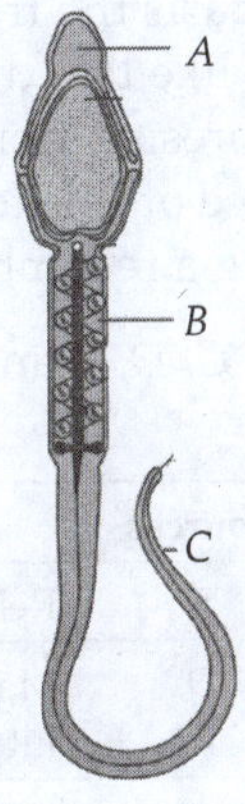

(i) Name this structure, along with parts labelled *A*-*C*.

(ii) How does part *A* help in the process of achieving successful fertilisation?

Or Mention the fate of corpus luteum and its effect on the uterus in the absence of fertilisation of the ovum in human female.

19. The graph given below shows the percentage of the use of ART methods, i.e. ZIFT and GIFT in 15 years. Interpret the graph and explain how these methods are releated to the aspects of reproductive health?

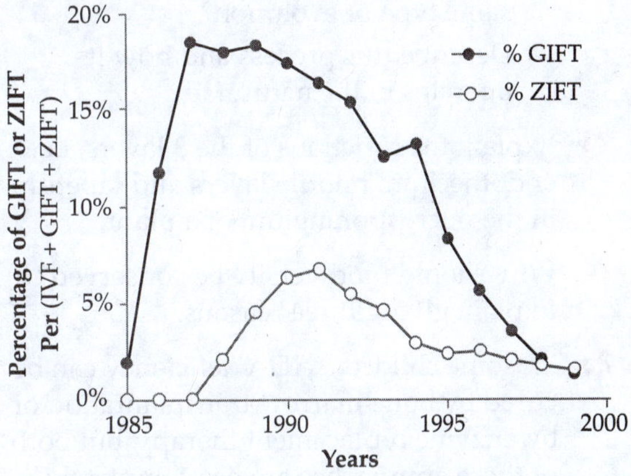

20. Why are sacred groves highly protected?

21. If the sequence of nitrogen bases in the coding strand of DNA in a transcription unit is

5′ – A T G A A T G – 3′

What would be the sequences of bases in its RNA transcript? Explain the changes that occur in the transcript.

Or

Give an example of a gene which is responsible for multiple phenotypic expressions. What are such genes called? State the cause that is responsible for such an effect.

Section C Short Answer Type Questions

22. Refer to the figure given below and answer the following questions.

P

Q

(i) Name the process by which Q came into existence. Where else you seen the same type of evolution?

(ii) Describe this process and how it operates in the nature?

23. Explain the functions of the 3 layers, i.e. endothecium, middle layers and tapetum in the microsporangium of a plant.

24. Why should biodiversity be conserved? Explain giving three reasons.

25. 'In some children, ADA deficiency can be cured by bone marrow transplantation or by enzyme replacement therapy, but both of these approaches are not completely curative'. Justify the statement.

26. (i) What is a detritus food chain made up of ? How do they meet their energy and nutritional requirements?

(ii) It is possible that a species may occupy more than one trophic level in the same ecosystem at the same time. Explain with the help of one example.

27. Given below is an autoradiograph of DNA segments, obtained from gel electrophoresis.

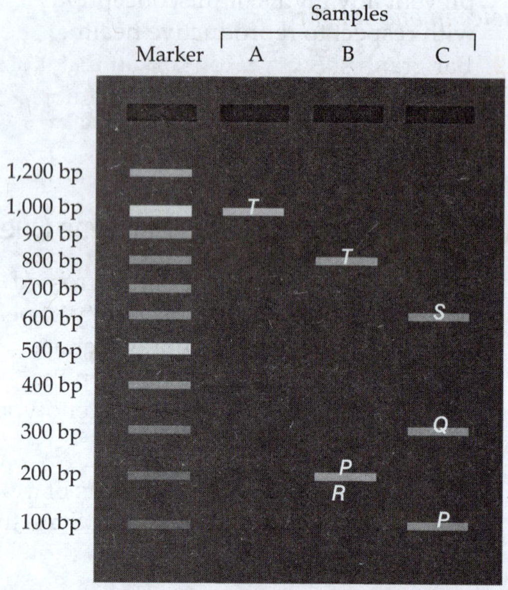

(i) In this autoradiograph, the ladder sequence measures approx. 1200 base pairs, which band will correspond to 600 bp?

(ii) On what basis the fragments get separated like this during gel electrophoresis? Mention one significance of this technique while conducting a recombinant molecule.

28. Identify *A*, *B*, *C*, *D*, *E* and *F* in the table given below.

Hormones	Sources	Functions
A	*B*	Release of ovum
C	*D*	Maintain corpus luteum
E	*F*	Act on sertoli cells

Section D Case Based Questions

Q. Nos. 29 and 30 are case-based questions. Each question has 3 subparts with internal choice in one subpart.

29. Bar graph shows reason for not using of modern contraception methods among current married women.

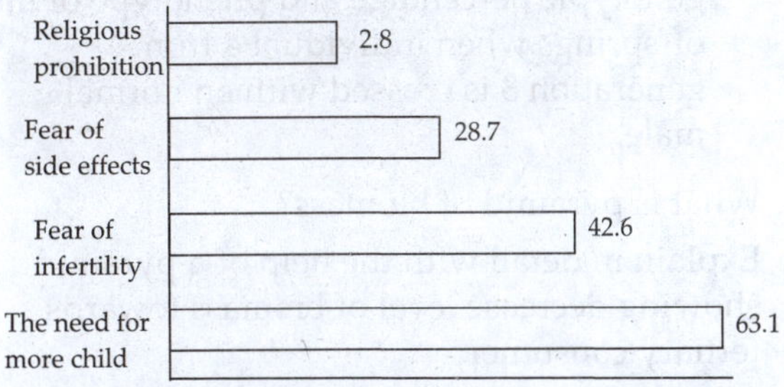

(i) On the basis of the above histogram, what will be the impact of this scenario on the population of a country? [1]

(ii) What can be the ideal contraceptive method for them? Support your answer by giving a suitable reason. [1]

(iii) Why is birth control so important? [2]

Or

(iii) Give the example of following
(a) Non-medicated IUDs
(b) Barrier method [2]

30. An experiment was conducted to measure the time taken by a person in response after seeing light. This person was given an alcoholic drink after every half hour and test was repeated.

The given below graph shows the result over two hours.

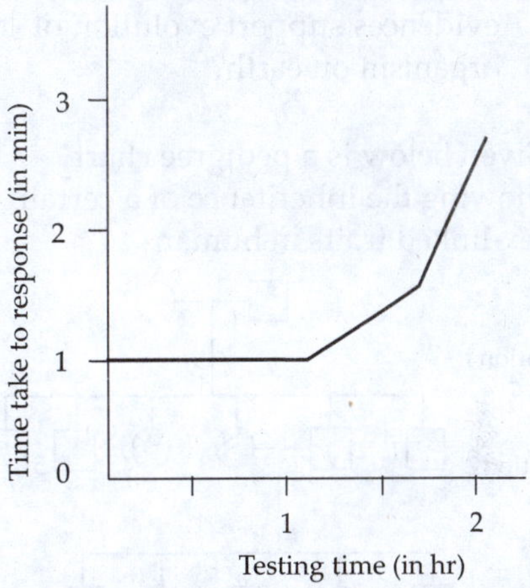

(i) With reference to the above graph, what difference was observe after one hour? [1]

(ii) What can be the reason for the observations that you made in (i)? [1]

(iii) Write down the effect of alcohol consumption. [2]

Or

(iii) If regular dose of alcohol is discontinued. What would be the affect of it on individual? [2]

SP-09

Section E Long Answer Type Questions

31. (i) Name the causative organisms and symptoms for the following diseases
(a) elephantiasis (b) common cold
(c) amoebiasis

(ii) How can public hygiene help to control infectious diseases?

Or

(i) How does the application of the fungal genus, *Glomus*, to the agricultural farm increases the farm output?

(ii) Explain the significant role of the genus *Nucleopolyhedrovirus* in an ecological sensitive area.

32. (i) Anthropogenic actions hasten evolution. Explain with the help of suitable example.

(ii) How do palaeontological evidences support evolution of organism on earth?

Or

Given below is a pedigree chart showing the inheritance of a certain sex-linked traits in humans.

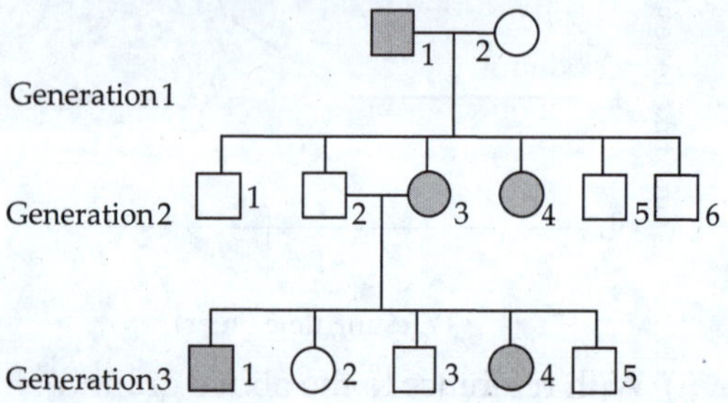

(i) On the basis of the inheritance pattern exhibited in this pedigree chart, what conclusion can you draw about the pattern of inheritance?

(ii) If the individual 1 from generation 3 married a normal female, what would be the probability of their daughter being a carrier?

(iii) Draw a Punnett square and give the genotypic percentage and phenotype of the offsprings when individual 4 from generation 3 is crossed with an normal male.

33. What is pyramid of biomass?

Explain in detail with the help of a pyramid showing decrease level of biomass towards tertiary consumer.

Or Draw and explain a logistic curve for a population of density (*N*) at time *t* whose intrinsic rate of natural increase is *r* and carrying capacity (*K*).

Explanations in Topper's Style

My Commitment *I affirm that I am reviewing these solutions only after I have solved the Sample Question Paper 9 on my own. My purpose of looking the solutions is solely to verify whether my answers/solutions were correct or not and to identify my mistakes in case my solutions were wrong or I could not solve that.*

1. (a) The polar bodies are formed during oogenesis in females to conserve cytoplasm for ovum which ensures that the ovum contains the most of cytoplasm. [1]

2. (b) Bacteria is able to produce human insulin because genetic code is nearly universal in all organisms. For example, the codon AGG specifies amino acid arginine in bacteria, animals and plants. [1]

3. (c) Polygenic inheritance and pleiotropy are correctly matched while, the others can be corrected as

In incomplete dominance, the F_1-hybrid does not resemble either of its parents.

In heterozygous organism both alleles expresses themselves completely in codominance. [1]

4. (d) Evolutionary divergence is marked by the development of different functional structure originating in organisms that arises from the common ancestral form. [1]

5. (d) A biocontrol agent relies on natural predation, not on chemicals. According to Intergrated Pest Management (IPM), these should be species-specific in nature and should be inactive on the non-target organisms in contrast of chemical pesticides that kills both useful and harmful life forms indiscriminatively. [1]

6. (d) When an infected female *Anopheles* bites a healthy person, *Plasmodium* in the form of 'sporozoites' are transmitted from saliva of mosquito into the human body. Thus, one can look for the sporozoites of the malarial parasite in the saliva of the infected female *Anopheles* mosquito. [1]

7. (a) Tropics regions lie near to the equator. As a result, they receive more solar energy, have warm temperatures with high humidity. This makes the climate stable, which allows many species to flourish over the period of time. This is why tropics are greatest biodiversity regions. [1]

8. (b) The correct sequence of events in genetically modifying an organism is as follows

(iii) → (i) → (ii) → (iv) [1]

9. (a) Genetic engineering includes techniques which alter the chemistry of genetic material (DNA and RNA) to induce the expression of genes which will give the desired products. [1]

10. (c) Option (c) is incorrect as of the two sperm cells, one sperm fertilises the egg cell, forming a diploid zygote, the other sperm fuses with the two polar nuclei, forming a triploid cell that develops into the endosperm. Together, these two fertilisation events in angiosperms are known as double fertilisation. [1]

11. (c) Statements (i) and (iv) are incorrect and can be corrected as

The law of dominance is used to explain the expression of only one of the parental characters in a monohybrid cross in the F_1 and expression of both in the F_2.

Turner's syndrome is caused due to the absence of one of the X chromosomes, i.e., 45 with XO. [1]

12. (b) The large holes in 'Swiss cheese' are due to the production of a large amount of CO_2 by a bacterium named *Propionibacterium shermanii.* [1]

13. (a) Both Assertion and Reason are true and Reason is the correct explanation of Assertion.

The early embryos in a vertebrates share remarkable similarities to the extent that human embryo is difficult to differentiate from the embryos of chick, lizard, frog or fish in early stages. This is explained by biogenetic law proposed by Haeckel. It describes that ontogeny recapitulates phylogeny, i.e. the development of embryo is the recapitulation of ancestral sequence. [1]

14. (a) Both Assertion and Reason are true and Reason is the correct explanation of Assertion.

Introduction of sex education in schools should be encouraged. This helps in conveying correct information to young children about sex related aspects. Instead of behaving false facts or myths which can develop knowledge of right and wrong practices. [1]

15. (a) Both Assertion and Reason are true and Reason is the correct explanation of Assertion.

The pyramid of number of pond ecosystem is upright, because the base of this pyramid is occupied by the maximum number of phytoplanktons (autotrophs) and number of individuals gradually decreases towards the primary and secondary consumers, respectively. [1]

16. (a) Both Assertion and Reason are true and Reason is the correct explanation of Assertion.

The two chains of DNA have antiparallel polarity. This is because one chain has a free phosphate moiety at the 5′ end of the ribose sugar and another chain has a free 3′ OH moiety at the 3′ end. [1]

17.

(Pure Tall) TT × (Pure Dwarf) tt **Parents**

(T) (t) **Gametes**

Tt **F_1-generation** (Selfing)

Tt × Tt

♀ \ ♂	(T)	(t)
(T)	TT (tall)	Tt (tall)
(t)	Tt (tall)	tt (dwarf)

F_2-generation

Phenotypic ratio Tall : Tall : Tall : Dwarf (3 :1)

Genotypic ratio TT : Tt : Tt : tt
(1 : 1 : 1 : 1)
(1 : 2 : 1) [2]

Or

The genotypes of the parents of a child suffering from thalassemia are as follows

Mother → $Th^B\ Th^{B+}$
Father → $Th^B\ Th^{B+}$ [1]

Thalassemia is an autosomal-linked recessive disease, which results in reduced rate of synthesis of one of the globin chains of haemoglobin. The disease is controlled by a single pair of allele, Th^B and Th^{B+}. Th^B codes for normal B-protein and Th^{B+} codes for an abnormal B-protein. Only homozygous individuals for Th^{B+} ($Th^{B+}\ Th^{B+}$) show the diseased phenotype. [1]

18. (i) The structure is of human sperm (a male gamete). Parts labelled from *A*-*C* are as follows

A - Acrosome,
B - Mitochondria
C - Tail [1]

(ii) Part *A*, (i.e. the acrosome) lies at the tip of the nuclei. It contains hydrolytic enzymes which helps in penetrating the layers of ovum and perform fertilisation by the fusion of haploid nucleus of sperm and ovum. [1]

Or In the absence of fertilisation, the corpus luteum degenerates and does not secrete progesterone. Lack of progesterone causes disintegration of the endometrium leading to menstruation and thus, a next cycle starts. [2]

19. According to the given graph, the GIFT gained popularity quickly, but has become less common in several years. On the other hand, ZIFT is used by couples in later years, but it has never been as popular as GIFT.

Both ZIFT and GIFT are the methods of assisted reproductive technology, which are used to correct the problems related to infertility in both the sexes.

In the process of ZIFT, zygote upto 8-blastomeres stage are placed in the oviducts and allow to grow normally while in the process of GIFT, ovum are collected from a donor and transferred into the Fallopian tube of another female who cannot produce one. [2]

Value Points

For getting maximum marks, following value point should be added in answer.

Briefly describe the process of ZIFT and GIFT.

20. Sacred groves are highly protected because

(i) They have cultural and religious significance. Protecting these areas is a way to honor and preserve cultural and religious traditions.
(ii) They are often integral to the identity and heritage of local communities.
(iii) They harbor rare, endangered and endemic species of plants and animals. [2]

21. The sequence for the template strand can be 3′ – TACTTAC – 5′. Hence, the sequence of bases in the RNA transcript strand, following Chargraff's rule will be

5′ – A U G A A U G – 3′

As the *m*RNA sequence would be complementary to the template. Excepting the base thymine (T), which gets replaced by uracil (U) at all positions. [2]

Or Pleiotropy is the phenomenon in which a single gene exhibits multiple phenotypic expressions. The genes exhibiting pleiotropy are called pleiotropic genes.

Pleiotropism occurs mainly because of mutation in a particular gene, e.g. In garden pea, starch synthesis, size of starch grains and shape of seeds is controlled by the single gene.

The genotypes and phenotypes of the trait are as follows

BB–Round seeds, large starch grains.

Bb–Round seeds, intermediate size starch grains.

bb–Wrinkled seeds, small starch grains. [2]

22. (i) This process is called adaptive radiation. It has been observed in the evolution of finches living in the Galapagos Island. [1]

(ii) Adaptive radiation comes into play when a single or a small group of ancestral species rapidly diverses into a large number of descendants with different adaptive forms.

These forms exhibit modification in organ structures which are basically similar to ancestral species, but adapted to exploit the resources in their habitats or support their lifestyles. Adaptive radiation thus, leads to divergence where the development of different functional forms occurs from a common ancestral form. [2]

23. The function of the three layers are as follows

(i) **Endothecium** It serves as a protective layer and aids in the dehiscence of anther to allow the discharge of pollen from the plant. [1]

(ii) **Middle layers** It is protective in function and also store reserve food during early stages of microspore development. [1]

(iii) **Tapetum** It provides nutrition to the pollen grains. [1]

24. Biodiversity should be conserved for the following reasons

(i) It plays a major role in many ecosystem services that nature provides. [1]

(ii) We derive countless direct economic benefits from nature including resources for food, raw materials and products of medicinal importance. [1]

(iii) The ethical argument for conserving biodiversity relates to protect millions of plant, animal and microbe species with whom we share this planet our motal responsibility. [1]

25. Adenosine Deaminase (ADA) deficiency is an inherited disorder that damages the immune system.

ADA deficiency leads to the accumulation of toxic purine degradation byproducts, which affects lymphocytes and lead to adenosine deaminase-deficient severe combined immuno deficiency. It is traditionally cured using two approaches *viz*., enzyme replacement therapy and bone marrow transplant.

In enzyme replacement therapy, an intramuscular injection containing the missing enzyme is injected weekly or monthly.

In bone marrow transplant, bone marrow laden with missing enzyme is transplanted from sibling donor. Both of these approaches are not completely curative.

In former, painful weekly injections are to be taken regularly and it may not be effective over time.

The latter procedure require suitable donor which is not easily available all the time. Over these two procedures, gene therapy can provide significant long term benefits to patients and can provide complete cure. [3]

> **Value Points** For getting maximum marks, following value point should be added in answer. Define ADA and how it's cured?

26. (i) Detritus food chain is made up of decomposers, i.e., some bacteria and fungi.

They meet their energy and nutrient requirements by degrading the dead organic matter of detritus. [1]

(ii) A single species may occupy more than one trophic level at the same time in an ecosytem because, the trophic level of species represents the functional level of species in the energy flow. The preference of food habit depends upon the available food. For example, sparrow is a primary consumer when it eats seed and secondary consumer when feeds on insects and worms. [2]

27. (i) The bands (*P* - *T*) corresponding to 600 bp length is band *S*. [1]

(ii) In gel electrophoresis, the cut pieces of DNA separates on the basis of size, shape and molecular weight. An electric current is passed through the gel. Since, DNA carries negative charge, thus it gets attracted towards the positive charge and moves toward the anode. The smaller fragments move faster as they experience lesser friction than the longer ones. In RDT, electrophoresis is used to purify and separate the DNA fragments cut by specific restriction enzyme. These sequences are used in creation of recombinant DNA. [2]

28. In the given table, *A, B, C, D, E* and *F* are identified as

A→ LH
B→ Pituitary gland
C→ Progesterone
D→ Ovaries
E→ FSH
F→ Pituitary gland [3]

29. (i) It will cause the population to grow, leading to population explosion. [1]

(ii) The ideal contraceptive method is male condoms that are up to 98% effective in preventing pregnancy and does not have any side effects. [1]

(iii) Birth control is also known as contraception. They are important because they allow individuals and couple to decide when to have children and helping to plan the timing and size of their families. It also helps to as it reduces pregnancy-related morbidity and mortality. [2]

Or

(iii) (a) **Non-medicated IUDS**- Lippes loop.

(b) **Barrier method**- condom, cervical caps and vaults. [2]

30. (i) It is observed that after one hour, the person takes more time to response after seeing light. [1]

(ii) Alcoholic drinks made the person react more slowly as it affect the central nervous system. [1]

(iii) The effect of alcohol consumption includes euphoria, peptic ulcer, gastric carcinoma, hepatitis, liver failure, liver cell carcinoma, etc. [2]

Or

(iii) If regular dose of alcohol is discontinued, it would lead to anxiety, shakiness, nausea, sweating and sometime it can be so severe that it may be become life threatening too. [2]

31. (i) The causative agents and symptoms of the following diseases are as follows

(a) **Elephantiais** *Wuchereria bancrofti*

Symptoms of this disease include severe swelling occurs, typically in the legs, but it can also affect the arms, breast and genitalia. [1]

(b) **Common cold** Rhino virus.

Symptoms of this disease include nasal congestion and discharge, sore throat, hoarseness, cough, headache and tiredness. [1]

(c) **Amoebiasis** *Entamoeba histolytica.*

Symptoms of this disease include constipation, abdominal pain and cramps, stool with excess mucous and blood. [1]

(ii) Maintenance of public hygiene includes the following

- keeping body and surroundings clean.
- consumption of clean drinking water, fruits and vegetables, etc.
- proper disposal of waste and excreta.
- regular cleaning and disinfection of tanks and other water reservoirs, etc.

All the above measures help to control the increase in vectors of infectious diseases and their breeding places. Thus, there would be reduced chances of transmission of infectious diseases. [2]

Or

(i) The application of *Glomus* to agricultural field increases the farm output by increasing the nutrient availability to the crops. *Glomus* develops symbiotic association with the roots of plants called mycorrhiza. It absorbs phosphorus from the soil and passes it to the plant it is associated with. In return, it derives sugars from the plant cells for its survival.

Thus, it acts as a biofertilisers. This association has other advantages like

(i) Resistance to salinity and drought.

(ii) Tolerance to salinity and drought.

(iii) Increase in plant growth and development. [2½]

(ii) *Nucleopolyhedrovirus*, a genus of baculovirus is useful in controlling many insects and other arthropods.

They are species specific narrow spectrum bioinsecticides with no side effects on plants, mammals, birds, fish and non - target insects. Therefore, they serve as an important component of integrated pest management programme in dealing with ecological sensitive areas. These properties are useful in organic farming. [2½]

32. (i) Human activites, i.e., anthropogenic action are found to enhance evolution. For example, Excessive use of DDT as a fertilisers in crops resulted in the evolution of DDT resistant mosquitoes.

- When DDT was used first time, many mosquitoes died, but few survived.
- Survived mosquitoes showed resistance to DDT and reproduced even in the presence of DDT.
- Offsprings produced by these mosquitoes were also resistance to DDT.
- Hence, DDT is not effective on mosquito population today. [2]

Similarly, evolution of antibiotic resistant microbes has occurred due to the overuse of antibiotics. [1]

(ii) Palaeontology is the study of past life based on fossil records. The study of fossil reveals the type of life forms existed in the past and highlights the course of evolution of living organisms. The distribution of fossil supports the concept of evolution. It shows that the structure of wings becomes more complex overtime from earliest to recent times. From the fossil records it has been concluded that evolution has taken place from the simple to complex forms in a gradual manner. [2]

Or

(i) The pattern of inheritance is X-linked dominant. It is a mode of genetic inheritance by which a dominant gene is carried on the X-chromosome. [1]

(ii) If the individual 1 from generation 3 married a normal female, then the probability of their daughter being a carrier is 50% as both the daughters will be diseased.

The schematic representation of the pedigree is as follows

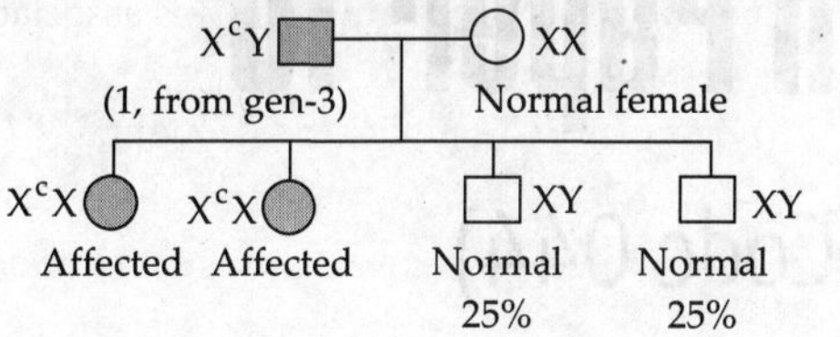

[2]

(iii) If individual 4 from generation 3 is crossed with an affected male the cross obtained will be as given below

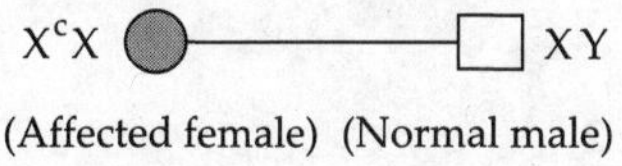

Parents X^cX × XY

Gametes (X^c) (X) × (X) (Y)

↓

Progeny

	X^c	X
X	X^cX	XX
Y	X^cY	XY

F_1-generation

Genotypic Percentage

X^cX = 25%, X^cY = 25%

XX = 25%, XY = 25%

Phenotypic Percentage

X^cX – Affected female, XX – Normal female

X^cY – Affected male, XY – Normal male. [2]

33. Biomass is the total dry mass or organic matter in organisms or ecosystem. A pyramid of biomass shows the mass of organic material at each trophic level. [1]

The biomass of the successive trophic levels decreases progressively due to the loss of energy at each successive level. Respiration and excretion are the two main processes in which both energy and biomass are lost at each stage of a food chain. The total biomass of food from the producer is the largest and total biomass of food available to higher trophic levels becomes smaller and smaller. Higher trophic levels, therefore usually contains very small numbers of large organisms with a low total biomass per unit area of the ecosystem. [2]

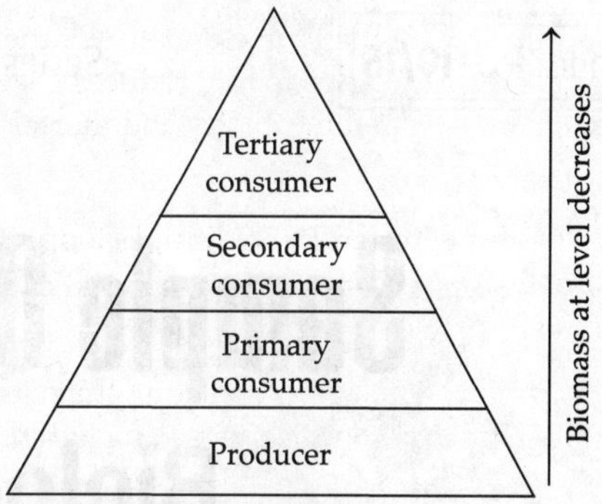

Pyramid of Biomass

[2]

Or The logistic curve for a population density (N) can be explained as

- Population initially shows a lag phase and then shows a phase of acceleration or exponential growth, followed by the phase of deceleration.
- Population can grow exponentially for a certain period of time and then assumes a steady state, as the resource availability becomes limited at some point of time.
- Every environment has resources to support a particular maximum number of individuals, called its carrying capacity (*K*). Beyond that, there is no increase in the size or density of a population.
- A population showing logistic growth shows a sigmoid curve, when the number of individuals is plotted as a function of time.
- Equation can be described as

$$\frac{dN}{dt} = rN\left(\frac{K-N}{K}\right)$$

Where, N = Population density at time t

r = Intrinsic rate of natural increase

K = Carrying capacity.

- The model is more realistic in nature, because no population can sustain the exponential growth indefinitely. [3]

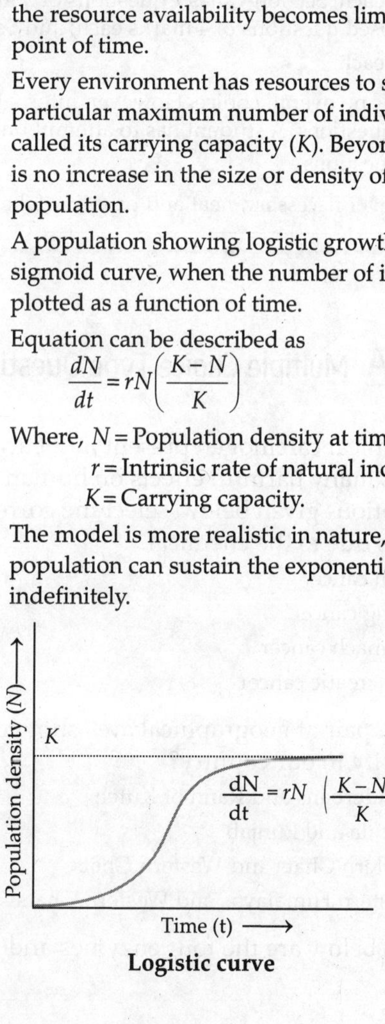

Logistic curve

[2]

SQP Code : PB-10/15	Series *i*-Succeed 10-25/15	Roll No.

Sample Question Paper 10

Biology 12th (Code 044)

General Instructions

1. All questions are compulsory.
2. The question paper has five sections and 33 questions.
3. Section-A has 16 questions of 1 mark each; Section-B has 5 questions of 2 marks each; Section-C has 7 questions of 3 marks each; Section-D has 2 case-based questions of 4 marks each; and Section-E has 3 questions of 5 marks each.
4. There is no overall choice. However, internal choices have been provided in some questions. A student has to attempt only one of the alternatives in such questions.
5. Wherever necessary, neat and properly labelled diagrams should be draw.

Time : 3 Hrs.

Max. Marks : 70

Section A Multiple Choice Type Questions

1. A chemical carcinogen present in tobacco smoke shows many harmful effects on human body. Out of the options given below, select the correct answer that results due to the chemical.
   (a) Skin cancer
   (b) Lung cancer
   (c) Stomach cancer
   (d) Pancreatic cancer

2. Which pair of geographical area show maximum diversity in our country?
   (a) Sunderbans and Rann of Kutch
   (b) Kerala and Punjab
   (c) Eastern Ghats and Western Ghats
   (d) Eastern Himalayas and Western Ghats

3. Given below are the four enzymes and their activities.

	Enzymes	Activities
A.	*Taq* DNA polymerase	1. Stable above 86°C
B.	Exonuclease	2. Cleaves the ends of linear DNA
C.	Protease	3. Degeneration of proteins
D.	Chitinase	4. Breakdown of fungal cell wall

How many of there are correctly matched?
(a) 2 (b) 1
(c) 4 (d) 3

4. When two similar species live in the same area, they may evolve to become more different in order to
(a) drive the other species to extinction
(b) reduce genetic variation
(c) reduce competition
(d) use up the other species resources

5. In humans, at the end of the first meiotic division, the male germ cells differentiate into which of the following cell division stage?
(a) Spermatogonia
(b) Spermatids
(c) Primary spermatocytes
(d) Secondary spermatocytes

6. The number of chromosomes in female and male honeybees are
(a) 32 and 32, respectively
(b) 16 and 16, respectively
(c) 32 and 16, respectively
(d) 16 and 32, respectively

7. Which one of the following exhibits least productivity?
(a) Salty marshes (b) Oceans
(c) Grasslands (d) Coral reefs

8. Identify the structure given below.

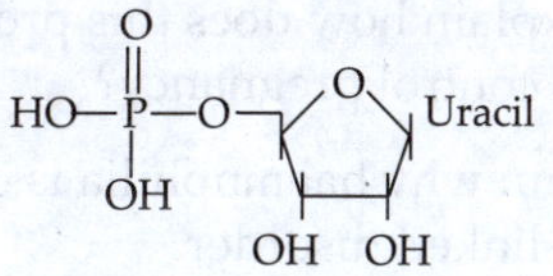

(a) Nucleoside, Uridylic acid
(b) Nucleotide, Inosinic acid
(c) Nucleoside, Inosinic acid
(d) Nucleotide, Uridylic acid

9. Select the incorrect match from the following.
(a) Copper releasing IUDs - Cu7
(b) Hormone releasing IUDs - Multiload 375
(c) Non - medicated IUDs - Lippes loop
(d) Non - steroidal - Saheli

10. Read the four statement given below and select the option having two correct statements.
(i) Each ovary is covered by a thick epithelium which encloses the ovarian stroma.
(ii) Fimbriae helps in collection of the ovum after ovulation.
(iii) The labia majora are paired folds of tissue under the labia minora.
(iv) Myometrium exhibits strong contraction during delivery of the baby.
(a) (i) and (ii) (b) (ii) and (iv)
(c) (i) and (iii) (d) (iii) and (iv)

11. Select the option that has the correct sequence of events of the technique of DNA fingerprinting.
(i) Digestion of DNA by restriction endonucleases.
(ii) Separation of DNA fragments by electrophoresis.
(iii) Isolation of DNA
(iv) Hybridisation
(v) Transferring of separated DNA fragments.
(vi) Detection of hybridised DNA fragments.

Options
(a) (ii) $\rightarrow$ (i) $\rightarrow$ (iii) $\rightarrow$ (v) $\rightarrow$ (iv) $\rightarrow$ (vi)
(b) (iii) $\rightarrow$ (i) $\rightarrow$ (ii) $\rightarrow$ (v) $\rightarrow$ (iv) $\rightarrow$ (vi)
(c) (i) $\rightarrow$ (iii) $\rightarrow$ (v) $\rightarrow$ (iv) $\rightarrow$ (vi) $\rightarrow$ (ii)
(d) (iii) $\rightarrow$ (ii) $\rightarrow$ (i) $\rightarrow$ (v) $\rightarrow$ (vi) $\rightarrow$ (iv)

12. The diagram below shows the structure of a flower.

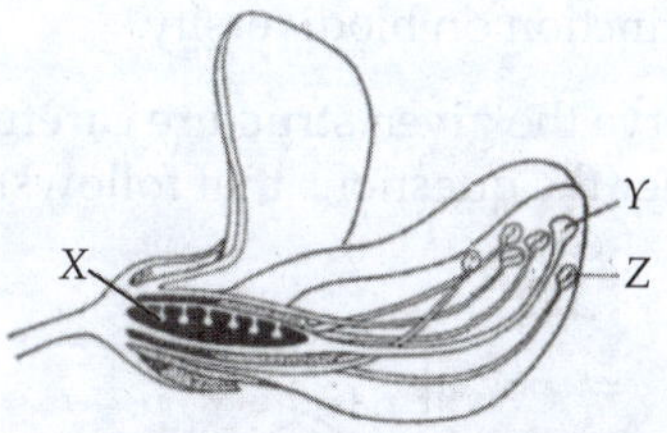

One of the part shows the site of pollination and the other part shows the site of fertilisation. Choose the correct option from the given table.

	Pollination	Fertilisation
(a)	Y	X
(b)	X	Z
(c)	X	Y
(d)	Y	Z

Question Nos. 13 to 16 consist of two statements, Assertion (A) and Reason (R). Answer these questions by selecting the appropriate option given below.

(a) Both Assertion and Reason are true and Reason is the correct explanation of Assertion
(b) Both Assertion and Reason are true, but Reason is not the correct explanation of Assertion
(c) Assertion is true, but Reason is false
(d) Assertion is false, but Reason is true

13. Assertion (A) Amniocentesis technique is frequently used in fetal disease treatment in India.

Reason (R) This technique can be used for sex-determination of child.

14. Assertion (A) Synthesis of daughter or new strand occurs continuously along the parent strand $3' \rightarrow 5'$.

Reason (R) DNA polymerase can polymerise nucleotides in $3' \rightarrow 5'$ direction on $5' \rightarrow 3'$ strand.

15. Assertion (A) Biotechnology produces transgenic microorganisms that function as microfactories for proteins.

Reason (R) Transgenic microorganisms can be developed by inserting genes encoding for desired protein product using recombinant DNA technology.

16. Assertion (A) Ecosystem are exempt from the second law of thermodynamics.

Reason (R) Ecosystem need a constant supply of energy to synthesise the molecules they require, to counteract the universal tendency towards increasing disorderlines.

Section B Very Short Answer Type Questions

17. Biodiversity must be conserved as it plays an important role in many ecosystem services that nature provides. Explain any two services of the ecosystem.

Or

Explain, taking one example, the effect of coextinction on biodiversity.

18. Observe the given structure carefully and answer the questions that follows.

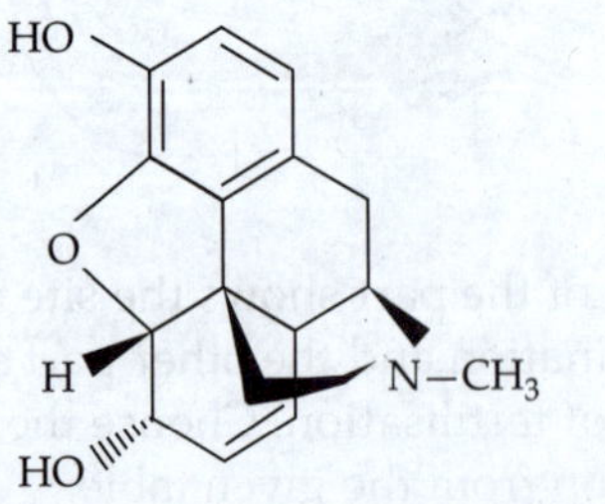

(i) What is the name of the chemical compound? What kind of drug is it?
(ii) What are the physical properties of this compound?

Or Name and explain the two types of immune responses in humans.

19. (i) Name the surgical process used for female contraception.
(ii) Explain how does this process help to control pregnancy?

20. Explain why haemophilia is considered a sex-linked disorder?

21. (i) Write the steps involved in Polymerase Chain Reaction (PCR).
(ii) Write two important applications of PCR.

Or A recombinant vector with a gene of interest inserted within the gene of β-galactosidase enzyme and is introduced into a bacterium.

Explain the method that would help in selection of recombinant colonies from non-recombinant colonies. Why is this method of selection referred to as insertional inactivation?

Section C Short Answer Type Questions

22. Study the *m*RNA segment given below, which is complete and to be translated into a polypeptide chain.

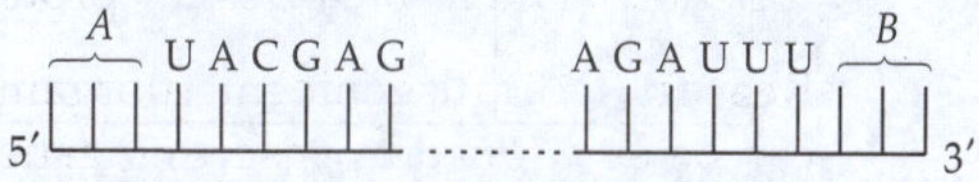

(i) Write the codons '*A*' and '*B*'. What do they code for?

(ii) How peptide bond formed between two amino acids in the ribosome?

23. Explain the role of restriction endonucleases, gel electrophoresis, selectable marker in pBR322 in biotechnology.

24. The size of a population for any species is not a static parameter and keeps on changing with time. It depends on the factors such as food availability, predation pressure and adverse weather.

(i) Explain death rate in a population by taking a suitable example.

(ii) Write the other two characteristics, which only a population shows but an individual cannot.

25. State the effect of carcinogens on human body. Name the carcinogenic ionising and non-ionising radiations. Mention their carcinogenic effects.

26. Identify *A*, *B*, *C*, *D*, *E* and *F* in the table given below.

Organisms	Bioactive molecules	Uses
Monascus purpureus (yeast)	*A*	*B*
C	*D*	Antibiotic
E	Cyclosporin-A	*F*

27. Pollination is the transfer of pollen grain from male reproductive part to the female reproductive part. This later enables fertilisation and production of seeds. This process of pollination is mainly facilitated by pollinating agents such as air, water, animals, etc. But if the flowers are closed or prefer self-pollination then plant's itself become the pollinating agents. Based on the type of pollinators pollen grains have developed different feature.

(i) Write the characteristic features of anther, pollen and stigma of wind pollinated flowers.

(ii) How do flowers reward their insect pollinator? Explain.

28. How do 'implants' act as an effective method of contraception in human females? Mention its one advantage over contraceptive pills.

Section D Case Based Questions

Q. Nos. 29 and 30 are case-based questions. Each question has 3 subparts with internal choice in one subpart.

29. The data below shows the function of immune system towards an antigen X?

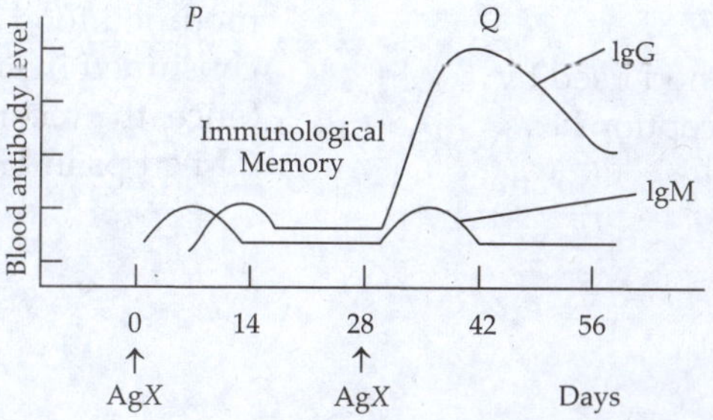

(i) With reference to the above graph, explain the response generated by our immune system at *P*? [2]

(ii) Evaluate the efficacy of *Q* towards antigen X. [2]

Or

(ii) Our immune system helps to protect us against virus and bacteria. Which cells of the immune system that helps in this function? [2]

30. The graph given below shows how natural selection process acts on peppered moth during industrial revotution.

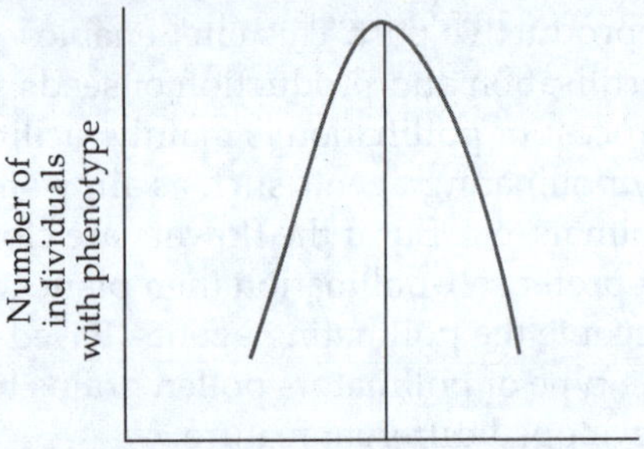

(A)

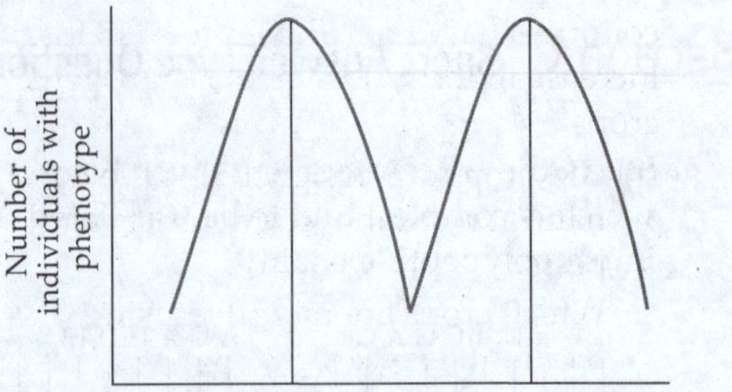

(B)

(i) With the reference to above graph, under the influence of which type of natural selection would graph *A* become like graph *B*. [1]

(ii) Who suggested natural selection as the mechanism of evolution? [1]

(iii) How can you explain that the large number of individuals acquires mean character value in terms of graph *A*? [2]

Or

(iii) What could be the likely reason for new variations arising in a population? [2]

Section E Long Answer Type Questions

31. (i) FSH, LH, oestrogen and progestogen are some of the main female hormones. Determine their levels during ovulatory phase and during pregnancy.

(ii) Also give reason to justify your answer.

Or

(i) Explain one application of each one of the following.

(a) Amniocentesis

(b) Lactational amenorrhea

(c) ZIFT

(ii) Name the barrier method used by female it prevent conception?

32. A GM crop can contain a gene that has been artificially inserted instead of the plant acquiring it through pollination. The resulting plant is said to be genetically modified although in reality all crops have been genetically modified from their original wild state by domestication, selection and controlled breeding over long periods of times.

In 1994, calgene's delayed-ripening tomato (*Flavr Savr*) became the first genetically modified food crop to be produced and consumed in an industrialised country. Since, the recorded commercialisation of GM crops in 1996 to 2018, several countries have contributed to ~ 113 fold increase in the global area of transgenic crops.

(i) GM crops are designed to develop natural resistance from insects and pests.
Which crops are modified using *Bacillus thuringiensis*?

(ii) List five advantages of GMOs to a farmer.

(iii) State that foods derived from genetically modified crops should be tested for possible reactions in people. Explain.

Or

(i) Evaluate the efficiency of Golden rice to meet the daily intake of vitamin-A on people.

(ii) The GM crops are the best solution to overcome issues develop due to conventional breeding. Discuss.

(iii) List the changes that are done to genetically modified plants.

33. (i) Draw a well-labelled diagram depicting process of transcription in eukaryotes.

(ii) Name the major types of RNAs and explain their role in the process of protein synthesis in a prokaryote.

Or

(i) Discuss the role of enzyme DNA ligase plays during DNA replication.

(ii) Draw a well-labelled diagram of process of transcription in bacteria depicting initiation, elongation and termination.

Explanations in Topper's Style

My Commitment *I affirm that I am reviewing these solutions only after I have solved the Sample Question Paper 10 on my own. My purpose of looking the solutions is solely to verify whether my answers/solutions were correct or not and to identify my mistakes in case my solutions were wrong or I could not solve that.*

1. (b) Lung cancer is due to the chemical carcinogen present in tobacco smoke. [1]

2. (d) Eastern Himalayas and Western Ghats are geographical areas that show maximum diversity in our country. [1]

3. (c) All four pairs are correctly matched. [1]

4. (c) According to the mechanism of resource partitioning, if two species compete for the same resources, they could avoid competition by choosing different times for feeding or different foraging patterns. [1]

5. (d) At the end of the first meiotic division, the male germ cells differentiate into secondary spermatocytes. [1]

6. (c) Sex-determination in honeybee is called haplo-diploid sex-determination system.

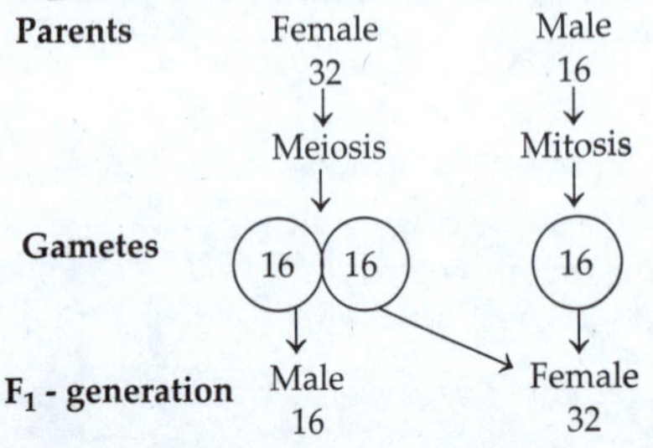

7. (b) In oceans, there are lots of nutrients, but no sufficient sunlight is available in deep areas, hence oceans have least productivity. [1]

8. (d) The structure is a nucleotide called uridylic acid. [1]

9. (b) option (b) is incorrectly matched and can be corrected as

Multiload 375 is a copper releasing IUDs.
Progestasert and LNG - 20 is a hormone releasing IUDs. [1]

10. (b) Statements (ii) and (iv) are correct, while statements (i) and (iii) are incorrect and they can be corrected as

- Each ovary is covered by a thin epithelium which encloses the ovarian stroma.
- The labia minora are paired folds of tissue under the labia majora. [1]

11. (b) The correct sequence of events of the technique of DNA fingerprinting is as follows

(iii)→(i)→(ii)→(v)→(iv)→(vi) [1]

12. (a) Pollination takes place at the surface of the stigma (*Y*), while fertilisation takes place within the ovary (*X*). [1]

13. (b) Both Assertion and Reason are true, but Reason is not the correct explanation of Assertion. It can be explained as

Amniocentesis is used for fetal sex-determination and diagnosing disorders based on chromosomal pattern in the amniotic fluid surrounding the developing foetus.

This technique is banned in India at present due to its misuse in increased female foeticides. [1]

14. (c) Assertion is true, but Reason is false. Reason can be corrected as

DNA polymerase can polymerise nucleotides only in $5' \rightarrow 3'$ direction. [1]

15. (a) Both Assertion and Reason are true, but Reason is the correct explanation of Assertion.

Transgenic microorganisms can be developed by inserting genes encoding for desired protein products using recombinant DNA technology. These transgenic organisms functions as living microfactories that produce proteins like human insulin, human growth hormones, etc. Production of proteins from such organisms is easier, more efficient and cost effective[1]

16. (d) Assertion is false, but Reason is true. Assertion can be corrected as

Ecosystems are not exempt from the second law of thermodynamics. [1]

17. The two ecosystem services are as follows

(i) Forest ecosystem mitigates droughts and floods and provides oxygen. [1]

(ii) The wildlife helps in the pollination of crops, without which fruits/seeds will not produced. [1]

Or Coextinction refers to the extinction of a species, if the plant and animal species associated with it in an obligatory relationship also gets extinct. For example, coevolved plant-pollinator mutualism as in case of *Pronuba yuccasella* and *Yucca*. If one partner is on the verge of extinction, the other partner will also get extinct. [2]

18. (i) The chemical compound given is morphine. It is an effective sedative, analgesic and painkiller. [1]

(ii) Morphine is obtained from the latex of poppy plant. It is white, odourless and bitter crystalline compound. [1]

Or Immune responses are of two types

(i) **Primary response** The reaction of the body's immune system to the first attack of microbe (antigen) is called primary immune response. It is slow and less intense. [1]

(ii) **Secondary response** The reaction of the body's immune system to any subsequent infection of the same microbe is termed as secondary immune response. It is fast and intense. [1]

19. (i) The surgical process of contraception that is used by female is tubectomy. [1]

(ii) Tubectomy controls pregnancy by permanently preventing the egg from meeting the sperm. In this procedure, a surgeon cuts ties or seals the Fallopian tubes, which are the pathways that egg travels from ovaries to uterus. [1]

20. Haemophilia is a sex-linked disease because gene responsible for this disease is carried on the X chromosome. Since males have one X and one Y chromosome (XY) and females have one pair of X chromosome (XX), the inheritance pattern of the gene is different for each sex. It is transmitted from an unaffected carrier female to some of the male offspring. Here, the males are always affected, but the female rarely becomes haemophilic. For female to be haemophilic, her mother has to be atleast a carrier and father should be haemophilic. [2]

> **Value Points** In order to gain maximum marks students should also include the reason of female for not or rarely being haemophilic.

21. (i) The steps involved in Polymerase Chain Reaction (PCR) are as follows

- Denaturation
- Annealing
- Primer extension/elongation [1]

(ii) Two important applications of PCR are as follows

- The amplification of gene fragments.
- Detecting genetic diseases and mutations associated with cancers. [1]

Or The recombinant colonies can be differentiated from non-recombinant colonies by their inability to produce colour in the presence of a chromogenic substrate. The recombinants do not produce any colour, while the non-recombinants produces a blue colour with a chromogenic substrate in the medium. It occurs because of the presence of β-galactosidase in the former and its absence in recombinants cells. The enzyme β-galactosidase become inactivated on insertion of recombinant DNA, within the coding sequence of enzyme. Thus, the method is called insertional inactivation. [2]

22. The codons A and B are as follows

(i) *A*-AUG, *B*-UAA / UAG/ UGA

AUG codes for methionine and also act as initiator. UAA/UAG/UGA does not code for any amino acid, but brings about termination of polypeptide synthesis. [1]

(ii) In the large subunit of ribosome, there are two sites in which subsequent amino acids bind to and come close enough for the formation of peptide bond. It is catalysed by the enzyme called peptidyl transferase. [2]

23. **Restriction endonucleases** These are the bacterial enzymes that cut *ds*DNA into fragments after recognising and binding to the specific nucleotide sequences, known as recognition site. These enzymes are used to form recombinant molecules of DNA. [1]

Gel electrophoresis is the technique which allows the separation and visualisation of fragments of DNA on an agarose gel matrix. [1]

Selectable markers in pBR322 helps in the identification and selection of transformants. pBR322, an *E. coli* cloning vector has two antibiotic resistance genes, i.e. for ampicillin and tetracycline, which act as selectable marker. [1]

24. (i) Death rate or mortality is expressed as the number of deaths of individual in a population per year. For example, if 80 individuals in a laboratory population of 800 fruitfly died in a week, then death rate is $\frac{80}{800} = 0.1$ per fruitfly/week. [2]

(ii) Characteristics of population, not exhibited by individual are

(a) Population size or Density.

(b) Population interactions. [1]

> **Value Points** In order to attain maximum marks, students should follow the given point
> While explaining death rate with an example, students must first define the death rate to give the clarity of the term.

25. Carcinogens can transform normal cells into cancerous cells. [1]

Carcinogenic ionising radiations are X-rays and gamma rays. Carcinogenic non-ionising radiations are UV-rays. [1]

These radiations cause DNA damage by changing the base sequences, i.e. mutations that lead to transformation of normal cells into cancerous cell. [1]

26. In the given table, A, B, C, D, E and F are identified as

A–Statins,

B–They are used as blood cholesterol lowering agents.

C–*Penicillium notatum*

D–Penicillin

E–*Trichoderma polysporum*

F–Used as an immunosuppressive agent in organ transplant patients. [½ × 6]

27. (i) The wind pollinated flowers are usually in inconspicuous having versatile anthers. The pollen grains are usually smooth-walled, relatively light, small and dry and are produced in large quantities. The stigmas on the other hand are comparatively large protruding and often feathery. [1½]

(ii) Flowers reward their insect pollinators through several mechanisms, primarily by providing food sources such as nectar and pollen.

Insects like bees, butterflies, and humming birds are attracted to the nectar and in the process of feeding transfer pollen from one flower to another. [1½]

28. Subcutaneous 'implants' contains synthetic progesterone and are placed under the skin. They are an effective contraceptive method as they check ovulation and thicken cervical mucus to prevent sperm transport. [2]

'Subcutaneous implants' are more advantageous than contraceptive pills as they are long lasting and once implanted, they are effective for up to 5 years. [1]

Common Mistake

Students may get confused between contraceptive pills and implants.

Contraceptive pill is a type of birth control that is designed to be taken orally by women.

Contraceptive implant is an implantable medical device used for the purpose of birth control.

29. (i) The *P* is identified as a primary immune response. It occurs when an antigen comes in contact with our immune system for the first time. Our body learns about this antigen, produce antibodies and keeps memory cells against it. Level of antibodies reaches peak in 7-10 days. Thus, it is of low intensity. [2]

(ii) *Q* represents the secondary immune response which develops due to a subsequent encounter with X. At this point, an immunological memory is already present due to memory cells. This results in the generation of a quick and an intense immune response towards antigen X (usually 2-3 days). With each subsequent exposure, the response gets more efficient and individual becomes resistant to the pathogen. [2]

Or

(ii) The immune cells are B-cell and T-cells. B-cells generate memory cells which keeps memory of the first exposure to antigen and helps in generating more intense response in subsequent infections T-cells fight the antigen. [2]

30. (i) Graph *A* would become like graph *B* under the influence of the disruptive and selective type of natural selection. [1]

(ii) Charles Darwin suggested natural selection as a mechanism of evolution. [1]

(iii) Graph *A* shows stabilising natural selection. For instance, the large number of individuals acquire mean character value, i.e. variation is much reduced. This thus operates by favouring optimal environmental conditions where competition is not severe. [2]

Or (iii) Because individual at the extremes contribute more offspring compared to those in the centre and produce two peaks in the distribution of a trait which leads to new variations arising in a population. [2]

31. (i)
- The levels of FSH and LH are high during ovulation and low during pregnancy.
- The levels of progesterone are low during ovulation high pregnancy.
- The levels of oestrogen remain high during ovulation as well as pregnancy. [2]

(ii) During ovulatory phase, the level of FSH and LH are at peak as they play a major role in development of ovarian follicles and to cause those follicles to rupture. But during pregnancy, soon after implantation there level drops down in order to maintain pregnancy.

During ovulatory phase if fertilisation do not takes place then the progesterone level drops down which result in shedding of endometrium. But if fertilisation occur successfully then to maintain pregnancy, level of progesterone increases.

Oestrogen level remain high in both ovulatory and pregnancy. [3]

Or (i) (a) Amniocentesis is often performed to diagnose chromosomal abnormalities and developmental disorders of foetus.

(b) Lactational amenorrhea is the absence of menstruation during the period of intense lactation following parturition. Since ovulation does not occur in this period, the chances of conception are nil. It is a natural method to avoid unwanted pregnancy.

(c) **ZIFT** (Zygote Intra Fallopian Transfer) is related to embryo transfer in the test tube programme. In this technique, the zygote or embryo up to 8 blastomeres is transferred into the Fallopian tube. [3]

(ii) The barrier method used by female are diaphragms, cervical caps and vaults.

These barriers are made up of rubber that are inserted into the female reproductive tract to cover during coitus. [1]

They prevent conception by blocking the entry of sperm through the cervix. [1]

32. (i) Crops modified using *Bacillus thuringiensis* are corn, cotton, tomato, rice, potato and soyabean. In there, the insect resistant gene is transferred from *Bacillus thuringiensis* to make them insect and pest-resistant. [1]

(ii) **Five advantages of GMOs to a farmer are as follows**

(a) Crops become more tolerant to abiotic stresses like cold, drought, salt and heat.

(b) Dependence on chemical pesticides has reduced.

(c) Helped to reduce post-harvest losses.

(d) Efficiency of mineral usage increased in plants, preventing early exhaustion of fertility of soil.

(e) Enhanced nutritional value of food, e.g. vitamin-A enriched rice. [2]

(iii) Genetically modified crops should be tested for possible reactions in people, because these crops are prepared by the insertion of gene of the other species into their DNA.

So, there is a possibility that they can cause some health issues, i.e. allergies due to release of new kind of proteins. Hence, GM crops should be tested. [2]

Or (i) Golden rice stands a very good chance of being able to deliver the recommended daily allowance of vitamin-A (after conversion from β-carotene) to all people. It can be seen that Golden rice varieties could fully provide the daily needs. [1]

(ii) The agro-chemicals have harmful effects on the environment and they are expensive for farmers especially in the developing countries.

Hence, the best solution to overcome all these issues is the development and use of Genetically Modified (GM) crops. [2]

(iii) Genetically Modified (GM) plants undergo a variety of changes to enhance their characteristics. These changes include

- Increased resistant to pest and diseases
- Herbicide tolerance
- Enhanced nutritional content
- Stress tolerance [2]

33. (i)

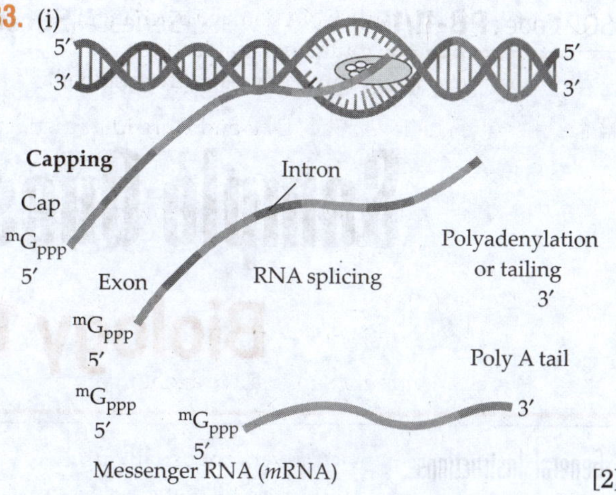

[2]

(ii) There are three major type of RNAs involve in the process of protein synthesis in prokaryotes, i.e. *m*RNA, *t*RNA and *r*RNA. There role in the process of protein synthesis is described below

(a) **Role of *m*RNA** The order and sequence of amino acids are defined by the sequence of bases in the *m*RNA. It stores the genetic information from DNA. [1]

(b) **Role of *t*RNA** It acts as an adapter molecule. It brings amino acid and reads the genetic code.[1]

(c) **Role of *r*RNA** It is formed in nucleolus and it forms 80% of total RNA present inside the cell. It is also the most stable type of RNA. *r*RNA is associated with structural organisation of ribosomes (*r*RNA forms about 60% of weight of ribosomes), which are seats of protein synthesis. [1]

Or (i) During replication, DNA ligase facilitates the joining of Okazaki fragments in lagging DNA strands together by catalysing the formation of phosphodiester bond. It also plays an important role in repairing single strand breaks in duplex DNA. [2]

(ii)

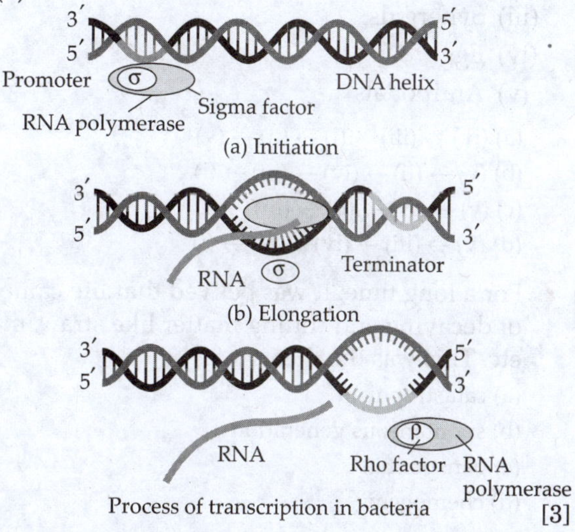

Process of transcription in bacteria [3]

SQP Code : **PB-11/15**

Series ***i*-Succeed 11-25/15**

Roll No. | | | | | | | | |

Sample Question Paper 11

Biology 12th (Code 044)

General Instructions

1. All questions are compulsory.
2. The question paper has five sections and 33 questions.
3. Section-A has 16 questions of 1 mark each; Section-B has 5 questions of 2 marks each; Section-C has 7 questions of 3 marks each; Section-D has 2 case-based questions of 4 marks each; and Section-E has 3 questions of 5 marks each.
4. There is no overall choice. However, internal choices have been provided in some questions. A student has to attempt only one of the alternatives in such questions.
5. Wherever necessary, neat and properly labelled diagrams should be draw.

Time : 3 Hrs.

Max. Marks : 70

Section A Multiple Choice Type Questions

1. Select the option that has the correct sequence of occurrence of different cells in a mature embryo sac (from chalazal to micropylar end).

(i) Filiform apparatus
(ii) Polar nuclei
(iii) Synergids
(iv) Egg
(v) Antipodals

(a) (iv) → (iii) → (i) → (ii) → (v)
(b) (v) → (ii) → (iv) → (iii) → (i)
(c) (v) → (iv) → (ii) → (iii) → (i)
(d) (v) → (iii) → (iv) → (ii) → (i)

2. For a long time, it was belived that life came out of decaying and rotting matter like straw, mud, etc. This was the theory of

(a) catastrophism
(b) spontaneous generation
(c) panspermia
(d) chemogeny

3. Select the incorrect match from the following.

(a)	Golden rice	1. Enriched with vitamin-A
(b)	*Bt* cotton	2. Increased shelf life
(c)	α-1-antitrypsin	3. Treat emphysema
(d)	Rosie cow	4. Protein-enriched milk

4. The impact of loss of biodiversity include

(a) decline in plant production
(b) lowered resistance to environmental perturbations
(c) increased variability in ecosystem processes like plant productivity, water use, pest and disease cycles
(d) All of the above

5. What is the fate of the male gametes discharged in the synergid?

(a) All fuse with the egg
(b) One fuses with the egg and other fuses with central cell nuclei
(c) One fuses with the egg and other fuses with synergid nucleus
(d) One fuses with the egg and other degenerate in the synergid

6. hCG, hPL and relaxin are produced in women. The production of these hormones takes place
(a) at the time of puberty
(b) only during pregnancy
(c) during menstruation
(d) at the time of menopause

7. Read the four statements given below and select the option having two incorrect statements.
(i) Stratification is the vertical distribution of different species occupying different levels.
(ii) NPP minus respiration loss is GPP.
(iii) Decomposition is largely an oxgen - requiring process.
(iv) In the process of fragmentation, water soluble inorganic nutrients go down into the soil horizon.
(a) (i) and (ii) (b) (ii) and (iv)
(c) (i) and (iii) (d) (iii) and (iv)

8. Which among the species of fungi species are free-living that are very common in the root ecosystems?
(a) Statin
(b) *Staphylococci*
(c) *Trichoderma*
(d) *Clostridium*

9. An alcoholic drink produced without involving distillation process is
(a) brandy (b) wine
(c) whisky (d) rum

10. Which one of the following animals may occupy more than one trophic levels in the same ecosystem at the same time?
(a) Goat (b) Lion
(c) Frog (d) Sparrow

11. Which of the following is a recessive trait for a character chosen by Mendel in garden pea?
(a) Violet flower colour
(b) Yellow pod colour
(c) Axial flower position
(d) Tall stem height

12. The limitations of ecological pyramids include all the following except
(a) They do not take into account the same species belongining to two or more trophic levels
(b) They assume a simple food chain and do not consider food webs
(c) They do not represent relationships between organisms at different trophic levels
(d) Saprotrophs are not given any place in the ecological pyramids

***Question** Nos. 13 to 16 consist of two statements- Assertion (A) and Reason (R). Answer these questions by selecting the appropriate option given below*
(a) Both Assertion and Reason are true and Reason is the correct explanation of Assertion.
(b) Both Assertion and Reason are true, but Reason is not the correct explanation of Assertion.
(c) Assertion is true, but Reason is false.
(d) Assertion is false, but Reason is true.

13. **Assertion** (A) The embryo with 8 to 16 blastomeres is called a morula.
Reason (R) The morula continues to divide and transforms into trophoblast.

14. **Assertion** (A) AUG acts as a stop codon for the nucleotide sequence.
Reason (B) AUG codes for methionine.

15. **Assertion** (A) *Lactobacillus* increase nutritional value of milk.
Reason (R) Curd and yoghurt have higher vitamin content than milk.

16. **Assertion** (A) Majority of insect - pollinated flowers are large, colourful, fragrant and rich in nectar.
Reason (R) The flowers pollinated by flies and beetles secrete foul odours to attract these animals.

Section B Very Short Answer Type Questions

17. A patient showed symptoms of sustained high fever, stomach pain and constipation, but no blood clot in stools. Name the disease and its pathogen. Write the diagnostic test for the disease. How does the disease get transmitted?

Or Name the two special types of lymphocytes in humans. How do they differ in their roles in immune response?

18. What is the role of sacred groves in the protection of biodiversity ?

Or List the features that make a stable biological community.

19. The following graph depicts changes in two population of herbivores, i.e. *A* and *B* in a grassy field.

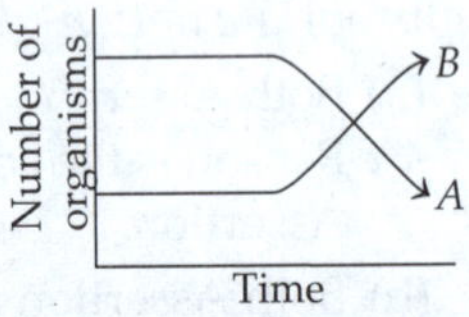

Can you suggest a possible reason for the changes observed in the graph?

20. (i) Write the dual purpose served by deoxyribonucleoside triphosphates in polymerisation.

(ii) Which one of an intron and an exon is the reminiscent of antiquity?

Or There was no atmosphere on the early earth. It was supposed to be formed about 4.5 billion years back in the solar system. Various theories of origin of life was given, one of them was Oparin-Haldane theory.

State two postulates of Oparin and Haldane's theory with reference to the origin of life.

21. In the flow chart given below, parts *A*, *B* and *C* shows the hormonal factors responsible for the ovarian changes during menstrual cycle. Study the chart and answer the questions that follows.

Primary follicle
↓ *A*
Graafian follicle
↓ *B*
Ova
↓ C
Corpus luteum

(i) Name the parts *A*, *B* and *C* which represents the hormonal factors responsible for the events.

(ii) State the impact of this hormones in female body.

SP-11

Section C Short Answer Type Questions

22. The image below shows an elephant in a zoological park.

(i) What significance does the conservation strategy hold?

(ii) What is the difference between *in situ* and *ex situ* conservation?

(iii) What are the few example of *in situ* and *ex situ* conservation?

23. (i) What is 'withdrawal' syndrome'? List any two symptoms of this condition.

(ii) Write the scientific name of the source plant of the drugs - marijuana and hashish and mention their effects on human body.

24. (i) Why are molecular scissors so called? Write their use in biotechnology.

(ii) Name the enzyme that are used for the isolation of DNA from bacterial and fungal cell for recombinant DNA technology.

25. (i) What is aminoacylation? State its significance.

(ii) Where does peptide bond formation occur in a bacterial ribosome and how?

26. Choose any three microbes from the following, which are suited for organic farming and is in great demand these days for various reasons. Mention one application of each one choosen.

Mycorrhiza, *Monascus, Anabaena, Rhizobium, Methanobacterium, Trichoderma.*

27. A codon is a trinucleotide sequence of DNA or RNA that corresponds to a specific amino acid. The genetic code describes the relationship between the sequence of DNA bases in a gene and the corresponding protein sequence that it encodes.

(i) (a) What is degeneracy?

(b) 'Starting codon is universal'. Justify.

(ii) Which feature of genetic code allows bacteria to produce human insulin by recombinant DNA technology?

28. Identify *A, B, C, D, E* and *F* in the table given below.

Phenomenon	Examples	Characteristics
A	*B*	Fruit develop without fertilisation
C	*D*	seeds develop without fertilisation
Polyembryony	*E*	*F*

Section D Case Based Questions

Q. Nos. 29 and 30 are case-based questions. Each question has 3 subparts with internal choice in one subpart.

29. A chromosome disorder associated either with an extra chromosome 21 or an effective trisomy for chromosome 21. Clinical manifestation include short stature, protruding tongue, small ears, short broad hands, fifth finger clinodactyly and moderate to serve mental retardation.

(i) On the basis of the given information, name the disorder that person is suffering from. [1]

(ii) What type of mutation is seen in this syndrome? [1]

(iii) If this syndrome is recognised during birth. What are the physical traits that can be seen? [2]

Or

(iii) Is this syndrome more common in males or females? Explain. [2]

30. The data given below, shows the concentration of alcohol in blood of drunkard.

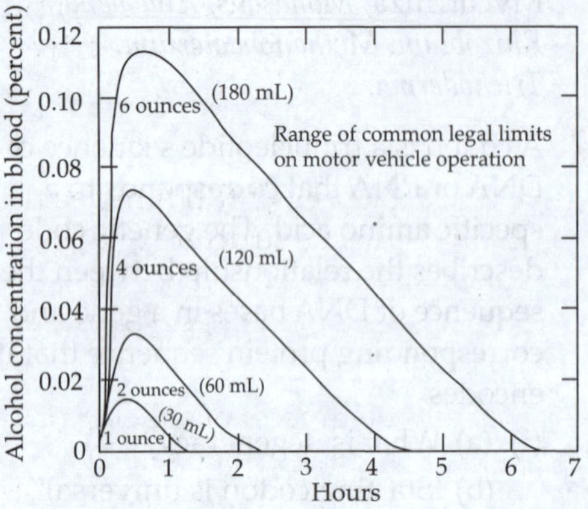

(i) With reference to the above graph, at which time the concentration of alcohol in blood will be highest? [1]

(ii) At which time will it have the lowest concentration of alcohol in blood? [1]

(iii) What are some common symptoms experienced during alcohol withdrawal. [2]

Or (iii) What are some of the major health effects associated with excessive alcohol consumption? [2]

Section E Long Answer Type Questions

31. The biological activity of insulin was tested using an assay in *in vitro*, using HepG2 cell under hyperglycemic conditions. In this assay, 3 concentrations were used for the standard insulin and crude biosynthesised human insulin : low (50 µg/mL), medium (100 µg/mL) and high (150 µg/mL).
A graph illustrating the above conditions are given below.

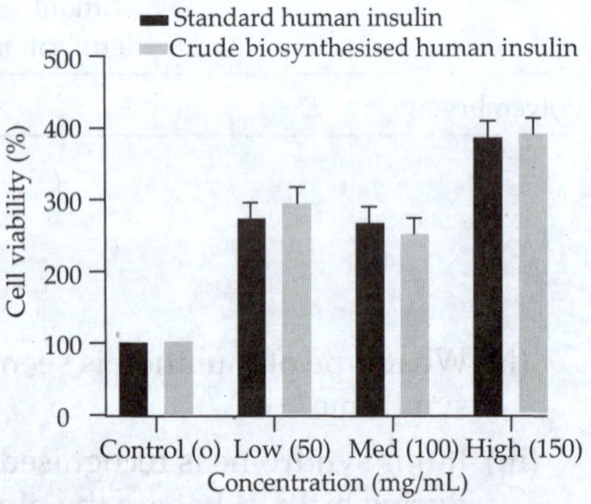

(i) By studying the above graph discuss the efficiency of crude biosynthesised human insulin at low concentration, i.e. 50 µg/mL.

(ii) At which concentration, both the insulin are equally efficient?

(iii) Using the above information, suggest why we should always use control in assay?

(iv) Describe the basic structure of the insulin molecule.

Or In recombinant technology, the desired genes for administration is/are selected, followed by selecting a perfect vector into which the desired gene is to be integrated and *r*DNA is formed.
The recombinant cells can be multiplied in large scale using a continuous culture system and can be achieved by using a bioreactor.

These are large vessels, 100-1000L in which raw materials are biologically converted into specific products, individual enzymes, etc. using microbial plant, animal or human cells.

A bioreactor provides optimum conditions for the growth of the desired product. These conditions include temperature, pH, substrate, etc.

(i) Which conditions apart from the temperature, pH and substrate are provided by the bioreactor?

(ii) Name the components of a bioreactor.

(iii) Write the name of two bioreactors.

(iv) What is the purpose of sparged stirred tank bioreactor?

32. Amniocentesis was first introduced as a mean of detecting the severity of rhesus (Rh) isoimmunisation about 50 years ago. Invasive prenatal diagnosis and particularly amniocentesis was introduced into clinical practice as the mid-trimester diagnostic investigation of choice.

Amniocentesis remains the most common invasive prenatal diagnostic procedure today. However, this technique is legally banned now.

(i) This test is based on what principle?

(ii) Explain why this procedure is banned now?

(iii) Which diseases can be diagnosed by this process?

Or Trace pollen grain development from sporogenous tissue in the anther.

33. Workout a typical Mendelian dihybrid cross and state the law that he derived from it.

Or

(i) Draw a diagram of *t*RNA molecule and describe its structure and function.

Why is it referred to as an adapter molecule?

(ii) Explain the process of splicing of *hn*RNA in a eukaryotic cell.

Answer Key

1. (b)	**2.** (b)	**3.** (b)	**4.** (d)	**5.** (b)	**6.** (b)	**7.** (b)	**8.** (c)	**9.** (b)	**10.** (d)
11. (b)	**12.** (c)	**13.** (c)	**14.** (d)	**15.** (a)	**16.** (c)				

Scan this QR code from your mobile phone to get the explanations of this paper.

SQP Code : **PB-12/15** Series ***i*-Succeed 12-25/15** Roll No.

Sample Question Paper 12

Biology 12th (Code 044)

General Instructions

1. All questions are compulsory.
2. The question paper has five sections and 33 questions.
3. Section-A has 16 questions of 1 mark each; Section-B has 5 questions of 2 marks each; Section-C has 7 questions of 3 marks each; Section-D has 2 case-based questions of 4 marks each; and Section-E has 3 questions of 5 marks each.
4. There is no overall choice. However, internal choices have been provided in some questions. A student has to attempt only one of the alternatives in such questions.
5. Wherever necessary, neat and properly labelled diagrams should be draw.

Time : 3 Hrs.

Max. Marks : 70

Section A Multiple Choice Type Questions

1. A cancer patient was admitted to the hospital. Out of the four options given below, select the substance given to the patient in order to activate their immune system and destroy the tumour?
   (a) Histamine (b) Morphine
   (c) Interleukin (d) α-interferon
2. Select the incorrect match from the following
   (a) Productivity- measured in $Kcalm^{-2}$
   (b) Standing crop - current biomass in an ecosystem
   (c) Stratification - vertical layering of different species
   (d) Catabolism- degradation of detritus into inorganic substance
3. Which of the following is a specialised procedure to form an embryo in the laboratory in which sperm is directly injected into the ovum.
   (a) ZIFT (b) GIFT (c) ICSI (d) ET
4. Which of the following is not observed in biodiversity hotspots?
   (a) Endemism
   (b) Accelerated habitat loss
   (c) Lesser interspecific competition
   (d) Species richness
5. Select the option that has correct sequence of events of development of human embryo
   (i) eyelashes
   (ii) heart
   (iii) major organ
   (iv) limbs and digits
   (v) hair
   (a) (ii) → (i) → (iv) → (v) → (iii)
   (b) (i) → (iii) → (iv) → (ii) → (v)
   (c) (ii) → (iv) → (iii) → (v) → (i)
   (d) (ii) → (iii) → (iv) → (v) → (i)
6. Which of the following option is correct for the haploid content human genome?
   (a) 2.2×10^4 bp (b) 3×10^9 bp
   (c) 6×10^9 bp (d) 20,000–25,000 bp

7. Which of the following is the ultimate energy source for all ecosystem?
(a) Producer
(b) Carbohydrate
(c) Solar radiation
(d) Organic molecule

8. Following pedigree chart shows

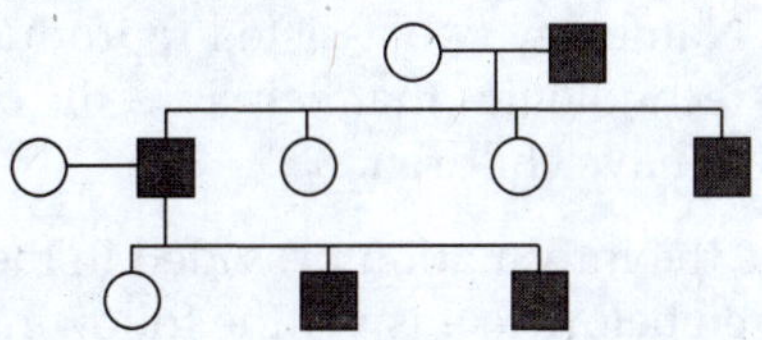

(a) character is carried by Y-chromosome
(b) character is sex-linked recessive
(c) character is sex-linked dominant
(d) character is recessive autosomal

9. When some human organs like heart, eye, liver, kidney fail to function satisfactorily, transplantation is the only remedy to enable the patient to live a normal life. The type of immunity responsible for graft rejection by a recipient body is
(a) innate immunity
(b) humoral immunity
(c) cell mediated immunity
(d) interferons

10. Which of the following bacterium is used for the isolation of the enzyme *Taq* polymerase and restriction endonuclease, respectively?

	***Taq* polymerase**	**Restriction endonuclease**
(a)	*Thermus aquaticus*	*Escherichia coli*
(b)	*Agrobacterium tumefaciens*	*Haemophilus influenzae*
(c)	*Streptomyces albus*	*Thermus aquaticus*
(d)	*Escherichia coli*	*Haemophilus influenzae*

11. On the rocky sea coasts of Scotland, the larger and competitively superior barnacle *Balanus* dominates the intertidal area and excludes the inferior barnacle *Chathamalus* from that zone. The kind of interaction exhibited in this case is
(a) predation (b) parasitism
(c) competition (d) mutualism

12. Read the four statements given below and select the option having two incorrect statements.
(i) Polyploidy occurs due to gain of a chromosome.
(ii) Multiple alleles can be found only when population studies are made.
(iii) Grasshopper is an example of XO type sex-determination.
(iv) Deletion and insertion of base pair of DNA, cause point mutations.
(a) (i) and (iii) (b) (ii) and (iv)
(c) (i) and (iv) (d) (ii) and (iii)

Question *Nos. 13 to 16 consist of two statements- Assertion (A) and Reason (R). Answer these questions by selecting the appropriate option given below.*

(a) Both Assertion and Reason are true and Reason is the correct explanation of Assertion
(b) Both Assertion and Reason are true, but Reason is not the correct explanation of Assertion
(c) Assertion is true, but Reason is false
(d) Assertion is false, but Reason is true

13. **Assertion** (A) Pollen grain of angiosperm is considered as the male gametophyte.
Reason (R) Pollen grain contains stigma, style and ovary.

14. **Assertion** (A) *Hind* II is a restriction enzyme.
Reason (R) It is responsible for the cleavage of DNA sequence.

15. **Assertion** (A) Each antibody is represented by H_2L_2.
Reason (R) Each antibody molecule has four nucleotide chains, two small called light chains and two longer called heavy chains.

16. **Assertion** (A) In a wildlife sanctuary, collection of timber, harvesting of minor forest products and private ownership rights are allowed.
Reason (R) A wildlife sanctuary is an *ex-situ* approach of biodiversity conservation.

Section B Very Short Answer Type Questions

17. Explain monohybrid cross taking seed coat colour as a trait in *Pisum sativum*. Work out the cross up to F_2-generation.

Or Name a disorder a human suffers from as a result of monosomy of the sex chromosome. Give the karyotypes and write the symptoms.

18. The figure given below shows a HIV virus.

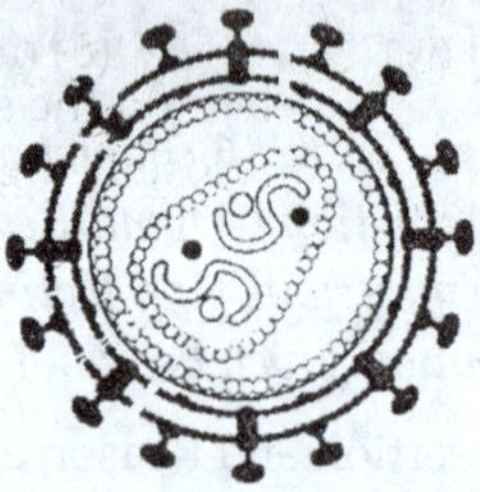

(i) Which type of cells does the HIV virus primarily target?

(ii) State how is it possible for HIV virus having no DNA infects the host cell which possess viral DNA?

Or Name any two techniques used to detect the cancer of internal organs and write about any one of them.

19. (i) How do prickles help cactus to survive in desert?

(ii) In a pond, there were 200 frogs. 40 more were born in a year. Calculate the birth rate of the population.

20. (i) Why is Cu - T considered a good contraceptive device to space children?

(ii) Name any two assisted reproductive technologies that help infertile couples to have children.

21. Use the information provided in the table given below to answer the following questions.

Lactose	Glucose	*Lac* repressor	*Lac* operon expression level
Present	*X*	Inactive	Very high
Y	Present	Inactive	Medium
Absent	Absent	Active	Very low
Absent	Absent	Active	Very low

(i) Fill the gap in *X* and *Y*.

(ii) How does the *lac* operon regulate the expressions of gene involved in lactose metabolism and what role does lactose play in this regulatory process?

Or Is haemophilia in humans a sex-linked or autosomal disorder? Workout a cross in support of your answer.

Section C Short Answer Type Questions

22. (i) Identify parts *A* and *B* from the given diagram. Also mention their role in male reproductive system.

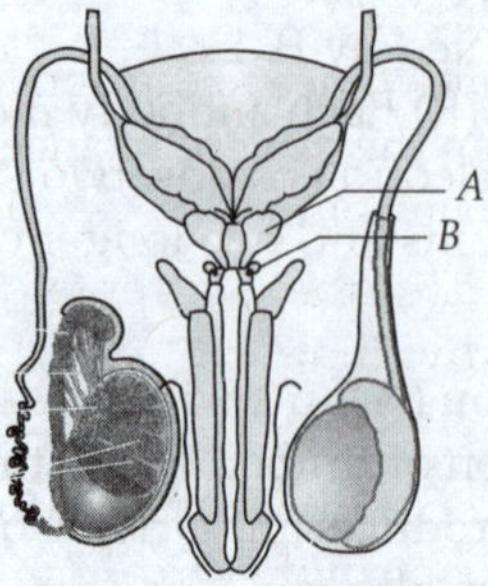

(ii) Why are scrotum situated outside the abdominal cavity? Also mention the path followed by sperm.

23. Explain the uses of plasmid DNA, recognition sequence and gel electrophoresis in biotechnology.

24. Seed is the basis of our agriculture. Dehydration and dormancy of mature seeds are crucial for storage of seeds. It can be used as food throughout the year and also to raise crop in the next season.

(i) Why does it is crucial for seed to undergo dormancy?

(ii) Give an example of a very old viable seed which is excavated from Arctic Tundra, in which the seed germinated and flowered after an estimated record of 10,000 years of dormancy.

25. (i) Bottled fruit juices are clearer as compared to those made at home. Explain.

(ii) Name a free-living and a symbiotic bacterium that serves as biofertiliser. Why are they called so?

26. Identify *A*, *B*, *C*, *D*, *E* and *F* in the table given below.

Characteristics of plant	Pollinating agents	Examples
Pollen grains are non-sticky	*A*	*B*
C	Water	*D*
Large and colourful flowers	*E*	*F*

27. (i) State any two criteria for determining biodiversity hotspots. Name any two hotspots designated in India.

(ii) Why is tropical environment is able to support greater species diversity ?

(iii) Why are thalassemia and haemophilia categorised as Mendelian disorders? Write the symptoms of these diseases. Explain their pattern of inheritance in humans.

28. A considerable amount of lactose is added to the growth medium of *E. coli*. How is the *lac* operon switched on in the bacteria? Mention the state of the operon when lactose is digested.

Section D Case Based Questions

Q. Nos. 29 and 30 are case-based questions. Each question has 3 subparts with internal choice in one subpart.

29. Mendelian disorders are mainly determined by alteration or mutation in the single gene. These disorders are transmitted to the offspring of the same lines as we have studied in the principle of inheritance. The pattern of inheritance of such mendelian disorders can be traced in a family by the pedigree analysis. Most common and prevalent mendelian disorders are haemophilia, cystic fibrosis, sickle-cell anaemia, colour blindness, phenylketonuria, thalassemia, etc.

(i) Which mendelian disorder is also known as royal disease and why? [2]

(ii) Cystic fibrosis is an autosomal recessive genetic disorders. What are the chances that the child would have the disease if any one of the parent is a carrier of the faulty cystic fibrosis gene?. [2]

Or

(ii) If the father in a family has a disease while the mother is normal, only the daughters inherited by this disease, not the sons. Name this type of disease? [2]

30. The data below shows the symptoms of common cold by an individual after the exposure of causative virus.

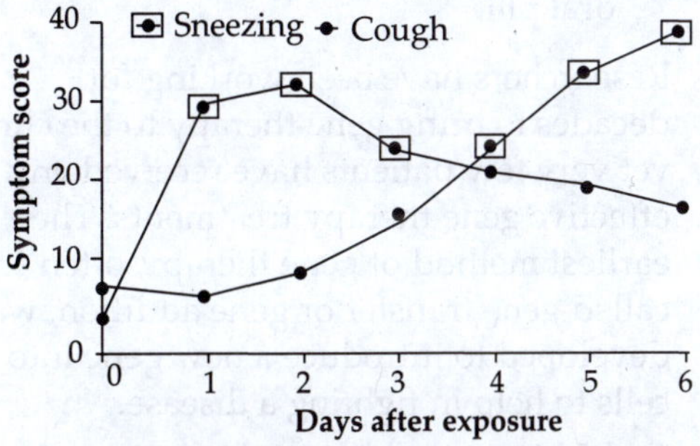

(i) How will the virus affect the immune system? [1]

(ii) With reference to the above graph explain the pattern of sneezing in common cold. [2]

(iii) How does the virus enter the body of an individual? [1]

Or

(iii) How do antibiotics help to fight common cold? [1]

Section E Long Answer Type Questions

31. (i) Explain and illustrate the phases in oogenesis.

(ii) After the formation of secondary oocyte, if sperm does not fertilise the egg, what will happen then? Explain.

Or (i) A woman has certain queries as listed below, before starting with contraceptive pills. Answer them.

(a) What do contraceptive pills contain and how do they act as contraceptives?

(b) What schedule should be followed for taking these pills?

(ii) State one reason, why breast feeding the baby acts as a natural contraceptive for the mother?

(iii) Name two hormones that are constituents of contraceptive pills. Why do they have high and effective contraceptive value? Name a commonly prescribed non-steroidal oral pill.

32. Researchers have been working for decades to bring gene therapy to the clinic, yet very few patients have received any effective gene therapy treatments. The earliest method of gene therapy, often called gene transfer or gene addition, was developed to introduce a new gene into cells to help in fighting a disease.

(i) List two advantages of using gene therapy for treating disorders.

(ii) For treating ADA deficiency, the gene therapy is carried out. How is this carried out and help the patient to overcome the disorder?

(iii) If the gene therapy is performed at embryonic stages, how will this have a positive effect on the children?

Or

(i) Why is it essential to have a selectable marker in a cloning vector?

(ii) How is an exonuclease functionally different from an endonuclease? Give an example of any two endonucleases.

(iii) Write the role of *ori* and restriction site in a cloning vector pBR322.

33. (i) Draw a schematic representation of a dinucleotide. Label the following

(a) The component of a nucleotide

(b) 5′ end

(c) N-glycosidic linkage

(d) Phosphodiester linkage

(ii) Describe the role of RNA polymerases in transcription in bacteria and in eukaryotes.

Or

It is sometimes observed that the F_1-progeny has a phenotype that does not resemble either of the two parents and has intermediate phenotype. Explain by taking a suitable example and working out the cross upto F_2- progeny.

SP-12

Answer Key

1. (d)	**2.** (a)	**3.** (c)	**4.** (c)	**5.** (c)	**6.** (b)	**7.** (c)	**8.** (a)	**9.** (c)	**10.** (a)
11. (c)	**12.** (c)	**13.** (c)	**14.** (a)	**15.** (c)	**16.** (c)				

Scan this QR code from your mobile phone to get the explanations of this paper.

SQP Code : **PB-13/15** Series *i*-**Succeed 13-25/15** Roll No. | | | | | | | | |

Sample Question Paper 13

Biology 12th (Code 044)

General Instructions

1. All questions are compulsory.
2. The question paper has five sections and 33 questions.
3. Section-A has 16 questions of 1 mark each; Section-B has 5 questions of 2 marks each; Section-C has 7 questions of 3 marks each; Section-D has 2 case-based questions of 4 marks each; and Section-E has 3 questions of 5 marks each.
4. There is no overall choice. However, internal choices have been provided in some questions. A student has to attempt only one of the alternatives in such questions.
5. Wherever necessary, neat and properly labelled diagrams should be draw.

Time : 3 Hrs.

Max. Marks : 70

Section A Multiple Choice Type Questions

1. Many athletes take drug before playing sports to enhance their performance. Out of the options given below, select the correct drug that help the athlete to increase their energy.

(a) Opioids
(b) Cannabinoids
(c) Barbiturates
(d) Lysergic Acid Diethylamide (LSD)

2. Select the option that has the correct sequence of order of different parts of sperm.

(i) Acrosome (ii) Plasma membrane
(iii) Neck (iv) Nucleus
(v) Middle piece

(a) (ii) → (iv) → (v) → (i) → (iii)
(b) (ii) → (i) → (iv) → (iii) → (v)
(c) (i) → (ii) → (iv) → (v) → (iii)
(d) (i) → (iv) → (ii) → (v) → (iii)

3. $A \xrightarrow{\oplus}$ Population density $\xleftarrow{\ominus} B$.

If A increases population density and B decreases it, then choose the correct option of A and B.

(a) A can be mortality which brings positive change in population density
(b) B can be emigration which brings negative change in population density
(c) values of A and B can never be equal
(d) Both (b) and (c)

4. Which among the following enzyme is used in polymerase chain reaction?

(a) DNA dependent RNA polymerase
(b) RNA dependent DNA polymerase
(c) DNA dependent DNA polymerase
(d) RNA dependent RNA polymerase

5. Which of the following is used as 'clot buster' for removing clots from blood vessels of patient who have undergone myocardial infarction?
(a) Ethanol
(b) Statins
(c) Cyclosporin-A
(d) Streptokinase

6. Pyramid of number is
(a) always upright
(b) always inverted
(c) either upright or inverted
(d) neither upright nor inverted

7. Two different species cannot live for long duration in the same niche or habitat. This law is called as
(a) Allen's law
(b) Gloger's rule
(c) Weismann's theory
(d) Competitive exclusion principle

8. Find out correct equations shown in the graph.

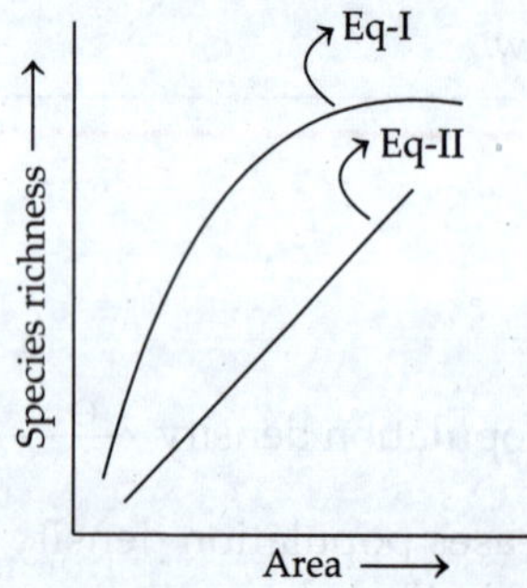

Species-area relationship

(a) I-$S = CA^Z$; II-$\log S = \log C + Z \log A$
(b) I-$\log S = \log C + Z \log A$; II-$S - CA^Z$
(c) I-$S = CA^Z + \log C$; II-$\log S = \log C + Z \log A$
(d) I-$S = CA^Z$; II-$\log S = \log C + Z \log A$

9. Select the incorrect match from the following.
(a) Francis Crick - Central dogma of molecular biology
(b) Frederick Griffith- Transforming principle
(c) Alfred Hershey and Marth Chase- Proved semi -conservative nature of DNA replication
(d) Avery, Macleod and McCarty - Biochemical characterisation of transforming principle

10. What can be the possible blood group of progeny whose father and mother are of A and B group respectively ?
(a) A and B (b) AB only
(c) All except O (d) A, B, AB and O

11. Which of the following is used in the production of the recombinant hepatitis-B vaccine?
(a) *Streptococcus* (b) *E.coli*
(c) Yeast (d) *Microsporum*

12. Read the four statements given below and select the option having two incorrect statements.
(i) The 'Roquefort cheese' are ripened by growing a specific bacteria on them.
(ii) 'Toddy' is made by fermenting sap from palms.
(iii) Bread is one of the oldest food items in which microbes were used.
(iv) The LAB play very beneficial role in checking disease-causing microbes.
(a) (i) and (ii) (b) (ii) and (iv)
(c) (i) and (iii) (d) (iii) and (iv)

***Question Nos.** 13 to 16 consist of two statements, Assertion (A) and Reason (R). Answer these questions by selecting the appropriate option given below.*
(a) Both Assertion and Reason are true and Reason is the correct explanation of Assertion
(b) Both Assertion and Reason are true, but Reason is not the correct explanation of Assertion
(c) Assertion is true, but Reason is false
(d) Assertion is false, but Reason is true

13. **Assertion** (A) Sticky ends forms covalent bonds with their complementary counter parts.
Reason (R) Sticky ends are formed when the restriction enzyme cuts the DNA little away from the centre of the palindrome.

14. **Assertion** (A) Nicotine, caffeine, quinine, strychnine and opium are produced by plants as defence against grazers and browsers.
Reason (R) Thorns of *Acacia* and cactus are most common physiological means of defence.

15. **Assertion** (A) All biodiversity hotspots if put together, cover less than 2% of the earth's land area.

Reason (R) The strict protection of the hotspots could reduce the ongoing mass extinction by almost 2%.

16. **Assertion** (A) Intra Cytoplasmic Sperm Injection (ICSI) is a procedure to form an embryo *in vitro*.

Reason (R) In ICSI, sperm is directly injected into the ovum.

Section B Very Short Answer Type Questions

17. During a field trip, one of your friend in the group suddenly became unwell, she started sneezing and had trouble in breathing.
Name and explain the term associated with such sudden responses. What would the doctor recommend for relief?

Or Why is *Rhizobium* categorised as a symbiotic bacterium? How does it act as biofertilisers?

18. Write the specific location in the palindromic sequence and the bond that is cut by *Eco*RI.

Or Why is proinsulin so called? How is proinsulin different from functional insulin in humans?

19. In the figure given below, the diagram of human sperm is shown. Study the figure and answer the questions that follows.

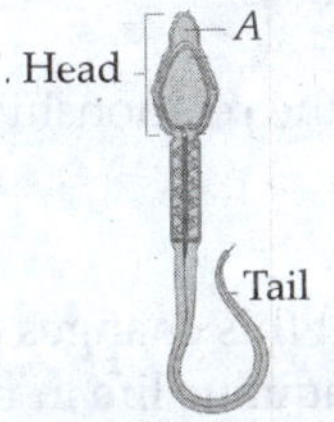

(i) Name the part labelled as *A* and state its significance.

(ii) State what will happen if a sperm fails to contact an ovum within a specific period?

20. (i) In the global biodiversity the number of mosses/ferns are so few? Give reason.

(ii) How do fungi that are heterotrophs sustain themselves as a large population?

21. (i) How do normal red blood cells become elongated and sickle - shaped in structure in a person suffering from sickle - cell anaemia?

(ii) XX-XY type of sex-determination is an example of male heterogamety or female heterogamety? Justify your answer.

Or

Name the enzyme and state its property that is responsible for continuous and discontinuous replication of the two strands of a DNA molecule.

Section C Short Answer Type Questions

22. Study the figure of a *Lac* operon given below.

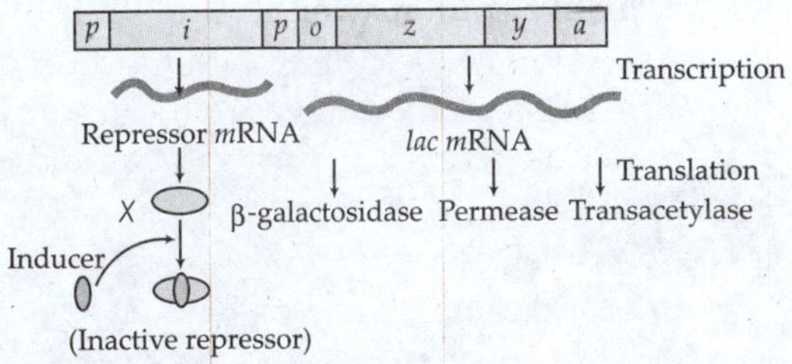

(i) Name the molecule '*X*' synthesised by *i* gene. How does this molecule get inactivated?

(ii) When will the transcription of this gene stop? Which one of the structural genes code for β-galactosidase?

23. (i) How would the gene flow or genetic drift affect the population in which either of them happen to take place?

(ii) List the two main propositions of Oparin and Haldane.

SP-13

24. (i) Describe any two devices in a flowering plant which prevent both autogamy and geitonogamy.

(ii) List the post - fertilisation events in angiosperms.

25. Many secondary metabolites of plants have medicinal properties.

It is their misuse that creates problems'. Justify the statement with an example.

26. (i) Indiscriminate diagnostic practices using X-rays, etc. should be avoided. Give one reason.

(ii) Why are adolescents especially advised not to smoke?

How does smoking affect the functioning of the body?

27. Identify *A*, *B*, *C*, *D*, *E* and *F* in the table given below

Biocontrol agents	Characteristics	Target species
A	Excellent candidates for species specific, narrow spectrum insecticidal application	*B*
Trichoderma species	*C*	*D*
E	secretes *Bt* toxin	*F*

28. State the functions of *ori*, *rop* and *Hind* III sites in the cloning vector pBR322.

Section D Case Based Questions

Q. Nos. 29 and 30 are case-based questions. Each question has 3 subparts with internal choice in one subpart.

29. Two blood samples of suspects 'A' and 'B' were sent to the forensic department along with sample 'C' from the crime scene. The forensic department was assigned the responsibility of running the samples and matching the samples of the suspects with that of the sample from the scene of the crime and thereby identifying the culprit.

(i) In genetic fingerprinting, what does the 'probe' refers to? [1]

SP-13

(ii) How does polymorphism arise in a population? [1]

(iii) What does 'minisatellite and micro satellite' mean in relation to DNA fingerprinting. [2]

Or (iii) State the steps involved in DNA fingerprinting in a sequential manner. [2]

30. Study the graph given below and answer the questions that follows

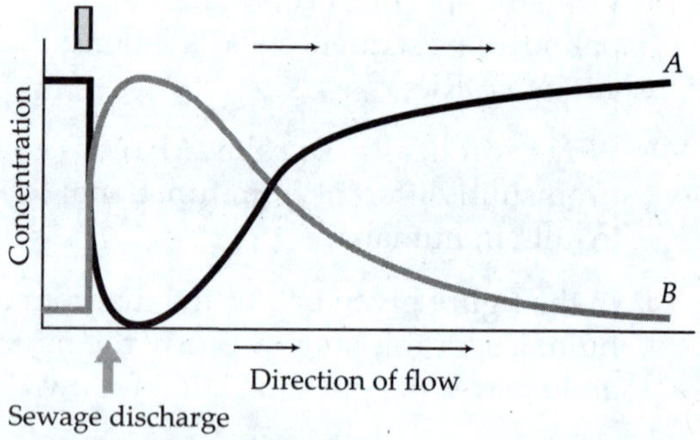

(i) What is the relationship between *A* and *B*? [1]

(ii) How will this changes between *A* and *B* affect aquatic life in river? [1]

(iii) Name the factors which affect dissolved oxygen. [2]

Or

(iii) Does the sewage treatment require aerobic conditions all through out? Justify your answer. [2]

Section E Long Answer Type Questions

31. The table given below shows the different genotypes of human ABO blood types. After thoroughly examining the table, find the genotype and phenotype of the offsprings. Also explain the phenomenon associated with ABO blood groups.

Allele from parent I	Allele from parent 2	Genotype of offsprings	Phenotype of offsprings
I^A	I^A	–	–
I^A	I^B	–	–
I^A	i	–	–
I^B	I^A	–	–
I^B	I^B	–	–
I^B	i	–	–
i	i	–	–

Or (i) Differentiate between a template strand and coding strand of DNA.

(ii) A DNA segment has a total of 1000 nucleotides, out of which 240 of them are adenine containing nucleotides. How many pyrimidine bases this DNA segment possesses?

32. For cultural reasons modern contraception has been slower to gain acceptance in Ethiopia. Knowledge about contraception and abortion is limited as family and community settings as it is socially disapproved. By 2000 only 4% of Ethiopian females aged 15-49 used contraception. Little is known of Sexually Transmitted Disease (STD) prevalance in Family Planning (FP) attenders in Africa in general and Ethiopia in particular, even through attenders of Family Planning Clinics (FPCs) are appropriate target groups for epidemiological studies and control programmes.

(i) Name the complication that arises due to late detection of STDs.

(ii) Explain how STDs can be prevented by self-consciousness?

(iii) Mention early symptoms of STDs.

Or

(i) What stimulates pituitary to release the hormone responsible for parturition? Name the hormone.

(ii) When and where do chorionic villi appear in humans? State their function.

(iii) Name the hormones produced only during pregnancy in human female. Mention their source organs.

33. (i) Explain the steps involved in *r*DNA technology.

(ii) Draw a well-labelled diagram sparged stirred-tank bioreactor.

Or

(i) Differentiate between somaclones and somatic hybrids. Give one example of each.

(ii) Draw a well-labelled diagram depicting maturation of pro-insulin into insulin.

Answer Key

1. (b) **2.** (b) **3.** (d) **4.** (c) **5.** (d) **6.** (c) **7.** (d) **8.** (a) **9.** (d) **10.** (d)
11. (c) **12.** (c) **13.** (d) **14.** (c) **15.** (c) **16.** (b)

Scan this QR code from your mobile phone to get the explanations of this paper.

SQP Code : **PB-14/15** Series ***i*-Succeed 14-25/15** Roll No. | | | | | | | |

Sample Question Paper 14

Biology 12th (Code 044)

General Instructions

1. All questions are compulsory.
2. The question paper has five sections and 33 questions.
3. Section-A has 16 questions of 1 mark each; Section-B has 5 questions of 2 marks each; Section-C has 7 questions of 3 marks each; Section-D has 2 case-based questions of 4 marks each; and Section-E has 3 questions of 5 marks each.
4. There is no overall choice. However, internal choices have been provided in some questions. A student has to attempt only one of the alternatives in such questions.
5. Wherever necessary, neat and properly labelled diagrams should be draw.

Time : 3 Hrs.

Max. Marks : 70

Section A Multiple Choice Type Questions

1. Saheli is a non-steroidal, once a week pill with high contraceptive value. Its mode of action involves

(a) increasing phagocytosis of sperms
(b) supressing the fertilising capacity of sperms
(c) inhibiting ovulation and implantation
(d) inhibiting maturation of ova

2. How does the HIV affect the body of a person?

(a) By reducing the number of blood platelets
(b) By reducing the number of WBCs
(c) By increasing the rate of HIV multiplication
(d) By reducing the number of T_H cells

3. Select the incorrect match from the following.

Methods of ARTs	Modes of action
(a) Intra-cytoplasmic	1. Sperm is injected into the cytoplasm of an ovum
(b) ZIFT	3. Transfer of zygote into oviducts
(c) IVF	4. External fertilisation followed by embryo transplant in Fallopian tube
(d) ICSI	5. Sperm is directly injected into ovum

4. Epicotyl has a shoot apex and a few leaf primordial enclosed in a hollow foliar structure called as the

(a) coleoptile
(b) scutellum
(c) coleorhiza
(d) perisperm

5. The impact of loss of biodiversity include

(a) decline in plant production
(b) lowered resistance to environmental pertubations
(c) increased variability in ecosystem processes like plant productivity, water use, pest and disease cycles.
(d) All of the above

6. The secondary host of *Plasmodium* is
(a) female *Anopheles* (b) female *Culex*
(c) male *Anopheles* (d) man

7. On what basis an area would be classified as a hotspot?
(a) Disrupted network of interaction
(b) Number of endemic species and degree of threat
(c) Habitat destruction
(d) Presence of alien species

8. Plants are more easily manipulated by genetic engineering than are animals because
(a) genes can be inserted into animal cells by microinjection
(b) plant genes do not contain introns
(c) totipotency is a feature generally associated with plant cell and not with animal cells
(d) more vectors are available to transfer *r*DNA into plant cells

9. Select the option that has the correct sequence of order of structure of different parts of seed.
(i) Endosperm (ii) Coleorhiza
(iii) Plumule (iv) Radicle
(v) Coleoptile
(a) (iii) → (i) → (v) → (iv) → (ii)
(b) (i) → (iii) → (v) → (ii) → (iv)
(c) (i) → (v) → (iii) → (iv) → (ii)
(d) (i) → (ii) → (v) → (iii) → (iv)

10. Read the four statements given below and select the option having two correct statements.
(i) Jawless fish probably evolved around 500 mya.
(ii) Reptiles lay thick - shelled eggs which do not dry up in sun unlike those of amphibians.
(iii) *Tyrannosaurus rex* was about 20 feet in height and had huge fear some dagger like teeth.
(iv) *Homo erectus* hides to protect their body and buried their dead.
(a) (i) and (ii) (b) (ii) and (iii)
(c) (i) and (iv) (d) (iii) and (iv)

11. Wine and beer produced directly by fermentation whereas brandy and whisky require both fermentation and distillation. This is because
(a) distillation prolongs storage
(b) distillation improves quality
(c) fermentation is inhibited at an alcohol level of 10-18%
(d) distillation purifies the beverage

12. Which of the following pyramids is generally inverted?
(a) Pyramid of numbers in grassland
(b) Pyramid of energy
(c) Pyramid of biomass in forest
(d) Pyramid of biomass is a sea

***Question Nos.** 13 to 16 consist of two statements, Assertion (A) and Reason (R). Answer these questions by selecting the appropriate option given below.*
(a) Both Assertion and Reason are true and Reason is the correct explanation of Assertion.
(b) Both Assertion and Reason are true, but Reason is not the correct explanation of Assertion.
(c) Assertion is true, but Reason is false.
(d) Assertion is false, but Reason is true.

13. **Assertion** (A) In plants, apomixis is a form of asexual reproduction that mimics sexual reproduction.
Reason (R) Apomixis involves the production of seeds with the fusion of gametes.

14. **Assertion** (A) Primary productivity of desert ecosystem is less in comparison to grassland ecosystem.
Reason (R) Primary productivity depends on the plant species inhabiting a particular area.

15. **Assertion** (A) *E. coli* having pBR322 with DNA insert at *Bam*HI site cannot grow in medium containing tetracycline.
Reason (R) Recognition site for *Bam*HI is present in tet ^{R} region of pBR322.

16. **Assertion** (A) Earliest organisms that appeared on the earth were non-green and presumably anaerobes.

Reason (R) The first autotrophic organisms were the chemoautotrophs that never released oxygen.

Section B Very Short Answer Type Questions

17. A man with colourblind father marries a woman whose father was also colourblind. What are the chances that their first born girl child would have colour blindness?

Or

A template stand is given below. Write down the corresponding coding strand and the *m*RNA strand that can be formed, along with their polarity.
3′ ATGCATGCATGCATGCATGCATGE-5′

18. Explain the events in a normal woman during her menstrual cycle from 13-15 days and 16-23 days.

Or

Differentiate between albuminous and non-albuminous seeds, giving on example of each.

19. A cross was carried out between two pea plants showing the contrasting traits of height of the plants. The results of the cross showed 50% parental characters.

(i) Work out the cross with the help of a Punnett square.

(ii) Name the type of the cross carried out.

20. In the artificially constructed pBR322 vector,

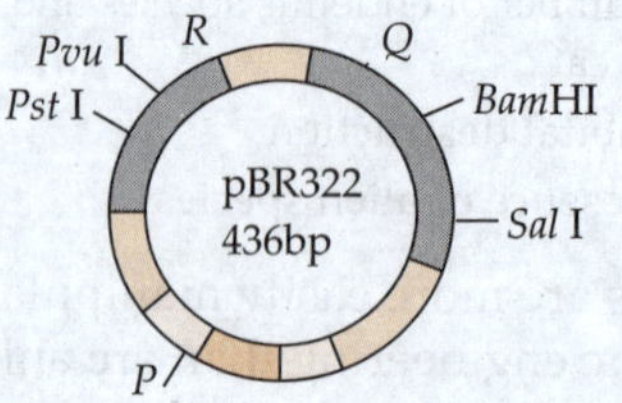

(i) Why the recombinant molecule will not be formed if the '*P*' is missing from the above vector?

(ii) In what way does the absence of *R* and *Q* will affect the selection of transformed cells? Discuss.

21. About 80,000 J of energy is received. Assuming that, draw a food chain in a terrestrial ecosystem depicting the transfer of energy at all 4 trophic levels. Also mention why the food chain cannot be longer than 4-5 trophic levels?

Or In a botanical garden of a city there is a huge banyan tree growing on which hundreds of birds and thousands of insects live.

(i) Draw the pyramid of number for this community. Comment giving reason.

(ii) If the pyramid of energy is drawn for same situation, what will be its shape? Justify your answer.

Section C Short Answer Type Questions

22. Given below is a figure of a plant which is used to obtain '*X*' drug.

(i) Name the plant whose flowering branch is shown above.

(ii) Many secondary metabolites of plants have medicinal properties. It is their misuse that creates the problem. Justify the statement.

23. Identify *A*, *B*, *C*, *D*, *E* and *F* in the table given below.

Organisms	Biological Name	Organic acid (Product)
A	*B*	Citric acidts
C	*Lactobacillus*	*D*
E	*F*	Butyric acid

24. About 2 mya, a common ancestor of Drawin finches arrived in the Galapagos. Over time, this ancestral species evolved into 15 distinct species with different beak sizes and shapes adapted to different food sources.

(i) Identify and describe the process of evolution observed in this case.

(ii) Name the scientist who observed this pattern of evolution. Give another example of the similar case.

25. Define operon. Explain the functions of inducer and repressor in an operon.

26. (i) Condoms are better contraceptives than pills. Justify the statements.

(ii) (a) Define sterilisation or surgical method of contraception to cause any side effects?

(b) Why tubectomy and vasectomy methods are generally not recommended to couples?

27. A farmer grow two varieties of crop in fields '*A*' and '*B*'. He grew normal tobacco plant in field *A* and GM crops in field *B*. He observed that nematode attacked only in field *A*, whereas crops in field *B* remains unaffected.

(i) Name the nematode responsible for affecting the crops of field '*A*'.

(ii) How did the crops of field '*B*' remain unaffected?

(iii) Name the vector used to introduce specific genes into the host plant.

28. There are many animals that have become exinct in the wild, but continue to be maintained in zoological parks.

(i) Which type of biodiversity conservation is observed in this case?

(ii) Explain any other two ways, which help in this type of conservation.

Section D Case Based Questions

Q. Nos. 29 and 30 are case-based questions. Each question has 3 subparts with internal choice in one subpart.

29. Study the pedigree chart given below.

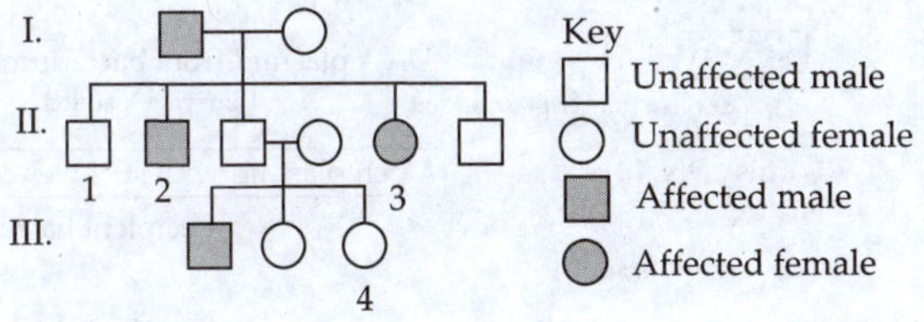

Answer the following questions.

(i) On the basis of the inheritance pattern represented by this pedigree chart, what is your conclusion with respect to the given disease/trait? [1]

Or (i) What will happen to the female who is homozygous for this trait? [1]

(ii) (a) To a couple where the female is unaffected and the male is affected, what will be the the genotype of the offspring they have? Show the same by using a genetic cross. [1]

(b) If a carrier female marry an affected male then what would be the genotype of the offspring? [1]

(iii) What would happen to the male children of the couple where woman is a carrier for this trait and man is normal? Explain with the help of a cross. [1]

30. When a microorganism invades a host, a definite sequence of events usually occur leading to infection and disease, causing suffering to the host. This process is called pathogenesis. Once a microorganism overcomes the defense system of the host, development of the disease follows a certain sequence of events as shown in the graph. Study the graph given for the sequence of events leading to appearance of a disease and answer the questions that follow.

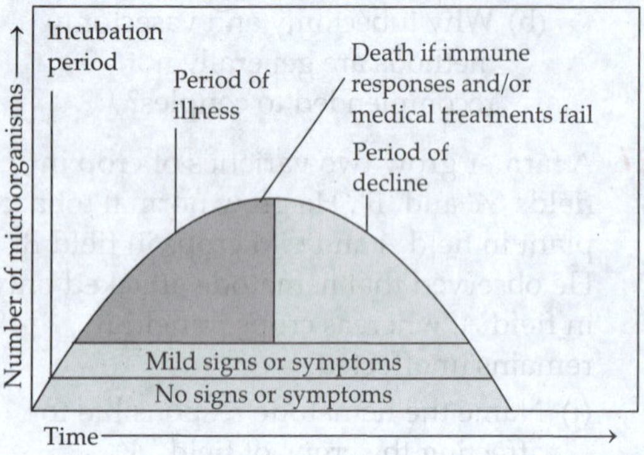

(i) In which period, according to the graph there are maximum chances of a person transmitting a disease / infection and why? [2]

(ii) Study the graph and write what is an incubation period?
Name a sexually transmitted disease that can be easily transmitted during this period.
Name the specific type of lymphocytes that are attacked by the pathogen of this disease. [2]

Or

(ii) Draw a schematic labelled diagram of an antibody. [2]

Section E Long Answer Type Questions

31. (i) Explain the phenomenon of codominance and multiple allelism in human population.

(ii) Linkage and crossing over of genes are alternatives of each other. Justify with the help of an example.

Or

(i) How is the phenotypic ratio of F_2 - generation in a dihybrid was is different from monohybrid cross?

(ii) Explain the role of regulatory gene, operator, promoter and structural genes in *lac* operon when *E. coli* is growing in a culture medium with the source of energy as lactose.

32. Almost any disease causing organisms such as bacteria, virus, fungi, prions, etc. or their toxins can be used as biological weapons.

Historical biological weapons programmes have included efforts to produce aflatoxin, anthrax and many others. In the bioweapon industry, genetic engineering is used to create new pathogenic strains through increased survivability, infertility, virulence, etc.

(i) In their natural state, the organisms or toxins do not have the efficiency to cause the large scale damage as compared to their bioweapon forms. Explain, how are these natural forms turned into bioweapons?

(ii) Genetic modification to this extent can have unpredictable or unforeseen risks to the living forms and the environment. Comment.

Or The steps involved in the formation of recombinant DNA using a plasmid and host bacterial cell are shown below.

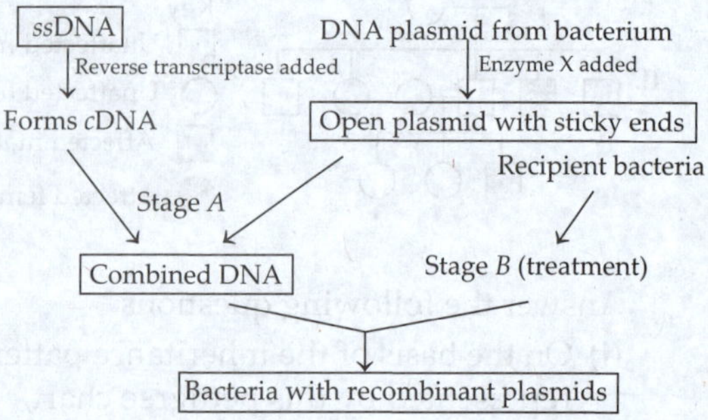

(i) The plasmid vector is cut with an enzyme to create sticky ends. Discuss why was this necessary?

(ii) What will be your strategy to select the transformed plasmids from those cells who have not picked up the gene of interest?

33. Male and female gametes in human beings differ from each other in terms of both structure and function. Enumerate some major differences between the two, along with their diagrams.

Or

Plan an experiment and prepare flowchart of the steps that you would follow to ensure that the seeds are formed only from the desired sets of pollen grains. Name the type of experiment that you carried out. Also write the importance of such experiments.

Answer Key

1. (c)	**2.** (d)	**3.** (c)	**4.** (a)	**5.** (d)	**6.** (d)	**7.** (b)	**8.** (c)	**9.** (c)	**10.** (c)
11. (c)	**12.** (a)	**13.** (c)	**14.** (a)	**15.** (a)	**16.** (b)				

Scan this QR code from your mobile phone to get the explanations of this paper.

SQP Code : **PB-15/15** Series *i*-**Succeed 15-25/15** Roll No.

Sample Question Paper 15

Biology 12th (Code 044)

General Instructions

1. All questions are compulsory.
2. The question paper has five sections and 33 questions.
3. Section-A has 16 questions of 1 mark each; Section-B has 5 questions of 2 marks each; Section-C has 7 questions of 3 marks each; Section-D has 2 case-based questions of 4 marks each; and Section-E has 3 questions of 5 marks each.
4. There is no overall choice. However, internal choices have been provided in some questions. A student has to attempt only one of the alternatives in such questions.
5. Wherever necessary, neat and properly labelled diagrams should be draw.

Time : 3 Hrs.

Max. Marks : 70

Section A Multiple Choice Type Questions

1. Both parents are carrier for thalassemia, which is an autosomal recessive disorder.
Out of the four options given below, select the correct option that shows the chance of pregnancy resulting in an affected child.

(a) 25% (b) 100%
(c) No chance (d) 50%

2. Which of the following is not included in the biodiversity hotspots of India?

(a) Indo-Burma (b) Himalayas
(c) Western Ghats (d) North Indian Plains

3. Condoms are 98% effective when used correctly. Identify the method of birth control and its mechanism from the given table.

	Methods	Mechanisms
(a)	Barrier	Creates a barrier between egg and sperm
(b)	Chemical	Prevents eggs from traveling down the fallopian tubes
(c)	Hormonal	Paralyses sperm after ejaculation
(d)	Surgical	Cuts the urethra so that no sperm can emerge

4. 'Golden rice' developed through transgene approach, is enriched with

(a) high glutenin content
(b) high lysine content
(c) high vitamin-A content
(d) high methionine content

5. Elephantiasis, a chronic inflammation that results in gross deformities, is caused by which of the following pathogens?

(a) *Ascaris*
(b) *E. coli*
(c) *Trichophyton*
(d) *Wuchereria*

6. *Monascus purpureus* is a yeast used commercially in the production of
(a) citric acid
(b) streptokinase for removing clots from the blood vessels
(c) blood cholesterol lowering agents
(d) ethanol

7. Methanogens grow anaerobically on cellulosic material. The product(s) produced during this kind of growth is/are
(a) methane
(b) methane and hydrogen
(c) methane and carbon dioxide
(d) methane, carbon dioxide and hydrogen

8. An urn-shaped population age pyramid represents which of the following type of population?
(a) Static population
(b) Extinct population
(c) Growing population
(d) Declining population

9. Select the incorrect match from the following
(a) Endemism - Species confined to a particular region and not found anywhere else
(b) Biosphere reserve - Unique and biodiversity rich areas that are legally protected
(c) Biodiversity hotspots - Regions with high diversity and accelerated habitat loss
(d) Sacred groves - Area where plants are grown for scientific study

10. Select the option that has the correct sequence of pathway taken by sperm to fertilise an egg.
(i) Uterine cavity
(ii) Cervical canal
(iii) Vagina
(iv) Isthmus
(v) Ampulla
(a) (iii) → (ii) → (i) → (v) → (iv)
(b) (v) → (iv) → (ii) → (ii) → (i)
(c) (iv) → (v) → (ii) → (i) → (iii)
(d) (iii) → (ii) → (i) → (iv) → (v)

11. Read the four statements given below and select the option having two correct statements.
(i) Retroviruses have an envelope enclosing the DNA genome.
(ii) Computed tomography uses x-rays to generate a 3-D image of the internals of an object.
(iii) Cannabinoid receptors are mainly present in the gastrointestinal tract.
(iv) Cocaine is obtained from *Erythroxylum coca*, native to South America.
(a) (i) and (iii) (b) (ii) and (iv)
(c) (i) and (ii) (d) (iii) and (iv)

12. In the following human pedigree, the filled symbols represent the affected individuals. Identify the type of given pedigree.

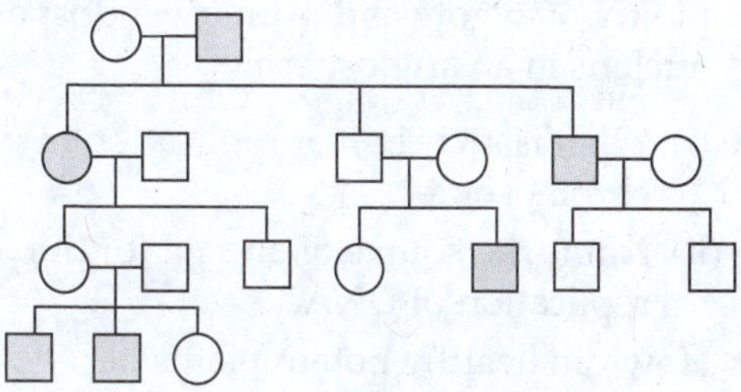

(a) X-linked dominant
(b) Autosomal recessive
(c) Autosomal dominant
(d) X-linked recessive

Question *Nos. 13 to 16 consist of two statements- Assertion (A) and Reason (R). Answer these questions by selecting the appropriate option given below.*
(a) Both Assertion and Reason are true and Reason is the correct explanation of Assertion
(b) Both Assertion and Reason are true, but Reason is not the correct explanation of Assertion
(c) Assertion is true, but Reason is false
(d) Assertion is false, but Reason is true

13. **Assertion** (A) Flowers are the sexual reproductive organs in flowering plants.
Reason (R) Various embryological processes of plants occur in a flower.

14. **Assertion** (A) At F_2 stage in a monohybrid cross, both parental traits are expressed in the proportion of 3:1.

SP-15

Reason (R) The contrasting parental traits show blending at F_2 stage.

15. **Assertion** (A) Repetitive sequences make up very large portion of human genome.

Reason (R) They do not have direct coding function in the genome.

16. **Assertion** (A) In case, a species becomes extinct, the plant and animal species associated with it in an obligatory way also become extinct.

Reason (R) When a host fish species becomes extinct, its unique assemblage of parasites also become extinct.

Section B Very Short Answer Type Questions

17. (i) Name the type of fruit apple is categorised under and why?

(ii) Suggest two advantages to a farmer using apomictic seeds of hybrid varieties.

Or Mention the reasons for difference in ploidy of zygote and primary endosperm nucleus in an angiosperm.

18. (i) What is an origin of replication in a chromosome?

(ii) Name the source of energy for the replication of DNA.

Or How can healthy potato plants be obtained from a desired potato variety which is virus infected? Explain

19. Primary productivity is the amount of biomass or organic matter produced per unit area over a time period by plants. It has two aspects, i.e. Gross primary productivity (GPP) and Net primary productivity (NPP).

(i) What is the difference between net and gross primary productivity?

(ii) Why primary productivity varies in different types of ecosystem? Explain.

20. In snapdragon a cross between true-breeding red flowered (RR) plants and true - breeding white flowered (rr) plants resulted in a progeny with all pink flowers.

(i) The appearance of pink flowers is not known as blending. Why?

(ii) What is this phenomenon known as?

21. Given below is the outline structure of a drug.

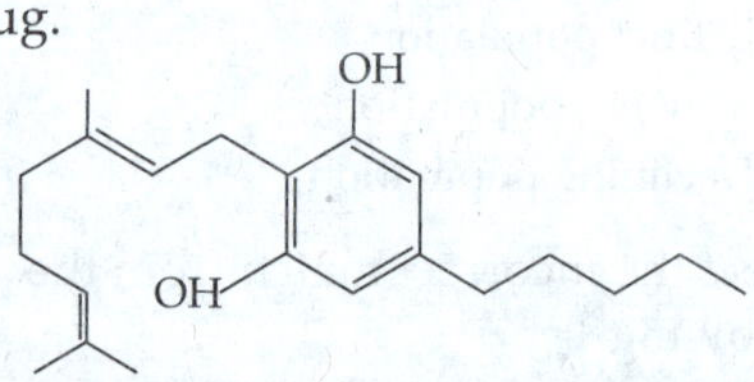

(i) Which group of drugs does thisstructure represent and which organ of the body will be affected by these drugs?

(ii) What are the modes of consumption of these drugs?

Or (i) Name any one symbiont, which serves as biofertiliser. Mention its specific role.

(ii) What are methanogens? Name the animals in which methanogens are present.

SP-15

Section C Short Answer Type Questions

22. Observe the diagram of human male reproductive system.

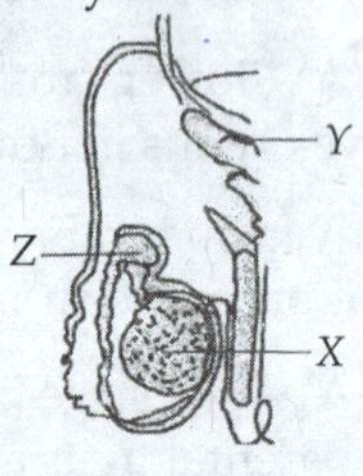

(i) Identify *X*, write its location in the body.

(ii) Also mention what the accessory gland *Y* represents and what is its secretion?

(iii) Name and state the function of *Z*.

23. Explain the menstrual, follicular and luteal phases of menstrual cycle in human female.

24. (i) Name two groups of organisms which constitute 'flocs'. Write their influence on the level of BOD during biological treatment of sewage.

(ii) 'Before releasing the wastewater into water bodies it should be treated' Elaborate.

25. (i) Write the source of cocaine and marijuana.

(ii) Explain the effects of some drugs on human body.

26. How can Hardy - Weinberg equilibrium be affected? Explain by giving three reasons.

27. Scientists have succeeded in recovering healthy sugarcane plants from a diseased one.

(i) Name the part of the plant used as explant by scientists.

(ii) Describe the procedure the scientists followed to recover the healthy parts.

28. Identify *A*, *B*, *C*, *D*, *E* and *F* from the following.

Conservation stratergy	Type	Number/Property
A	*B*	448
C	*D*	Gametes are preserved in viable conditions
E	*In-Situ*	14
F	*Ex-Situ*	Seeds are kept for a long period

Section D Case Based Questions

Q. Nos. 29 and 30 are case-based questions. Each question has 3 subparts with internal choice in one subpart.

29. Study the diagrammatic representation of the experimental setup used by SL Miller for his experiment.

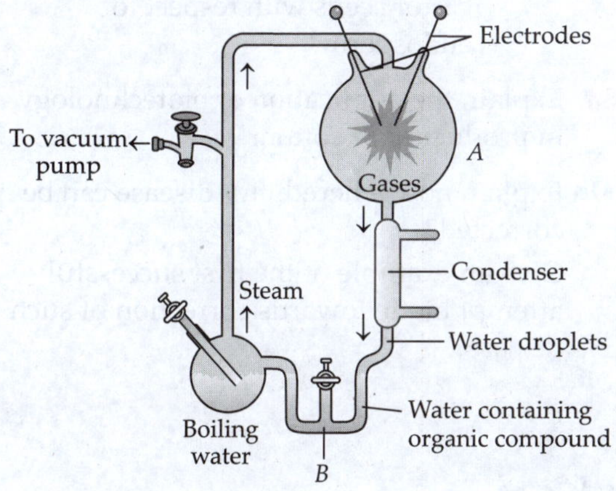

(i) (a) On the basis of the given diagram, write the different gases contained in the flask.

(b) The condition(s) required for the reaction to occur in the flask *A*. [1]

(ii) What type of organic molecule did he collect in the water at *B*? [1]

(iii) What does he concluded from the experiment? [2]

Or

(iii) How did his experiment work in favour of Oparin and Haldane's hypothesis? [2]

30. The data below shows the age and sex of the suspected cholera cases recorded in the Kasese District of Uganda.

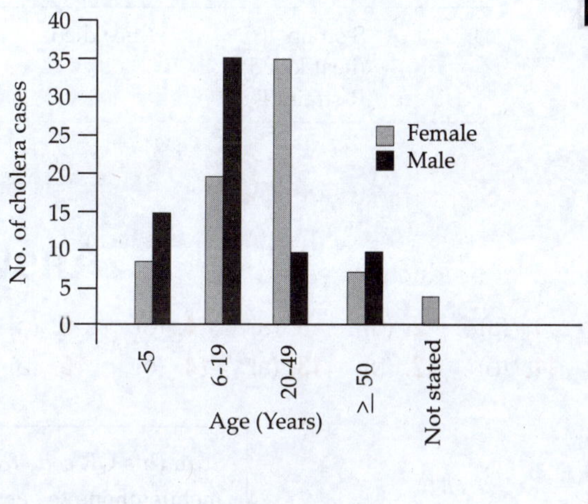

(i) With reference to the above data who suffered the most with cholera in the younger generation? [1]

(ii) What is the mechanism of transmission of *Vibrio cholerae*? [1]

(iii) What advice should be given to the citizens for the prevention of cholera? [2]

Or (iii) What are the public health solutions for the global problem of epidemic cholera? [2]

Section E Long Answer Type Questions

31. (i) Name a blood related autosomal Mendelian disorder. Why is it called Mendelian disorder? How is the disorder transmitted from parents to offspring?

(ii) Write the type of sex-determination mechanisms the following crosses show

(a) Female XX with male XO.

(b) Female ZW with male ZZ.

Or

Given below are the observations of Griffith experiment. Analyse the obervations and briefly explain each result/observation.

Situations	Strain (injected into mice)	Results
1.	S-strain	Mice died
2.	R-strain	Mice lived
3.	S-strain (heat-killed)	Mice lived
4.	S-strain (heat-killed) + R-strain (live)	Mice died

32. (i) (a) How is ART helpful, if the male partner has low sperm count in ejaculate?

(b) Also which ART is prescribed to woman who cannot produce ovum, but can provide suitable environment for fertilisation?

(ii) Draw a well-labelled diagram depicting tubectomy.

Or (i) Draw a diagrammatic sectional view of an embryo of grass and label the following

(a) Radicle (b) Coleorhiza

(c) Epiblast (d) Scutellum

(ii) (a) Describe the endosperm development in coconut.

(b) How are pea seeds different from castor seeds with respect to endosperm?

33. Explain the application of biotechnology in producing *Bt* cotton.

Or Explain how a hereditary disease can be corrected?

Give an example of the first successful attempt made towards correction of such disease.

Answer Key

1. (a)	**2.** (d)	**3.** (a)	**4.** (c)	**5.** (d)	**6.** (c)	**7.** (d)	**8.** (d)	**9.** (d)	**10.** (d)
11. (b)	**12.** (b)	**13.** (a)	**14.** (c)	**15.** (b)	**16.** (a)				

Scan this QR code from your mobile phone to get the explanations of this paper.

Knowledge Booster Zone

Welcome to the Knowledge Booster Zone !

This section is dedicated to enhancing your understanding of key concepts. Here, you will find chapter-wise revision notes designed to solidify your **foundational knowledge**. Use these notes to review and reinforce what you've learned, ensuring you're well-prepared for each topic.

Progress Tracker Tick the papers as you complete them.

- ☐ Sexual Reproduction in Flowering Plant
- ☐ Human Reproduction
- ☐ Reproductive Health
- ☐ Principles of Inheritance and Variations
- ☐ Molecular Basis of Inheritance
- ☐ Evolution
- ☐ Human Health and Diseases
- ☐ Microbes in Human Welfare
- ☐ Biotechnology: Principles and processes
- ☐ Biotechnology and its Applications
- ☐ Organisms and Population
- ☐ Ecosystem
- ☐ Biodiversity and Its Conservation

Chapter 1 Sexual Reproduction in Flowering Plants

1. Sexual Reproduction

It is a process of development of new organisms due to the fusion of male and female gametes.

It occurs through flowers in plants. Such plants are called **angiospermic** or **flowering plants.**

Male gametes are found in pollen grains and produced in the anthers of the flower. Female gametes are found in ovules and produced in the ovary of the flowers.

2. Flower

It is the site of sexual reproduction in flowering plants. Male and female reproductive structure can be found in the same individual plant. A typical flower consists of four whorls or floral appendages, attached on the receptacle, viz.

A. Calyx
B. Corolla
C. Androecium
D. Gynoecium

3. Pre-Fertilisation Events

It includes the development of male and female gametophyte.

A. **Male Reproductive Part** It consists of a stamen, microsporangium and a pollen grains.

(i) A typical stamen has two main parts, i.e. an **anther** and a long slender structure called **filament**. Anther is generally a bilobed structure with each lobe having two thecae (dithecous). Thus, it has two patches of sporogenous tissue (bearing microsporangia) in each theca which develops and becomes pollen sacs that contain pollen grains. Ploidy level of Pollen Mother Cell (PMC) is diploid i.e., 2n.

(ii) **Structure of Microsporangium** Transversely, a microsporangium appears circular in outline. It is generally surrounded by four layers, i.e. the epidermis, endothecium, middle layers and tapetum (nourishing tissue) enclosing the microspore mother cells.

(iii) **Pollen grains** are known as **male gametophytes**. Each pollen grain has a two-layered wall, i.e. sporoderm.

The outer layer is hard and known as **exine**. It is made up of sporopollenin which is one of the most resistant organic material known. Pollen grains are well preserved as fossils because of the presence of sporopollenin. The inner layer is thin, called as **intine**. It is composed of cellulose and pectin.

(iv) **Microsporogenesis** The formation of **microspores** from a pollen mother cell by meiotic division is called microsporogenesis.

Pollen grains are released by dehiscence of an anther.

These microspores later develop into microgametophytes or matured pollen grains, by the process of microgametogenesis. Each pollen grain has two cells, i.e. generative cell and vegetative cell. The vegetative cell is large and irregular shaped nucleus. It has abundant reserve food. The generative cell is small, spindle-shaped and floats in the cytoplasm of the vegetative cell. In over 60 per cent of angiosperms, pollen grains are shed at 2-celled stage and in remaining species, the generative cell dividies mitotically to give rise 10 the two male gametes before pollen grains are shed (3-celled stage).

(v) Viability of pollen grains depends on temperature and humidity, also viability varies from species to species.

Pollen grains have great economic importance as they are rich in nutrients and are used to increase performance of athletes and race horses.

It is possible to store pollen grains of a large number of species for years in liquid nitrogen (–196° C).

B. **Female Reproductive Part** The gynoecium represents the female reproductive part. It consists of pistil, megasporangium (ovule) and embryo sac.

(i) **Pistil** Each pistil consists of stigma, style and ovary.

Stigma is meant to receive pollen grains, **style** is the slender part below the stigma and the basal swollen part of style is called **ovary**.

(ii) **Ovule** (megasporangium) is attached to the placenta of the ovary, by a stalk called **funicle**. **Hilum** is the junction between ovule and **funicle**. Each ovule contains one or two protective envelopes, called **integuments**.

Micropyle is present at the tip while chalazal lies opposite to the micropylar end representing the basal part of ovule containing food reserves.

(iii) **Megasporogenesis** It is the process of formation of megaspores from megaspore mother cell by meiotic division.

In a majority of flowering plants one of the megaspore is funciton while the other there degenerate. This is called **monosporic development**.

Embryo sac or female gametophyte is formed when the nucleus of functional megaspore divides mitotically to form two nuclei, which move to the opposite poles and form 2-nucleate embryo sac, which later results into the formation of 4-nucleate and further 8-nucleate stage. These mitotic divisions are strictly free nuclear i.e. This developmental process of the functional megaspore is known as **megagametogenesis**.

The matured embryo sac contains 7-cells and 8-nuclei (polygonum type). The 6 out of 8-nuclei get surrounded by cell wall and are organised into cells. Group of three cells present towards the micropylar end, constitute the egg apparatus, i.e. two synergids and one egg cell. The 3-cells of the chalazal end are called **antipodal cells.**

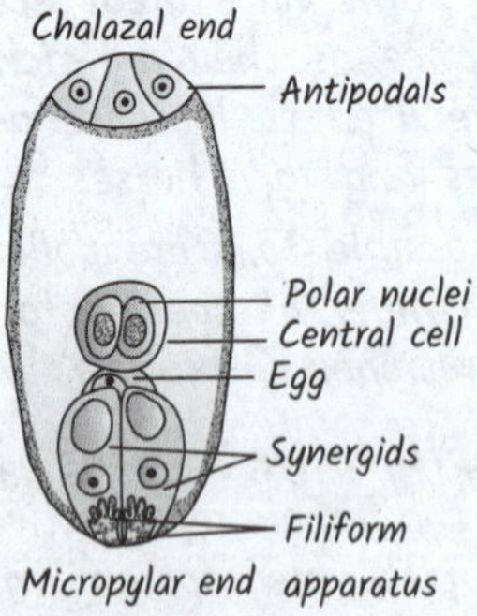

Mature Embryo sac

4. Pollination

Transfer of pollen grains from anther to stigma of a pistil is called pollination. Stamen and other whorls fall down after pollination.

A. **Self-Pollination** When pollen grains reach to the stigma of the same flower **(autogamy)** or to the stigma of the another flower of the same plant, **(geitonogamy)**, it is known as self-pollination.

It is found in both unisexual and bisexual flowers. Adaptations for self-pollination are homogamy and cleistogamy.

B. **Cross-Pollination** or **Allogamy** (Xenogamy) In this pollination, pollen grains of one plant reach to the stigma of flower of another plant of the same species. It involves two plants of the same species to produce seeds. **Unisexuality**, **dichogamy**, **self-sterility**, **heterostyly**, **dioecy** and **herkogamy** are the specific adaptations in flowering parts to prevent self-pollination. These are also known as **outbreeding devices**. Pollen grains require some agencies to reach to the stigma. These agencies are grouped as follows

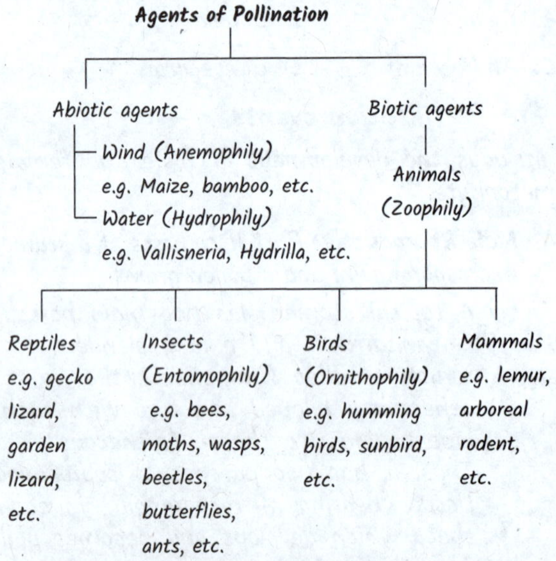

Pollination by water is quite rare in flowering plants and is limited to about 30 genera mostly monocotyledons. The fallest flower of **Amorphophallus** (the flower itself is about 6 feet in height) provide floral rewards in providing safe place to lay eggs.

5. Pollen-Pistil Interaction

It is an essential step in fertilisation of angiosperms because it determines the compatability and incompatability of pollen and pistil. It generally includes the events from the deposition of pollen on the stigma till the pollen tube enters ovule.

This pollen-pistil interaction comprises of three stages

(i) Recognition of compatible pollen

(ii) Growth of pollen tube

(iii) Entry of pollen tube into the ovule

Artificial Hybridisation

It is the crossing of different species to generate a progeny by combining desirable characters for commercially superior varieties. This process involves

(i) **Emasculation** It is the removal of anther before its dehiscence.

(ii) **Bagging** involves covering an emasculated flower in a bag to prevent its contamination by unwanted pollen grains.

6. Fertilisation

It occurs just after pollination. Fusion of male and female gametes is called fertilisation. Pollen tube enters in ovary and after fertilisation embryo is formed.

7. Double Fertilisation

It was discovered by **SG Nawaschin** in Fritillaria and Lilium plants in 1898. It involves two fusions, in which, one of the male gametes fuses with egg cell and forms diploid zygote. This is called **syngamy**. The other male gamete fuses with polar nuclei and forms (3n) triploid Primary Endosperm Nucleus (PEN). So, this is called **triple fusion**.
Formation of a triploid endosperm to nourish the developing embryo is the significance of double fertilisation in angiosperms.

8. Post-Fertilisation : Structure and Events

The major post-fertilisation events include development of endosperm and embryo, maturation of ovules into seeds and ovary into fruit. These events take place soon after double fertilisation.
Endosperm development is of three types, i.e. nuclear type, cellular type and helobial type. Out of these, nuclear type is the most common one in which the PEN undergoes repeated mitotic divisions without cytokinesis. At this stage, endosperm is called **free endosperm nucleus**.
Development of an embryo takes place at the micropylar end of the embryo sac. The zygote development gives rise to proembryo and later globular, heart-shaped stages to develop into mature embryo.
Embryos are of two types, i.e. dicot embryo, which consists of two cotyledons and monocot embryo, which consists of only one cotyledon (called **scutellum**), e.g. rice, maize, etc.

9. Development of Seed and Fruit Formation

After fertilisation, ovary converts into fruit. The wall of ovary develops into pericarp, a fleshy part of fruits. It has three layers, i.e. epicarp, mesocarp and endocarp.
Types of fruits are as follows

A. **False fruits** are derived from ovary along with thalamus or other accessory floral parts, e.g. apple, cashewnut, strawberry, etc.

B. **True fruits** are derived from ovary of flower, e.g. mango and tomato.

Ovule converts into seed which consists of seed coat, cotyledon and embryonal axis. The seed coat contains two layers, i.e. outer called **testa** (hard) and inner called **seed coat** or **tegmen**.
Two types of mature seeds are

(a) **Non-albuminous** in which endosperm is completely consumed e.g. in pea and groundnut.

(b) **Albuminous** that retain part of endosperm, e.g. castor and maize.

10. Special Modes of Reproduction

A. **Apomixis** Sometimes embryo and sporophyte develop without fusion of male and female gametes or without gametophyte formation, this is called apomixis.

B. **Polyembryony** The process of developing more than one embryo in one seed is called polyembryony. It occurs as a result of presence of more than one embryo sac in the ovule or due to the development of embryo sac from the cell other than egg cell. e.g. lemon an orange.

C. **Parthenocarpy** When development of fruit in plants occurs without pollination and fertilisation, it is called parthenocarpy. As a result of this process, seedless fruits so developed are called **parthenocarpic fruits**, e.g. grapes, banana, pineapple, papaya, etc.

11. Significance of Seed and Fruit Formation

Seeds are basis of agriculture and can be stored for long period of time. Fruits protect seed from mechanical injury. They provide food to animals who act as pollinating agents.

Chapter 2 Human Reproduction

Humans are sexually reproducing viviparous organisms, i.e. giving birth to young ones. They are unisexual, i.e. male and female sexes are separate.

1. Human Reproductive Organs

These organs are divided into primary sex organs and secondary sex organs. Primary sex organs produce gametes and sex hormones while secondary sex organs play an important role in reproduction.

2. Male Reproductive System

It is located in the pelvic region. It consists of following organs

A. **Primary Sex Organs** Testes are primary sex organs in men.

(i) **Microscopic Anatomy of Testes** These are the site where formation of male gametes or sperms takes place. These are suspended in the scrotum by **spermatic cords**. Each testis is divided into 200-300 compartments called **testicular lobules**. Each lobule contains 1-3 convoluted seminiferous tubules, blood vessels and nerves.

(ii) **Scrotum** is a pouch of deeply pigmented skin arising from the lower abdominal wall present between legs. It keeps the temperature of testes about 2-2.5°C lower than the internal body temperature, which is essential for sperm production, i.e. spermatogenesis. It remains connected with abdomen or pelvic cavity by **inguinal canals**.

(iii) **Seminiferous tubule** is the structural and functional unit of testis consisting of two specialised cells. They are as follows

- **Sertoli cells** (nurse cells) are pyramidal cells which provide nutrition to germinal cells.
- **Male germ cells** produce spermatogonia by mitotic division which grow into primary spermatocytes.

Region outside the seminiferous tubules called **interstitial spaces** contain blood vessels and interstitial cells or the **Leydig cells**. These cells secrete hormones called **androgens.**

B. **Secondary Sex Organs** It consist of the following organs

(i) **The tubuli recti** are straight tubules which join to the end of seminiferous tubules. It opens into a network of wider irregular tubules called **rete testis** which opens in **vasa efferentia**. It opens into epididymis and carries sperms outside the body.

(ii) **Epididymis** is a mass of long narrow closely coiled tubules lying along the inner side of each testis. It temporarily stores immature sperms. It helps sperms in attaining maturity, acquiring motility and fertilising capacity.

(iii) **Vasa deferentia** emerge from cauda epididymis on each side. They leave the scrotal sac and enter the abdominal cavity through inguinal canal.

(iv) **Ejaculatory ducts** are two short tubes each formed by the union of the duct from a seminal vesicle and the vas deferens.

(v) **Urethra** provides a common pathway for the passage of urine and semen.

C. **Male Accessory Glands** These are of following types

(i) **Prostate gland** is a single large gland that surrounds the urethra. It secretes a milky secretion with pH 6.5 which forms 20-30% of semen volume. The secretion contains lipids, enzymes, citric acid, etc.

(ii) **Seminal vesicles** secrete mucus and a watery alkaline fluid that contains fructose (acts as an energy source for sperms). It accounts for 60% of semen volume. **Prostaglandins** stimulate uterine contractions for sperm movement.

(iii) **Bulbourethral or Cowper's gland** secretes mucus and alkaline fluid into urethra. The mucus helps in lubrication of penis and neutralises urinary acids present in vagina.

D. **External Genitalia** It consists of **penis**. It is the male copulatory organ.

3. Female Reproductive System

It is located in pelvic cavity. It consists of following organs

A. ***Primary Sex Organs*** *Ovaries are primary sex organs in women.*

(i) ***Microscopic Anatomy of Ovaries*** *They produce female gametes (ovum) and several female hormones, i.e.* ***ovarian hormones****. The broad ligament of uterus attaches ovaries by double-layered fold of peritoneum called* ***mesovarium****.*

(ii) *These are covered by cubical epithelium, i.e. germinal epithelium. These cubical epithelia enclose ovarian stroma and it is divided into two zones, i.e. peripheral cortex and inner medulla.*

B. ***Secondary Sex Organs*** *They constitute following organs*

(i) ***Fallopian tubes*** *(oviducts) are 10-12 cm long and consist of*

(a) ***Infundibulum*** *is broad and funnel-shaped with its motile and finger-like projections called* ***fimbriae****.*

(b) ***Ampulla*** *is the widest and longest part of Fallopian tube.*

(c) ***Isthmus*** *is short, narrow and thick-walled portion that follows ampulla.*

(d) ***Uterine part*** *passes through uterine wall and communicates with uterine cavity.*

(ii) ***Uterus*** *is 7.5 cm long and 5 cm wide. It is like an inverted pear in shape. It lies between urinary bladder and rectum. It receives ovum from the Fallopian tube and forms placenta for the development of foetus. The cervix is narrow opening of uterus into vagina.*

(iii) ***Vagina*** *is about 10 cm long. It is adapted for receiving male's penis during copulation, for allowing menstrual flow and for serving as a birth canal during parturition.*

(iv) ***External genitalia*** *are collectively known as* ***vulva*** *which consists of mons pubis, clitoris and hymen.*

C. ***Accessory Glands*** *They contain a pair of Bartholin's gland. It occurs on each side of vaginal orifice.*

These glands correspond to Cowper's gland of the male and secrete a clear and viscous fluid during sexual excitement. Its secretions serves as a lubricant during copulation.

D. ***Mammary Glands*** *These are paired structures, i.e. breast in females.* ***Breast*** *are rounded paired structures located ventrally lying over the thoracic region.*

- *The glandular tissue of each breast is divided into 15-20* ***mammary lobes*** *containing clusters of* ***mammary alveoli****, which open into mammary tubules.*
- *Each breast contains a nipple in its middle, which is surrounded by circular and pigmented area called* ***areola****.*

4. Gametogenesis

It is the process of formation of haploid gametes from the undifferentiated diploid germ cells in the gonads for sexual reproduction. It is of two types, i.e. spermatogenesis in males and oogenesis in females.

A. ***Spermatogenesis*** *is the formation of spermatozoa (sperms) in testes which originate from Primordial Germ Cells (PGCs). It includes following stages*

(i) ***Multiplication Phase*** *In this phase, the undifferentiated germ cells present on the inner wall of seminiferous tubules of the testes increase in number by repeated mitotic divisions.*

(ii) ***Growth Phase*** *In this phase, some of the spermatogonia differentiate into primary spermatocytes.*

(iii) ***Maturation Phase*** *Each of these primary spermatocytes undergoes first meiotic division and produces two secondary spermatocytes (23 chromosomes) each. They further undergo second meiotic division to produce haploid spermatids. The spermatids transform into spermatozoa (sperms) by the process of* ***spermiogenesis****.*

(iv) ***Differentiation Phase*** *After spermiogenesis, sperms get embedded in Sertoli cells and are finally released from the seminiferous tubules by* ***spermiation****.*

> ***Structure of Sperm*** *A mature spermatozoa is a microscopic tadpole-shaped of about 2-5 μm in diameter and 6 μm long. It consists of head, neck, middle piece and a tail. A cap-like structure is present over the head of sperm. It contains hydrolytic enzymes that helps sperm in penetration during fertilisation.*

B. **Oogenesis** is the process of formation of a mature female gamete. The production of eggs in females begins before birth, i.e. during embryonic development stage, but is completed only after fertilisation. The following phases complete the process

(i) **Multiplication Phase** Cells of germinal epithelium undergo mitotic division producing undifferentiated germ cells called **oogonia** or **egg mother cells**. They get temporarily arrested at prophase-I of meiotic division. These cells (at this stage) are called **primary oocytes**.

(ii) **Growth Phase** Each primary oocyte when get surrounded by a single layer of granulosa cells is called **primary follicle**. At puberty stage, 60,000-80,000 primary follicles are left in each ovary. The primary follicles get surrounded by more layers of granulosa cells and new theca to form **secondary follicles**.

(iii) **Maturation Phase** During this phase, the secondary follicle transforms to tertiary follicle. These are characterised by a fluid cavity called **antrum**. The primary oocyte within tertiary follicle grows in size and completes its meiotic division to produce two daughter nuclei, i.e. **secondary oocyte** (larger haploid cell) and **first polar body** (tiny cell). The tertiary follicle further changes into a mature follicle or Graafian follicle. The secondary oocyte forms a new membrane called **zona pellucida** around it and starts its second meiotic division, but remains in metaphase-II till a sperm invades into it. The release of the secondary oocyte from the ovary is called **ovulation**.

Structure of Ovum Human female produces non-motile and rounded cell called **ovum**. It is yolk-free, i.e. alecithal. It contains abundant cytoplasm called **ooplasm** with large nucleus called **germinal vesicle**.

Hormonal Control of Gametogenesis

The pituitary hormones viz. Luteinizing Hormone (LH) and Follicle Stimulating Hormone (FSH) under the influence of Gonadotropin Releasing Hormone (GnRH, a hypothalamic hormone) regulates the process of gametogenesis in human males and females.

5. Menstrual Cycle

It is reproductive cycle in female primates, e.g. monkeys, apes and human beings. At puberty, the beginning of first menstruation is called **menarche**. In females, the menstruation is repeated at an average interval of about 28/29 days. This cycle stops at around 50 years of age and the stage is called **menopause**. The cycle consists of following four phases

(i) **Menstrual** (Bleeding) **Phase** It lasts for 3-5 days. The unfertilised egg undergoes autolysis which reduces LH level and causes regression of corpus luteum. The endometrial lining of uterus breaks down due to the deficiency of progesterone. The blood vessels rupture causing bleeding through vagina.

(ii) **Proliferative** (Follicular) **Phase** It lasts for 14 days. The primary follicles in ovary grow to become fully mature **Graafian follicles**. The endometrium regenerates through proliferation. The changes in the ovary and uterus induce changes in FSH and oestrogen.

The secretion of LH and FSH increases gradually during follicular phase.

(iii) **Ovulatory Phase** Both LH and FSH attain a peak in the middle of cycle (about 14th day). Rapid secretion of LH induces rupture of Graafian follicle and thereby release of ovum, i.e. ovulation.

(iv) **Luteal** (Secretory) **Phase** It lasts for about 10 days. The remaining parts of Graafian follicle transform into **corpus luteum**. It secretes large amounts of progesterone essential to maintain the endometrium.

6. Fertilisation

It takes place in the ampullary–isthmic junction of the Fallopian tube. The process of fusion of sperm with an ovum resulting in formation of zygote (2n) is called fertilisation.

7. Cleavage and Embryo Development upto Blastocyst Formation

After fertilisation, the meiotic division starts as zygote moves through the isthmus of the oviduct towards the uterus, forming 2, 4, 8, 16 daughter cells called **blastomeres**.

This process is called **cleavage**. The embryo with 8-16 blastomeres forms **morula** (32 cells) which at later stage transforms into **blastocyst**. This process is known as **blastulation**.

The outer layer arrangement of blastomeres in blastocyst is called **trophoblast** and inner group of cells is called **inner cell mass**.

8. Implantation

Around 6th day of fertilisation, blastocyst attaches to uterine wall and becomes embedded in endometrium of uterus. This is called **implantation** and leads to **pregnancy**.

9. Placenta Formation

It is the structural and functional unit between mother and foetus and is formed by foetal and maternal tissues. Its functions are as follows

(i) Provides nutrients and oxygen to the developing embryo.

(ii) Removes CO_2 and waste material from the embryo.

(iii) Acts as an endocrine tissue and produces several hormones like hCG, hPL, oestrogen, progesterone, etc.

10. Embryonic Development

Following changes take place in embryo after implantation. Inner cell mass of blastula differentiates into an outer layer called **ectoderm** and inner layer called **endoderm**. Mesoderm develops between these two layers.

> Kidney, heart, gonads and blood originate from mesodermal layer.
> These three layers give rise to tissues and organs. By the end of 9 months of pregnancy, the foetus becomes fully developed and is ready for delivery.

11. Extraembryonic Membrane

These are the thin protective layers enclosing the embryo inside the uterus. There are four layers, the amnion, yolk sac, allantois and chorion.

The chorion is outermost layer that helps in formation of placenta. It also helps in attachment of embryonic blastula to uterine wall.

12. Pregnancy or Gestation Period

The time duration, after the last day of menstruation to the day of parturition is known as gestation period or pregnancy. Its about 270 to 280 days in humans.

1st month – Heart formed

2nd month – Develops limbs and digits

End of 12 weak – Major organ system formed (1st trimester)

5th month - Appearance of hair

The first movements of the foetus is usually observed during the fifth month.

13. Parturition

It is the process of delivery of foetus. It is induced by the oxytocin hormone, produced due to the foetal-ejection reflexes.

14. Lactation

The production and release of milk by the mammary glands of female after birth of a young one is called lactation. Pituitary hormone prolactin, regulates production of milk, whereas the oxytocin acts as milk let-down hormone responsible for ejaculation of colostrum.

15. Colostrum

It is the first milk, produced by mammary gland after delivery, under influence of prolactin hormones. It is rich in proteins, energy and sexual antibodies like IgA. Thus, it provides passive immunity to the newborn.

Chapter 3 Reproductive Health

1. Reproductive Health

It refers to the state of healthy reproductive organs with normal functions. According to WHO, reproductive health can be defined as the total well-being in all aspects of reproduction, i.e. physical, emotional, social and behavioural.

Need for Reproductive Health

To aware society about sex related matters, sexually transmitted diseases, their transmission, control and to encourage pre-natal as well as post-natal care and to improve maternal and infant mortality rates.

2. Reproductive and Child Healthcare (RCH) **Programmes**

These programmes are for creating awareness among people about various aspects of family planning. They provide facilities and support to buildup a reproductively healthy society.

Some measures taken for RCH are

(i) Use of audio-visual and print media

(ii) Introduction of sex education

(iii) Educate about sexually transmitted diseases

(iv) Instruct people about pre and post-natal care

Note Family planning programmes were initialised in India in 1951 for healthy society development and were periodically assessed over past decades.

3. Population Explosion

The rapid increase in population over a relatively short period is called **population explosion**. Expected reasons for the population explosion may be

(i) A rapid decline in death rate (mortality).

(ii) A reduction in the Maternal Mortality Rate (MMR).

(iii) Decline in Infant Mortality Rate (IMR).

(iv) Increase in number of people of reproductive age.

Consequences of Overpopulation Some direct consequences of overpopulation are enhanced food demand, unemployment and poverty.

4. Birth Control (Contraception)

Need of birth control is essential to minimise and reduce the consequences of population explosion.

The regulation of conception by preventive methods or devices that limit the number of offsprings is called **birth control** or **contraception**. An ideal contraceptive should be user-friendly, easily available, effective, reversible with no or least side effects and non-interfering with the sexual drive/desire and/or the sexual act of the user.

Methods of Birth Control

(i) **Natural/Traditional Methods** These are based on the principle of avoiding chances of meeting sperms and ovum, e.g.

(a) **Period abstinence** (10-17th days of menstrual phase)

(b) **Coitus interruptus** or withdrawal

(c) **Lactational amenorrhea** (absence of menstruation).

(ii) **Barrier Methods** These prevent sperms and ovum from physically meeting with each other in order to prevent fertilisation, e.g. condoms, cervical caps, diaphragms and vaults.

(iii) **Chemical Methods** Spermicides available in the form of cream, jellies and foams are usually used along with the above stated barriers to increase their contraceptive efficiency.

The spermicides include lactic acid, citric acid, boric acid, zinc sulphate and potassium permanganate.

(iv) **Intrauterine Devices** (IUDs) are a form of long term, reversible contraceptive methods. These are categorised as

(a) **Copper releasing IUDs**, e.g. Cu-T, Cu-7, Multiload-375 and Paragard. Copper ions released from IUDs make uterus unsuitable for implantation.

(b) **Hormone releasing IUDs**, e.g. Progestasert, LNG-20 and Mirena.

(c) **Non-medicated IUDs**, e.g. Lippes loop.

(v) **Oral contraceptives** are preparations of hormones either progesterones or progesteron-oestrogen combinations in the form of pills, e.g. **Saheli**. These medicines inhibit ovulation and fertilisation.

They also modify the quality of cervical mucus to prevent or retard the entry of sperms. The emergency contraceptive oral pills are i-pill, pill-72, unwanted-72.

(vi) **Implants** Capsule/Implants are surgically placed under skin. These act similarly to oral contraceptives by blocking ovulation, e.g. Norplant is synthetic progesterone.

(vii) **Injection Contraceptives** These are the injection which are given at every 3 months interval. It slowly releases hormone which prevents ovulation, e.g. Depo-Provera injections.

(viii) **Surgical methods** are terminal methods used by male and female partner to prevent any more pregnancies. These are available in the form of **tubectomy** in women and **vasectomy** in men.

5. Medical Termination of Pregnancy (MTP)

MTP is intentional or voluntary termination or abortion of pregnancy before full term or before foetus becomes viable.Government of India legalised MTP in 1971 with some strict conditions to avoid its misuse.

It is prescribed only in certain cases, when pregnancy is fatal for either mother or child or both; and in cases of contraceptive failure or in cases of sexual molestations.

6. Sexually Transmitted Diseases (STDs)

These are the diseases that are mainly passed from one person to another during sexual activities. These are called as **venereal Diseases** (VDs) or Reproductive Tract Infections (RTIs).

These can be prevented by avoiding unprotected sexual intercourse. Some common STDs are genital herpes, trichomoniasis, syphilis, gonorrhoea, chlamydiasis, genital wart, hepatitis-B and AIDS. Early symptoms of STDs are swelling in genital regions, itching, fluid discharge, etc.

STDs like hepatitis-B and HIV can also be transmitted by the following measures

(i) Sharing of contaminated injection needles, surgical instruments, etc., with infected persons.
(ii) Transfusion of blood.
(iii) From infected mother to foetus.

Preventive Measures for STDs

Prevention from STDs is possible and one can avoid these infections by following the simple principles mentioned below

(i) Avoid sex with unknown/multiple partners.
(ii) Always use condoms during coitus.
(iii) Use sterilised needles and syringes.
(iv) Awareness about STDs.
(v) In case of doubt, consult a doctor as early as possible for early detection and get completely treated if diagnosed with disease.

7. Infertility

It is also one of the major aspects of reproductive health. It is mainly of two types

(i) **Primary infertility** refers to those who never had children.
(ii) **Secondary infertility** refers to a situation, when a couple had children or achieved pregnancy previously, but are unable to conceive the next time.

Some common causes of infertility in males are

- low semen quality
- oligospermia (low sperm count)
- azoospermia (absence of sperms)
- sexual dysfunction and cryptorchidism

Some common causes of infertility in females are

- polycystic ovarian syndrome
- damage or blockage of Fallopian tube
- age-related factors
- uterine problems
- previous tubal ligation.

8. Assisted Reproductive Technologies (ARTs)

ARTs include IVF, ICSI, ZIFT, etc., which now provide hope to many infertile couples.

(i) **In Vitro Fertilisation** (IVF) **or Test Tube Baby Programme** It is a technique of initiating the fertilisation process outside the female body. It is followed by the **embryo transfer** in which the embryo is placed inside the uterus with the intention to establish pregnancy.

(ii) **ZIFT and IUT** When the 8-celled blastomere stage embryo obtained by in vitro fertilisation is transferred into the Fallopian tube, the process is termed as **Zygote Intra Fallopian Transfer** (ZIFT). If more than 8-celled blastomere stage is placed directly into the lining of uterus for further development is called **Intra Uterine Transfer** (IUT).

(iii) **In Vivo Fertilisation** In this, embryos are formed when the fusion of the gametes takes place within the female body.

This could also be used to assist those females who cannot conceive.

(iv) **Gamete Intra Fallopian Transfer** (GIFT) The ovum collected from donor is transferred to the Fallopian tube of another female, who cannot produce ova, but can provide a suitable environment for fertilisation and further development. This is termed as Gamete Intra Fallopian Transfer (GIFT).

(v) **Intra Cytoplasmic Sperm Injection** (ICSI) In this, a single sperm is carefully injected into an egg using a microneedle. It is beneficial in case of male infertility, where sperm count is low.

(vi) **Artificial Insemination** (AI) It is a technique in which semen is collected from husband or healthy donor and then artificially introduced into vagina or uterus (IUI or Intra Uterine Insemination) of the female.

Amniocentesis is a medical procedure used in prenatal diagnosis of chromosomal abnormalities (genetic defects) and foetal infection. Unfortunately, this technique is being misused for sex-determination. If the sex determined comes out to be a girl, people undertake actions that lead to female foeticide. Thus, this procedure has certain legal restrictions in countries like India.

Chapter 4 Principles of Inheritance and Variations

'Like begets like' *is an important and universal phenomenon of life. It means that living beings produce offsprings of their own kind. The branch of science, which deals with the study of hereditary traits and variations is termed as* ***Genetics****.*

Inheritance *is the process by which characters of traits are passed from parent to their progeny (heredity), i.e. from one generation to the next. It is the basis of heredity.* ***Gene*** *is the unit of inheritance.*

Variation *is degree by which progeny differs from their parents.*

1. Genetic Terminology

- ***Chromosomes*** *are the hereditary vehicles which store genetic information in the form of genes. They are composed from condensed and super coiled chromatin of a cell. The chromosomes involved in the determination of sex of an organism are called* ***sex chromosomes****, while those which regulate other physical and physiological characteristics of an organism are called* ***autosomes****. Homologous chromosomes refer to a set of one maternal and one paternal chromosomes which are similar in length, gene position and centromere location, they pair up at the time of metaphase of cell division.*
- ***Gene*** *or* ***factor*** *is a structure located on chromosomes, which transfers a hereditary character from one generation to another generation. It is a unit of DNA..*
- *The alternative forms of genes for a single trait or character are called* ***alleles****, e.g. colour of flower (red and white), stem height (tall and dwarf). The allele which is expressed in heterozygous as well as its homozygous condition, it is called* ***dominant allele*** *whereas the one which is expressed only in its homozygous condition is called* ***recessive allele****.*
- ***Phenotype*** *is the physical appearance of an individual, while* ***genotype*** *is the complete genetic constitution of an individual.*
- ***Homozygous*** *A diploid condition, in which both alleles are same, e.g. TT, tt.*
- ***Heterozygous*** *A diploid condition, in which both alleles are different, e.g. Tt.*
- ***Monohybrid Cross*** *A cross in which only one pair of character is taken for study.*
- ***Dihybrid Cross*** *A cross in which two pairs of characters are taken for study.*
- ***Reciprocal Cross*** *A cross where sexes of parents are reversed.*
- ***Back Cross*** *A cross between homozygous dominant parent and F_1-hybrid progeny is known as back cross.*
- ***Test Cross*** *A cross between homozygous recessive parent and F_1-hybrid progeny is known as test cross. By this cross, it can be identified that a plant is homozygous or heterozygous.*

2. Mendel's Experiments

Mendel conducted his experiments on garden pea for seven years to investigate inheritance pattern. He had applied the statistical analysis and the mathematical logic to his experiments.

Reasons for Mendel's Success *Mendel's experiments were successful because he focussed only on one character at a time and the cross-breeding was done between the parents of purelines. The plant selected has easily detectable contrasting characters, thus he selected seven pairs of contrasting characters and all related as dominant and recessive.*

3. Mendelian Inheritance

On the basis of his observations, Mendel proposed two general rules to consolidate his understanding of inheritance in monohybrid cross. These laws are given below

A. ***Law of Dominance*** *It states following rules*
   - (i) *Characters are controlled by discrete units called* ***factors****.*
   - (ii) *Factors occur in pairs.*
   - (iii) *In a dissimilar, pair of factors, one member of the pair is dominant, while the other is recessive.*

B. ***Law of Segregation*** *It states that the parents contain two alleles during gamete formation. The factors or alleles of a pair segregate from each other, such that gamete receives only one of the two factors.*
   The following table shows the phenotypic and genotypic ratio(s) of the F_2 progeny produced

from the monohybrid cross in a pea plant, for better understanding of the above two laws

Generations/Ratio	F_2 for Monohybrid cross
Phenotypic	3 : 1
Genotypic	1 : 2 : 1

C. **Law of Independent Assortment** It states that when two pairs of traits are combined in a hybrid, segregation of one pair of characters is independent of the other pair of characters at the time of gamete formation. It also gets randomly rearranged in the offsprings producing both parental and new combinations of characters. The following table explains the law of independent assortment on the basis of ratio(s) of the F_2 progenies produced from a dihybrid cross in a pea plant.

Generations/Ratio	F_2 for Dihybrid cross
Phenotypic	9 : 3 : 3 : 1
Genotypic	1 : 2 : 1 : 4 : 2 : 2 : 1 : 2 : 1

4. Deviations from Mendelism

All patterns of inheritance could not be explained on the basis of Mendel's principles which are as follows

(i) **Incomplete Dominance** It is a phenomenon in which phenotype of the F_1-hybrid offspring does not resemble any of the parent, but is an intermediate between the expression of two alleles in their homozygous state. Phenotypic ratio is 1 : 2 : 1, e.g. flower colour in Mirabilis jalapa.

(ii) **Codominance** It is a phenomenon in which two alleles express themselves independently when present together in an organism, e.g. ABO blood grouping in humans.

(iii) **Multiple Alleles** More than two alternative forms (allele) of a gene occupying the same locus on a chromosome in a population are known as multiple alleles. e.g. ABO blood grouping.

Human Blood Groups, their Genotype and Transfusion

Blood groups	Antigen in RBC	Antibody in Plasma	Can give Blood to	Can take Blood from	Gene Type
O (universal donor)	None	a,b	O, A, B, AB	O	$I^o I^o$
A	A	b	A, AB	O, A	$I^A I^A$ or $I^A I^o$
B	B	a	B, AB	O, B	$I^B I^B$ or $I^B I^o$

(iv) **Polygenic Inheritance** The inheritance of a trait is controlled by multiple genes where each gene contributes a little to the phenotype, e.g. human skin colour.

(v) **Pleiotropy** It is the phenomenon in which a single gene may produce multiple or more than one phenotypic effects, e.g. sickle-cell anaemia, white eye in Drosophila.

5. Chromosomal Theory of Inheritance

It was proposed by **Boveri** and **Sutton** in 1902. It is a fundamental unifying theory of genetics, which identifies chromosomes as the carriers of genetic material.

6. Crossing Over

The exchange of genetic material between non-sister chromatids of homologous pair chromosomes is known as **crossing over**.

Linkage and Recombination The physical association of two genes is called **linkage** while the generation of non-parental gene combinations is called **recombination**.

7. Sex-Determination

The establishment of sex through differential development in an individual at the time of zygote formation, is called sex-determination.

There are following types of sex-determination mechanisms observed in various organisms

Male Heterogamety

(i) **XX-XO** type is seen in insects like grasshopper, etc. It is an example of male heterogamety because in this male produces two different types of gametes either with or without X-chromosome.

(ii) **XX-XY** type is seen in insects like Drosophila melanogaster and humans. Males have XY type chromosomes, while females have XX type chromosomes.

Female Heterogamety

(i) **ZZ-ZW** type is seen in birds, fowls and fishes. It is an example of female heterogamety because female produces two different types of gametes.

(ii) **ZZ-ZO** type female is heterogametic (ZO) and male is homogametic (ZZ), e.g. in butterflies and moths.

Haplo-diploidy is a sex-determination mechanism in which males develop from unfertilised eggs and are haploid. Females develop from fertilised eggs and are diploid. It is common in insects like honeybee, wasps, etc.

Note
- In Drosophila melanogaster (fruit fly), the sex is determined by the ratio of sex chromosomes with the autosomes, i.e. the ratio theory or the genetic balance theory of Bridges.
- On the basis of type of allosomes present in the gamete, the parents can be of two types
  (i) Homogametic produces similar gametes.
  (ii) Heterogametic produces different gametes.

- **Sex-Determination in Human** Males have two types of gametes, i.e. X and Y, while females have only one type of gamete, i.e. XX. If an ovum gets fertilised with a sperm carrying X-chromosome, the zygote will develops into a female (XX). If an ovum fertilises with a sperm carrying Y-chromosome then it will develop into a male (XY). Hence, the type of sperm, which fertilises the ovum determines the sex of a child.

8. Sex-Linked Inheritance

It is the phenomenon of appearance of trait which occurs due to the presence of an allele either on the X or on the Y-chromosome. The sex-linked inheritance can be of following two main types

(i) **X-linked inheritance** which includes the genes located on X-chromosomes, e.g. haemophilia, colour blindness.

(ii) **Y-linked inheritance** which includes the genes located on Y-chromosomes. This can occur only in males (not in females), e.g. baldness, outgrowth of hairs on ears.
- **Sex-linked Inheritance in Drosophila** In this inheritance eye colour is associated with sex of parents.
- Morgan concluded from his experiments that only X-chromosome carries the gene for eye colour and is therefore, it is a X-linked or sex-linked trait.
- Similarly, the wing type in Drosophila, is usually controlled by an **autosomal gene**. However, it was found that miniature and rudimentary wings are **sex-linked traits**, with poor viability.

9. Mutation

It is sudden, stable and inheritable change in genetic material or DNA sequences of an organism. The organism which undergoes mutation is called **mutant**.

The factors, i.e. chemical and physical stimulants which induce mutations are called **mutagens**, e.g. UV-radiations, etc.

The mutations are of following types

(i) **Spontaneous mutations** originate spontaneously and are generally produced naturally by mutagenic agents such as atomic particles, rays, temperature, electric currents, etc. Their frequency of occurrence is relatively low.

(ii) **Induced mutations** are induced artificially by subjecting organisms to the mutagens such as high energy radiations, chemicals, etc. Their frequency is comparatively higher.

(iii) **Substitution mutations** are caused by the replacement of a base pair of a nucleotide. These may be further divided as
- **Transition** purine base is replaced by another purine and a pyrimidine base replaced by another pyrimidine base.
- **Transversion** A purine is replaced by a pyrimidine and vice-versa.
- **Point mutation** arises due to the change in single base pair of DNA.
- **Frameshift mutation** refers to deletions and insertions of base pairs in DNA.

The loss or gain of a segment of DNA, results in **structural alteration in chromosomes** because genes are located on the chromosomes.

When the members of a homologous pair of chromosomes fail to segregate during meiosis, **aneuploidy** occurs, i.e. loss or gain of one or more chromosomes. Due to this, there may be **monosomy** (i.e. lack of one chromosome of normal complement) or **trisomy** (i.e. three instead of normal two chromosomes) of a chromosome.

Polyploidy occurs when there is failure of cytokinesis after telophase stage of cell division. It results in increase in a whole set of chromosomes in an organism.

10. Pedigree Analysis

The analysis of traits in several generations of a human family in the form of a family tree or a diagram is known as pedigree analysis.

11. Human Genetic Disorders

The disorders or illness which are caused by one or more abnormalities in autosomes or sex chromosomes of a person are called **autosomal disorders** and **sex-linked disorders**, respectively. It can be divided into the following

I. **Mendelian Disorders** These are determined by alteration or mutation in a single gene. These disorders can be recessive or dominant.

Some diseases are described below

A. **Colour Blindness** Person suffering from this disorder is not able to distinguish between red and green colour. Gene controlling colour blindness is located on X-chromosome and is recessive.

B. **Haemophilia** (bleeder's disease) Person suffering from this disorder is not able to form blood clots when hurt or wounded. The continuous bleeding causes death of the person. This disorder is caused due to X-linked recessive gene.

C. **Sickle-cell Anaemia** It is an autosomal-linked recessive trait that occurs due to the substitution of an amino acid in the β-globin chain of haemoglobin.

D. **Phenylketonuria** (PKU) is an inborn error metabolism, which is inherited as an autosomal recessive trait. Its gene is associated to the 12th chromosome.

E. **Thalassemia** is an autosomal recessive disease, which occurs due to the either mutation or deletion of genes. It results in reduced rate of synthesis of one of the globin chains of haemoglobin.

II. **Chromosomal Disorders** These are caused by the absence, excess or abnormal arrangement of one or more chromosomes.

Some of the disorders are described below

(i) **Down's Syndrome or Mongolism** It is caused by the presence of an extra copy of chromosome number 21 in autosomes, i.e. trisomy. Therefore, individual suffering from Down's syndrome are short statured, furrowed tongue with slow motor mental development.

(ii) **Turner's Syndrome** It is caused by the absence of one X-chromosome in female. The females have 45 (44+X) chromosomes. Uterus is less developed, short height and webbed neck are the symptoms.

(iii) **Klinefelter's Syndrome** It is due to the presence of an extra copy of X-chromosome in males like 44+XXY, 44+XXXY, etc. The symptoms include under developed testes, presence of breast-like structures, little growth of hair on face and body, sterility (no sperm formation), mental retardedness, etc.

Chapter 5 Molecular Basis of Inheritance

1. Search for Genetic Material

Frederick Griffith, carried out a series of experiments with Streptococcus pneumoniae and discovered the genetic material as the transforming principle.

Avery, **MacLeod** and **McCarty** worked to determine the biochemical nature of Griffith's transforming principle. They proved that DNA is the hereditary material.

Hershey and Chase's experiment with bacteriophage gave the proof that DNA is the genetic material that is passed from one generation to the next.

2. DNA as Genetic Material

DNA acts as a genetic material in most organisms. It is a long polymer of deoxyribonucleotides. It codes for all the metabolic processes of life.

RNA acts as genetic material in viruses and viroids and helps in the transfer and expression of information in cellular organisms. It functions as messenger RNA (mRNA) for the translation of proteins.

3. Structure of DNA and RNA

In 1869, **Johannes Friedrich Miescher** had discovered the DNA. Later in 1953, **James Watson** and **Francis Crick** proposed the double helix model of DNA from the X-ray photographs of **Wilkins** and **Franklin** (1953).

Nucleic Acids These are long polymers of nucleotides. Two types of nucleic acids are found in living systems, i.e. RNA and DNA.

Nucleoside and Nucleotide A nucleoside is formed when a nitrogenous base is linked to a pentose sugar through a N-glycosidic linkage.

A nucleotide is the basic unit of DNA and RNA and is composed of a nitrogenous base, a pentose sugar and a phosphate group. **Nitrogenous bases** are of two types, i.e. purines (adenine, guanine) and pyrimidines (cytosine, uracil, thymine).

RNA contains uracil in place of thymine.

Two types of sugars are present in RNA and DNA, i.e. ribose and deoxyribose, respectively.

- RNA functions as adapter, structural and as a catalytic molecule.
- RNA also acts as a genetic material in some viruses.
- Although both RNA and DNA can act as genetic material, but DNA being chemically and structurally more stable, is a better choice.
- RNA was the first to evolve and DNA was derived from RNA.
- Adenine pairs with thymine through two H-bonds, while the guanine pairs with cytosine through three H-bonds. This makes one strand complementary to the other.

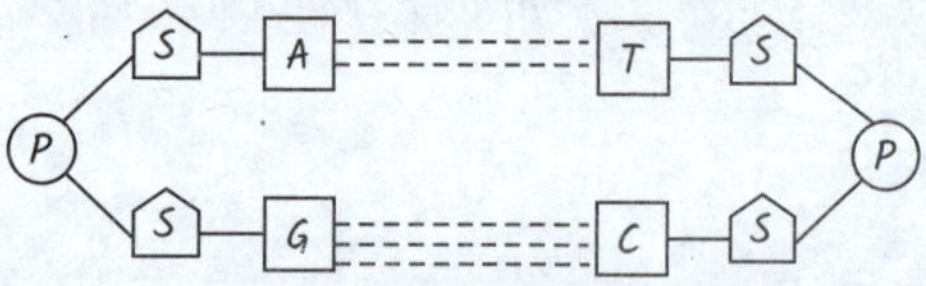

Polynucleotide chain

Chargaff's base equivalence rule, states that purine and pyrimidines are present in equal amount in DNA, i.e.

$$\frac{A+G}{T+C}=1$$

4. DNA Packaging

(i) In **prokaryotic cells,** DNA (negatively charged) is held together with some proteins (positively charged) in a region known as **nucleoid**.

(ii) In **eukaryotic cells**, there is a set of positively charged proteins called **histones** which are organised to form a unit of eight molecules called **histone octamer**. The negatively charged DNA is wrapped around the positively charged histone octamer to form a structure called **nucleosome** which is the unit of compaction.

5. Packaging of Chromatin

The packaging of chromatin at higher level requires additional set of proteins that are collectively called as **Non-Histone Chromosomal (NHC) proteins**.

6. Euchromatin and Heterochromatin

Some regions of chromatin which is loosely packed (stain light) is called euchromatin (active chromatin). In some regions, chromatin is densely packed (stain dark), so it is called heterochromatin (inactive chromatin).

7. Central Dogma of Molecular Biology

Francis Crick proposed the 'central dogma' in molecular biology, which states that genetic information flows in the following manner

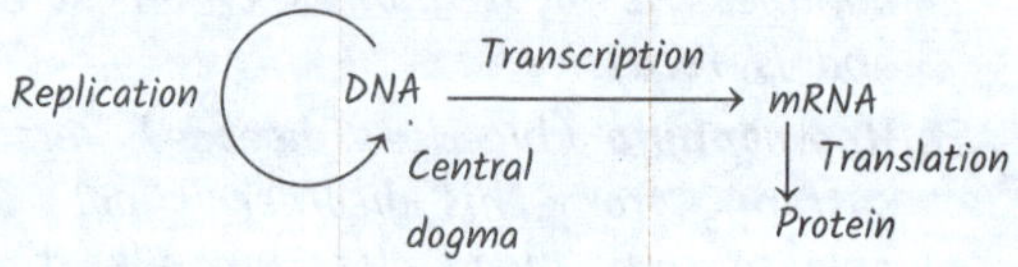

Temin and **Baltimore** discovered the reverse transcription in certain viruses which are exception to central dogma. According to which genetic information flows as

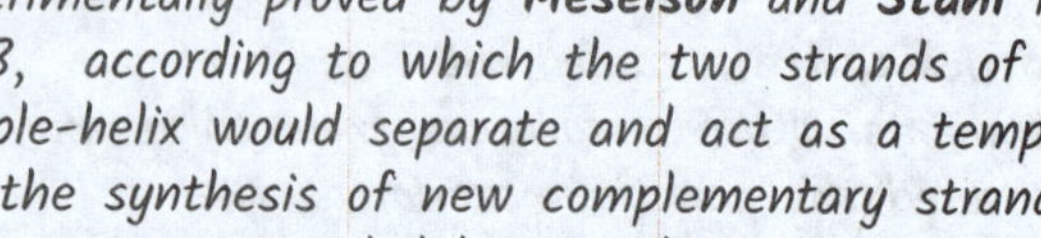

8. DNA Replication

The DNA replicates semiconservatively. This scheme was proposed by **Watson** and **Crick**, but experimentally proved by **Meselson** and **Stahl** in 1958, according to which the two strands of double-helix would separate and act as a template for the synthesis of new complementary strands. The process is guided by complementary H-bonding. The process is catalysed by various sets of enzymes which are as follows

(i) **DNA dependent DNA polymerase,** uses DNA template to catalyse the polymerisation of deoxyribonucleotides.

(ii) **DNA helicase**, unwinds DNA strands for the formation of a replication fork.

(iii) **DNA ligase,** facilitates the joining of DNA strands together by catalysing the formation of phosphodiester bond.

On 3′ → 5′ strand, replication is **continuous** and on 5′ → 3′ strand, it is **discontinuous** and leads to the formation of Okazaki fragments.

DNA replication begins at a specific and fixed position of DNA molecule known as **origin of replication.**

9. Transcription in Eukaryotes and Prokaryotes

Transcription is the process of copying genetic information from one strand of the DNA into RNA. In this only a segment of DNA or only one out of the two strands is copied into RNA.

(i) **In prokaryotes** like bacteria, the transcribed mRNA is functional, so it can be directly translated.

(ii) In eukaryotes, the genes are split. The coding sequences, i.e. exons are interrupted by non-coding sequences, i.e. introns. Introns are removed and exons are joined together to produce functional RNA. This is called splicing. A transcription unit in DNA has three regions, i.e. a promoter, the structural gene and a terminator.

Note Cistron is the segment of DNA, which codes for a polypeptide.

10. Post Transcriptional Modifications

Heteronuclear RNA (hnRNA) The hnRNA undergoes two additional processes

(i) **Capping,** where methyl guanosine triphosphate, is added to the 5′ end of hnRNA.

(ii) **Tailing,** where adenylate residues (200-300) are added at 3′ end in a template independent manner.

Types of RNA

There are following three types of RNA, i.e. **messenger RNA** (mRNA) which provides the template for translation, **transfer RNA** (tRNA), which brings amino acids and reads the genetic code and **ribosomal RNA** (rRNA), which plays structural and catalytic role during translation.

11. Genetic Code

It is the relationship between the sequence of nucleotides on mRNA and the sequence of amino acids in the polypeptide chain.

(i) **Artificial Synthesis of Genetic Code**
Dr. Har Gobind Khorana, developed a chemical method for the synthesis of RNA molecule with defined base combination to develop a genetic code.

(ii) **Important Features of Genetic Code** It has following features

- Genetic code is **unambiguous** and **specific**, i.e. one codon codes for only one amino acid. **Codon** is triplet and degenerate.
- The genetic code is **universal**, i.e. one codon codes for the same amino acid in all organisms.
- AUG codon has dual functions, i.e. it codes for the amino acid **methionine** (met) and also acts as an **initiator** codon.
- Three codons do not code for any amino acid, hence they function as stop codon, e.g. UAA, UGA, UAG.

Note tRNA is an adapter molecule which could read the code on one end and on the other end could bind to the specific amino acid. tRNA has five loops, i.e. anticodon loop, amino acid acceptor end, T-loop, D-loop and variable loop. It is a clover leaf-shaped molecule.

12. Translation

The process of polymerisation of amino acids to form a polypeptide is known as translation. In protein synthesis, tRNA, mRNA and ribosomes are required.

(i) **Ribosomes** exist as two subunits in inactive state, i.e. small subunit and large subunit.

(ii) Different phases of translation are

- Initiation of polypeptide synthesis.
- Elongation of polypeptide chain.
- Termination of polypeptide synthesis.

13. Gene Expression and Regulation

Regulation of gene expression occurs at various levels. Gene expression results in the formation of a polypeptide.

(i) In **prokaryotes**, it is regulated by the rate of initiation of transcription and in **eukaryotes**, regulation is achieved at the following four levels

- Transcriptional level (formation of primary transcript).
- Processing level (regulation by splicing)

- Transport of mRNA from nucleus to the cytoplasm.
- Translational level.

(ii) **Operon** is a transcriptionally regulated system, where a polycistronic structural gene is regulated by a common promoter and regulatory genes, e.g. lac (lactose) operon, ara (arabinose) operon, his (histidine) operon, val (valine) operon, etc. Lac **operon** model was proposed by Francois Jacob and Jacque Monod.

(iii) **Lac operon** is the prototype operon in bacteria, which codes for the enzymes responsible for the metabolism of lactose.

The operon is regulated by the amount of lactose in the medium, where the bacteria are grown. Therefore, this regulation can also be viewed as regulation of enzyme synthesis by its substrate.

14. Human Genome Project

The human genome project was a mega 13 year project coordinated by the U.S department of energy and the National Institute of Health.

15. Rice Genome Project

Rice was the first crop whose genome was sequenced. It was a project of 10 years. It provided an excellent opportunity to illustrate the impact on plant biology and breeding. The knowledge of genetic code of rice helps breeders to develop strains of the crop with specific characteristics (e.g. stress tolerance, disease resistance or high yield).

16. DNA Fingerprinting

It is a technique to find out variations in individuals of a population at DNA level. It works on the principle of polymorphism in DNA sequences. It has immense applications in the field of forensic science, genetic biodiversity, evolutionary biology and kinship relationships. The technique has the following steps

(i) DNA isolation

(ii) Amplification

(iii) Separation of DNA fragments by electrophoresis

(iv) Blotting (transfer of the separated DNA fragments to synthetic membranes like nylon or nitrocellulose)

(v) Hybridisation

(vi) Autoradiography

Chapter 6 Evolution

1. Evolution

It is the sequence of gradual changes from simple life forms to complex forms, i.e. from primitive organisms that lived over million of years ago to new organisms that exist today.

2. Origin of Life

Our earth originated about **4.6 billion years ago**, whereas the origin of life on earth occurred 4 billion years after its formation.

The **Big-Bang theory** (given by **Abbe Lemaitre** in 1931) explains about the origin of earth as a terrible explosion resulting in the formation of universe or cosmos.

3. Ancient Theories for Origin of Life

(i) **Special Creation** It states that god has created the life.

(ii) **Cosmozoic Theory** It states that life arose from the spores or panspermia which came from outer space.

(iii) **Spontaneous Generation Theory** According to this, the life originated from abiotic substances spontaneously. Therefore, this theory is also called as theory of **abiogenesis** or **autobiogenesis.**

(iv) **Theory of Biogenesis** It states that life has originated from pre-existing life and it was supported by **F Redi**, **Spallanzani**, **L Pasteur** and others.

(v) **Louis Pasteur** rejected the theory of spontaneous generation. He demonstrated that life evolved from pre-existing life by his swan-neck flask experiment.

(vi) **Theory of Chemical Evolution** It was given by **Oparin** and **Haldane.** According to them, first form of life originated in reducing environment that lack oxygen, from pre-existing, non-living organic molecules (e.g. RNA, protein, etc.) i.e. **chemical evolution** and then it led to the formation of life, (i.e. **biological evolution**).

On primitive earth, organic macromolecules aggregated due to the intermolecular attractions and got precipitated as colloidal particles in hot pre-biotic soup, which were termed as **coacervates.**

Protobionts were the protocells or the nucleoproteinoid molecules which resemble the present day virus and viroids.

(vii) **Miller and Urey's Experiment** (Evidence of Chemical Evolution) **Stanley Miller** (1953) performed a simple experiment under the guidance of **Harold Urey**. They inoculated water vapour along with hydrogen, methane and ammonia (in 2 : 2 : 1 ratio) in a flask and provided an electric discharge by tungsten's electrode.

The amino acids such as glycine, alanine, etc., were formed in their experiment. By this experiment, it was proved that C, H, O and N in various forms can give rise to complex compounds.

4. Modern Concept of Origin of Life or Biological Evolution

It refers to the origin of first living cell from non-living chemical complexes.

5. Evidences for Biological Evolution

A. **Palaeontological evidences** come from the study of fossils. The fossils are the remains of past organisms preserved in sedimentary rocks.

(i) **Fossil records/Inscriptions** are the remains or impressions of the hard parts of ancient plants and animals on rocks and mountains. The process by which animals or plants become a fossil is called **fossilisation**.

'Study of fossils' is called **palaeontology**.

(ii) **Geological time scale** By the study of fossils occurring in different strata of rocks, geologists have evolved a geological time scale which gives time and course of evolution of life on earth.

B. **Comparative Anatomy and Morphological Evidences** These show the similarities and differences among the organisms of today and those that existed many years ago. This can be achieved by the study of following evidences

(i) **Homologous organs** are the organs which having same structural design and origin but different functions, e.g. forelimbs of some animals like whales, bats and cheetah, mouth parts of various insects, etc.

(ii) **Analogous organs** are the organs which are anatomically different but functionally similar, e.g. wings of butterfly and birds. Analogy is based on convergent evolution.

(iii) **Vestigial organs** are rudimentary and non-functional organs that were earlier functional in ancestors.

Divergent Evolution It refers to the development of different functional structures from a common ancestral stock in order to adapt to different environmental conditions.

Convergent Evolution Development of similar morphological characters in the organisms of different lineages at same geographical regions is called convergent evolution.

C. **Biochemical evidences** (Molecular evidences) suggest that the similarities in proteins and genes performing a common function among diverse organisms indicates a common ancestry, e.g. common genetic code is shared universally.

D. **Embryological evidences** suggest that some organisms that show common descent embryological patterns (i.e. ontogeny repeats phylogeny), on which they later build their adult patterns. This was first observed by **von Baer** and later reinterpreted by Haeckel in the form of **recapitulation** or **biogenetic law.**

E. **Biogeographical evidences** suggest that the species restricted to a region develop unique features leads to formation of a biogeography, i.e. geographical distribution of flora and fauna. Also, species present in separated regions show similarity of ancestry. This can be explained with the help of **adaptive radiation**. It is an evolutionary process in which an ancestral stock gives rise to new species adapted to new habitats and new ways of life, e.g. Darwin's finches, marsupials of Australia and placental animals in Australia.

6. Theories and Mechanism of Evolution

Various theories were put forward by scientists to explain the evolutionary mechanism.

(i) **Lamarckism or Theory of Inheritance of Acquired Characters** Lamarck published a book named 'Philosophie Zoologique' in 1809 to *propose this theory. It states that each organism acquires many characters in his lifetime from the environment he lives in. These acquired characters are inherited by the offspring to form a new species gradually.*

Any organ which is used more, slowly enlarges in size and the organ which is not used, degenerates, e.g. degeneration of legs of snake, elongation of neck in giraffe. This theory was highly criticised.

(ii) **Modern Lamarckism** August Weismann in 1892 proved using genetics and theories of inheritance that characters, present in genotype of an individual are transmitted to next generation by inheritance. This theory was named as **Theory of Continuity of Germplasm.**

(iii) **Darwinism or Theory of Natural Selection** Darwin concluded that the fitness of individual ultimately refers to its reproductive fitness. Thus, those organisms which are better or adapt well will survive more in nature just like long neck girraffe were selected as they were better adapted. Hence, this is called **natural selection.** He also explained that different species descending from common ancestor get adapted into different habitats. This is called **branching descent**. Therefore, natural selection and branching descent are two important concepts of Darwinism.

Malthus proposed a theory of human population growth, in which he stated that natural calamities (positive checks) balances the over population of a species.

Darwin alongwith **Alfred Wallace** jointly propounded the 'Theory of natural selection' in 1958. It was based on following factual observations

(a) Limited natural resources, stable population (except for seasonal fluctuations).

(b) Variations (in sexually reproductive animals).

(c) Reproductive isolation, etc.

- **Industrial Melanism** An example of evolution by natural selection. It was observed in peppered moths (Biston betularia) in 1859s in England.
  Before industrialisation, white-winged moths were more in number compared to dark-winged moths. After industrialisation, dark-winged moths increased in number, as they were able to camouflage themselves from predators on tree trunks turned darker due to the air pollution (soot and dust particles).
  The white-winged moth population declined due to the easy detection by predators. Thus, in a mixed population, better adaptable species are selected by nature to grow while others are eliminated.
- **Chemical Resistance** The excessive use of chemicals leads to development of resistance in organisms to chemicals. Such as mosquito larva and bacteria developed resistance for DDT and antibiotics, respectively. These organisms are selected naturally due to the favourable variation.

(iv) **Neo-Darwinism** (Modern Synthetic Theory of Evolution) Modern synthetic theory is actually a form of modern Darwinism. It states that the origin of species is based on the interaction of genetic variation in a population, natural selection and reproductive isolation.

(v) **Mutation Theory of Hugo de Vries** He studied and carried out experiments on a plant, evening primrose (Oenothera lamarckiana).

He proposed the mutation theory of evolution on the basis of his observations. de Vries proposed that evolution can also occur due to the sudden large changes (variations) occurring in a population which caused speciation and called it **saltation** (single step large mutation).

7. Hardy-Weinberg Principle

According to it, the allele frequencies in a population are stable and remain constant from generation to generation. This is called **genetic equilibrium.**

It is expressed as $p^2 + q^2 + 2pq = 1$

[i.e. binomial expansion of $(p+q)^2$]

8. Agents of Evolutionary Change

There are following factors which affect the Hardy-Weinberg's principle and the basic mechanisms through which biological evolution takes place

(i) **Genetic Drift** (Random Drift) It is a change that occurs in allelic frequencies by chance. Sometimes due to the changes in allele frequency in new population, some different species are formed. This is called **founder effect** and the original drifted population is called **founder**.

Change events like natural calamities may eleminate a specific allele from entire population, this phenomenon is called **bottle-neck effect**.

(ii) **Gene Flow or Migration** It is the movement of alleles from one population to another.

(iii) **Natural Selection** It occurs due to the inheritance of variations. It leads to the survival of those who best fit in an environment. It can be of three types, i.e. stabilised, directional and disruptive.

(iv) **Genetic Recombination** During gametogenesis, crossing over in meiosis leads to new combination of genes.

(v) **Mutations** They cause genetic variations over a long period of time and leads to additon of new genes in gene pool.

9. Account of Evolution

The cellular forms of life first appeared on earth around 2000 million years ago (mya).

A. **Evolution of Plants**

Plants appeared first on lands before animals.

Bryophytes were the first plants to colonise land followed by vascular plants.

Vascular plants (pteridophytes and gymnosperms) first originated in **Silurian period**.

Herbaceous lycopods and **arborescent lycopods** evolved from Zosterophyllum of **Palaeozoic era**.

Psilophyton is the common ancestor for horsetails, ferns and gymnosperms.

B. **Evolution of Animals**

Animals evolved around 500 mya and first animals were invertebrates. Jawless fish and amphibious fish with stout and strong fins were found on earth around 350 mya.

The Jurassic period is called **age of reptiles,** i.e. around 200 mya. Mammals appeared in Triassic period and the first mammals were like shrews.

10. Human Evolution

The fossil evidences indicate that origin of man occurred in Central Asia, China, Java and India (Shivalik hills).

The human population took place as follows

Human Ancestors	Time of Origin	General Features
Dryopithecus	20-25 mya	Ape-like, hairy, ate soft fruits and leaves. Arms and legs of same length, large brain.
Ramapithecus	14-15 mya	More man-like, walked more erect, teeth like modern man.
Australopithecus (The first ape man)	3-4 mya	Probably lived in East African grasslands and ate fruits, hunted with stones, weapons, brain capacity was 400-600 cc.
Homo habilis (Handy man)	2 mya	Fossils found in East Africa, first hominid, i.e. human being- like, brain capacity 650-800 cc, did not eat meat.
Homo erectus (Java man)	1.5 mya	Fossils found in Java in 1891, brain capacity 900 cc, probably ate meat.
Homo sapiens neanderthalensis (Primitive man)	1,00,000-40,000 years ago	Known as Neanderthal man. Fossils found in East and Central Asia, brain size 1400 cc, used hides to protect body, buried their dead. They became extinct 25,000 years ago.
Homo sapiens (Modern man)	75,000-10,000 years ago (ice age)	Arose in Africa, developed cave art around 18,000 years ago, agriculture started around 10,000 years back and thus human settlement and civilisation started.

Cro-Magnon man is the closest to modern man, that was excavated from France in 1868. Its physique is similar to modern man with cranial capacity of 1650 cc (more than modern man).

Chapter 7 Human Health and Diseases

1. Health

According to World Health Organisation (WHO), health is state of physical, mental and social well-being and not merely an absence of disease or infirmity. .

2. Diseases

It is defined as any disorder or hindrance that arises in normal functioning of the body and brain.

Factors causing disease are called **causative agents** or **pathogens** or **germs** like bacteria, virus, fungi, protozoans, etc., Diseases can be classified as given below

A. **Congenital or Inherited Diseases** These are the diseases which are inherited from generation to generation, e.g. haemophilia, colour blindness, sickle-cell anaemia, etc.

B. **Acquired Diseases** These diseases develop after birth due to the many factors like causative agent, deficiency of nutrients or hormones, etc., e.g. kwashiorkor, marasmus, night blindness, scurvy, cancer, addiction, arthritis, allergy, etc.

Acquired diseases are further classifed as

(i) **Communicable Diseases** (Infectious Diseases) These diseases can be transmitted from infected person to a healthy person, e.g. malaria, typhoid, cold, amoebiasis, AIDS, gonorrhoea, syphilis, hepatitis, etc.

(ii) **Non-communicable Diseases** (Non-Infectious Diseases) These diseases cannot be transmitted from person to person and are not caused by pathogens. They are caused by nutritional deficiency, malfunctioning of organs, etc., e.g. cancer, scurvy.

3. Some Common Infectious Diseases in Humans

The diseases caused by infections are classified on the basis of pathogens involved, i.e. causative agents. Some common diseases are given below

A. Bacterial Diseases

(i) **Enteric fever or Typhoid** is caused by bacterium Salmonella typhi. It enters the small intestine through contaminated food and water.

Symptoms include fever (39-40°C), weakness, stomach pain, constipation, headache and loss of appetite.

Widal test is used to diagnose typhoid fever.

(ii) **Pneumonia** The causative agents of pneumonia are Streptococcus pneumoniae and Haemophilus influenzae. Pneumonia infects the alveoli of the lungs due to which the alveoli get filled with fluid leading to problem in breathing.

Symptoms are fever, chills, cough and headache.

(iii) **Plague** is caused by Pasteurella/Yersinia pestis and is also called **black death**.

(iv) **Diphtheria** is caused by Corynebacterium diphtheriae and is characterised by difficulty in breathing due to infection in the mucous membrane of upper respiratory tract.

B. Viral Diseases

(i) **Common cold** is caused by rhinoviruses. These viruses majorly affect nose and respiratory tract, but not the lungs. The infection is transmitted through droplets resulting from coughing or sneezing of an infected person.

Symptoms include nasal congestion and discharge, sore throat, hoarseness, cough, headache, tiredness, etc.

(ii) **Chikungunya** is caused by chikungunya virus. It is transmitted by the bite of Aedes aegypti mosquito. **Symptoms** include sudden onset of fever, crippling joint pains, lymphodenopathy, etc. The fever is typically biphasic.

(iii) **Dengue** is caused by Flavivirus and transmitted by the bite of female Aedes and Culex mosquito. There is no proper treatment for dengue fever, but analgesics are provided to the patients to reduce the effect of fever.

Symptoms are high fever, headache, nausea, pain in joints and vomiting.

(iv) **AIDS** (Acquired Immuno Deficiency Syndrome) is a fatal disease. It is caused by HIV (Human Immunodeficiency Virus), which is a member of group of viruses called **retrovirus**.

It spreads from one person to other via body fluids.

The virus replicates in the macrophages by reverse transcription to infect helper T-lymphocytes. Thus, count of T-lymphocytes decreases in the patient and it becomes immunodeficient and cannot protect himself/herself from other severe infections.

It is symptomised by recurring infections, loss of weight and appetite, fatigue, diarrhoea, swollen lymph nodes, etc.

HIV can be transmitted through sexual contact, sharing infected needles, transfusion of contaminated blood and from infected mother to foetus through placenta.

HIV infection can be diagnosed by **Enzyme Linked Immuno Sorbent Assay** (ELISA), **Polymerase Chain Reaction** (PCR) and Western blotting methods.

There is no treatment for HIV, but use of antiviral drugs can only prolong the life of patient, but cannot prevent death.

Prevention and Control
Blood banks should be screened for HIV, use of disposable needles and syringes, use of condoms during coitus and promote regular checkup for HIV.

C. Protozoan Diseases

(i) **Malaria** This is caused due to the infection of a protozoan, i.e. Plasmodium in the form of sporozoites. It has two hosts

(a) **Primary host** (for asexual cycle) is human.

(b) **Secondary host** (for sexual cycle) is female Anopheles.

Different species of Plasmodium are P. ovale, P. falciparum, P. vivax and P. malariae.

Haemozoin is released into blood due to the rupture of RBCs during the infection of Plasmodium vivax at every 24 hours.

Symptoms are shivering chills, headache, muscle ache, nausea, vomiting, diarrhoea and in severe cases anaemia and jaundice.

(ii) **Amoebiasis** (Amoebic Dysentery or Enteritis) This disease is caused by protozoan Entamoeba histolytica found in large intestine of human. This is a hostile parasite, whose infectious stage is trophozoite. It is transmitted by housefly. It transmits the parasite from faeces of an infected person to food and water.

Symptoms include constipation, abdominal pain, cramps, stools with excess mucus and blood clots.

D. Helminthic Diseases

(i) **Ascariasis** This disease spreads by helminth parasite Ascaris lumbricoides (unhostile), which is an intestinal parasite. It is transmitted through contaminated water, vegetables, fruits, etc.

Symptoms are internal bleeding, muscular pain, fever, anaemia and blockage of intestinal passage.

(ii) **Filariasis** (Elephantiasis) This disease is caused by Wuchereria bancrofti and W. malayi. This is a bi-hostile parasite, i.e. primary host is human, secondary host is female Culex fatigans mosquito.

Symptoms include chronic inflammation that develops slowly. When worms live for many years inflammation arises mostly in lymphatic vessels of the lower limbs, even genital organs also get affected.

E. Fungal Diseases

Ringworms are caused by fungi like Microsporum, Trichophyton and Epidermophyton. They are generally acquired by soil or by direct contact with contaminated articles used by infected person.
Symptoms include dry scaly lesions on various parts of body such as skin, nails and scalp with intense itching.

4. Preventive Measures for Infectious Diseases

(i) **Personal Hygiene** Regular bathing, consumption of clean drinking water, food, etc.

(ii) **Public Hygiene** Proper disposal of waste and excreta, periodic cleaning and disinfection of water reservoirs, pools, etc.

(iii) **For vector borne diseases such as malaria** includes eradication of vectors and destroying their breeding sites. It can be done by using mosquito nets and repellents, avoiding stagnation of water, introducing fishes like Gambusia in ponds that feeds on mosquito larvae and spraying of insecticides in open water bodies.

(iv) **For Air Borne Diseases** Avoid contact with infected persons or their belongings.

(v) **Vaccination and immunisation** utilises the property of 'memory' of immune system. During vaccination, antigenic proteins or weakened pathogens are injected in the body, where they neutralise the causal agent. When immunisation is achieved by injecting preformed antibodies (e.g. snake bite), it is called **passive immunisation.**

5. Non-Infectious Disease

Cancer

Normal body cells show a property called **contact inhibition** by virtue of which body cells stop their growth and cell division on coming in contact with other cells. Cancerous cells do not have this property due to which they continue to divide forming **tumours** or **neoplasm.**

(i) **Tumour** is a mass of cells formed due to the uncontrolled division of cells. These are of two types

- **Benign tumour** remain confined to their original location and does not spread in the entire body.
- **Malignant tumour** is the mass of proliferating cells, called **neoplastic** or **tumour cells**. These grow rapidly, invade and damage the surrounding normal cells by proliferating to other body parts through blood and body fluids. This cancerous activity of malignant tumours is called **metastasis**.

(ii) **Causes of Cancer** It is caused due to some agents called as **carcinogens**. These are as given below

- **Physical agents** include X-rays, γ-rays, UV-rays.
- **Chemical agents** include tobacco smoke, benzene fumes, etc.
- **Biological agents** are cancer causing viruses called **oncogenic viruses**. These have genes called viral **oncogenes**. Other genes are called cellular oncogenes (c-onc) or **proto-oncogenes.**

(iii) **Cancer Detection** It can be detected by following methods

- Blood and bone marrow tests
- Biopsy
- Radiography
- Computed Tomography (CT) scan
- Magnetic Resonance Imaging (MRI)
- Monoclonal antibodies

(iv) **Treatment of Cancer** The various methods involve in the treatment of cancer are given as

- Surgery
- Radiotherapy
- Chemotherapy

6. Immunity

It is the ability of the host to fight against the disease causing agents. It is of two types

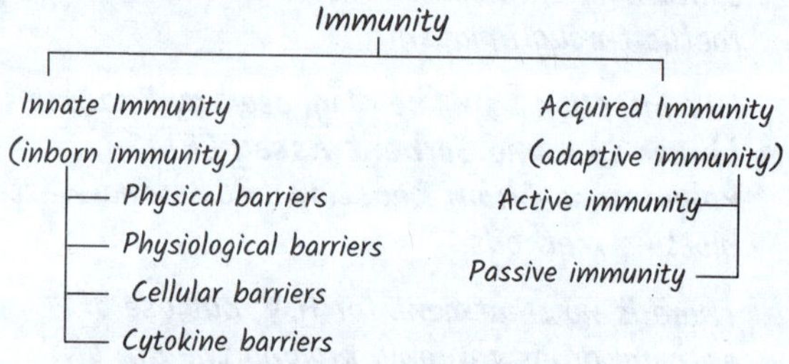

(i) **Innate immunity** refers to all defence elements with which an individual is born. It is non-specific.

(ii) **Acquired immunity** is pathogen specific immunity. It is not present from birth, but develops during an individual's life time.
Acquired immunity is further classified as

(a) **Active Immunity** It is the immunity developed by the body when exposed to the antigens, which may be living or dead microbes or other proteins. Antibodies are produced by the body in this case. It may be artificial or natural.

(b) **Passive Immunity** It is the immunity bestowed by antibodies that are directly given to the body. It is fast, but lasts only for few days. For example, Antibodies (IgG) received by foetus from mother through placenta.

Note The small protein molecules synthesised in the body during viral infection are called **interferons**. They provide semi-specific protection to the body.

7. Immune Responses

Following are two major types of immune responses

(i) **Primary Response** It occurs when a body encounters a pathogen for the first time. It is of low intensity. After every primary response, cell memory stores the details of the encounter.

(ii) **Secondary/Anamnestic Response** Subsequent encounters with the same pathogen elicit secondary response. It is highly intense and aided by the memory of the primary encounter. The primary and secondary responses are carried out with the help of T-lymphocytes and B-lymphocytes.

The immune response mediated by B-lymphocytes is called **humoral immune response** while the immune response mediated by T-lymphocytes is called **Cell-Mediated Immunity** (CMI).

8. Antigens and Antibodies

Antigens (immunogens) are substances which enter the body and stimulate the production of antibodies. They bind to antibody with the help of covalent bond.

Antibodies These are immunoglobulins, Y-shaped proteins composed of heavy and light chains linked by sulphide bonds. They are produced in response to antigenic stimulation. Different types of antibodies are IgG, IgA, IgM, IgE and IgD.

Note A **vaccine** is either a cell suspension or a byproduct excreted by the cell. The vaccines, when introduced into the body, stimulate the production of antibodies.

9. Allergies

The exaggerated or hypersensitive response of the immune system to certain agents in the environment is called **allergy** and its causing elements are called **allergens**, e.g. dust, mites, pollens, dried animal skin which are constantly shed, etc. Sneezing, watery eyes, running nose are common symptoms.

The antibodies produced in response to allergens are of IgE type.

10. Autoimmunity

It is the state, where body loses the ability to distinguish between self and non-self cells. The body's immune system goes off the track and starts destroying self cells and molecules.

This results in **autoimmune diseases**, e.g. rheumatoid arthritis, Addison's disease, Hashimoto's disease, etc.

11. Immune System in the Human Body

It consists of lymphoid organs, tissues, cells and antibodies.

(i) **Primary lymphoid organs** are **bone marrow** and **thymus** where immature lymphocytes differentiate and proliferate.

(ii) **Secondary lymphoid organs** are the sites for the interaction of lymphocytes with antigen, which then proliferate to become effector cells. The organs are **spleen, lymph nodes** and **Mucosal Associated Lymphoid Tissue** (MALT).

12. Adolescence

It refers to the period of rapid growth, physical and mental development from childhood to adulthood.

A. Some drugs which are commonly abused are

(i) **Opioids** are obtained from the latex of poppy plant Papaver somniferum. These are psychotropic drugs which can affect central nervous system and gastrointestinal tract, e.g. heroin, morphine.

(ii) **Cannabinoids** are obtained from the inflorescences of the plant Cannabis sativa. They affect the cannabinoid receptors in brain, e.g. hemp, hashish, charas and ganja.

(iii) **Coca alkaloid** or **Cocaine** (coke or crack) is obtained from Erythroxylum coca. It interfers with transport of dopamine and produces a sense of euphoria and energy.

(iv) **Barbiturates** are sedative-hypnotic drugs, generally depressants to which CNS is most sensitive. They reduce anxiety and induce sleep, e.g. mephobarbitone.

(v) **Tobacco** is obtained from tobacco plant (Tabacum nicotiana) and has nicotine which stimulates adrenal gland.

B. **Effects of Drugs and Alcohol Abuse** The effects are as follows

(i) Behavioural changes, unsocial attitude, lack of interest in social activities, voilent, depression, withdrawal and isolation.

(ii) Lack of hygiene, appetite, weight loss, loss of interest in hobbies.

(iii) Drop in academic performance and absence from school and college.

(iv) Mental and financial crisis which leads to habit of stealing.

(v) Chronic damages to nervous system causes liver cirrhosis, cardiac problems and respiratory issues.

C. **Reason for Drug Addiction** Peer pressure family history, apathy, for excitement and adventure or to get rid of frustration and depression or to increase physical or mental performance, etc.

D. **Prevention and Control**

(i) Parents should understand their children.

(ii) Parents and teachers both should educate and counsel the child about the effects of abuses.

(iii) Affected person should seek professional help of psychologist, doctors and also go rehabilitation to get rid of problems.

Chapter 8 Microbes In Human Welfare

1. Microbes

These are the major components of biological systems on the earth. These are microscopic, single-celled, tiny creatures that are very small and can only be seen under the microscope. Protozoans, virus, bacteria, algae (small plant groups) and fungi are various microorganisms. Study of microorganisms is called **Microbiology**. Microbes perform various beneficial activities and are also responsible for various diseases.

2. Microbes in Household Products

They are used in household products in day-to-day life, e.g. **curd** is made by Lactobacillus, commonly called **Lactic Acid Bacteria** (LAB). It grows in milk and converts it into curd. The **dough** which is used for making food items such as dosa, idli, cakes and bread are also fermented by bacteria or yeast (Saccharomyces cerevisiae).

(i) **Cheese** is also made by using microbes. Different varieties of cheese are known by texture, flavour and taste. These specifications come from Propionibacterium shermanii in **Swiss cheese** and Penicillium roqueforti in **roquefort cheese**.

(ii) **Toddy** is a traditional drink of Southern India. It is made by fermenting sap from palm trees, coconut, etc.

Note The small amount of curd added as raw material to convert milk into curd is known as **inoculum**.

3. Microbes in Industrial Products

A variety of microbes are used to synthesise a number of products valuable to human beings, e.g. beverages and antibiotics. For industrial production, microbes are grown in large vessels called **fermentors** or **bioreactors**.

(i) **Fermented Beverages** Saccharomyces cerevisiae (commonly called as **Brewer's yeast**) is used for producing food, drinks and bakery products, and is also used in the production of alcohol, alcohol-free drinks and bread.

(ii) **Antibiotics Production** Microorganisms are used in the production of antibiotics (Anti-against, bio-life) which suppress the growth of other microbes, e.g. penicillin. It was the first antibiotic discovered by **Alexander Fleming**, when he was working on Staphylococcus bacteria.

It is obtained from a mould called Penicillium notatum. Some other antibiotics were also purified like streptomycin (Streptomyces griseus), terramycin (Streptomyces rimosus), fumagillin (from Aspergillus fumigatus), etc.

Note Judicious use of antibiotics is an approach to maximise the therapeutic efficiency and minimise the antibiotic-resistance in microorganisms.

(iii) **Chemicals, Enzymes and Other Bioactive Molecules** Microbes are being used for commercial and industrial production of certain chemicals like alcohols, organic acids, enzymes and other bioactive molecules. Some of them are given below

Organic Acids Produced by Microbes

Acids	Microbes
Citric acid	Aspergillus niger (fungus)
Acetic acid	Acetobacter aceti (bacterium)
Butyric acid	Clostridium butylicum (bacterium)
Lactic acid	Lactobacillus (bacterium)
Ethanol	Saccharomyces cerevisiae (yeast)

Enzymes and their Functions

- **Lipase** is used in laundry detergents.
- **Pectinase** and **protease** are used in bottled juices.
- **Streptokinase** (Streptococcus bacterium) used as clot buster (to remove clots).

Bioactive Molecules and their Uses

- **Cyclosporin-A** (Trichoderma polysporum fungi) is used as immunosuppressive agent (for organ transplant patients).
- **Statins** (Monascus purpureus yeast) are used as blood cholesterol lowering agents.

4. Microbes in Sewage Treatment

In sewage treatment, several microbes are used in the treatment of wastewater, viz. heterotrophic microbes like bacteria, fungi, protozoans, etc., which are naturally present in the sewage. All discarded materials, domestic wastes, agriculture wastes, human excreta, etc., are needed to be treated in **Sewage Treatment Plants** (STPs).

This treatment is carried out in following two stages

(i) **Primary Treatment** It is the physical removal of large and small particles from the sewage. It is done through filtration and sedimentation. All grit (soil and small pebbles) are removed by sedimentation in settling tanks. All solids that are settled down at the bottom are known as **primary sludge**. It traps lots of microbes and debris. The supernatant forms **effluent**.

(ii) **Secondary Treatment or Biological Treatment** It involves the use of microbes for treatment of polluted water, polluting microbes and carbonic products present in sewage. The primary effluent is passed into large aeration tanks where it is constantly agitated mechanically. This allows the growth of the microbes into flocs (masses of bacteria associated with fungal filament to form mesh-like structures), which consume the major part of the organic matter present in the effluent. It significantly reduces the **BOD** (Biochemical Oxygen Demand) of the effluent.

As the BOD of the waste matter is reduced to 10-15% of raw sewage, it is passed into settling tank. The sediment of settling tank is called **activated sludge**. The effluent of secondary treatment is now sent to anaerobic sludge digesters.

Here anaerobic microbes (methanogens) digest the organic mass and aerobic microbes (bacteria and fungi) and produce gases like methane (CH_4), hydrogen sulphide (H_2S), carbon dioxide (CO_2), etc., during decomposition. These gases form **biogas**.

5. Microbes in Biogas Production

Microbes like methanogens and Methanobacterium are used for the production of '**biogas**' which is used as an energy source.

The major part of biogas consists of methane (50-70%). Other constituents of biogas are CO_2 (30-40%), small amount of hydrogen, nitrogen, ethylene, acetylene, ethane, propane and a very little amount of hydrogen sulphide (H_2S).

The excreta of cattle, i.e. **cattle dung** (commonly known as **gobar**) is rich in methanogenic bacteria, which are used in the generation of biogas or **gobar gas**.

Biogas plant optimises the utilisation of manure, waste and other organic feed stock by converting these biomasses into energy and valuable biofertilisers.

Biogas production technology was developed in India by **Khadi and Village Industries Commission** (KVIC) and **Indian Agricultural Research Institute** (IARI).

6. Microbes as Biocontrol Agents

It is the useful biological method for controlling plant diseases and pests. There are the few examples of biological control agents.

(i) Bacillus thuringiensis is a soil bacterium, which produces crystals of a protein in its endospore form. This protein kills insects like cotton bollworm and other termites, butterflies, ants, etc.

(ii) **Ladybird** and **dragonflies** are useful to get rid of aphids and mosquitoes, respectively.

(iii) Trichoderma are free-living fungi that are very common in the root ecosystems. They also act as biocontrol agents.

(iv) **Baculoviruses** belonging to the genus-Nucleopolyhedrovirus act also as biological control agents.

Note ***Chemical Pesticides*** *They cause environmental contamination and their bioaccumulation may also cause development of resistant pest.*

7. Microbes as Biofertilisers

Different types of microbes increase the nutrient content of soil via their biological processes.

These are known as biofertilisers. These are responsible for increasing plant growth. Some organisms such as bacteria, fungi and cyanobacteria enrich the nutrient quality of the soil.

The main sources of biofertilisers are as follows

(i) **Bacteria Symbiosis**, e.g. Rhizobium, **free-living** in the soil, e.g. Azotobacter and Azospirillum.

(ii) **Fungi Symbiosis**, e.g. Mycorrhiza.

(iii) **Cyanobacteria Symbiosis**, e.g. Anabaena and Azolla.

(iv) **Free-living**, e.g. Nostoc, Oscillatoria and blue-green algae.

> **Integrated Pest Management** (IPM) is an approach that involves economic control of pests by encouraging natural pest control mechanisms.

Chapter 9 Biotechnology: Principles and processes

1. Biotechnology

It is an integrated branch of biology which deals with the techniques of using live organisms or enzymes isolated from organisms, in order to produce different products and processes useful to humans. The term 'biotechnology' was coined by **Karl Ereky** in 1917. It encompasses both traditional and modern biotechnology.

2. Principles of Biotechnology

Two core techniques that enabled birth of modern biotechnology are

A. **Genetic Engineering** It refers to the techniques used for modification of chemical nature of genetic material (DNA/RNA) and their introduction into another organism (host) to change the phenotypic characters of that organism. **Paul Berg** is known as the **Father of Genetic Engineering.**

B. **Sterilisation Methods** These methods are used to maintain microbial contamination-free conditions in chemical engineering processes to enable the growth and manipulation of only the desired microbes or cells. It is used to get large quantities of products like vaccines, enzymes, antibiotics, etc.

3. Recombinant DNA Technology (RDT)

It is a technique of genetic engineering which combines two genes from two different sources to create new recombinant gene. Recombinant DNA was first created by **Stanley Cohen** and **Herbert Boyer** in 1972.

Tools of Recombinant DNA Technology The key tools involved in RDT are

A. **Enzymes** are involved in genetic engineering which simplify this complex process. The various enzymes involved are

(i) **Restriction Enzymes** (Molecular scissors) **Arber, Smith** and **Nathan** discovered the restriction enzyme. These enzymes are used for cutting of DNA at specific locations during recombinant DNA technology.

Restriction enzymes belong to a larger class of enzymes called **nucleases**, which are of two types, i.e.

(a) **exonucleases** remove nucleotides from the ends of the DNA (either 5′ or 3′) in one strand of duplex.

(b) **endonucleases** make cuts at specific position within DNA.

These are named with first letter from the genus and next two letters belongs to name of species from which they are obtained, e.g. Eco RI, is obtained from E. coli bacterium.

(ii) **DNA Ligases** (Molecular glue) These enzymes repair broken DNA by joining two nucleotides.

(iii) **Alkaline Phosphatase** (AP) This enzyme removes the phosphate group from the 5′ end of a DNA molecule, leaving a free 5′ hydroxyl group, which prevents unwanted self-ligation of vector DNA molecules during the formation of recombinant DNA.

(iv) **DNA Polymerases** This enzyme helps in in vitro synthesis of complementary DNA (cDNA) strand on DNA templates.

B. **Cloning Vectors** The DNA molecule that can carry a foreign DNA segment and replicate inside the host cell is called as a **vector**.

These vectors have the ability to replicate within bacterial cells independent of the control of chromosomal DNA.

Following vectors are commonly used in recombinant DNA technology.

(i) **Plasmids** These are small, autonomously replicating usually circular, extrachromosomal double-stranded DNA molecule that occurs in many bacteria and some yeasts, e.g. E. coli containing vector pBR322.

(ii) **Bacteriophages** These are viruses which infect bacteria. They are used as the vector because of very high copy number of their genome within the bacterial cells.

- **Bacterial Artificial Chromosome** (BAC) vectors are artificial vectors, produced from natural extrachromosomal plasmid of E. coli to carry genes of interest, similarily **Yeast Artificial Chromosome** (YAC) vectors are synthesised from segments of yeast DNA and linear plasmid of bacteria to carry genes of interest.

Features of a Good Cloning Vector

(a) **Origin of replication** (ori) is sequence where replication begins.

(b) **Selectable markers** help in identifying or selecting transformants and eliminating the non-transformant. Several genes like antibiotic resistance genes, are used as marker genes for selection of recombinants.

Transformation is a procedure through which piece of DNA is introduced into the host bacterium.

> **Blue/White screening or Insertional/ Inactivation** is a methodology to differentiate recombinants from non-recombinants on the basis of their ability to produce colour in the presence of a chromogenic substrate.

(c) **Cloning sites** (recognition sites) are generally required to link foreign or alien DNA with vector.

Ligation of foreign DNA is carried at restriction site present in one of the two **antibiotic resistance genes**. This process includes inactivation of **antibiotic resistance gene** and insertional inactivation.

(iii) **Vectors for Cloning Genes in Plants and Animals** In plants, the Tumour inducing (Ti) plasmid of Agrobacterium tumefaciens (a pathogen of several dicot plants) is used as a cloning vector (in vivo gene cloning). The proper vector for cloning in animal cells is SV40.

Similarly, retrovirus, adenovirus, papilloma virus are also used as a cloning vector in animals because of their ability to transform normal cells into **cancerous cells**.

C. **Competent Host Organism** (For Transformation with Recombinant DNA) DNA is a hydrophilic molecule, so it cannot pass through cell membranes. In order to force bacteria to take up the plasmid, the bacterial cells must first be made **competent.** The competency is the ability of a cell to take up foreign DNA. The cells can be made competent by following methods

(i) Heat shock (direct method)

(ii) Microinjection

(iii) Biolistic/Gene gun

4. Processes of Recombinant DNA Technology

It involves various steps in a specific sequence.Stages of recombinant DNA technology are described below

(i) **Isolation of Genetic Material** (DNA) In majority of organisms, DNA is the genetic material. The isolation of DNA can be achieved by treating bacterial cells/plant or animal tissues with enzymes such as **lysozyme** (bacteria), **celiulase** (plant cells) and **chitinase** (fungus).

RNA and proteins can be removed by **ribonuclease** and **protease**.

(ii) **Cutting of DNA at Specific Locations** It is generally performed by incubating purified DNA molecule with the restriction enzyme. This is done at the optimal conditions for that specific enzyme.

(iii) **Separation and Isolation of DNA Fragments** The cutting of DNA by restriction endonucleases results in the formation of fragments of DNA, which are separated by a technique known as **gel electrophoresis**. The separated DNA fragments can be visualised only after staining the DNA with **Ethidium Bromide** (EtBr) followed by exposure to UV-radiation. Thus, the bright orange coloured bands of DNA can be visualised.

(iv) **Amplification of Gene Interest using PCR** (in vitro gene cloning) In this stage, several replicas of useful genes are synthesised by using two sets of primers, a DNA polymerase enzyme and dNTPs by an in vitro method known as **Polymerase Chain Reaction** (PCR). It was developed by **Kary Mullis** in 1985.

This method involves three processes, viz., denaturation, annealing and extension.

(v) **Ligation of DNA Fragment into a Vector**

This process requires a vector DNA and a source DNA. In order to obtain sticky ends, both of these should be cut with the same endonuclease, after which, both are ligated by mixing vector DNA, gene of interest and enzyme **DNA ligase** to form the **recombinant DNA/ hybrid DNA.**

(vi) **Insertion of Recombinant DNA into Host Cells/Organisms**

It can be achieved by several methods, before which the recipient cells are made competent to receive DNA, by heat shock or gene gun method. A recombinant DNA containing gene for resistance to an antibiotic is transferred to host cells to produce ampicillin resistant cells. These cell contain ampicillin resistant gene which can be used as **selectable markers**.

(vii) **Obtaining or Culturing the Foreign Gene Product**

The desired protein encoded gene is expressed in the heterologous host, it is called **recombinant protein**. The cells harbouring cloned genes of interest are grown on a small scale in the laboratory. These cell cultures are used for extracting the desired protein using various separation techniques.

5. Bioreactors

These are the large volume vessels (approximately 100-1000 L). A bioreactor provides the optimal conditions for achieving the desired product by providing optimum growth conditions like temperature, pH, substrate, salts, vitamins and oxygen.

- The components of a bioreactor include an agitator system, an oxygen delivery system, a foam control system, a temperature control system, pH control system and a sampling port to withdraw culture periodically.
- The most commonly used bioreactors are stirring type bioreactor, simple stirred-tank bioreactor and sparged stirred-tank bioreactor.

6.Downstream Processing

After completion of the biosynthetic phase, the product has to be subjected through a series of processes before it is ready for marketing as a finished product.

The processes include, separation and purification of products, which are collectively called the downstream processing.

Chapter 10 Biotechnology and Its Applications

1. Biotechnology

It is useful to humans in producing various products by using microbes, plants, animals and their metabolic machinery.

This became possible due to Recombinant DNA Technology (RDT), in which valuable and useful manipulation of genes in various living species is done to obtain desirable products at a large scale.

The critical research areas of biotechnology are

(i) To provide the best catalyst in the form of **improved organisms**, usually a microbe or a pure enzyme.

(ii) To create optimal conditions through **engineering for a catalyst** to act.

(iii) Downstream processing technologies to **purify the organic compounds**.

2.Biotechnological Applications in Agriculture

Green revolution succeeded in increasing the food supply however, it was not sufficient. To feed the increasing population of the world, we need to enhance our food production. The most of the agrochemicals are harmful on the environment and organic farming is expensive for farmers. Therefore, the best solution to overcome these issues are to develop **Genetically Modified** (GM) foods or crops.

The plants, bacteria, fungi and animals whose genes have been altered by manipulation are called **Genetically Modified Organism** (GMO). These are also called **transgenic organisms**, as they contain and express one or more foreign genes, called **transgenes**. A cell which contains and expresses a transgene is known as **transgenic cell**.

GM plants have developed various changes as given below

(i) More tolerant to abiotic conditions (like cold, salt and heat). The transgenic Arabidopsis is more tolerant to drought conditions.

(ii) Use of chemical pesticides and fertilisers has been reduced.

(iii) Reduces post-harvest losses.

(iv) Enhances nutritional value of food.

I. Bt **Crops** Such type of crops are being produced by biotechnological methods. These plant species are pest resistant.

Bt is a type of antitoxin, which is produced by Bacillus thuringiensis or Bt bacteria. It is a soil bacterium, which was discovered by Japanese scientist **Ishiwata** in 1902. Gene of Bt toxin is transferred into plants by extracting it from the bacterium. The plants so produced are pest resistant. Bacillus thuringiensis forms protein crystals (Cry) during a particular phase of their growth. These crystals contain a toxic **insecticidal protein**.

Hence, due to the formation of specific toxin in the plants (crops) against a particular group of insects the pesticides are no longer required. Such types of crops are called Bt **crops**.

A. **Bt Cotton** Bt toxin gene is isolated from the bacteria and is transferred to the plants/crops. In this way, Bt cotton plants are formed. Bollworms do not affect Bt cotton and thus its production increases. The gene forming Bt toxin is called cry **gene**. It is of various types

(i) cry IAc and cry IIAb control cotton bollworms.

(ii) cry IAb controls corn borer.

B. **Bt Brinjal** In Bt brinjal, the cry gene present in soil bacterium Bacillus thuringiensis is inserted. Protein synthesised by this gene, prevents Fruit and Shoot Borer (FSB) insect attacking on brinjal. Thus, the production of brinjal increases.

II. **Pest-Resistant Plants** A nematode Meloidogyne incognita infects the roots of tobacco plants, which reduces the production of tobacco.

The strategy adopted to prevent its infection is based on the process of **RNA interference** (RNAi). RNAi takes place in all eukaryotic organisms as a method of cellular defence.

3. Nutrition Rich Crops (Biofortification)

It is defined as a technique that is used for breeding to increase the nutritional value of food crops. This can be either done through conventional breeding or through geneticengineering.

The objective behind this is to improve the protein quality, quantity, oil content and vitamin content, etc.

e.g. **Golden rice** Scientists have developed a rice variety which is rich in vitamin-A by making changes in the genes. It is called **golden rice**.

4. Biotechnological Applications in Medicines

The recombinant DNA technological processes have made immense impact in the area of healthcare by enabling the mass production of safe and more effective therapeutic drugs. Some examples are given below

(i) **Genetically Engineered Insulin** This has lead to the sufficient availability of insulin for the management of adult onset of diabetes.

Human insulin is not easily available and animal insulin if used in human, can cause allergic reactions.

In humans, insulin is translated in its inactive form, which contains three peptide chains viz., A, B and C. C-peptide chain is an extra stretch of polypeptide which makes the insulin molecules inactive. It is later removed during maturation of insulin. In 1983, **Eli Lilly an American company**, prepared two DNA sequences corresponding to A and B chains of human insulin and introduced *them in plasmids of E. coli to produce insulin chains.*

Chains A and B were produced separately, extracted and combined by creating disulphide bonds to form human insulin, i.e. humulin.

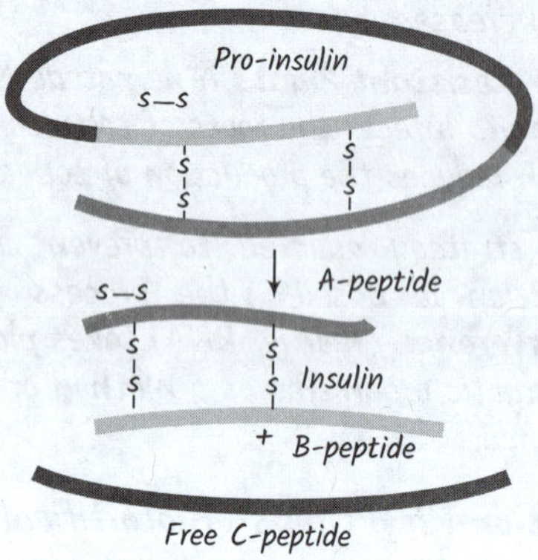

Maturation of pro-insulin into insulin after the removal of C-peptide (simplified)

(ii) **Production of Vaccines through Genetic Engineering** Such vaccines are called **recombinant vaccines**. These are also called as **subunit vaccines** or **second generation vaccines**, e.g. vaccines for hepatitis-B, vaccine for polio virus.

(iii) **Gene Therapy** It is the replacement of a defective or faulty gene with normal healthy ones to correct a genetic disorder. It is used to correct **Adenosine Deaminase** (ADA) deficiency which leads to **Severe Combined Immuno Deficiency** (SCID), as follows

- Lymphocytes are isolated from the blood or bone marrow of the patient and grown in a culture outside the body.
- A normal ADA gene is isolated from normal cells.
- This normal functional ADA gene is then introduced into the cultured lymphocytes, which are subsequently returned to the patient.
- These cells have a limited life, so the patient requires repeated infusion of such genetically engineered lymphocytes.
- However, the replacement of faulty gene in the bone marrow of early foetal stage could be a permanent cure to this disease.
- Gene therapy is also used to prevent cystic fibrosis diseases.

(iv) **Stem Cell Technology** It is known to be the most rapidly developing field that combines the efforts of cell biologists and geneticists for treatment of malignant and non-malignant cells by using stem cells.

The potential applications of stem cell include organ and tissue regeneration, bone marrow transplantation, brain disease treatment, etc.

(v) **Molecular Diagnosis** For effective treatment of diseases, early diagnosis and understanding its pathophysiology is very important. By using conventional methods of diagnosis (serum and urine analysis), early detection of diseases is not possible.

Note **Recombinant DNA technology** (employs DNA/RNA probes for diagnosis), **PCR** (Polymerase Chain Reaction) and Enzyme-Linked Immuno-Sorbent Assay (ELISA) are some of the techniques that serve the purpose of early molecular diagnosis. ELISA is based on the principle of antigen-antibody interaction.

5. Transgenic Animals

Those animals whose genome have been modified by genes obtained from other species are called transgenic animals or Genetically Modified (GM) animals.

Benefits of Transgenic Animals

(i) Study of normal physiology and development.

(ii) Study of diseases like cancer, cystic fibrosis, etc.

(iii) To obtain biologically improved products, e.g. α-1 -antitrypsin used to treat emphysema; **Rosie**, the first transgenic cow to produce human protein (α-lactalbumin) enriched milk.

(iv) To ensure vaccine safety.

(v) For chemical safety testing, mice are the most commonly used organisms for transgenic experiments.

6. Ethical Issues in Applications of Biotechnology

- Genetic modification of organisms can have unpredictable results when such organisms are introduced into an ecosystem.
- The GM crops may lead to the change in the evolutionary patterns.
- Accidentally new infectious agents can be formed.

7. Biopatent

- The patents are granted for biological entities or the products derived from them are called biopatents.
- A patent is the right granted by a government to an inventor to prevent others from the commercial use of his invention.
- The modification/usage of living organisms for public services. For example, food (medicine) has also created problems with patents granted for the same. In order to control these issues, the Indian Government has setup organisations such as **Genetic Engineering Approval Committee** (GEAC).

8. Biopiracy

It refers to the use of bioresources by multinational companies and other organisations without proper authorisation from the countries and people concerned, without compensatory payment.

Some nations are developing laws to prevent such unauthorised exploitation of their bioresources and traditional knowledge.

For example, USA granted a patent of Basmati rice variety which is indigenous to India. Similarly German and Japanese companies are the chief biopirates in world.

9. Biowar

- War which is fought by bioweapons against humans, their crops and animals are called biowar.
- **Biosafety issue** measures taken to prevent any risk to plant, animals and microbes from transgenic organisms are known as biosafety.

Chapter 11 Organisms and Population

1. Population

A group of organisms living in the same area at the same time and can interbreed is called a population.

Population Attributes

Main attributes of the population are as follows

(i) **Density** Total number of individuals present in a unit area or volume at a specific time, is called density.

Its formula is $D = \frac{N}{S}$

Where, D = Density, N = Total number of individuals in a region and S = Total size or area of the region.

(ii) **Birth Rate or Natality** Number of individuals born in a population in a given time period is called birth rate.

(iii) **Death Rate or Mortality** Number of individual dying in a population in a given time period is called **death rate**.

(iv) **Sex Ratio** The number of females and males per 1000 individuals at the given time is called as sex ratio.

2. Age Pyramid

Population at any given time is composed of individuals of different ages. When the age distribution (per cent individuals of a given age or age group) is plotted for the population, this is called age pyramid. The age pyramids of human population generally show the age distribution of males and females. These are of three types

(i) Expanding (ii) Stable (iii) Declining

3. Population Growth

The size of a population for any species is not a static parameter, it keeps changing with time. It depends on factors such as food availability, predation pressure and adverse weather.

The population growth can fluctuate due to the following four reasons

(i) **Natality** refers to number of births during given period.

(ii) **Mortality** refers to number of deaths during a given period.

(iii) **Immigration** is the number of individuals of the same species that have come in to the habitat from elsewhere.

(iv) **Emigration** is the number of individuals of the population who left the habitat and moved somewhere else.

So, if N is the population density at time t, then its density at time t + I is

$$N_{t+1} = N_t + [(B+I) - (D+E)]$$

where, N = Population density, t = Time,

B = *Birth rate*
I = *Immigration,*
D = *Death rate*
E = *Emigration.*

From the above equation we can see that population density will increase, if $(B + I)$ is more than $(D + E)$.

4. Growth Curves

To study the behaviour and pattern of different human population, there are following two models of population growth.

(i) ***Exponential growth*** *is calculated as*

$$dN/dt = (b - d)N$$

Let, $(b - d) = r$, *then,* $dN/dt = rN$

where, N is population size, b is birth per capita, d is death per capita, t is time period and r is intrinsic rate of natural increase.

r is an important parameter that assesses the effects of biotic and abiotic factors on the population growth.

Exponential growth curve is J-shaped and occurs when resources like food and space are unlimited.

(ii) ***Logistic Growth*** *A given habitat has enough resources to support a maximum possible number. This is called* ***carrying capacity*** *(K) for that particular species.*

The logistic growth shows sigmoid (S-shaped) curve and this type of growth is called ***Verhulst-Pearl Logistic Growth.*** *It is calculated as*

$$dN/dt = rN\left(\frac{K - N}{K}\right)$$

where, N is population density at time t, K is carrying capacity and r is intrinsic rate of natural increase.

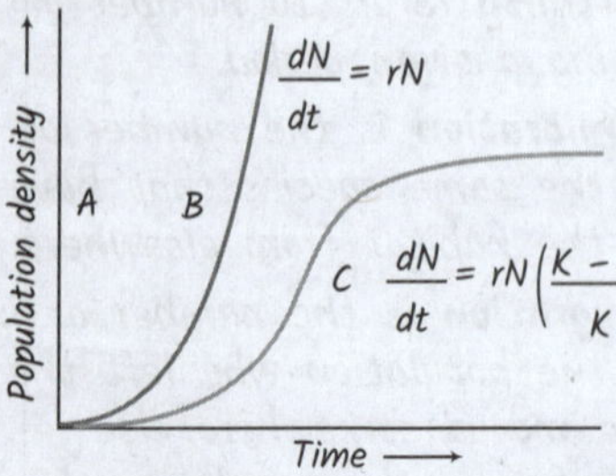

Population growth curve a when responses are not limiting the growth, plot is exponential, b when responses are limiting the growth, plot is logistic Kis

> ***Life History Variations***
> *Populations evolve to maximise their reproductive fitness or Darwinian fitness (high r value) in the habitat where they live. Under a particular set of selection pressures, organisms evolve towards the most efficient reproductive strategy. The rate of breeding varies from species to species.*

5. Population Interactions

In nature, living organisms such as animals, plants and microbes, cannot live in isolation and therefore, interact in various ways to form a biological community. ***Interspecific interactions*** *occur between the populations of two different species living together within a community.*

A. ***Predation*** *It is an interspecific interaction, where an animal (predator) kills and consumes the other weaker animal (prey). It is a biological control method, e.g. tiger (predator) and deer (prey). Roles of predators are*

(i) *Provide population stability.*
(ii) *Maintain species diversity in a community.*

Defences developed in prey species to avoid predation are as follows

(i) *Preys are cryptically coloured, i.e. camouflaged, e.g. insects and frogs.*
(ii) *They produce poisonous toxins, e.g. monarch butterfly secretes chemical during caterpillar stage and Calotropis secrete cardiac glycosides.*
(iii) *25% of insects are phytophagous, i.e. feed on plant sap. Therefore, plants have also evolved by developing thorns, e.g. Acacia and Cactus.*

B. ***Competition*** *It occurs when closely related species compete for the same resources that are limited.*

Gause's competitive exclusion principle *states that two closely related species competing for the same resources cannot co-exist indefinitely and the competitively inferior one will be eliminated eventually. This may hold true in case of limited resources.* ***Resource partitioning*** *is a mechanism evolved by competing species for co-existence.*

In ***interspecific competition****, the feeding efficiency of one species is interfered by inhibitory effect of other, i.e.* ***interference.***

Competitive release *is a phenomena, in which the competitively inferior species expand its distribution abruptly when the competitively superior species is removed.*

C. ***Parasitism*** *It is the mode of interaction between two species in which one species (parasite) depends on the other species (host) for food and shelter and damages the host. In this process, one organism is benefitted (parasite), while the other is being harmed (host).*

Types of Parasites *These are broadly divided into following main types*

(i) ***Ectoparasites*** *are present on the external surface of the host organism for food and shelter, e.g. lice on humans, ticks on dogs, copepods in marine fishes, etc.*

(ii) ***Endoparasites*** *live inside the host's body at different sites like liver, kidney, lungs, etc., for food and shelter, e.g. tapeworm, liver fluke, Plasmodium, etc. The life cycles of endoparasites are more complex because of their extreme specialisation.*

> ***Brood parasitism*** *is a phenomena in which one organism (like cuckoo) lays its eggs in other organism's (like crow's) nest for their hatching.*

D. ***Commensalism*** *It is the interaction between two species, where one species is benefitted and the other is neither harmed nor benefitted. Some examples of commensalism are*

(i) *An orchid growing as an epiphyte on a mango tree gets shelter from mango tree.*

(ii) *Barnacles growing on the back of whale are benefitted by movement of whales to different locations, this provides them food as well as shelter.*

E. ***Mutualism*** *It is an interaction that confers benefit to both the interacting species. Some examples of mutualism are*

(i) *Lichens represent an intimate mutualistic relationship between a fungus and photosynthesising algae or cyanobacteria.*

(ii) *Mycorrhizae show close mutual association between fungi and the roots of higher plants, e.g. Glomus genus.*

(iii) *Mediterranean orchid Ophrys employs 'sexual deceit' to get pollinated by a species of bee.*

F. ***Amensalism*** *It is an interaction between different species in which one species is harmed and the other is neither benefitted nor harmed, e.g. Penicillium, a mould secretes penicillin which kills bacteria, but the mould remains unaffected.*

Chapter 12 Ecosystem

1. Ecosystem

It is a functional unit of nature, where living organisms interact among themselves and also with their surrounding physical environment.

The concept of ecological system was put forward by ***Karl Mobius*** *(1877). The term ecosystem was coined by* ***AG Tansley*** *(1935).*

According to him, the ecosystem is a system which is exhibited by the inter-relationships between abiotic and biotic components of its environments.

It is considered as an interactive system, which can be either natural or artificial.

(i) ***Natural Ecosystem*** *These are capable of maintaining and operating themselves, without the interference of man. They are further classified into terrestrial and aquatic types.*

(ii) ***Artificial Ecosystem*** *These are maintained and manipulated by man for different purposes, e.g. cropland, aquarium, etc.*

2. Components of an Ecosystem

The ecosystem consists of the following components

(i) ***Biotic Components*** *These are comprised of animals, plants and microorganisms and have the following main parts*

- ***Producers*** *The green plants which make their own food by photosynthesis are called producers, e.g. all green plants and the green algae.*
- ***Consumers*** *All heterotrophic animals obtain their food from green plants directly or indirectly. They are also called*

*as **heterotrophs**.The consumers may be of following types*

*(a) **Primary consumers** The consumers that feed on plants directly, are called primary consumers or **herbivores**, e.g. rabbit, rat, squirrel, goat, cattle, etc.*

*(b) **Secondary consumers** Those animals, which feed on other animals, who eat plants are called secondary consumers. These are also referred to as **primary carnivores**, e.g. dogs, cats, foxes and most birds, etc.*

*(c) **Tertiary consumers** These are animals who feed on secondary consumers for their nutrition.*
*These are also referred to **secondary carnivores**, e.g. lions, snakes and seals, etc.*

> ***Omnivores*** *They depend on both producers and consumers, for their food, e.g. pig, bear, etc.*
> ***Detritivores*** *They depend on dead and decaying organic matters for obtaining their food, e.g. vultures, earthworm.*

- ***Decomposers*** *These obtain their food by decaying dead organic matter, e.g. bacteria and fungi. These are also called **saprobes** or **mineralisers**.*

*(ii) **Abiotic Components** These include temperature, water, light and soil.*

3.Structure and Functions of Ecosystem

Two important structural features of an ecosystem are

*(i) **Species composition** is calculated by the characteristic identification and enumeration of plants and animals of an ecosystem.*

*(ii) **Stratification** is the vertical distribution of different species occupying different levels in an ecosystem, e.g. trees occupy top vertical strata or layer of a forest, shrubs at the second and herbs and grasses occupy the bottom (third) layer.*

4. Functions of Ecosystem

The important functional aspects of an ecosystem are productivity, decomposition and energy flow.

A. Productivity of an Ecosystem

*The rate of synthesis of biomass by any trophic level per unit area in unit time is called its **productivity**. It is expressed in terms of $g^{-2} yr^{-1}$ or $(kcal\ m^{-2})\ yr^{-1}$.*

*Productivity of an ecosystem can be categorised as **primary** and **secondary** productivity.*

*(i) **Primary Productivity** It is the amount of biomass or organic matter produced per unit area over a time period by plants during photosynthesis. It is expressed in terms of weight (g^{-2}) or energy $(kcal\ m^{-2})$. The total sum of organic matter synthesised by primary producers via photosynthesis is called **gross primary productivity**.*
*The organic matter/energy stored by the primary producers after utilisation of some energy for respiration is called **net primary productivity**. It is a part of gross primary productivity.*

Net primary productivity =
Gross primary productivity
– Respiratory loss by plants

*(ii) **Secondary Productivity** It is the rate of new organic matter synthesised by the consumers. It is smaller than primary productivity and tends to decrease with an increase in trophic level.*

***Ecological efficiency** is the amount of energy received by one trophic level from the previous trophic level in an ecosystem.*

B. Decomposition

It is the process of breaking down of complex organic matter into inorganic substances like water, carbon dioxide and nutrients by decomposers.

***Detritus** is the raw material of the decomposition.*

It involves following steps during its process

*(i) **Fragmentation** It is a process of breakdown of detritus into small particles by detritivores, e.g. earthworms.*

*(ii) **Leaching** It is the process by which water soluble inorganic nutrients leach into soil horizon and get precipitated as unavailable salts.*

*(iii) **Catabolism** It is the process of degradation of detritus into simple organic material by the action of bacterial and fungal enzymes and then their further conversion into simpler inorganic compounds.*

*(iv) **Humification** It is a process that leads to accumulation of a dark coloured amorphous and*

colloidal substance called **humus**, which is highly resistant to microbial action and undergoes decomposition at a very slow rate.

(v) **Mineralisation** It is the process of degradation of humus by microbial action and release of inorganic nutrients.

Factors affecting decomposition are as follows

(a) **Chemical Decomposition of Detritus** Decomposition is slow if detritus is rich in lignin and chitin but it is quicker if detritus is composed of nitrogen and sugar.

(b) **Climatic Factors** Temperature and soil moisture are the most important climatic factors.

C. Energy Flow

The sun is the only source of energy for all ecosystems on earth. Out of the incident solar radiation, less than 50% of it, is **Photosynthetically Active Radiation** (PAR).

Plants and photosynthetic bacteria (autotrophs) use only 2% of sun's radiant energy to produce food from simple inorganic materials.

Food Chain

It is a sequence of population of an ecosystem through which the food and its contained energy passes through levels, with each member becoming the food of a later member in the sequence.

The food chain present in nature is of two types

(i) **Grazing Food Chain** (GFC) begins with producers which capture solar energy and pass on energy into food chain through photosynthesis, e.g.

Grass ⟶ Goat ⟶ Man
(Producer) (Primary consumer) (Secondary consumer)

(ii) **Detritus Food Chain** (DFC) begins with dead organic matter and consists of decomposers mainly **fungi** and **bacteria**, e.g.

Dead leaves ⟶ Wood louse ⟶ Black bird
(Producer) (Primary consumer) (Secondary consumer)

Food Web

A network of cross connecting food chains involving producers, consumers and decomposers are termed as a food web. It maintains a kind of homeostasis in an ecosystem to make it stable.

Trophic Level

All organisms occupy a particular place in their natural surrounding or in a community according to their feeding relationship among organisms. The particular place of an organism in food chain is called trophic level.

The following diagram shows the various trophic levels in an ecosystem.

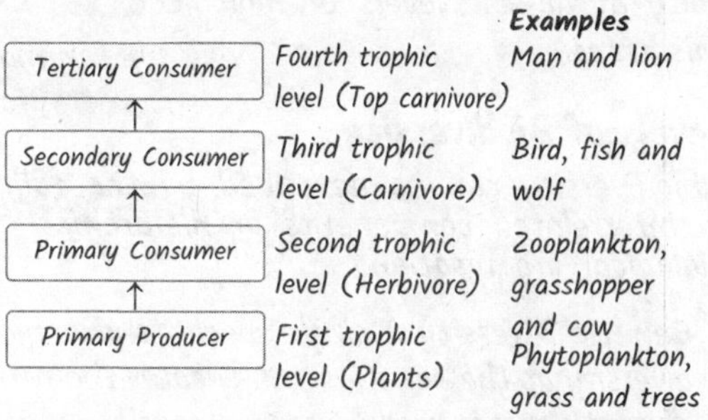

> **Standing crop** is the mass of living material at a particular level at a specific time. It is measured as the mass of living organisms (or biomass) in a unit area.
> **Ten per cent law** was given by **Lindemann** in 1942. It states that at each step of food chain, 10% of energy is transferred to next level while remaining is lost as heat and respiratory losses.

Ecological Pyramids

It is a graphical representation of an ecological parameters like biomass, energy or number of individuals present at various trophic levels of food chain.

The concept of ecological pyramid was given by **Charles Elton** (1927).

The ecological pyramids are of three types

(i) **Pyramid of number** represents the total number of organisms at each trophic level. It is always upright but inverted in tree ecosystem.

(ii) **Pyramid of biomass** refers to the total weight of the organisms in each trophic level. It can be upright or inverted.

(iii) **Pyramid of energy** expresses the total energy of the organisms in each trophic level. It is always upright and unidirectional.

Chapter 13 Biodiversity and Its Conservation

1. Biodiversity

It refers to the **variety** and **variability** of living organisms on the planet, earth. It can also be defined as the variety of life forms, gene pools and habitats found in an area. The term 'biodiversity' was popularised by socio-biologist **Edward Wilson** (1992) to describe the combined diversity at all the levels of biological organisations.

2. Levels of Biodiversity

The biodiversity can be described by the following three interrelated components or hierarchical levels of biological organisation.

A. **Genetic Diversity** A single species shows high diversity at the genetic level. Greater the genetic diversity among organisms of a species, more sustenance it has against the environmental disturbances.

Genetic diversity within the species creates different sub-species, variety, breed, forms, etc., e.g. different varieties of mangoes.

B. **Species Diversity** It is the diversity at the species level or the measure of the variety of species and their relative abundance within a region, e.g. Western Ghats have more amphibian species diversity than Eastern Ghats.

The two important measures of species diversity are

(i) Species richness

(ii) Species evenness

C. **Ecological Diversity** It refers to the diversity at ecological level. Due to the presence of more varieties of ecosystems and habitats, i.e. rainforest, desert, wetlands, mangroves, coral reefs, alpine meadows, etc., India has a greater ecological diversity than Scandinavian countries (e.g. Norway).

3. Magnitude of Biodiversity

According to **International Union of Conservation of Nature** (IUCN) 2004, the total number of plant and animal species described, so far is more than 1.5 million.

More than 70% of all the species recorded are animals, while plants comprise not more than 22% of the total.

Insects are the most species rich taxonomic group in animal kingdom, making more than 70% of the total animals. It means that out of every 10 animals, 7 are insects on the earth.

4. Patterns of Biodiversity

It is not uniform throughout the world. It varies with change in latitudes and altitudes. Following are the patterns of biodiversity

A. **Latitudinal Gradients** Species diversity decreases as we move away from the equator towards the poles. It means biodiversity is more at lower latitude (equator) than the higher latitude (poles).

It means that tropics (latitudinal range 23.5°N to 23.5°S) have more species than temperate or polar areas.

The various hypothesis for greater biodiversity in tropics are given below

(i) Frequent glaciation in temperate killed various species but tropics have remained undisturbed.

(ii) Temperate environment is seasonal while tropical regions have constant environmental conditions.

(iii) Due to the more solar energy in tropics, higher productivity leads to species diversity.

B. **Species-Area Relationships Alexander von Humboldt** observed that within a region, species richness had increased with increasing explored area, but only upto a limit. The relationship between species richness and an area turns out to be a rectangular hyperbola for wide taxonomic variety (e.g. birds, bats, fishes in freshwater). On a logarithmic scale, the relationship is a straight line and described by the following equation,

$$\log S = \log C + Z \log A$$

where, S = Species richness, A = Area

Z = Slope of the line (regression coefficient)

C = Y-intercept

The value of Z lies between 0.1-0.2, regardless of the taxonomic group or the region.

5. Importance of Species Diversity to the Ecosystem

A stable community shows following characteristics

(i) It does not show too much of variations in the year-to-year productivity.

(ii) It must be either resistant or resilient to occasional disturbance (man-made or natural).

(iii) It must be resistant to invasion by alien species.

David Tilman through his long-term ecosystem experiments using outdoor plots provided some concrete evidences of link between species richness and stable community. According to him, more species diverse communities show almost constant productivity in total biomass and also contribute to higher productivity.

Paul Ehrlich gave **rivet popper hypothesis** to help understand the contribution of species richness. He compared each species with rivet in the body of an aeroplane.

6. Loss of Biodiversity

The International Union for Conservation of Nature and Natural Resources (IUCN) was founded in 1948. Its headquarter is at Switzerland. It works in the field of nature conservation and sustainable use of natural resources. IUCN Red List of threatened species is an inventory of global conservation status of biological species, which is compiled in **Red Data Book**. It was initiated in 1963.

IUCN Red List (2004) enlists the **extinction** of 784 species (including 338 vertebrates, 359 invertebrates and 87 plants) in the last 500 years.

Some examples are Dodo (Mauritius), Quagga (Africa), Thylacine (Australia), Steller's sea cow (Russia) and three sub-species of tiger (Bali, Javan and Caspian).

Extinction refers to disappearance of any living species from earth. Species which are on the verge of extinction in near future are termed as **endangered organisms**.

A. **Effects of Loss of Biodiversity** Loss of biodiversity may lead to

(i) Decline in plant production.

(ii) Lower resistance and resilience to environment perturbations such as drought.

(iii) Increased variability in ecosystem processes such as plant productivity, water use, pest and disease cycles, etc.

B. **Causes of Loss of Biodiversity** Human activities have accelerated the rate of extinction of species from the earth. The four major causes also called the **Evil Quartet** are responsible for the loss of biodiversity.

(i) Habitat loss and fragmentation

(ii) Over-exploitation

(iii) Alien (Exotic) species invasions

(iv) Coextinctions

7. Reasons for Conserving Biodiversity

The reasons for conservation of biodiversity can be grouped into three categories

(i) **Narrowly Utilitarian** Humans desire countless direct economic benefits from nature, therefore it must be conserved.

(ii) **Broadly Utilitarian** Biodiversity plays a major role in ecosystem services. Thus, conservation is necessary.

(iii) **Ethical Argument** Every species has an intrinsic value even if it is not of any economic value to us. It is our duty to pass this biological legacy in good order to future generations.

8. Biodiversity Conservation

It can be briefed into two ways, In situ conservation and Ex situ conservation.

A. Ex situ **conservation** In this type of conservation, the animals are kept outside their natural home in a special care unit. Hence, it is known as ex situ conservation. Ex situ conservation includes off-site collections and gene banks. They are as follows

(i) **Gene Bank** The genes of the rare, endangered and desired quality of plants and animals are conserved at a safe place. This is known as gene bank.

(ii) **Cryopreservation** In this technique, the germplasm of threatened and endangered species is kept at very low temperature (–196°C) in liquid nitrogen. In this process, the biological activities, mitosis and the genetic changes stop. It is known as **cryopreservation**. Seed banks are setup to the preserve seeds of such plant species.

Zoos, botanical gardens, Wildlife Safari Park, etc., are other methods of ex situ conservation.

B. In situ **Conservation** In this process, the species are kept in their natural homes for conservation. It includes following protected areas

(i) **National Parks** To provide safe homes for wildlife, Central Government has established National Parks. In these parks any type of human interference is prohibited. The property available in these parks cannot be used for commercial purpose.

First Indian National Park is Jim Corbett National Park, which is situated in Uttarakhand.

(ii) **Wildlife Sanctuaries** To provide safety to wildlife, sanctuaries are setup. In these sanctuaries, residing communities are allowed for the limited cutting of trees, collection of forest products, etc.

(iii) **Biodiversity Hotspots** These are regions with very high levels of species richness and high degree of **endemism** and also regions of accelerated habitat loss. There are 34 international biodiversity hotspots in the world out of which three are located in India.

(a) **Eastern Himalayan Region** This is situated in the Northern and Eastern parts of India. This includes Assam, Nepal, Sikkim and Bhutan. Temperate forests are found in it.

(b) **Western Ghats** These include regions of Karnataka, Maharashtra, Kerala and Tamil Nadu. Evergreen forests are found near the sea coasts.

(c) **Indo-Burma** It extends from Bhutan to Myanmar covering most of the North-Eastern India.

(iv) **Biosphere Reserves** These are special category of protected areas of land and/or coastal environments, wherein people are an integral component of the system.

They represent a specified area zonated for particular activity. These consist of core zone (no human activity), buffer zone (limited human activity), manipulation zone (several human activities are allowed).

(v) **Sacred Groves** These are small group of forests with special religious importance in a particular culture and are also of mythological importance, e.g. Aravalli Hills of Rajasthan, etc.

A Ramsar site is a wetland site designated as of international importance under the Ramsar convention (i.e. a convention on wetlands). It is the intergovernmental treaty that provides the framework for the conservation and wise use of wetlands and their resources established in 1971 in Iran. Currently, India has 26 Ramsar sites like Kolleru Lake (Andhra Pradesh), Deepor Beel (Assam), Pong Dam Lake (Himachal Pradesh), etc.

9. People Participation for Biodiversity Conservation

These activities are seen since past. These include various movements like Chipko Movement, Appiko Movement, etc.

Biodiversity rich countries expect to reap more benefits from the increasing resources put into **bioprospecting**, i.e. exploration of molecular, genetic and species-level diversity for obtaining products of economic importance.

50 MPQs Most Probable Questions

This section features questions meticulously compiled by expert teachers with extensive experience, based on examination trends over the past five years. These questions are likely to appear in the 2025 examination. However, we strongly recommend that you prepare the entire syllabus to ensure comprehensive readiness.

Chapter 1 Sexual Reproduction in Flowering Plants

Q.1 In the diagram given below identify "*a*"," *b*", "*c*" and "*d*" and mention their function.

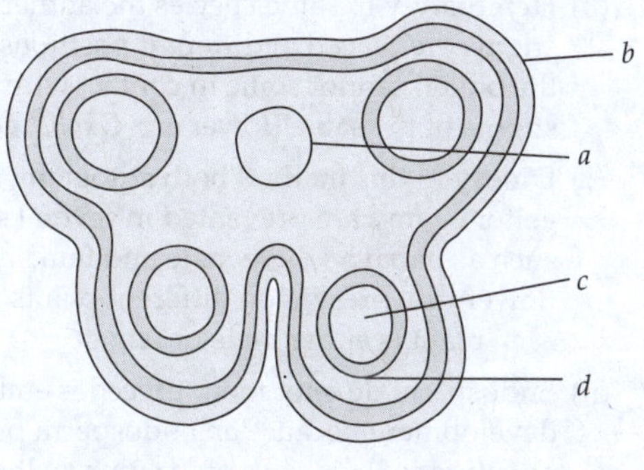

Ans. (a) **Connective** The portion of sterile tissue of anther that forms the body. The function is to connect the anther thecae with each other.

(b) **Epidermis** The outermost protective layer of anther.

(c) **Sporogenous tissue** It forms pollen grains.

(d) **Tapetum** The innermost layer of anther that provides nourishment to the developing pollen grains.

Q.2 Mention the ploidy of the different types of cells present in the female gametophyte of an angiosperm.

Ans. Synergids (2 no;s)- haploid

Egg (one)- haploid

Central cell (one) - diploid (has two polar nuclei which are haploid)

Antipodals (three)- haploid.

(Explanation - A female gametophyte or an embryo sac has seven cells and eight nuclei. There are, one egg cell, 2 synergids, 3 antipodal cells and single central cell. The central cell has two nuclei.)

Q.3 (a) Trace the development of Megaspore Mother Cell (MMC) upto the formation of mature embryo sac in the flowering plant.

(b) Draw a labelled diagram of structure of mature embryo sac.

Ans. **Megasporogenesis**

- The formation of female gametophyte embryo-sac is called megasporogenesis.
- Megaspore is the first cell of the female gametophyte.
- The megaspore increases in size and its nucleus divides mitotically into two nuclei, which moves apart to the opposite poles. Thus, a 2-nucleate embryo sac is formed.
- The two daughter nuclei undergoes another mitotic division, giving rise to the 4 nuclei stage. The 3rd mitotic division gives rise to 8 nucleate 7 celled embryo sac.
- The central cell contains two nuclei known as polar nuclei.
- The three nuclei at the micropolar region form the egg apparatus.
- In the egg apparatus, the middle cell is the largest cell and is called oosphere /egg or ovum while other two naked cells adjoining the egg cell are called synergids.
- The three nuclei at the Chalazal end are surrounded by cytoplasm and cellular wall. These are called antipodal cells.
- Female gametophyte is 7 celled 8 nucleate as it consists of 7 cells but 8 nuclei (2 nuclei in polar cell).

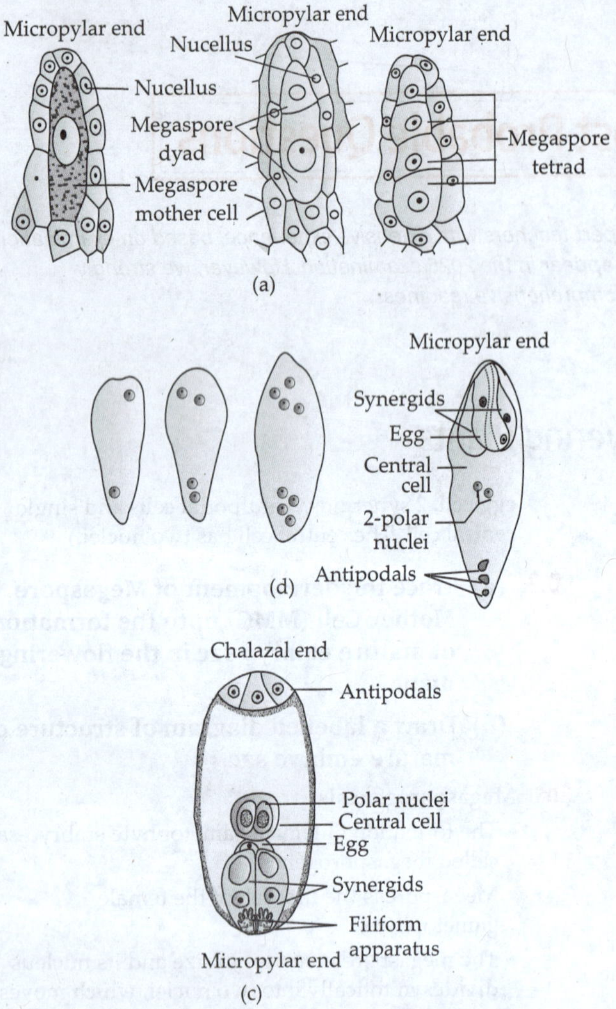

Q.4 **(i) Make a list of any three outbreeding devices that flowering plants have developed and explain how they help to encourage gross pollination?**

(ii) Why does endosperm development precede embryo development in angiospermic seeds?

Ans. (i) The three outbreeding devices that the flowering plants have developed to encourage grass pollination are

(a) **Dichogamy** In some bisexual flowers the anther and stigma do not mature at the same time, i.e. either the anther mature earlier than the stigma (protogamy) e.g. sunflowers, sweet pea, etc. or the stigma matures earlier than the anthers (protogyny) e.g. Magnolia custard apple, etc.

(b) **Heterostyly** In same species the anther and stigma are placed at different positions so that the pollen cannot come in contact with the stigma of the same flower e.g. *Oxalis,* etc.

(c) **Dioecy** In this method both autogamy and geitonogamy are prevented in several species such as papaya where male and female flowers are present on different plants i.e. each plant is either male or female.

(ii) Endosperm development precedes embryo development because an endosperm provides nutrition to the developing embryo. It is an adaptation to provide ensured nutrition to the developing embryo.

Chapter 2 Human Reproduction

Q.5 Mention the location and function of Sertoli cells and Leydig cells in humans.

Ans. Sertoli cells are present in the seminiferous tubules. They provide nutrition to the germ cells or sperms.

Leydig cells are present in the region called interstitial spaces outside the seminiferous tubules. They synthesise and secrete androgen (testosterone).

Q.6 Identify the figure given below, and the part labeled (*A*) and (*B*). Mention the fate of the structures.

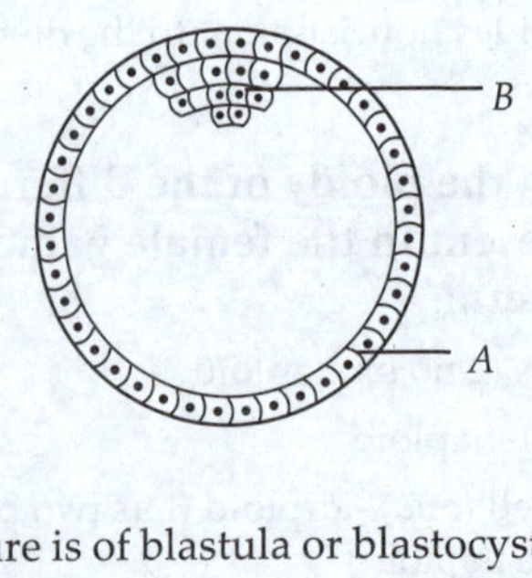

Ans. The figure is of blastula or blastocyst.

A- Trophoblast

B- Inner cell mass.

The trophoblast nourishes and protects the embryo while inner cell mass differentiates into ectoderm, mesoderm and endoderm.

Q.7 Study the graph given below and answer the questions that follow.

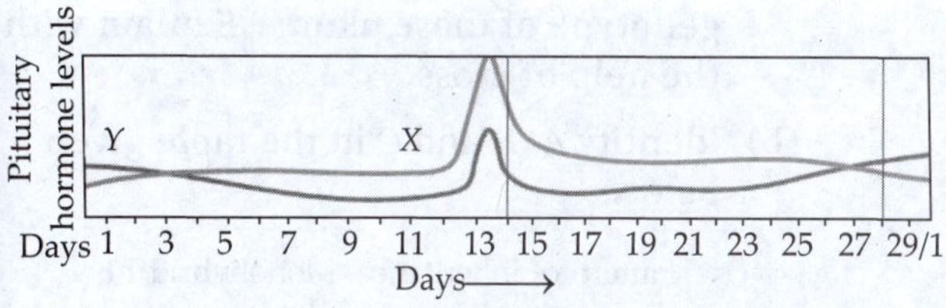

Menstrual cycle

(a) Name and function of the hormones *X* and *Y*.

(b) Explain the ovarian events under the influence of these hormones.

Ans. Hormone X is Luteinising Hormone (LH).

Hormone Y is Follicle Stimulating Hormone (FSH).

(i). FSH is secreted by the anterior pituitary, which stimulates the ovarian follicle to secrete oestrogen, which in turn stimulates the proliferation of the endometrium of the uterine wall.

(ii) Both LH and FSH attain a peak level in the middle of the cycle (about 14th day).

The rapid secretion of LH leads to the maximum level during the mid cycle, called 'LH surge' induces rupture of graafian follicle, and thereby the release of ovum (ovulation).

(iii) The remaining cells of ovarian follicles are stimulated by the LH to transform into corpus luteum. The corpus luteum secretes large amount of progesterone, which is essential for maintenance of the endometrium.

Chapter 3 Reproductive Health

Q.8 Identify the figures. Label the parts "C" and "D". What is the importance of this method?

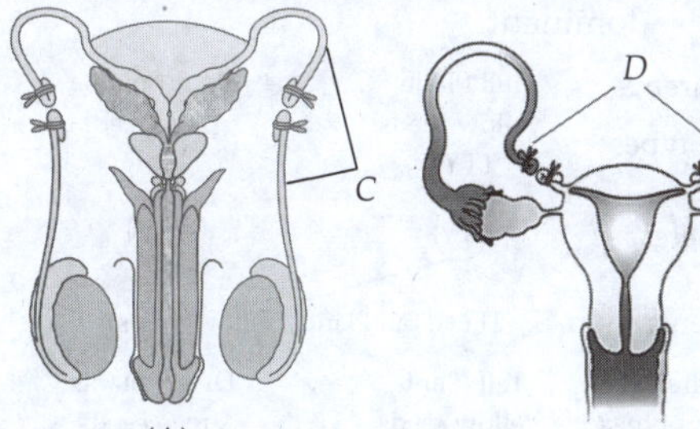

(A) (B)

Ans. The diagrams represent

A – Vasectomy, *B*- Tubectomy

The parts labeled as C and D are as follows

C- Vas deferens cut and tied.

D- Fallopian tubes cut and tied.

These are the surgical method of contraception that are safest but irreversible in nature.

Q.9 Reproductive Tract Infection (RTIs) are STDs, but all STDs are not RTIs. Justify with example.

Ans. Among the common STDs, hepatitis B and AIDS are not infections of the reproductive organs, though, their mode of transmission could be through sexual contact also or other diseases like gonorrhea, syphilis, genital herpes, are transmitted through sexual contact, and are also infections of reproductive tract.

Q.10 How are Assisted Reproductive Technologies helpful to humans? How are ZIFT and GIFT different from intra-uterine transfers? Explain.

Ans. The infertile couples could be assisted to have children through certain special techniques known as assisted reproductive technologies (ART).

ZIFT In this the zygote or early embryo with up to eight blastomeres is transferred into the Fallopian tube. This is called zygote Intra Fallopian Transfer (ZIFT).

GIFT It is the transfer of an ovum collected from a donor into the fallopian tube of another female who cannot produce one, but can provide suitable environment for fertilization and further development of the embryo.

Intrauterine Transfer (IUT) It refers to the introduction of embryo with more than eight blastomeres into the uterus of the female to complete its further development.

Chapter 4 Principles of Inheritance and Variation

Q.11 Study the figures given below and answer the question.

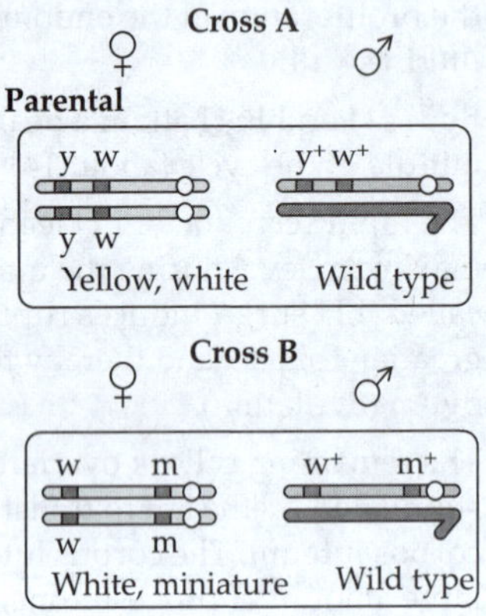

Identify in which of the crosses is the strength of the linkage between the genes higher. Give results in support of your answer.

Ans. (i) When the genes are linked.

(ii) The frequency of recombination will be higher.

(iii) True breeding lines are plants, which have undergone continuous self- pollination for several generations. These are homozygous for traits.

Q.12 Give an example of a gene responsible for multiple phenotypic expressions. What are such genes called? State the cause that is responsible for such an effect.

Ans. Gene causing phenylketonuria causes multiple phenotypic expressions. Such genes are called pleiotropic genes.

This effect of multiple phenotypic expressions is caused because pleiotropic gene affects metabolic pathways, resulting in different phenotypes.

Q.13 Name a disorder, give the karyotype and write the symptoms where a human male suffers as a result of an additional X-chromosome.

Ans. Klinefelter's syndrome. The karyotype is 44 + XXY. The common symptoms are as follows

(i) Sex of the individual is masculine, but possesses feminine characters.

(ii) A symptom is visible called gynecomastia, i.e., development of breasts.

(iii) Poor beard growth and often sterile.

(iv) Feminine pitched voice.

Q.14 (a) You are given tall pea plans with yellow seeds whose genotypes are unknown. How would you find the genotype of these plants? Explain with the help of cross.

(b) Identify *A*, *B* and *C* in the table given below.

	Pattern of inheritance	Monohybrid F1 phenotypic generations
(i)	Co – dominance	*A*
(ii)	*B*	The progeny resembled only one of the parents
(iii)	Incomplete dominance	*C*

Ans. (a) If all the plants of F_1 generations are tall, with yellow seeds, then the phenotype of the parent is homozygous dominant (Case i) if the plants in F_1 generation are in the ratio of 1:1:1:1 then the parent plant is heterozygous dominant.

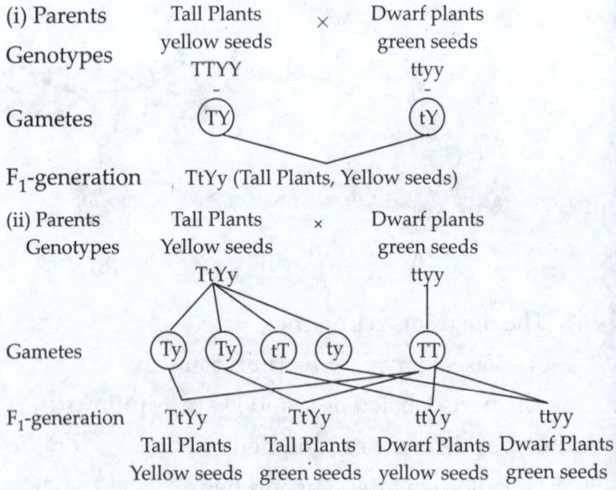

(b) *A* – Both the forms of a trait are equally expressed in F_1 generation.

B- Dominance

C- Phenotypic expression of F_1-generation is somewhat intermediate between the two parental forms of a trait.

Q.15 A normal visioned woman whose father is colour blind, marries a normal visioned man. What would be the probability of her(a) sons (b) daughters to be colour blind? Explain with the help of a pedigree chart.

Ans. The genotypes of parents are

Father → X^CY

Mother → XX

Colour blindness is the inability of an individual to differentiate between red and green colors.

Genotype of colour blindness: Colour blindness is recessive X- linked trait.

Females are affected by colour blindness only in the homozygous condition i.e. both X-chromosomes carry the recessive allele represented by the genotype (X^CX^C) and act as a carrier in heterozygous condition (X^CX). Males have only one X chromosomes and show colour blindness due to the presence of single recessive allele (X^CY).

Cross between a carrier woman and normal man for colour blindness

A normal visioned women may have XX or X^CX. In the given question, since her father is colour blind, she must have inherited his only one Xc chromosome and became a carrier of colour blindness XXc. When she marries a normal man (XY) without colour blindness, there is 50% probability that male progenies are colourblind as they inherit the allele of colour blindness allele from their mother. Similarly, 50% of female progenies are carriers. Therefore, every daughter has a normal vision.

Carrier woman and normal man will produce 50% colour blind sons and 50% carrier daughters.

	X^C	X
X	XX^C (Carrier daughter)	XX(Normal daughter)
Y	X^CY (Colour blind son)	XY(Normal son)

Pedigree chart

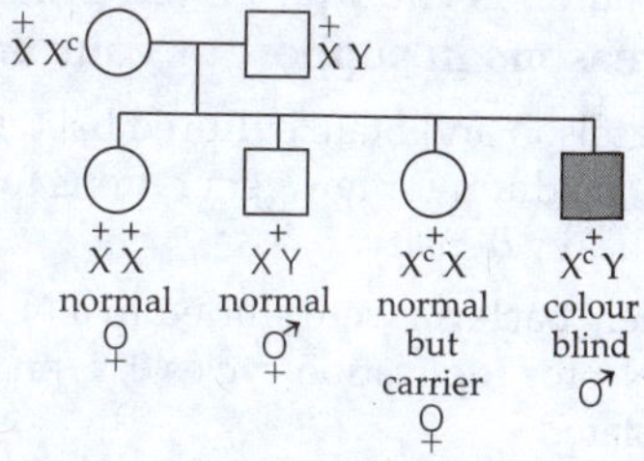

Final answer

Probability of colour blind sons = 50 %

Probability of colour blind daughters= 0 %

Chapter 5 Molecular Basis of Inheritance

Q.16 Explain the dual function of AUG codon. Give the sequence of bases it is transcribed from and its anticodon.

Ans. The dual function of AUG codon is that

(a) It codes for an amino acid methionine.

(b) It is an initiation codon.

The sequence of bases from which it is transcribed is TAC. Its anticodon is UAC.

Q.17 (a) DNA $\xrightarrow{A}$ *m*RNA $\xrightarrow{B}$ Protein $\xrightarrow[C]{\text{Proposed by}}$

Look at the above sequence and mention the events *A, B* and *C*.

(b) What does central dogma state in molecular biology? How does it different in some viruses?

Ans. The events *A, B* and *C* are identified as

(a) *A*- transcription *B*- translation and *C*-Francis Crick.

(b) Central dogma of molecular biology states that that information flows in the order as

DNA → RNA → proteins.

It differs in some viruses, called retroviruses, as the flow of information is in the reverse direction, i.e. from DNA to RNA.

Q.18 (a) Name the molecules 'X' synthesised by 'i' gene. How does this molecule get activated?

(b) Which of the structural genes codes for galactosidase?

(c) When will the transcription of this gene stop?

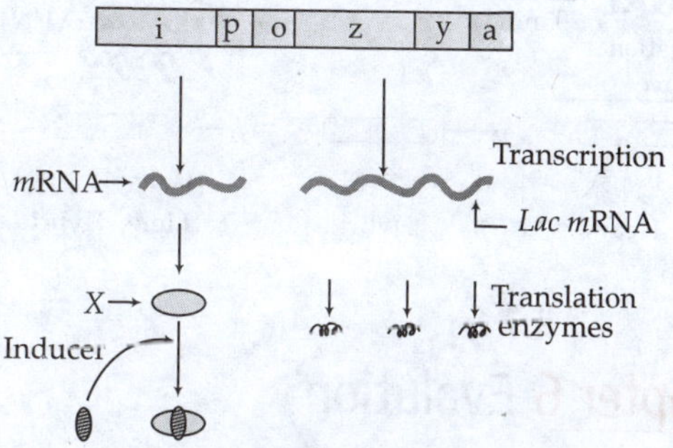

Ans. (a) The molecule *X* is a repressor. It gets inactivated when lactose inducer binds with the repressor molecule.

(b) *Z* gene codes for β-galactosidase.

(c) Transcription of the gene stops when lactose is absent and thus, repressor is free to bind with the operator.

Q.19 What did Meselson and Stahl observe when

(i) They cultured *E.coli* in a medium containing $^{15}NH_4Cl$ for a few generations and centrifuge the content?

(ii) They transferred one such bacterium to the normal medium of NH_4Cl and cultured for two generations?

(iii) What did Meselson and Stahl conclude from this experiment? Explain with the help of diagrams.

(iv) Which is the first genetic material? Give reasons in support of your answer.

Ans. (i) Meselson and Stahl cultured bacteria *E. coli* in a N^{15} medium for few generations to get the DNA of heavy density.

(ii) Then, bacteria were shifted to a N^{14} medium, DNA for replication cycles 0, 1, and 2 was isolated.

(iii) The key conclusion drawn from the Meselson-Stahl experiment was that DNA replication is semiconservative.

- Each DNA strand serves as a template for the synthesis of a new complementary strand.
- After replication, each newly synthesised DNA molecule contains one original (parental) strand and one newly synthesised (daughter) strand.
- This mode of replication ensures that the genetic information is successfully transmitted from one generation to the next.

Separation of DNA by centrifugation

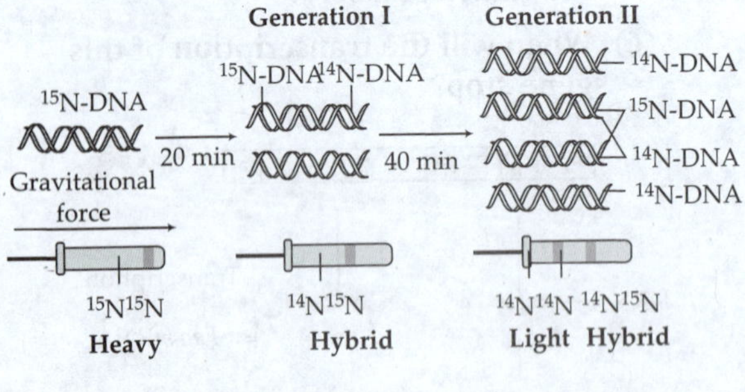

The Meselson-Stahl experiment provided direct experimental evidence supporting the semiconservative model of DNA replication, which is now widely accepted in molecular biology. This model has profound implications for understanding inheritance, genetic variability, and the molecular basis of life.

(iv) RNA is the first genetic material.

Reasons

(i) RNA is highly reactive and acts as a catalyst as well as a genetic material.

(ii) Essential life processes such as metabolism translation and splicing evolved around RNA.

(iii) It expresses itself through proteins.

Q.20 What is hnRNA? Explain the changes *hn*RNA undergoes during its processing to form *m*RNA.

Ans. *hn*RNA is the precursor of *m*RNA that is transcribed by RNA polymerase-ll and is called heterogeneous nuclear RNA.

Post-transcriptional changes includes

The hnRNA undergoes two additional processes called capping and tailing.

(i) **Capping** It is a process in which an unusual nucleotide methyl guanosine triphosphate is added to the 5′ end of *hn*RNA.

(ii) **Tailing** In this adenylate residues (about 200 – 300) are added at 3′ end in a template independent manner.

Now the *hn*RNA undergoes a process where the introns are removed and exons are joined to form *m*RNA by the process called splicing.

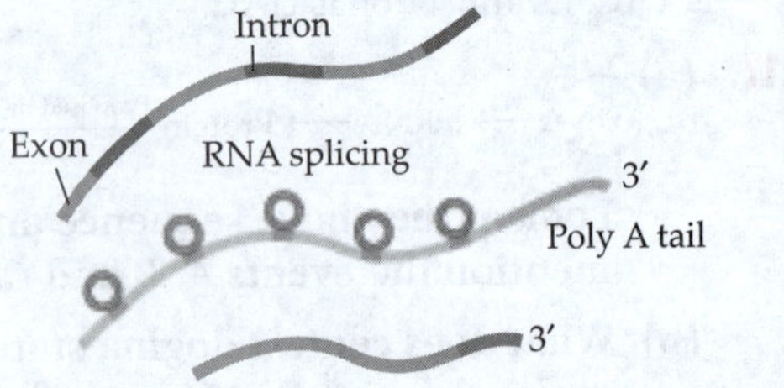

Chapter 6 Evolution

Q.21 Convergent evolution and divergent evolution are the two concepts explaining organic evolution. Explain each one with the help of an example.

Ans. **Convergent Evolution** When more than one adaptive radiation appeared to have occurred in an isolated geographical area and two or more groups of unrelated animals resembles each other for similar mode of life or habitat, it is called convergent evolution. Example, Australian Marsupials, Placental mammals.

Divergent Evolution In some animals, the same structures develop along different directions due to adaptation to different needs. This is known as divergent evolution for example, forelimbs of whales, bats, cheetah and human perform different functions, but have similar anatomical structures with similar bones arranged in similar segments.

Q.22 State Hardy -Weinberg principle of genetic equilibrium, knowing that genetic drift disturbs this equilibrium, mention what does this disturbance in genetic equilibrium leads to?

Ans. Hardy- Weinberg Principle states that the gene pool remains constant i.e., the allele frequencies in a population are stable and remains constant from generation to generation.

Genetic drift refers to change in the allele frequencies of a population occurring by chance. The change in allele frequency may be so different that the population becomes a different species. This effect is called founder's effect.

Q.23 Describe the experiment of S.L. Miller on the origin of life. Write the conclusion drawn at the end of the experiment.

Ans. Experiment was performed by S.L. Miller and H.C. Yuri in 1953.

Experiment setup In a closed flask containing CH_4, H_2, NH_3 and water vapours at 800°C. Electric discharge was created. The conditions were similar to those in the primitive atmosphere.

Observations: After a week, they observed the presence of amino acids and complex molecules such as sugars, nitrogen bases, pigments and fats in the flask.

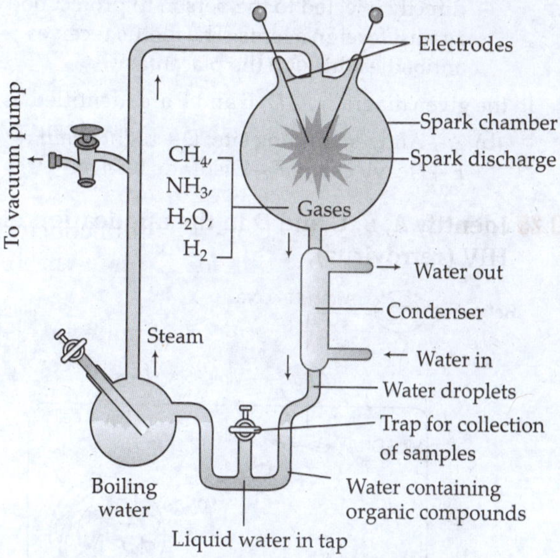

Diagrammatic representation of Miller and Urey's experiment

Conclusions

(i) It provides experimental evidence for the theory of chemical origin.

(ii) It showed that the first non-cellular form of life was created about 3 billion years ago.

(iii) It showed that non-cellular biomolecules exist in the form of DNA, RNA, polysaccharides and protein.

Chapter 7 Human Health and Diseases

Q.24 (a) List the two types of immunity a human body is born with. Explain the differences between the two types.

(b) Identify *A, D, E* and *F* in the diagram of an antibody molecule given below.

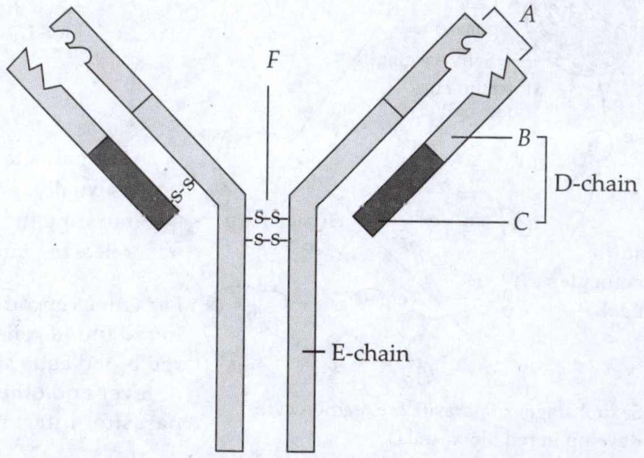

Ans. (a) The two types of immunity a human body is born with are innate and passive or acquired immunity.

Innate immunity is a non-specific type of defense that provides barrier to the entry of antigens.

Passive immunity is a pathogen specific type of defense in which readymade antibodies are directly injected to the person to protect body against foreign agents. The foetus receives antibodies through the placenta.

In the given diagram A, D, E and F are identified as

(b) *A*—Antigen binding site, *D*—Light chain, *E*—Heavy chain, *F*—Disulfide bridge.

Q.25 Identify *A, B, C* and *D* in the application of HIV (retrovirus).

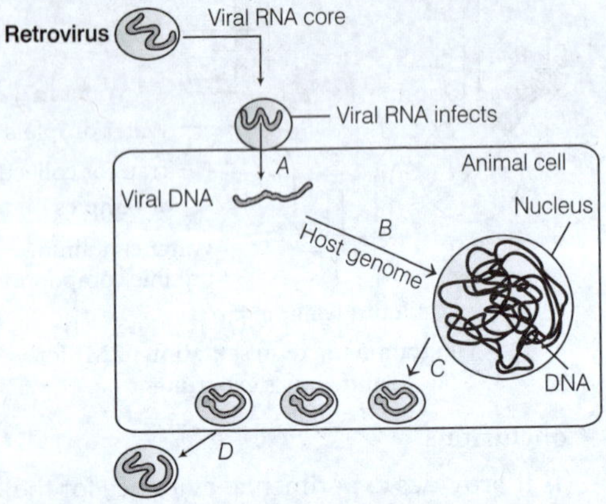

Ans. *A*- Reverse transcription.

B- Viral DNA incorporates into host genome.

C- New viral RNA produced by infected cell.

D- New viruses can infect other cells.

Q.26 To which category of cells do B-cells and T-cells belong? How do they differ from each other with reference to their formation and response to antigens? Which cells of these are affected by the pathogen like HIV?

Ans. B- cells and T- cells belongs to the category of lymphocytes i.e., leucocytes, (WBC).

S. No.	B-Lymphocytes	T-Lymphocytes
(i)	They mature in bone marrow.	They mature in Thymus Gland.
(ii)	They produces antibody against antigen.	They directly attach the antigen or direct B cells to produce antibody.
(iii)	They do not respond to organ transplantation.	They respond to organ transplantation.

HIV like pathogens destroys helper T-lymphocytes.

Q.27 Describe the asexual and sexual phases of life cycle of *Plasmodium* that causes malaria in humans.

Ans. *Plasmodium* completes its life cycle in two main phases as asexual phase which occurs in human blood and sexual phase that occurs in mosquitoes. The complete life cycle is described by the figure given below.

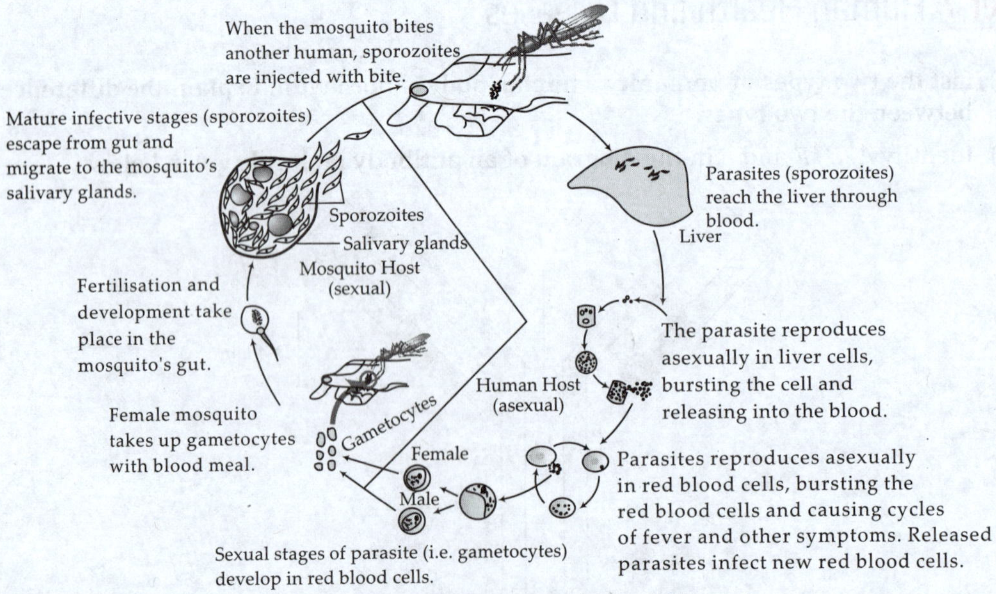

Stages in the life cycle of *Plasmodium*

Q.28 Write the source and the effect on the human body of the following drugs: morphine, cocaine, marijuana, LSD and tobacco.

Ans. Sources and effects of various drugs on the human body of and described here under

1. **Morphine**

Source Derived from the opium poppy plant *(Papaver somniferum)*.

Effect on the Human Body

It acts as a powerful analgesic (pain reliever) by binding to the opioid receptors in the brain and spinal cord.

- Long-term use can lead to tolerance, physical dependence, and addiction.

2. **Cocaine**

Source Extracted from the leaves of the coca plant *(Erythroxylum coca)*.

Effect on the Human Body:

- It interferes with the receptor of dopamine which is a neurotransmitter. It stimulates the central nervous and produces a sense of euphoria and its excessive dosage can cause hallucinations.
- Hallucinogens.
- Source derived from erergy the plants like *Atropa Belladonna* and *Datura*.
- **Effect on human body** Have effect on cerebrum and sense organs so are also called psychedelic drugs. They affect feelings, emotions perceptions and thoughts.

Tobacco

- **Source** Obtained from tobacco plant and can be smoked or chewed or used as a snuff.
- **Effect on human body** Stimulates adrenal gland to release adrenaline or nor-adrenaline into blood resulting in increasing the blood pressure and heart rate.

Chapter 8 Microbes in Human Welfare

Q.29 Microorganisms play an important role for the biological treatment of sewage". Justify.

Ans. Primary effluent is passed into a aeration tanks where oxygen is constantly pumped in and agitated. This allows the growth of useful aerobic microbes into flocs. The flocs are the masses of bacteria and fungal filaments. These microbes consumes organic matter in the affluent and reduce its biological oxygen demand (BOD).

Q.30 State the medicinal value and the bioactive molecules produced by *Streptococcus, Monascus* and *Trichoderma*.

Ans.

	Species name	Bioactive molecule produced	Medicinal value
(i)	*Streptococcus*	Streptokinase	Removes clot from the blood vessels.
(ii)	*Monascus purpureus*	Statin	Inhibits enzymes responsible for synthesis of cholesterol. So is used as cholesterol lowering agent.
(iii)	*Trichoderma polysporum*	Cyclosporin A	Immunosuppressive agents used in organ transplantation.

Q.31 Complete the given table.

Aspergillus niger	A
(ii)	Ethanol
(iii)	Cyclosporin-A
(iv)	Acetic acid
Monascus purpureus	(v)
Streptococcus	(vi)

Ans. (i) Citric acid
(ii) *Saccharomyces cerevisiae*
(iii) *Trichoderma polysporum* (iv) *Acetobacter aceti*
(v) Statin (vi) Streptokinase

Q.32 Why should biological control of pests and pathogens be preferred to be conventional use of chemical pesticides? Explain how the following microbes act as biocontrol agents?

(a) *Bacillus thuringiensis*

(b) *Nucleopolyhedrovirus*

Ans. Microbes as Biocontrol Agents

(a) ***Bacillus thuringiensis*** *(Bt)* This is a bacterium that produces crystal proteins (Cry toxins) toxic to certain insects. When insects ingest these proteins, the proteins become activated in the insect's alkaline gut, bind to the receptors on the gut cells, create pores, and cause cell lysis and death. Different strains of Bt produce different Cry proteins, each targeting specific insect groups like caterpillars, beetles, and flies.

Applications

- **Sprays** *Bt* is commonly formulated as a liquid spray. It is applied directly to plant surfaces where insect larvae feed. Once ingested, the *Bt* toxins act on the pest.
- **Granules** *Bt* can be formulated into granules and applied to soil or plant foliage, providing targeted delivery to pest habitats.
- ***Bt* Crops** Genetic engineering has incorporated *Bt* genes into crops like corn and cotton, enabling the plants to produce Bt toxins and protect themselves from specific pests.

(b) ***Nucleopolyhedrovirus*** They are used as biological control agents. These are excellent for species-specific, narrow spectrum insecticidal applications.

- Baculoviruses do not have any negative impact on plants, mammals, birds, fish or even on non-target insects.
- Thus, biological control agents are useful in overall integrated pest management programme, when beneficial insects have to be conserved or when an ecologically sensitive area is being treated.

Chapter 9 Biotechnology : Principles and Processes

Q.33 What is Ti plasmid? Name the organism where it is found? How Does it help in genetic engineering?

Ans. An extra-chromosomal DNA, which delivers gene of interest into variety of plants and acts as cloning vector is called Ti plasmid. They are present *in Agrobacterium tumifaciens* Ti plasmid vectors are used for genetic transformation in many dicot plants. The tumor causing plasmid of in *Agrobacterium tumifaciens* has been modified into a cloning vector, which is no more pathogenic to the plant, but is still able to use the mechanism to deliver gene of interest into the variety of plants.

Q.34 What are molecular scissors? Why are they so named? Write their use in biotechnology.

Ans. The restriction endonucleases are called molecular scissors as they cut the DNA segments at particular locations. For example, *Eco*RI.

The restriction enzymes cuts the DNA strand a little away from the center of the palindromic sites, But between the same two bases on the opposite strands. This leaves single stranded portions with overhanging stretches called sticky ends on each strand as they form hydrogen bonds with the complementary cut counterparts. This stickiness at the end facilitates the action of the enzyme DNA ligase.

Q.35 Explain the process of gel electrophoresis technique.

Ans. Gel electrophoresis is a technique for separating DNA fragments based on their size. Firstly, the sample of DNA is cut into fragments by restriction endonucleases.

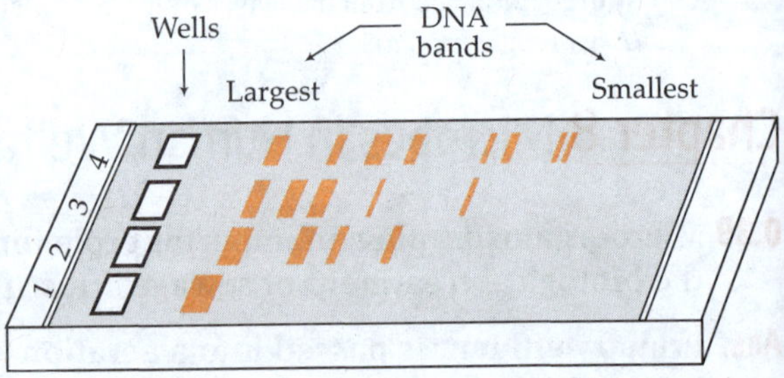

The DNA fragments being negatively charged can be separated by facing them to move towards the anode under an electric field through a medium/matrix.

Commonly used matrix is agarose, which is natural linear polymer of D-Galactose and 3, 6 anhydro- L-galactose, which is extracted from seaweeds.

The DNA fragments separate out (resolve), according to their size, because of the sieving property of agarose gel. Hence, smaller the fragment size, the farther it will move.

The separated DNA fragments are visualized after staining the DNA with ethidium bromide (EtBr) followed by exposure to UV radiation.

The DNA fragments are seen as orange-colored bands.

The separated bands of DNA are cut out and extracted from the gel piece. This step is called **elution.**

The purified DNA fragments are used to form recombinant DNA, which can be joined with cloning vectors.

Q.36 A schematic representation of polymerase chain reaction (PCR) upto the extension stage is given below. Answer the questions that follows.

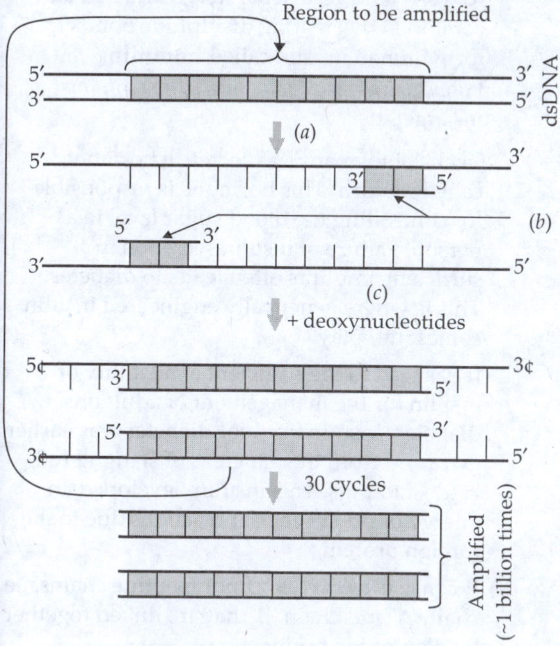

(i) Name the process 'a'.
(ii) Identify 'b'
(iii) Identify 'c' and mention its importance in PCR.

Ans. (i) *a*—Denaturation process
(ii) *b*—Primers
(iii) *c*—*Taq* DNA polymerase.

Taq polymerase is a thermostable enzyme which remains active during the high temperature required for extension of DNA

Q.37 What are bioreactors? List its components. What are two different types of bioreactors? Explain with diagram.

Ans. A **bioreactor** provides the optimal conditions for achieving the desired product by providing optimum growth conditions like temperature, pH, substrate, salts, vitamins and oxygen.

Components of Bioreactor

The components of a bioreactor are as follows

(i) An agitator system
(ii) An oxygen delivery system
(iii) A foam control system
(iv) A temperature control system
(v) pH control system
(vi) A sampling port to withdraw culture periodically.

Types of Bioreactor

The most commonly used bioreactors are of **stirring** type bioreactor. These are of two types

(i) **A simple stirred-tank bioreactor** is usually cylindrical or with a curved base to facilitate even mixing of reactor contents.

(ii) The **sparged- stirred-tank bioreactor** also facilitates the mixing of components and ensures oxygen availability throughout the bioreactor. Alternatively, air is bubbled through the reactor.

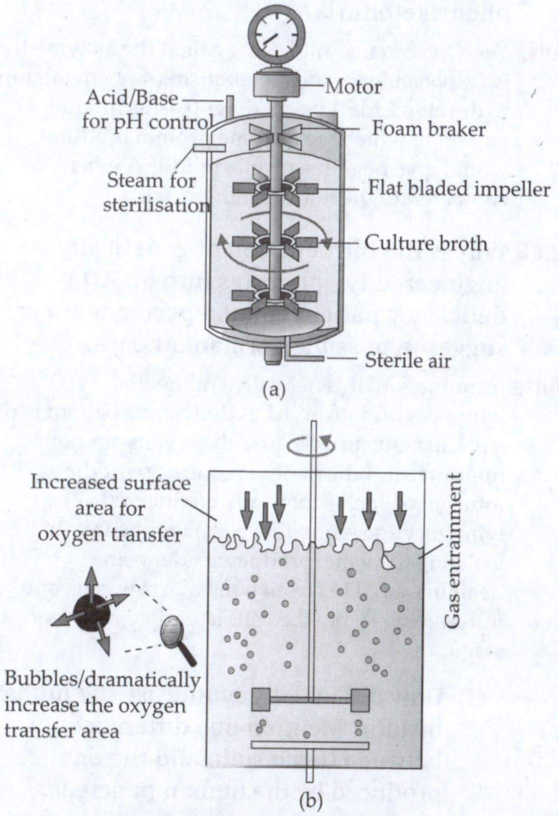

(a) Simple stirred-tank bioreactor
(b) Sparged stirred-tank bioreactor through which sterile air bubbles are sparged

Chapter 10 Biotechnology and Its Applications

Q.38 Name the genes responsible for making Bt cotton plants resistant to bollworm attack. How do such plants attain resistance against bollworm attacks? Explain.

Ans. *Bt* cotton has cryIAc /cryIIAb These genes produce crystal of protoxin. When bollworm bites the cotton fruits, it consumes the toxic insecticidal protein. The alkaline pH in its gut activates the toxin. The activated toxin binds to mid gut epithelial cells, resulting in the lysis of cells leading to the death of the insect.

Q.39 ELISA technique is based on the principles of antigen and antibody interaction. Can this technique be used in the molecular diagnosis of a genetic disorder such as phenylketonuria?

Ans. Yes. One can use antibody against the enzyme that is responsible for the metabolism of phenylalanine to develop ELISA based diagnosis technique. The patient in which the enzyme protein is absent would give negative results in ELISA when compared to the normal individual.

Q.40 Why is the introduction of genetically engineered lymphocytes into an ADA deficiency patient is not a permanent cure, suggest a possible permanent cure.

Ans. Introduction of genetically engineered lymphocytes into an ADA deficiency patient is not a permanent cure because these cells are not immortal and the patient requires periodic infusion of such genetically engineered lymphocytes. A possible permanent cure can be isolating the gene, producing adenosine deaminase (ADA) from bone marrow cells and introducing it into the cells at early embryonic stage.

Q.41 (i) How did Eli Lilly synthesise the human insulin? Mention one difference between this insulin and the one produced by the human pancreas.

(ii) Why is pro-insulin so called? How is insulin different from it?

Ans. (i) Synthesis of Human Insulin by Eli Lilly

In 1983, **Eli Lilly**, an American company prepared two DNA sequences corresponding to A and B-chains of human insulin and introduced them in the plasmids of *E. coli* to produce insulin chains. These chains (A and B) were produced separately, extracted and combined by creating disulphide bonds to form human insulin called **humulin**.

Difference Between Humulin and Natural Human Insulin:

β-cells of the pancreas secrete a hormone called **insulin**. This hormone is responsible for controlling the blood sugar level in a person. Failure of insulin secretion in sufficient amounts often leads to diabetes. This is where genetically engineered insulin comes into play.

It has lead to the sufficient availability of insulin for the management of adult onset diabetes. Insulin used for diabetes was earlier extracted from the pancreas of slaughtered cattle and pigs. This insulin developed an allergy or other types of reactions due to the foreign protein.

(ii) It consists of two short polypeptide chains, i.e. chain 'A' and chain 'B' that are linked together by disulphide bridges.

In mammals, including humans, insulin is synthesised as a **pro-hormone** (needs to be processed before it becomes a fully mature and functional hormone) which contains an extra stretch called the **C-peptide**.

This C-peptide is not present in the mature insulin and is removed during the maturation. Therefore, the main challenge for the production of insulin using *r*DNA techniques was getting insulin assembled into a mature form.

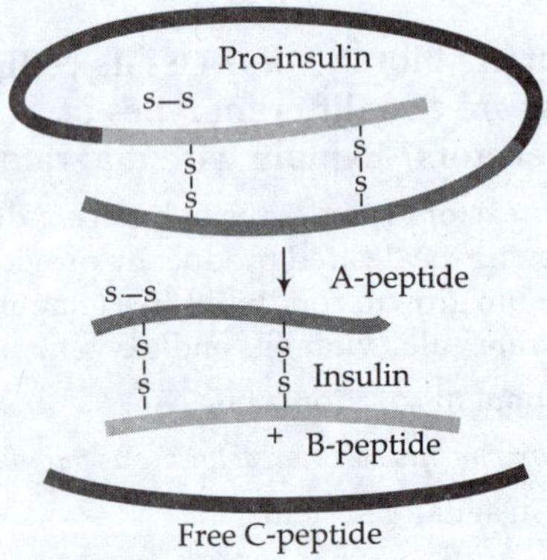

This conversion from proinsulin to insulin occurs in the pancreas before insulin is secreted into the bloodstream.

Chapter 11 Organisms and Populations

Q.42 Identify the curves '*A*' and '*B*', shown in the graph, given below, list the condition responsible for growth patterns, '*A*' and '*B*'.

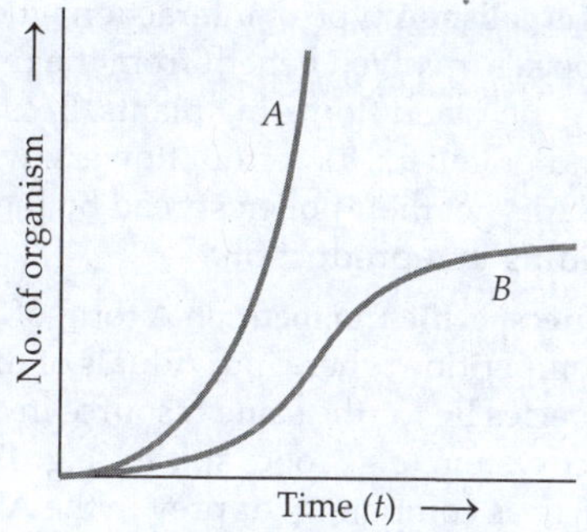

Population growth curve

Ans. Curve '*A*' represents exponential growth curve when the resources (food + space) are unlimited, this type of growth curve appears.

Curve '*B*' is logistic curve when the resources become limited at certain point of time this type of growth curve appears.

Q.43 (i) How does the Mediterranean orchid *Orphys* ensure its pollination by bees?

(ii) How is *Cuscuta* adapted to be a parasitic plant?

Ans. (i) The petals of the *Orphys* resembles the female of a bee species in size, colour and odour, etc. Male bee mistakes the *Orphys* for female bee and tries to copulate. Few pollen grains adhered with the body of the male bee fall over the stigma of the flower, thereby leading to pollination.

(ii) *Cuscuta* has lost its chlorophyll and leaves during evolution and thus it derives its nutrition from host plant. Thus, it is a parasite plant.

Q.44 (a) List the different attributes data population has and not an individual organism.

(b) What is population density? Explain any three different ways the population density can be measured with the help of an example each.

Ans. (a) Attributes of a population not found in an individual organism.

A population has certain attributes that an individual organism does not have. Some of them are given below

1. Population Size or Density

It is defined as the number of individuals of a species per unit area or volum

Population Density (PD)

$$= \frac{\text{Number of individuals in a region } (N)}{\text{Size of unit area in the region } (S)};$$

$$PD = \frac{N}{S}$$

However, population density need not necessarily be measured in numbers only. Although, the total number is the most appropriate measure of population density, but it is difficult to determine in some cases, e.g. there are 200 *Parthenium* (carrot grass) plants, but only a single huge banyan tree with large canopy.

This states that the population density of banyan is relatively low as compared to that of *Parthenium*. In such cases, the per cent cover or biomass is a more meaningful measure of the population size/density.

2. **Birth Rate or Natality** It is the number of births of new individuals per unit of population per unit time, e.g. if in a pond, there are 20 lotus plants last year and through reproduction, 8 new plants are added, taking the current population to 28. Then, birth rate = 8/20 = 0.4 offspring per lotus per year.

3. **Death Rate or Mortality** It is the number of loss of individuals per unit of population per unit time due to death or due to the different environmental changes, competition, predation, etc., e.g. if in a laboratory, population of 40 individuals, 4 fruitflies died during a week, then the death rate = 4/40 = 0.1 individuals per fruitfly per week.

4. **Sex Ratio** It is the number of females to males per 1000 individuals of a population in a given time, e.g. 60% of the population is females and 40% is males.

(b) **Population Density** refers to the number of individuals of a species per unit area or volume in a given habitat at a given time/period.

Methods of Measuring Population Density

(i) Biomass/% cover, e.g., Hundred *Parthenium* plants and 1 huge banayan tree.

(ii) Relative Density, e.g., Number of fish caught per trap from a lake.

(iii) Numbers, e.g., human population.

(iv) Indirect estimation, e.g., without actually counting/seeing them, e.g., tiger census based on pug marks and faecal pellets.

Q.45 Define the following terms and give one example for each.

(a) Commensalism **(b) Parasitism**
(c) Camouflage **(d) Mutualism**
(e) Interspecific competition

Ans. (a) **Commensalism** A type of ecological relationship where one species benefits while the other is neither benefitted nor harmed. e.g. Barnacles attaching to whales. The barnacles benefit by being transported to different feeding grounds, while the whale is unaffected.

(b) **Parasitism** A type of relationship where one organism (the parasite) benefits at the expense of the host, which is harmed. e.g. tapeworms in the intestines of mammals. The tapeworm absorbs nutrients from the host's intestine, depriving the host of essential nutrients.

(c) **Camouflage** An adaptation that allows organisms to blend in with their surroundings to avoid predation or to ambush prey. e.g. A chameleon changing its skin color to match its environment. This helps the chameleon avoid predators and sneak up on prey.

(d) **Mutualism** A type of interaction where both species involved benefit from the relationship. e.g. Bees and flowering plants. Bees get nectar and pollen for food from flowers, while the plants get their pollen spread by the bees, aiding in reproduction.

(e) **Interspecific Competition** A form of competition where individuals of different species lie for the same resource in an ecosystem (e.g., food, space). e.g. lions and hyenas competing for prey in the African Savanna. Both species hunt similar prey, and the competition can affect their survival and reproduction.

Chapter 12 Ecosystem

Q.46 Differentiate between

(a) Detritivore and decomposer
(b) Primary and secondary productivity

Ans. (a) Differences between detritivore and decomposer is as follows

Detritivore	Decomposer
They are the organisms which feed on dead and decaying organisms and break them into smaller particles. Example, earthworm.	They are the organisms, which secretes enzymes and breakdown complex organic matter into inorganic substances. Example, some bacteria and fungi.

(b)Difference between primary and secondary productivity is as follows

Primary productivity	Secondary Productivity
It is the amount of biomass or organic matter produced per unit area over a time period by plants during photosynthesis.	It is the rate of assimilation and formation of new organic matter by consumers.

Q.47 Explain various functions of ecosystem.

Ans. Various functions of ecosystem is as follows

(i) **Productivity** Conversion of inorganic material into organic material with the help of a solar energy by the autotrophs.

(ii) **Energy flow** Unidirectional movement of energy towards higher trophic level (and its dissipation and loss as heat to the environment).

(iii) **Decomposition** Fragmentation, leaching, catabolism, humification, mineralisation, by bacteria, fungi and flagellates (abundant at the bottom of lake).

(iv) **Nutrient cycling** Decomposition of dead matter to release the nutrients back to be re-used by the autotrophs.

Chapter 13 Biodiversity and Its Conservation

Q.48 What does an ecological pyramid indicate? Explain the three different types of upright pyramids in nature, with the help of an example of each.

Ans. An ecological pyramid is a graphical representation showing the relationship between different trophic levels in an ecosystem. It illustrates the distribution of biomass, numbers, or energy among the trophic levels from producers at the base to top predators at the apex.

There are three major ecological pyramids as discussed below

1. **Pyramid of Number** It represents the total number of organisms at each trophic level. It is always upright. Exception is a tree ecosystem, where the pyramid of number is inverted.

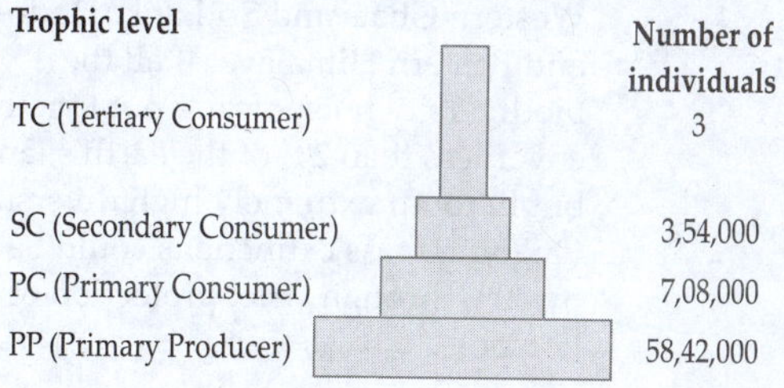

2. **Pyramid of Biomass** It represents total weight of the organisms in each trophic level. It can be
   (i) **Upright**, e.g. in grasslands.

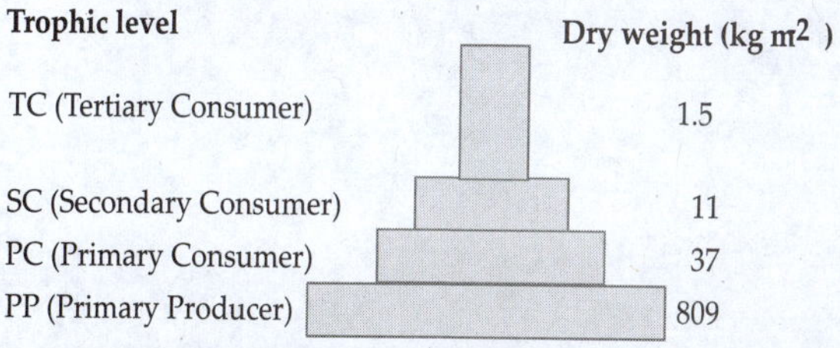

   (ii) **Inverted,** e.g. in pond ecosystem.

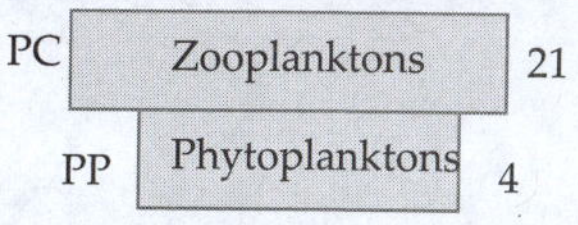

3. **Pyramid of Energy** It represents total energy of the organisms in each trophic level. Pyramid of energy is always **upright**. It can never be inverted, because when energy is transferred from a particular trophic level to the next trophic level, some energy is always lost as heat at each step.

   Each bar in the energy pyramid indicates the amount of energy present at each trophic level in a given time or annually per unit area.

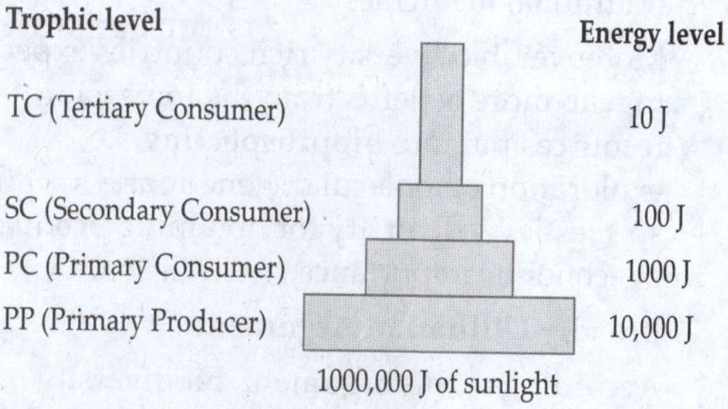

Q.49 Expand IUCN. What is IUCN red list? Give any two uses of this list.

Ans. IUCN stands for International Union for Conservation of Nature and Natural resources.

IUCN Red list is a catalogue of species and sub-species that are facing the risk of extinction. The two uses of this list are as follow

(i) It provides information and develop awareness about the importance of threatened species.

(ii) Identification and documentation of endangered species and so measures can be taken for their protection.

Q.50 (a) Why should we conserve biodiversity explain with reasons?

(b) Mention the importance of biodiversity hotspots.

Ans. (a) Conservation of biodiversity is essential for several reasons as given below.

Conservation of biodiversity is protection, upliftment and scientific management of biodiversity. It is maintains the biodiversity at the optimum level and derive sustainable benefits for the present as well as future generations.

Reasons for Conserving Biodiversity

There are many reasons for conservation of biodiversity, but all reasons are equally important. They can be grouped into three categories which are as follows

1. **Narrowly Utilitarian Argument**

These are based on obvious reasons. Humans derive countless direct economic benefits from the nature like food (cereals, pulses and fruits), firewood, fibre, construction material, industrial products (tannins, lubricants, dyes, resins and perfumes) and products of medicinal importance.

More than 25% of the drugs currently sold in the market worldwide are derived from plants and 25,000 plant species are used in traditional medicines.

Moreover, biodiversity rich countries expect to reap more benefits from the increasing resources put into **bioprospecting**, i.e. exploration of molecular, genetic and species-level diversity for obtaining products of economic importance.

2. **Broadly Utilitarian Argument**

According to this argument, biodiversity plays a major role in ecosystem services that nature provides.
Some of these are

(i) Production of oxygen, e.g. Amazon forests produce 20% of the total oxygen in the earth's atmosphere *via* photosynthesis.

(ii) Pollination of flowers without which fruits and seeds are not produced is provided by pollinator layer, i.e. bees, bumble bees, birds and bats.

(iii) Control of floods and soil erosion.

(iv) Intangible benefits of nature like aesthetic pleasures of watching spring flower in full bloom, walking through thick forest, listening to bulbul's song, etc.

3. **Ethical Argument**

Every species has an intrinsic value, even if it is not of any economic value to us. It is our moral duty to care for their well-being and pass on our biological legacy in good order to future generations. Moreover, many plants like tulsi and peepal have religious importance as well.

(b) Importance of biodiversity hotspots are as follows

- These are regions with very high levels of species richness, high degree of **endemism** (species confined to a region and not found anywhere else) and accelerated habitat loss. Thus, these are areas for maximum protection. Initially, 25 biodiversity hotspots were identified. Now, there are 34 hotspots all over the world.
- Out of these, hotspots in India lie in Western Ghats and Sri Lanka, Indo-Burma and Eastern Himalaya. If all the biodiversity hotspots are put together, they cover less than 2% of the earth's land area, but harbour extremely high diversity. Ongoing mass extinctions could be reduced by 30% through strict protection of these hotspots.